POSTCOLONIAL DEVELOPMENTS

Agriculture in the Making of Modern India

Akhil Gupta

DUKE UNIVERSITY PRESS   Durham / London 1998

© 1998 Duke University Press
All rights reserved
Printed in the United States of America on acid-free paper ∞
Typeset in Minion by Keystone Typesetting, Inc.
Library of Congress Cataloging-in-Publication Data appear
on the last printed page of this book.

For my parents
Jwala Prasad and Meena Gupta

Contents

Preface and Acknowledgments

This book demonstrates what the *postcolonial condition* means for the lives of rural people in north India. Since the Second World War, the everyday lives of poor people in the Third World have been thoroughly transformed by the Age of Development, during which has occurred some of the most ambitious national and international experiments in social engineering that the world has ever witnessed. What have these experiments meant to specific groups of people in different locations who are both the targets and the subjects of "development"? In this book I attempt to describe and analyze what development has meant to people living in one village in north India. The book explores the complex and conflicted formation of development institutions, ideologies, and practices in local, regional, national, and global spaces.

Postcolonial Developments differs from much of the literature on development in that it focuses primarily on how underdevelopment becomes a form of *identity* in the postcolonial world. I argue that underdevelopment is not merely a structural location in the global community of nations; rather, underdevelopment is also a form of identity, something that informs people's sense of self. Who people think they are, how they got that way, and what they can do to alter their lives have been profoundly shaped by the institutions, ideologies, and practices of development. In rural northern India, a pervasive feeling of being underdeveloped, of being behind the West, articulated with other identities of caste, class, region, gender, and sexuality, produces people's sense of their selves. I have termed this complex articulation of "backwardness" the *postcolonial condition;* thus, development is never a singular or monolithic "apparatus" that imposes itself on the rural poor.

An identity of "underdevelopment" is thoroughly imbricated in nationalism because the nation is largely assumed as the "natural" unit of analysis in the discourse of development. In the waning years of the twentieth century, however, this assumption of the nation-as-actor is being revised by the ascendance of a neoliberal global economic agenda. The neoliberal agenda, in turn, is being resisted by grassroots groups that object to the form of (mal)development encoded in neoliberal policies. Resistance to a globalizing agenda is generating responses which participate in nationalist discourse in some respects and which depart sharply from its premises in others. The challenge to ideas of the nation embodied in global neoliberalism and in the responses of grassroots groups to it problematizes the easy equation between "the grassroots" and "the local." Grassroots organizing has to be conceptualized in terms of a warped space that is no longer simply "local" or "global" but a little bit of each. And neoliberalism itself has to be contextualized within a much broader pattern of global regulation and government which extends far beyond the "economic" and which fundamentally alters the identities and everyday experiences of people.

A project such as this, which has involved several rounds of fieldwork and which has been written, rewritten, and revised in many different institutional contexts, involves debts, intellectual and personal, to many different people. Even if I could recall all the people who have contributed to this book in different ways, I would be unable to acknowledge my gratitude to them sufficiently.

The people to whom this study owes the most are the residents of Alipur, particularly Suresh, Sompal, and the Manager. They and their families welcomed me into their homes throughout my stay and in all my subsequent visits. I am especially grateful to the Manager and his family for housing me and for looking after me as they would one of their own.

When I first started writing my dissertation, Arjun Appadurai generously shared drafts of his work on agrarian questions in Maharashtra. More than anything else, it was these papers that enabled me to see the immense possibilities and potential of combining a sophistication in social theory with detailed empirical work in agriculture.

I have presented early and late drafts of some chapters to audiences in different parts of North America. An early version of Chapter 1 was presented in 1994 at the SSRC workshop "The Dynamics and Transmission of Development Ideas" held at the University of Michigan. I am grateful to Fred Cooper and Randy Packard for inviting me to that workshop and to Gillian Hart for her insightful comments. Subsequently, different parts of this long chapter were presented at the Center for International Security and Arms Control, Stanford University; at the South Asia Seminar, University of California, Berkeley; at the Center for Comparative Studies in History, Society, and Culture at the University of California, Davis; at the South Asia Seminar/Workshop at the University of Chicago; and at the Anthropology Department Colloquium at York University in Toronto. An early version of the last section of Chapter 3 was first presented on a panel entitled "Intersections: Minority Discourse/Area Studies/Cultural Studies" at the 1994 Annual Meeting of the American Anthropological Association in Atlanta. I thank Lisa Yoneyama for inviting me to be a part of that panel. I also thank David Lloyd for inviting me to present part of this chapter at the Center for European Studies at the University of California, Berkeley, in 1997. A preliminary version of a small part of Chapter 4 was first presented on a panel that I co-organized with Arun Agrawal entitled "Environmental Conflicts and the Negotiation of Identities in South and Southeast Asia" at the Annual Meeting of the Association for Asian Studies held in Honolulu, Hawaii, in 1996. Chapter 5 has had many incarnations. A preliminary version was first presented on a panel organized by George Collier called "Peasant Cultures and the Global Economy" at the International Congress of Anthropological and Ethnological Sciences in Mexico City in 1993. Obtaining an enthusiastic response from an international audience assured me that this chapter had an important role to play in this book. Subsequent versions have been presented at the Institute of Asian Research at the University of British Columbia, Vancouver; at the Jackson School of International Studies, University of Washington, Seattle; at the Agrarian Studies Seminar, Yale University; at the Cultural Analysis Colloquium, University of California, Santa Barbara; at the forum "Science and Media in Their Transnational Locations" organized by the Postdisciplinary Approaches to the Technosciences Resident Research Group at the Humanities Research Institute, University of California, Irvine; at the MIT Anthropology Program and the Center for International Studies' Peoples and States lectures series on Ethnic Identity and Conflict; at the Department of Environmental Science, Policy, and Management, University of California, Berkeley; at the University of Oregon's Anthropology Department colloquium series "Culture, Power, History"; at the MacArthur Workshop on Sustainability held at the University of Minnesota, Minneapolis; and at the

Department of Urban Planning, UCLA, Los Angeles. I am grateful to audiences at all these places for their comments and in particular to Hugh Gusterson for his discussion of my paper at MIT.

Many people were kind enough to give me comments on some chapters of the manuscript or the whole book in its early stages. I am particularly indebted to George Collier, Donald Moore, Arjun Appadurai, and one anonymous reviewer for Duke University Press for their comments on the entire manuscript. Their criticisms and suggestions helped make this a much better book. Jim Ferguson, Liisa Malkki, and Tanya Luhrmann read early versions of the Introduction and gave me many suggestions that proved invaluable in revising and rewriting it. The comments of Stacy Pigg and Prabhu Mohapatra on an oral presentation of the first chapter greatly aided in its conceptualization, and Renato Rosaldo provided many useful suggestions on that chapter as well. Inderpal Grewal, Aditya Behl, and Lawrence Cohen gave me excellent comments on Chapter 3, and Suzana Sawyer and Ann Gold provided detailed feedback on Chapters 3 and 4; Peter Vandergeest offered insightful criticisms of a talk crafted from Chapter 4; and Sanjeev Khagram provided extremely detailed and helpful comments on Chapter 5. The accounts of the Karnataka Farmers Association in Chapter 5 and the Epilogue owe a great deal to primary material collected by Mridula Udayagiri, which she was kind enough to share with me.

Despite the demands for authorship imposed by accrediting agencies, the production of a work such as this is a necessarily collaborative and social act. I wish to acknowledge all those who contributed to this project in their roles as students and colleagues. One group of people deserve special gratitude, namely, the students who served as research assistants during the final stages of the manuscript. Sameer Pandya and Aly Remtulla did an absolutely amazing job of reading the manuscript with a fine-tooth comb, making excellent suggestions for revision and locating and summarizing reference material. James Krapfl spent many long hours making the maps. Yoo-Jean Chi provided steady research assistance that consisted of a multitude of tasks. Rohan Chandran and Sandeep Jain were responsible for the charts.

I also thank my colleagues, first, at the University of Washington for providing me with a wonderfully supportive atmosphere in which to begin my academic career and, then, at Stanford University for helping advance my scholarly work. At the University of Washington, I owe a special debt to the chairs of the two departments where I worked, Frank Conlon of South Asian Studies and Joel Migdal of International Studies.

Resat Kasaba, Kathie Kasaba, Vicky Lawson, Michael Toolan, Christine Di Stefano, Val Daniel, Ruth Frankenberg, Lata Mani, Ted Swedenburg, and Biff Keyes sustained me intellectually and personally. At Stanford, George Collier was the kind of chair that every junior faculty member dreams of having; Jane Collier, Sylvia Yanagisako, Joan Fujimura, Paulla Ebron, Renato Rosaldo, Miyako Inoue, Carol Delaney, and Purnima Mankekar have provided a vibrant intellectual home in the Anthropology Department. Other scholars from related departments who have contributed to this book by their support and insights include Joel Beinin, Gordon Chang, Estelle Freedman, Gabrielle Hecht, Sharon Holland, Suvir Kaul, David Palumbo-Liu, Mary Pratt, Richard Roberts, and Debra Satz. Most important, I thank the staff in the Anthropology Department, who have helped me immensely during the time that I have been here, particularly Beth Bashore, who kept me connected during my year of fieldwork; Ellen Christensen, who has been a rock of support during some trying times; and Shannon Brown.

My early fieldwork was supported by the Center for Research in International Studies at Stanford, which gave me grants for both the fieldwork and the writing stages, and the Indian Council for Social Science Research (ICSSR). Subsequent field research was funded by the Fritz Endowment for International Studies at the University of Washington. Most of this book was written while I was a fellow at the Agrarian Studies Program at Yale University in 1993–94. I had the pleasure of spending the academic year with a superb group of fellows: Bob Baldwin, Catherine LeGrand, Prabhu Mahapatra, Alex Naty, David Nugent, Stacy Pigg, Ricardo Salvatore, and Paolo Squatriti. The atmosphere of constructive criticism and camaraderie at Agrarian Studies bore the stamp of everything that Jim Scott does; and the program strikes just the right mix of administrative minimalism and formal programming. No small part of its success owes to Kay Mansfield, whose care for the fellows' needs extended far beyond her formal duties. Other people at Yale to whom I am indebted for intellectual and social companionship are Angelique Haugerud, Gil Joseph, Bill Kelly, Patricia Passaro, Nancy Peluso, Donna Perry, Rukhsana Siddiqui, Helen Siu, K. Sivaramakrishna, and Bala Sivaramakrishna. Finally, without Akash Bhargava's help, we would not have found such a wonderful place to stay, nor would our stay there have been as enjoyable.

I also thank all the students who read parts of this manuscript in their courses and gave me extremely valuable feedback. Although I cannot mention the names of particular individuals, I am grateful to the students who responded to this manuscript in the 1996–97 academic year: in the graduate seminar "Topics in Political Economy" in the fall; in the seminar on the political economy of India in the spring; and in Michael Watts's graduate seminar on agrarian issues at the University of California, Berkeley. I have learned a great deal from the varied reactions to the book in these courses.

The work represented in this book would not have been possible without another group of collaborators: the graduate students with whom I have worked most closely over the last few years. They are Falu Bakrania, Federico Besserer, Tom Boellstorf, Carrie Bramen, Jackie Brown, Alicia Schmidt Camacho, Donna Daniels, Monica DeHart de Galicia, Alnoor Ebrahim, Elizabeth Enslin, Jack Ferguson, Michael Goldbach, Helen Gremillion, Stefan Helmreich, Aida Hernandez, Francisca James Hernandez, Sanjeev Khagram, Jana Sequoya Magdalena, Don Moore, Vivek Narayanan, Diane Nelson, Laura Nelson, Julie Olson, Amit Rai, Shankar Raman, Josie Saldanha, Victoria Sanford, Suzana Sawyer, Aradhana Sharma, Lok Siu, Gita Srinivasan, Rebecca Stein, Dori Tunstall, and Mridula Udayagiri.

A small group of South Asia scholars in the Bay Area have contributed more to this book than they could imagine. Many of us work in institutions where a critical mass of scholars working on the subcontinent is not available. In particular, I thank Aditya Behl, Lawrence Cohen, Inderpal Grewal, Ravi Rajan, Raka Ray, and Parama Roy.

I have been fortunate to know a terrific intellectual community in India, from whom I have learned a great deal. Colleagues and friends who have contributed to this project directly by their questions and comments or indirectly by their acute observations of contemporary India include Zoya Hasan, Sudipta Kaviraj, Uma Chakravarty, Shahid Amin, Niraja Gopal Jayal, Indivar Kamtekar, Urvashi Butalia, Kumkum Sangari, Rajiv Bhargava, Harpreet Mahajan, C. Rajamohan, Nirmala George, Gautam Bhatia, and Ritu Bhatia.

Librarians and library facilities at Stanford University, Yale University, the Library of Congress, the India International Center (IIC), George Washington University, and Goa University were critical for locating sources and references.

For their friendship and nurture, I thank those people who have provided me with the perspective that puts academic work and academic production in its proper place: Ethiraj Venkatapathy, Julia Jaroch, Tara Mohanan, K. P. Mohanan, Arun Kumar, Poornima Kumar, Jim Ferguson, Liisa Malkki, Ravi Oswal, Suruchi Oswal, Resat Kasaba, Kathie

Friedman Kasaba, Vikram Seth, Caren Kaplan, Prabhat Hajela, Aparna Mehrotra, Fernando Salas, Ashok Sangani, and Geeta Sangani.

I must thank my family, without whose support this book, like much else, would not have been possible: Jwala and Meena Gupta; and Anita, Rahul, and Shefali Aggarwal. After rounds of fieldwork, I looked forward to returning to Delhi to spend time with my in-laws, Kamla Mankekar and the late D. R. Mankekar. Were it not for their affection and support, my fieldwork would not have been so successful. I am sorry that my father-in-law did not live to see the finished book but grateful that a field site near Delhi provided me a brief opportunity to get to know him.

Finally, I owe the deepest gratitude to my partner, Purnima Mankekar, who has endured and participated in all stages of this project. We were married in the middle of my first long spell of fieldwork in 1984–85; since then, she has seen this project through its various stages, constantly giving advice, encouragement, and support over the years. It is safe to say that this would have been a very different and much weaker manuscript without her incisive intelligence and keen editorial eye. She read the drafts of all the chapters several times and, just as I was ready to abandon the manuscript, pushed me to reorganize the argument, clarify the prose, and sharpen the analysis. This book owes more to her than anyone else.

Introduction

I t was late July 1992, during my third extended field trip to the region around Alipur, a small village of approximately seven hundred people in western Uttar Pradesh.[1] Located in the flat, rich agricultural tract called the Doab (the region between the two great rivers of northern India, the Ganges and the Jamuna), Alipur has an economy based largely on agriculture. The monsoons were in full swing so the ground was muddy. But, after the blazing heat of summer, the verdant fields brought hope and relief. Carefully maintaining my balance on the mounds and raised irrigation canals, I walked through the fields to a little hamlet on the outskirts of the village. Ram Singh, an older, lower-caste (*jatav*) man, lived there, in a settlement founded by his grandfather and inhabited exclusively by his extended kin. Because he shared approximately fifty acres with his three brothers, he was a well-to-do farmer by local standards. Ram Singh had been involved in agricultural activities for almost all his life, and although most of the work was now done by Inder Singh, one of his adult sons, he continued to participate actively in farming.

When I reached the house, a cot was brought out and positioned carefully in the shadow of the house, next to the tube well.[2] Ram Singh had gone out but returned shortly, along with Inder Singh. With the tape recorder positioned between us, we began a wide-ranging conversation. I had interviewed Ram Singh in earlier field trips: he was an articulate and engaging speaker, in contrast to his son, whose comments I sometimes found hard to decipher. We had already been talking for about forty-five minutes when we broached the topic of the effect of the high-yielding varieties on the land; there was a momentary lull in the

Main road leading into Alipur, with the village pond to the right

conversation while I turned the tape around, and then we launched into the discussion, parts of which are reproduced below.

Like other places in northwest India, Alipur had witnessed a drastic transformation in agricultural practices after the introduction of the "green revolution," in which use of hybrid, high-yielding seeds had resulted in a fourfold increase in India's wheat output since the late 1960s. The green revolution combined the use of hybrid seeds with high doses of chemical fertilizer and intensive irrigation to obtain high yields.[3] Like the other farmers of Alipur, Ram Singh had planted only high-yielding varieties of wheat.

While talking about the effects of green revolution agriculture on the land, Ram Singh contrasted the properties of chemical fertilizer with manure or *desi* fertilizer:[4]

> Ram Singh: Earlier it was like this, that no one knew about [chemical] fertilizer and people used to apply desi fertilizer. Now, they mostly use market fertilizer: it makes the soil weak and deficient. Otherwise, organic manure was the thing used most widely. And it used to yield a very good output. Now people want even more output. They are pursuing [planting] two or three crops, so the soil is getting weaker because of the fertilizer, and the taste is diminishing in this way. Compared with before, there are no elements [*tatv*]

left in the land. Earlier, the land had a chance to relax [*sastavein*]; now who allows it to [do so]?

Inder Singh: Apart from that, the thing is that now organic manure [*bhooday kaa khaad*] is not applied. Animal manure [*pashuon kaa khaad*] made a lot of difference.

Ram Singh: If there was enough organic fertilizer for all our fields, we wouldn't touch market fertilizer.

Despite the near unanimity of evaluations regarding its superiority, manure was overshadowed by the vastly greater use of chemical fertilizers. Ram Singh maintained that the output had been "very good" with organic manure alone. Land had begun to be overused, however, which prevented the application of an adequate amount of manure. The amount of manure employed was rather small when compared with the amount of chemical fertilizer used.

The fact was that Alipur's farmers had become increasingly dependent on the use of chemical fertilizers. When I started fieldwork in 1984–85, farmers used rather low levels of chemical fertilizer. In fact, most farmers employed chemical fertilizer in quantities that agricultural scientists would have deemed suboptimal. But in 1991–92, farmers informed me that they were using increasing amounts of chemical fertilizer. Ram Singh, for example, said that "if you take market fertilizer, and keep using it, then the farming will be spoiled. It won't be able to produce output. These things have been investigated. [By contrast,] manure gives the soil strength. Since the new varieties have come, we have had to use [chemical] fertilizer. If we don't apply fertilizer, they won't give any production. The [quantity of] fertilizer we use depends on the amount of money we have; when we get more money, we apply more fertilizer. We now have to apply more fertilizer than before. Earlier, people used to put five kilograms per *bigha,* now they put ten, even twelve.[5] People keep using more fertilizer." At the same time as he complained of the need to use larger quantities of chemical fertilizer, however, Ram Singh also maintained that "the output is better and the prices are good, so there's been no loss to us." The data he advanced were not actual figures but the kind of rule-of-thumb guidelines most often used by farmers about the level of inputs.[6] Very similar figures were cited by other farmers in Alipur.

And why was manure so much more effective than chemical fertilizer in "strengthening" the soil? The difference lay in that, as compared with manure, chemical fertilizers released their heat suddenly. Inder Singh noted that with chemical fertilizer "the land remains hard, it makes the land swell at once. The organic manure gives it real strength, the other one just makes it swell." Ram Singh added, "Chemical fertilizer makes the crop shoot up [*fasal ko uthaanay waali cheez hai*], whereas organic manure makes for strength. Without strength, no matter how much fertilizer you put, the field won't give output; this is what we have determined from experience." Therefore what made manure so much better than chemical fertilizer was not just that manure released its heat slowly but that it strengthened the soil.

Ram Singh went on to voice one of the most common complaints made by people in Alipur; ever since they started using large quantities of chemical fertilizer, the *taste* of wheat had declined: "Earlier, no one knew about market fertilizer [*bazaar ki khaad*], and the wheat grown was desi wheat. Desi wheat was very good to eat. It had a lot of sweetness [*mithaas*]. It was very tasty [*swaadisht*]. But this [high-yielding hybrid] wheat is not as good. Is it the fertilizer, or is it something else? In terms of output, it does produce more. But it is not as tasty as desi wheat." He seemed unsure whether to attribute the blame to fertilizer. In turn, I was skeptical of his explanation. So I pushed him to clarify what he meant, asking whether the decline in tastiness was due to fertilizer or to the variety of wheat grown. His answer left no doubt: "No, fertilizer affects its taste. It is not tasty. The more fertilizer you put, the less tasty it will be [*jitnaa khaad pail dogay, utnaa swaadisht nahee rahegaa*], this is for sure. Of course, the output will go up." Ram Singh kept referring to the trade-off made to achieve higher productivity; what had been sacrificed was taste. The more chemical fertilizer one applied, the less tasty was the wheat. It is important to note, however, that "taste" did not reflect just the momentary sensation on the tongue. It was expressive of other properties (*gunas*) that the grain possessed.

I have presented fragments of a conversation with one farmer as an example of the agricultural discourse found in Alipur. In the course of administering a detailed survey of farming practices, I realized that a significant disjuncture existed between the discourse of farmers and the language of the survey forms that I had adapted from the protocols used by an agricultural research institute. It took me just a few days to learn to substitute "How much fertilizer did you put at the time of sowing?" for "Quantity of basal dressing" and to ask how much fertilizer they had put later where the form said, "Quantity of top dressing." But what I was completely unprepared for were the explanations that emerged when I pressed farmers to account for seeming discrepancies in the data. They spoke of fields, plants, and fertilizers in terms of whether they were hot or cold, drying or moisturizing. They told me about the declining "strength" of the land, its ability to "speak," its "taking hold of" and supporting certain crops. Ram Singh, for example, talked about the need for the soil to "relax" and "rest" and of the difference between the swelling of the land encouraged by chemical fertilizers and the longer-lasting strength imparted by manure. It is tempting to appropriate Ram Singh's explicit critique of chemical fertilizers' deleterious effects on the strength of the soil and the taste of crops into a set of structural oppo-sitions which pit a system of meanings and symbols that was "non-Western" or "indigenous" against the universalizing discourses of "the West." For example, to understand why Ram Singh associated the use of chemical fertilizers with the declining taste of wheat, one would need to appreciate the importance of a substantivist theory that connected the life of plants to human life (a fuller account of this theory is presented in Chapter 4). But whereas a strategy positing a different cultural "system" is useful in decentering and denaturalizing Western assumptions and can be employed in understanding Ram Singh's critique of market-based production, it fails to account for the enthusiasm with which farmers took up green revolution agriculture or for Ram Singh's assess-ment that, because the output was plentiful and prices good, "there's been no loss to us."

What is more important is that such a theory would find the ease with which farmers switched codes, speaking in the "system" of indigenous agronomy in one instance and the "system" of bioscience in the next, disconcerting. In explaining the declining strength of the soil, Ram Singh deployed a theory that emphasized the need for land to "relax" simultaneously with a theory that employed a bioscientific discourse according to which the soil had to be constituted of the "right combina-tion" of different elements. In a similar vein, he talked of the need to apply ever larger quantities of chemical fertilizer in the face of declining soil strength in order to sustain production, but he tempered that obser-vation with the note that the quantities of fertilizer applied depended mostly on the resources of the household. Different farmers offered compelling explanations of farming decisions, explanations that were based on a blend of "humoral agronomy"; "scientific" theories; the poli-tics of class, caste, and gender; and prevailing discourses of develop-ment and the role of the state.

Such situations, in which contradictory logics and incommensurable discourses are intermingled with one another, have, for the most part, evaded sustained analytic attention in the ethnographic literature. Anthropologists have become acutely aware that "difference" need not take the form of a "system" of otherness. Yet the question remains of how to deal with such redoublings and border crossings not as humorous asides but as a central analytic challenge.[7] How does one conceptualize impure, hybrid, incommensurable modes of thinking and being without filtering them of their messiness?

The rest of this book is an attempt to come to grips with this complex border zone of hybridity and impurity which I see as a central trait of what may be termed "the postcolonial condition."[8] To undertake an ethnographic exploration of "postcoloniality" means to pay close attention to the interconnections between divergent discourses and structural forces. For instance, "local" understandings of agriculture in Alipur were profoundly shaped by globally and nationally circulating discourses of development. When peasants in Alipur expressed astonishment that someone like me had come from a country where farming was so "advanced" to study their "backward" techniques of agriculture, they were articulating a distinction between the "developed" and the "underdeveloped" that has been the mainstay not just of international development discourse but also of the independent Indian nation-state. Instead of discounting farmers' declarations about their technological and economic "backwardness" on the grounds that such statements originated "outside" the village, I consider them to be *constitutive* of "local" lives and "local" systems of meaning in rural north India. Farmers were as likely to draw on—and contest—hegemonic meanings of development as they were to employ—and resist—dominant (that is, indigenous) understandings of agriculture. Was there, then, any good reason to regard discourses of development as "external" and indigenous knowledges of agronomy as "internal" to the lives of the inhabitants of Alipur?

In characterizing the situation of nonelite rural people in northern India as "the postcolonial condition," I am aware that I risk raking up recent controversies surrounding the use and abuse of the notion of "postcoloniality." In some institutional contexts in the First World academy, the adjective "postcolonial" has become an indiscriminate signifier for a depoliticized incorporation of "difference." It is used to refer to Third World nation-states (whether formally colonized or not); minorities and indigenous groups of the United States; and, sometimes, even settler colonies inhabited by immigrants from an overpopulated Europe—both where the colonizers are now a majority (such as the United States, Canada, and Australia) and where they are a minority (such as South Africa and the former Southern Rhodesia).[9]

Three questions continually haunt this idea of "the postcolonial." The first is the relationship between a body of "theory" that uses "postcolonial" as a prefix, and the conditions, states of being, or objects that are denoted by that term. Is there *a* "postcolonial condition" that gives rise to and is in turn described by "postcolonial theory"? Is "postcolonial theory" merely the agonistic output of diasporic intellectual elites from the Third World? We need to be careful not to confuse the sociology of the genesis of a particular body of theory with why that theory is sociologically important. The important question is whether "postcolonial theory" helps identify, describe, and analyze conditions—specifically "postcolonial" conditions—that are of great social significance in the contemporary world. And, if it does, a related question must be asked: How do such conditions articulate with global capitalism? Postcolonial theory has been variously described as being the cultural logic of late capitalism in the Third World (Dirlik 1994) and attacked for providing the theoretical tools to enact an evasion of the power of global capitalism (Miyoshi 1993).

The second question that haunts postcolonial scholarship is that of the relationship between the universalizing descriptive or theoretical claims embodied in the notion of a unitary *postcolonial theory,* and the particular conjunctures of history, culture, and place that are the basis of such a generalization. What is gained and what is obscured in describing both Latin American and South Asian societies as "postcolonial"—or in using that term to refer to diasporic populations from Africa, Latin America, and Asia in Europe and North America? Is the term useful in discussions about minority populations in the United States? Do the processes of colonization provide a thread that unites these disparate settings and the experiences of the people living and working in them, despite their palpable differences?

This brings me to the third question that the concept of "postcoloniality" raises, namely, the temporal connection to colonialism that is embedded in that term. Does "postcolonial" signify that colonialism is no more than a historical legacy in the present? Is the Third World now no longer subject to colonial or neocolonial modes of power and control? Would it be more fruitful to persist in emphasizing the continuing power of colonial discourses, institutions, and practices in the contemporary world by using terms such as "neocolonialism" or "imperialism" (see Hall 1996:247)? Does employing the term "postcolonial" make one complicitous in a forgetting or denial of those relations of inequality that owe their effectivity to colonial domination?[10] Ella Shohat has put the question most forcefully: "When exactly, then, does the 'postcolonial' begin? Which region is privileged in such a beginning?" (1992:103).[11]

A burgeoning body of literature has raised searching questions about "the postcolonial" and has proposed alternative formulations to that term in an attempt to come to grips with the contemporary world situation (see especially the work of Ahmad 1995; Bhabha 1984, 1994; and Spivak 1987, 1988a,b, 1990; readers on "postcoloniality" include Ashcroft, Griffiths, and Tiffin 1995 and Williams and Chrisman 1993; and for a representative sample of the debate on postcolonialism, see Appiah 1991; Chakrabarty 1992; Dirlik 1994; Frankenberg and Mani 1993; Hall 1996; Loomba and Kaul 1994; McClintock 1992, 1994; Miyoshi 1993; O'Hanlon and Washbrook 1992; Prakash 1992a; and Young 1990). "The postcolonial" has been used very differently across disciplines and in its application to diverse geographic territories. My aim in dealing with the questions raised above is not to attempt a resolution of the debate at the high level of generality usually employed but to take the more modest task of looking at the specificities of one cultural, historical, and geographic setting in northern India. This allows us to see how a conjunctural analysis might illuminate some of the questions surrounding "the postcolonial." I thus hope to move the debate beyond helpful, but also limiting, programmatic statements to sociologically compelling representations of societies and social movements. Although the core of this book is ethnographic in nature, I have drawn on sources from different disciplines to address an interdisciplinary audience. My goal is not so much to resolve the debates around the postcolonial, debates that may well be intractable, but to offer a detailed study that might enable a more nuanced framing of the issues. My objective, ultimately, lies less in defending or attacking "postcolonial theory" than in seeing what kinds of political action and activism are made possible by alternative descriptions of peasant life. Does it make sense to talk of "the postcolonial condition" when analyzing the everyday lives of the subaltern in such a country as India? If so, how can "postcolonial theory" help in representing or conceptualizing poor people's movements of resistance and social transformation?[12]

In this book, I attempt to delineate what "postcoloniality" might mean for one group of nonelite people in northern India. Colonial discourse bequeathed a set of dichotomies that were unusually "productive" in a Foucauldian sense in that they enabled the construction of a sociology that informed colonial institutions and practices. These colonial dichotomies continue to operate quite freely in the present, although perhaps not with the same valences. Of these dichotomies, that between modernity and tradition has proved to be the most enduring. The first axis—modernity—is associated with progress, development, "the West," science and technology, high standards of living, rationality, and order; the other axis—tradition—is associated with stasis or even stagnation, underdevelopment, the Orient, conventional tools and technologies, poverty, superstition, and disorder. Within this set of dichotomies, important realms of social life in "Third World" or "postcolonial" nation-states such as India have disappeared from analytic view. While being fundamentally shaped by colonial modernities, many of the everyday practices of the farmers I met in the village of Uttar Pradesh that I have named Alipur displayed a distinct lack of fit with the dichotomy of "modern" and "traditional."[13]

For the most part, these farmers were enthusiastic users of new irrigation technologies in the form of tube wells, of chemical fertilizers, and of scientifically bred, hybrid varieties of wheat. At the same time, their practice of agriculture was dependent on interpretations that drew largely from "indigenous" agronomical knowledges and categories. Was this a paradoxical situation that called for the ironic juxtaposition of "traditional" and "modern" practices? Or was it better seen as a mundane condition that constituted what Appadurai (1991) has creatively termed "alternative modernities" in the postcolonial world? Modernity may have been instituted as a global phenomenon through colonial capitalism, but it was, in the process, resisted, reinvented, and reconfigured in different social and historical locations. To emphasize the multivalent genealogies of "modernity" in colonial and postcolonial settings, therefore, is to emphasize that the "non-Western" is not just a residual trace of a vanishing "tradition" but a constitutive feature of *modern* life (Rai 1993).

One of the central arguments of this book is that the apparatus and discourse of development is a key to any definition of "the postcolonial condition." In the period after the Second World War, when the demise of direct colonial rule appeared inevitable, the apparatus of development institutionalized a new mode of global governmentality.[14] Inaugurated by the Bretton Woods institutions, a new era of global politics began that recognized the geographic division of the world into formally equal nation-states. It was no surprise that colonialism, as a system of geographic conquest among *competing* Western nation-states, should have spawned movements of resistance along national lines—the nation was immanent in colonial rule. As movements of independence in the Third World led to the universalization and naturalization of the order of nation-states, however, a different regime of domination and management replaced the explicit administrative and economic control exercised during official colonialism.[15] In this new regime of global governance, development discourses and institutions interpellated the newly independent nation-states of the Third World into particular temporal and spatial locations. Temporally, Third World nation-states were allochronistically positioned, that is, seen as being "behind" the West, as inhabiting a period that lay in the dim recesses of the history of the "developed" world. The term "allochronism," borrowed from Johannes Fabian (1983), labels the familiar process whereby regions in the Third World are thought to occupy the past, thereby denying that the poverty and underdevelopment of the many might be directly related to the current structures of inequality that result in growing wealth for the few.[16] Geographically, newly emerging nation-states, no matter what their position on the map, were located on "the periphery" of a world system whose center lay on the Euro-American axis.

Thus, in using the term "postcolonial condition," I index a specific set of locations articulated by the historical trajectories of European colonialism, developmentalism, and global capitalism. I prefer to employ "postcolonial condition" instead of "postmodern condition" (see Harvey 1989) because colonialism is not considered a central structuring principle in creating the postmodern condition.[17] According to Stuart Hall (1996:249): "In the restaged narrative of the post-colonial, colonisation assumes the place and significance of a major, extended and ruptural world-historical event. By 'colonisation,' the 'post-colonial' references . . . the whole process of expansion, exploration, conquest, colonisation and imperial hegemonisation which constituted the 'outer face,' the constitutive outside, of European and then Western capitalist modernity after 1492."

My emphasis on the postcolonial *condition* is intended to draw attention to a specific conjuncture that has shaped the lives and experiences of people in rural India. Thus, I am interested in the institutions and discourses which position subjects and which configure their experience in particular ways, and not just with a body of theory that may be labeled "postcolonial." I use postcolonial theory because it enables me to describe and analyze compellingly the condition of subaltern, rural people in India, their agricultural and ecological practices, and their forms of political organization, and not just because I find it a creative and innovative new theory (although that would have been a sufficient reason for using it).

In the first chapter, I show that what constitutes the experience of modernity as "postcolonial" in a country such as India is the acute self-awareness of this temporal lag and spatial marginality.[18] Development discourses, with their built-in teleologies and spatial hierarchies, created subject positions that reinscribed inequalities after the dismantling of formal domination with the end of colonial rule. Thus "development" is about the economic position of a nation-state relative to others, but it is also crucially a form of identity in the postcolonial world. To be "underdeveloped" or "developing" is to be backward, deficient, inadequate, behind. The most important way in which questions of identity are hinged to development is through the metonymic association of the human life cycle with the growth of the nation. If there is an enduring trope in development discourse, it is that which equates "development" with adulthood and "underdevelopment" with infancy and immaturity. The temporal lag of postcoloniality is inscribed onto developing nations, anthropomorphized as less-than-fully-formed subjects, whose growth and maturity has to be supervised and monitored by those who have reached adulthood—that is, by the West. In this way, development discourse has served to naturalize the control of the "underdeveloped" world by the West after the demise of formal colonial rule. Development discourse, therefore, not only has served to subject the Third World to Western control through a phalanx of institutions and treaties but has also created the "underdeveloped" as a subject and "underdevelopment" as a form of identity in the postcolonial world.

So far, I have spoken of "the postcolonial" condition in India almost entirely with respect to its imbrication in global discourses of development. This begs the following question: Is the formal end of colonial rule and the worldwide dissemination of the discourses and institutional forms of development *the* most important aspect of postcoloniality? And, if so, what is the relationship between postcoloniality and other global processes, such as that of world capitalism?[19] Further, does positing a relationship between postcoloniality and late capitalism automatically lead to an endorsement of the use of metanarratives?[20] In this book, I have employed two strategies to counter the (implicit) teleologies of metanarratives. But before explaining the two strategies, let me interject that I wish to guard against the hasty equation often made between macrological explanations and metanarratives. The postmodern critique of *metanarratives* has too often been extended to any explanation that seeks to account for *global* phenomena such as capitalism, confusing closure with scale. There is, thus, an inadvertent substitution of time for space, as a critique of certain uses of time in historical narrative is extended to that of the use of space in geographic explanation. In Marx's story about capitalism, those features are linked, as the teleological unfolding of the narrative of capital requires its worldwide expansion. But there is no reason to believe that nonteleological explanations about capitalism as a global phenomenon cannot be advanced. Hence, it is a mistake to assume that a critique of teleology stands in for a critique of macrological explanations. Some scholars have argued that a turn to "local" events and individual life narratives is a way to evade totalizing explanations. "Local" phenomena, however, are surely no less susceptible to totalizing, unsituated, and teleological representations than "global" ones.[21]

The first antiteleological strategy that I have employed is to demonstrate that resistances and contestations at different sites make the direction taken by macrological processes such as capitalism and postcoloniality uncertain: examining these narratives in any detail at a particular site shakes one's confidence in pronouncing the direction in which they are heading. My second antiteleological strategy is to reject a single characterization of "the postcolonial." In the chapters that follow, I have chosen to investigate what postcoloniality might mean for the rural majority in India by examining shifts in national agricultural policies, transformations in the world food economy, changes in discourses of development, the everyday practices of farmers in the village of Alipur, and peasant mobilization at the regional and national levels. In each chapter, the emphasis is on a slightly different aspect of the postcolonial condition.

To understand why certain kinds of agricultural policies were pursued, how they were implemented, and whether they were adopted by farmers, it is important to keep three different macrological frames in mind. The different temporalities of each macrological frame created moments of overlap but also periods of disjuncture, and it is precisely in the affinity and differentiation between these three macrologies that something called "postcoloniality" came into being for rural people. The first macrological frame, as mentioned above, is development discourse. After the attainment of independence in 1947, the nationalist

Congress government, with the help of international "development" experts and institutions, decided to pursue a strategy of modernization that relied on the rapid establishment of heavy industry. This development strategy was also shaped by the alliances and conflicts of the cold war, during which the Indian government followed a policy of non-alignment, a political stance mirrored in its adoption of a "mixed" economy that combined state planning with capitalism. The development path adopted during the postcolonial era, however, was contested by, among others, the better-off members of the peasantry, who perceived that they stood to lose from policies emphasizing industrial growth. As a consequence, these development policies were modified in different postindependence periods. Thus, any macrological account of the discourses, practices, and institutions of "development" must take into account its shaping by peasant resistance and activism: without an understanding of the effect of peasant resistance, therefore, we lose sight of the particular trajectory of "development" in India (see Chapter 1 for further details).

At the same time—and this is the second macrological frame considered in this book—the course of "development" was also defined by the changing nature of global capitalism. Regional differences in postcoloniality were perhaps most evident here. After the end of formal colonization, trade and multinational capital largely followed old colonial connections or neocolonial ones. For example, South Asia had closer links to British multinationals, whereas Latin America had a "special" relationship to the United States. But as capitalist production itself shifted from raw material extraction in the colonies to the export of Fordism for the exploitation of low-wage labor and then to the present era of flexible accumulation and just-in-time production, it has led to and been accompanied by profound shifts in industrial and agricultural policies in postcolonial nation-states. At particular moments, as in the pressure put by multilateral institutions on indebted governments to adopt neoliberal policies in the 1980s, transformations in global capitalism have worked in concert with changes in development orthodoxy and the politics of nation-states. With the beginning of a renewed phase of capitalist expansion built on the rapid development of communication technologies and the tighter interconnection of financial markets, multilateral institutions and development orthodoxy shifted to the advocacy of neoliberal positions such as the reduction of fiscal deficits, the lowering of protective tariffs, and the opening of all markets to multinational corporations. Further, the collapse of a tottering Soviet bloc shrank the room for maneuver available for Third World nation-states who could no longer play off the superpowers against each other. At other times, however, as in the import-substitution strategies adopted by many Latin American countries and India in the fifties and sixties, "development" strategies embedded in the ambitions of nationalist leaders had a much more agonistic relationship with the centers of capitalist production in the West.

The potential disarticulations between "development" and capitalism become even more complicated when one considers the third macrological frame that I wish to draw attention to here. When studying agriculture in an "underdeveloped" country like India, one needs to take into account major international transformations in the technology of food production. Using techniques first developed in the program to breed high-yielding varieties of corn in the United States, new varieties of wheat were discovered and successfully produced in Mexico and subsequently exported to India. These new wheats, called high-yielding varieties, or HYVs for short, but more popularly known as the green revolution, were dependent on high doses of fertilizer and water. After their introduction to India in 1967 on the heels of two years of severe drought and food shortages, national food grain production shot up to unprecedented new levels. This newfound self-sufficiency in food grains actually undermined the dumping of surplus production from the United States, cutting off a potentially lucrative market for multinational companies involved in grain production and transportation.[22] Any straightforward explanation following from the "interests" of agricultural capital would therefore be hard-pressed to explain the "export" of this new technology of food grain production. Two factors combined to produce the HYV strategy for national food self-sufficiency in the Third World. The first factor was the employment of the highly resource-intensive method of production geared to large commercial agriculture in the United States as a model; and the second factor was a paradigm of national development premised on mimicking the historical trajectory of industrial nation-states. Nationalism was thus not only assumed to be an overriding goal by Third World elites but also normalized as a universal project in the postcolonial world.

This particular configuration of "postcoloniality," centered on the project of national self-sufficiency under the tutelage of the "developed" world, is being reshaped in the last decade of the twentieth century. A new technology of agriculture based on genetic engineering is threatening to alter methods of food production drastically all over the world.

This time, however, there is a convergence between high-tech methods of food production, a neoliberal development regime, and late-capitalist firms interested in profiting from the sale of intellectual property rights. Hence there are shifts in the manner in which technologies of food production, the politics of nation-states, global regimes of development, and the organization of capital articulate with one another. Instead of reducing the explanation to one overriding principle, I have endeavored to maintain the tension between these phenomena, demonstrating how a conjunctural analysis of postcoloniality can attend to moments of both disarticulation and articulation.[23]

Chapter 1 charts the moments of interlinkage and conflict between discourses of development, the world food economy, and the high-yielding varieties program. I pay particular attention to the interweaving of these processes in India from the mid-sixties to the early nineties. I intend to demonstrate that a rich and complex story about the interconnections between "development," the world food economy, and the green revolution can be constructed to enable us to understand what the condition of postcoloniality might mean for nonelite, rural people in the Third World. My objective is to convey a sense of both the connections between these macrologies and the contingencies that shape them at particular times and places. The green revolution is a good example of a technological phenomenon whose global reach and importance was not a foregone conclusion. After the "success" of the green revolution in India's tropical climate, the program was vigorously promoted by an international agricultural consortium to other parts of the tropical Third World. Had the program failed in India, even if the reasons for its failure had little to do with the high-yielding varieties themselves, it is doubtful that the green revolution would have been as enthusiastically promulgated as a "global" phenomenon.

As my ethnographic analysis in Chapter 1 demonstrates, these "global" processes did not impose themselves on a pliant and unwilling peasantry: they were actively resisted, accepted, and modified in the process. The ethnography illuminates the extent to which a "global" discourse like "development" is profoundly transformed through crises of realization in different locations. In India, conflict between industrial and agricultural interests over definitions of development and about the implementation of development programs and who should benefit from them profoundly shaped the nature of agrarian "development." For instance, intraparty conflicts led Indira Gandhi to embark on a populist path in 1971; soon afterward, however, groups of well-to-do peasant cultivators seized on this populism and employed it quite successfully *against* the state. Peasant groups, therefore, contested a particular hegemonic configuration of "development" and, in the process, asserted their own populist strategy of development in which rural areas would receive a larger share of benefits than had historically been the case in postcolonial India. The fact that oppositional populism employed the rhetoric of development indicated the success of development discourse in shaping the terrain of argumentation; however, the destabilization of a hegemonic notion of "development" was surely an important indication of the failure of the functioning of some universal and unitary process. Thus, it is important to maintain the tension between the universalizing and globalizing power of development discourse and its disputed and contentious redeployment in particular cultural and historical locations. The first chapter draws on bodies of literature from many different disciplines—anthropology, sociology, comparative politics, literary theory, policy analysis, development studies, and history—to construct a conjunctural analysis of the role played by agriculture in discourses of national development and of postcoloniality.

In Chapter 2 I take a close look at the articulation of the green revolution—a state-sponsored technological transformation in the means of food production—with state-sponsored programs to bring the fruits of "development" to the poorest and lowest-caste people in rural India. I use narratives of village politics in Alipur, specifically those revolving around contests for the position of headman, as a means to analyze the links between the green revolution and the government's development schemes. Together, these processes have had far-reaching and sometimes quite unintended effects. Development discourses were central both to the green revolution, which was launched to increase agricultural production so as to preserve the sovereignty of the postcolonial nation-state, and to programs specifically targeted at lower-caste and poor people. In the context of severe class and caste inequalities in rural areas, one would expect rural elites to support subsidies for production but oppose subsidies and benefits for lower-caste and poor people. I show why rural upper classes actually ended up supporting government programs for the poor and how the substantial surpluses from serving as brokers in the implementation of government programs tremendously increased the stakes of winning the election for the headman's position, creating deep political divisions in village society. At the same time, government programs for lower castes have necessarily been ac-

companied by a progressive social rhetoric of anticasteism and economic equality. Growing economic opportunities that enabled lower
castes not to rely as heavily on agricultural labor in the village, together
with the rhetoric of social equality and the dependence of the upper
castes on the electoral support of the lower castes, led to a phenomenal
transformation in the confidence with which lower-caste people dealt
with erstwhile landlords and other socially superior groups. Younger,
lower-caste men, still primarily wage laborers, publicly criticized upper-
caste people, something that their fathers would not have dreamed of
doing. Lower-caste people also mounted a challenge to a vision of "development" in which it was assumed that economic change would trig-
ger transformations in caste and social relations. They criticized state
officials for not implementing development programs properly but also
condemned the slow pace of social change. In this way, they questioned
nationalist claims that the postcolonial state would liberate the nation
from the poverty and caste oppression that colonial rule had wrought.
Questioning the state's ability to bring about development was also to
put into doubt its claims to postcoloniality.

Contestations of the state's claims of fostering "development" reveal
that the postcolonial condition is distinguished by heterogeneous temporalities that mingle and jostle with one another to interrupt the teleological narratives that have served both to constitute and to stabilize
the identity of "the West." And what exactly does that mouthful—
"teleological narratives of identity formation"—mean? Chapters 3 and 4
are devoted to unpacking this formulation by ethnographically examining indigenous discourses of agronomy and ecology in one particular
postcolonial setting. In Chapter 3 I provide a close analysis of indigenous knowledges of agronomy and their relevance to the agricultural
practices of farmers in Alipur. As in other green revolution areas,
farmers in the village used chemical fertilizers and electric tube wells to
grow hybrid varieties of wheat. At the same time, their agronomical
interpretations stressed that the health of a plant depended on the properties that were transmitted to it from fertilizers, irrigation water, and
the wind and how those properties affected the balance of humors—of
hot, cold, dry, and wet elements—necessary for its good health. Moreover, humoral understandings were constantly intermingled with those
derived from "scientific" agriculture. When asked to account for particular agricultural decisions, farmers drew on "indigenous" and "scientific" understandings of agronomy as well as on the politics of class and
caste in production relations. For example, a farmer might explain why

he did not irrigate his crop by talking about his recent conflict with the neighbor who usually supplied him irrigation water. But, at the same time, he might also point to the fact that the land did not "demand" more water, and because he had not applied any "hot" fertilizer, he did not need to irrigate the land to "cool" it as often as may have been necessary for other farmers. An understanding of agricultural practices, therefore, could not simply be deduced on the basis of indigenous knowledges alone, nor were practices intelligible entirely from the perspective of the politics of production relations.

Indigenous knowledge and indigenous people have come to occupy a privileged place in development discourse as well as in antimodern discourses, especially in the last decade.[24] In the third chapter, I question the notion of the "indigenous" and make a series of closely related arguments about its promise and problems. Any critique of "indigenousness" has to confront a central dilemma, which I have tried to navigate especially carefully. My struggle in this book has been to point to the limitations inherent in the notion of "indigenousness," while recognizing the strategic importance of that form of identity and supporting the political movements based on claims to indigenousness forged by some of the most marginal and disempowered people in the world. My argument is based on the premise that a theory of cultural difference used by anthropologists to analyze "indigenous knowledge" and "indigenous people" that emphasizes systems of meaning can be separated from the political project of supporting the struggles of subaltern peoples, some of whom may indeed find it strategically efficacious to claim an "indigenous" identity. I employ theories of "postcoloniality" in the belief that a cultural theory which stresses the hybridities and impurities that are the legacy of colonialism and global capitalism and which recognizes the continuously transforming impact of global inequalities on the lives of marginal people in the Third World can better account both for the conditions in which claims to indigenousness are politically effective and for those situations which do not allow such claims to be mustered. By pointing out that "indigenous knowledge" is not a static or closed system but is itself heterogeneous, hierarchical, and infused by relations of power and inequality; that "indigenousness" is a conjunctural location rather than an essential identity; and that the effectiveness of "indigenous" identity depends on its *recognition* by hegemonic discourses of imperialist nostalgia, where poor and marginal people are romanticized at the same time that their way of life is destroyed: in this manner I intend to highlight that claims to indigenous identity are, as Spivak (1988b:13) has termed it, a "strategic essentialism." In other words, claims to indigenousness entail staking a terrain within an unfolding war of position. That raises the following set of questions for me: When theorists of culture see resistance to colonial, capitalist, and ecological domination primarily in terms of indigenousness, where does that leave the majority of the subaltern and most desperately poor people in the world who cannot claim such an identity? Can an understanding of cultural difference be robust enough to account, on the one hand, for why "indigenousness" turns out to be such an effective cultural identity for some marginalized groups in the contemporary world and, on the other hand, for why so many of the world's most disempowered people cannot be helped by such claims?

To give a flavor of the argument in Chapter 3, I contend that a close study of indigenous knowledges and practices of agronomy and ecology reveals that they do not stand in as clear an opposition to the West as their most ardent advocates and staunchest critics would like to believe. Both the proponents of Western science and those of indigenous knowledge accept the duality between "the West" and "the indigenous," differing mainly in that they affiliate with opposite poles of that duality. But in advancing a position in which the closure of narratives of the identity of the West is attained through its alterity with the indigenous, what is overseen, suppressed, or erased? What does a critical examination of the indigenous tell us about the postcolonial condition? Does the recent revival of interest in indigenous knowledges serve to construct "the modern" in the process of criticizing it? I argue that these uses of indigenous may be closer to the concept that it seems to have supplanted—the traditional—than its supporters would like to acknowledge. "The indigenous" and "the traditional" are distinguished by being outside of and resistant to "the modern." They are defined by their status as residual categories of the "modern," and it is therefore not surprising that they are most frequently to be found in postcolonial Third World locations. In fact, a longer history of "the indigenous" would show the critical role that it played in colonial and nationalist discourse. In both, the indigenous was the source of a lost, authentic, national culture that needed to be recuperated. Nationalists did not simply want a return to that authentic culture but an updated, modern version of it that would give national culture a distinctive position in the world of nation-states. The nationalist position found its echo in some versions of development discourse that sought to preserve or salvage indigenous knowledge as an eco-friendly, sustainable alternative to the ravages of modernist progress. One way to mobilize discourses of indigenous knowledge in analyzing the agricultural practices of the farmers of Alipur would have been to emphasize the use of humoral agronomy and substantivist theories. Yet this mode of analysis could not have accounted for the use of industrial inputs, the commingling of humoral accounts with bioscientific ones, or the manner in which development programs shaped farmers' agricultural decisions. It is precisely these unexpected intersections—the legacy of the modernist projects of colonialism, nationalism, and development—that I have identified as being central defining features of the postcolonial condition. Postcolonial theory provides the analytic framework to describe these hybrid discourses and practices and to delineate the intertwining of "local" practices with global and national projects of development. It unsettles the binaries of colonial and nationalist thought in pointing to the imbrication of the indigenous in modernist discourse (Hall 1996:244, 247).[25] Postcolonial theory, therefore, enables a different kind of understanding of indigenous practices and discourses, one which does not seek to determine whether something is authentic, original, or uncontaminated but which accepts cultural hybridity as a starting point in political projects that seek to empower subaltern, poor, and marginal groups. In my use of notions of "hybridity," I am careful to underscore that it denotes a *set* of locations that are formed by structural violence and stratified by different kinds of inequalities.

In Chapter 4, the analysis of indigenousness is extended to questions of ecology by examining farmers' practices and discourses surrounding land quality and water resources. Farmers in Alipur were often quite critical of the impact that green revolution agriculture had on the strength of the soil but were sharply divided as to the exact causes for why that had happened. Similarly, they were conscious that the groundwater level was falling very quickly and that if it continued to decline at the same pace, it would completely destroy agriculture in Alipur. Although there were many different explanations offered for the drop in the groundwater level, including the absence of normal amounts of rainfall, there was substantial agreement that the introduction of tube well technology had been the primary cause for the depletion of groundwater.

The declining strength of the soil and falling groundwater levels, in turn, were thought to have an adverse impact on the health of humans. According to villagers, this was due to the detrimental properties imparted to the grain by chemical fertilizers, the displacement of more nutritious grains by the monocropping of wheat, and the consumption of cheaper and less nutritious food because of the need to preserve cash for purchasing inputs. Indigenous understandings of the interlinkage between the health of the soil, the health of plants, and the health of humans, therefore, were combined with a critique of green revolution technologies and their associated market-based demands. At the same time, however, farmers also expressed their satisfaction with the increased incomes and surpluses that the new agricultural technology had generated. In this manner, farmers had conflicting and contradictory assessments of the effects of the most important and visible "development" intervention in their lives—the green revolution. As with agronomical knowledges, ecological practices and discourses were marked by their startling juxtapositions and hybrid explanations, precisely those markings of postcoloniality that I discuss in Chapter 3.

From the rather detailed and specific discussion of the ecology of agriculture in Alipur in Chapter 4, I shift perspective to a much more global scale in Chapter 5, which deals with the politics of global environmentalism, exemplified by the Rio Accords. Just as global phenomena such as the green revolution have serious implications for the ecological practices of farmers in Alipur, so do global environmental treaties threaten to alter the relationship between farmers and their use of resources. And just as farmers in Alipur participated in peasant groups that criticized an urban-centered, ecologically nonsustainable development model, global treaties and neoliberal regimes have spawned movements of resistance that are forging transnational alliances between peasants and other grassroots organizations across the world.

Chapter 5 raises questions about the effect of global environmental treaties on the everyday lives of subaltern peoples. Are environmental treaties, such as the Rio Accords, indeed produced for the "common benefit of humankind"? And, if so, why were so many of the purported (nonelite) beneficiaries in the Third World opposed to them? Or are such transnational accords as those signed at the Earth Summit better seen as novel forms of regulation and control that have become necessary with the transformation of the nation-state? In particular, I argue that environmental problems and global treaties draw our attention to the growing tension between nation and state. As all participants at the Earth Summit realized, environmental problems have raised new questions for a system of nation-states founded on the principle of territorially based sovereignty. This system of sovereign nation-states had become consolidated in Europe by the beginning of the eighteenth century (Tilly 1975a) and provided the basis of colonial competition and the orderly transition to a postcolonial world. Global environmental problems and treaties are problematizing this coupling of nation and state. I deploy Ruggie's (1993:165) notion of the *unbundling* of territory to suggest that the hyphen between nation and state has been put into question. My objective is to explore the implications of this phenomenon of the unbundling of territory for understandings of postcoloniality.

One of the most important consequences of the unbundling of territorially based sovereignty is that it problematizes theories of neocolonialism. It does so because notions of neocolonialism hark back to a model of competition between nation-states that formed the basis of colonialism.[26] Instead, I advance the strong claim that *if* the term "postcolonialism" is to be used to signal a temporal rupture—as that which comes *after* colonialism—then it may indeed be an appropriate marker of new forms of global regulation and control in the waning years of the twentieth century. The term "postcolonial" oscillates continuously between marking an era that comes after the demise of formal colonial rule and denoting an analytic approach that attempts to go beyond the binaries of colonial discourse. Whereas proponents of postcolonial theory wish to emphasize the latter aspect, critics have focused on the temporalizing claims implicit in the notion of "postcoloniality." In my discussion of the postcolonial condition so far, I have concentrated on the heterogeneous temporalities and cultural hybridities that go into constituting social life in postcolonial societies. The analysis I present in Chapter 5, however, suggests that we may be witnessing a more decisive temporal break with the order of nation-states that underlay colonialism than has been the case so far. Thus, *post*coloniality in the strong sense, as an era that goes beyond the world of colonialism, may now, as never before, be an appropriate indicator of global social relations.

While I have great sympathy with the view that the "post" in "postcolonialism" is too often taken to mean that colonial forms of domination have faded into the dim recesses of the past, is it possible that *elements* of colonialism have been taken intact and configured into a new series of global domination? In other words, I argue that despite the fact that particular features of social life display a continuity with colonialism, they have been reconstituted as part of a different *pattern* of global control in which the nation-state no longer promises to play the central role it once did. To speak of postcoloniality, then, is to speak of the decline of the entire order of competitive nation-states that nurtured and sustained colonialism. It has been appropriately noted that the term "postcolonial," most often used to mark the era initiated by formal decolonization, sometimes underappreciates the real continuities between the colonial period and its immediate aftermath. However, the decline of the *order* of nation-states made visible in global environmental problems and regulations does indeed appear to signify a fundamental shift that might justify the use of the "post" as a temporal marker. The processes described in Chapter 5, therefore, might very well indicate the consolidation of the "postcolonial condition," a global process of regulation and control that does not depend as centrally on the nation-state as did its predecessor.[27]

These shifts in the nature of "postcoloniality" draw attention to the imprint of differing tempos of the end of *formal* colonial rule on diverse places. This century has been marked by successive waves of loosely clumped decolonizations since the late forties. By the time the satellite states of Russia that constituted the former Soviet Union broke free from its direct control, in countries like India the heady optimism proclaiming the dawning of a new age, where anything was possible, had already faded into oblivion. By the end of the eighties, a generation of Indians with no direct experience of colonial rule, whom Salman Rushdie (1980) has evocatively termed "midnight's children," had grown into adults and occupied positions of power. The expectation of rapid "development" that would lead to India's formation as a "modern" nation had been replaced by a rather thorough questioning of the entire project of modernity (Nandy 1984, 1987a; Kothari 1990). Colonized elites who had seized the reins of the state after independence, convinced that the avarice of colonial rulers was keeping their nation poor, themselves expressed grave doubts about the project of "development." The "failure" of modernity has been articulated by activists and scholars in a variety of debates on topics as diverse as secularism, medicine, the environment, education, development, and science and technology (apart from the work of Nandy and Kothari already cited, see Alvares 1992; Das 1990; Marglin and Marglin 1990; Shiva 1988, 1991, 1993b; Visvanathan 1988). In my treatment of postcoloniality, I have chosen to focus on "development" because of the centrality of those discussions of modernity for the agricultural sector.

The faith in development, activated in the period after independence, had in common with colonialism a narrative of the telos of the nation-state. The questioning of development and of the project of modernity has also brought in its wake a questioning of the sanctity of the nation and a profound skepticism about the nationalist project. It is in the context of this "postcolonial condition"—the inability to realize the promise of a modern nation-state (Nandy 1992:264)—that we have to situate the emergence of theoretical currents such as subaltern studies and postcolonial theory. A full explanation of these intellectual trends lies beyond the scope of this book; obviously, any explanation would have to account for the multiple and complex intersections between intellectual production and changes in the social world.[28]

Profoundly shaped by the *failure* to constitute a modern nation that mimics the development trajectory of "the West," postcolonial theory has had much less influence in locations or with groups that have had a longer period of formal independence, such as parts of Latin America; among people who are still colonized, such as native peoples in North America; and in places where the optimism of nationhood has not yet led to the disillusionment of postcoloniality, as in the former Soviet Union and in South Africa. The differing tempos of decolonization are precisely what need to be emphasized in comparing or contrasting different postcolonial conditions; for this reason, it is a mistake to use "the postcolonial" as a synonym for "the Third World."

The differing tempos of decolonization draw our attention to the play of similarity and difference that has to be analytically maintained in any attempt to understand "the postcolonial" dilemma. On the one hand, it is important to see modernity, colonialism, capitalism, development discourse, and international science as *global* phenomena that have far-reaching and systematic consequences for the regions that they affect. On the other hand, it is crucial not to overlook the differences in the forms taken by these global phenomena in multiple locations, differences that arise from contestation, reworking, and rearticulation. The opposition between "the global" and "the local" itself depends on a spatialized dichotomy that needs to be questioned.

My concern, therefore, is not to replicate the implicit spatial hierarchy constructed in speaking of the articulation of "the global" with "the local." Even scholars who do not dismiss "the local" as irrelevant end up privileging "the global" as that which brings change, whether positive or negative, to "the local." Whether it is the capitalist world system or modern modes of bureaucratic organization, military force, systems of thought, or scientific knowledge, the directionality of change, at least as far as the Third World is concerned, is usually depicted as being one-sided: from "the West" to "the rest." These narratives very often fail to acknowledge that "the global" too originates from *some* location: Eurocentric assumptions are thus smuggled in at the same time that they are being theoretically disavowed. Chapter 5 consists of an analysis of discourses on the global environment, which reveal this mechanism of disavowal most clearly. Thus, the challenge in analyzing global/local interactions is to be able to acknowledge simultaneously the historical inequalities resulting from colonial control and capitalist expansion and yet acknowledge the overdetermined nature of particular conjunctures and the situatedness of the theoretical and popular discourses surrounding them.

A further step that we need to take in thinking about the relationship of the global and the local is to question the spatial assumptions that enable such a duality to be constructed. If we take the nation-state as an originary unit of spatial organization, does "the global" stand for that which lies beyond the nation-state and "the local" for that which lies within it? In other words, does this duality depend on a naturalization of the nation-state? If the dichotomy between the global and the local is implicitly shaped by the nation-state, what do changing configurations of the nation-state imply for this distinction? In the concluding chapter, I explicitly address this question by looking at new forms of governmentality and their corresponding modes of resistance that are making this distinction a problematic one at the end of the twentieth century.

As a diasporic subject ambivalently located within the spaces of nation-states, it would appear proper that I should find postcolonial theories and identities to be a compelling subject. Yet the research project that provided the data for this book was not motivated by an interest in postcolonial theory. A brief history of this project, the methods used in fieldwork, and the textual strategies that I have employed in writing this book might be useful in helping contextualize both its content and style.

I came to do anthropological research quite by accident. After high school, I followed the path usually taken by immigrants from the South Asian subcontinent by obtaining undergraduate and graduate degrees in engineering. But I found my interests shifting to "development," and when I undertook a Ph.D. in Engineering-Economic Systems at Stanford, I devoted a substantial chunk of my course work to understanding economic development. During my studies, I discovered that questions of power and inequality were peripheral to large areas of development studies and that the lives, hopes, and fears of the subaltern were rarely addressed in most disciplines that dealt with "development." I decided to conduct a research project for my dissertation that involved empirical work at the grass roots, and it was with this resolve that I first went to do fieldwork in the village of Alipur in 1984. The fieldwork was to be part of my project on the rate and direction of technical change in agriculture.

When I first reached Alipur, I found myself the object of some suspicion. Learning where I had come from, villagers quite naturally wanted to know "why the Americans had sent me there." Did I work for the CIA? Or perhaps I was not a foreign agent but one recruited by the Indian government to determine how much villagers ought to be taxed. When I tried to explain that I was studying agriculture, they were genuinely puzzled. Why would someone be sent from a country with such "advanced" agriculture to a place where there was hardly any machinery? What could possibly be learned from studying agriculture in such a "backward" place? But the elders remembered another young man who had come to "study" there almost two decades earlier. "He kept asking us questions—he wanted to know everything, including how many handheld hoes we had!" they recalled. "Do you want to do the same kind of study?" I was grateful to that earlier researcher in more ways than they realized.

After all, one of the reasons why I had chosen Alipur as a "good" field site was that there was a "baseline" socioeconomic survey that I could use to document the changes that had occurred in the last quarter of a century. The village had been surveyed initially by a team from an institution of agricultural economics in Delhi and then resurveyed several years later by another group from the same institution. After some searching, I finally managed to track down a researcher who had conducted one of the earlier surveys, who convinced me that the data he had collected were not trustworthy. It dawned on me that if I could not trust the data collected by an institution which specialized in this task, what degree of confidence could I possibly have in the "avalanche of numbers"[29] that was generated to produce knowledge about rural India by a variety of state bureaucracies since the late nineteenth century (B. Cohn 1987a; Appadurai 1993b)? I gave up the idea of measuring changes from a baseline and proceeded to fashion a very detailed survey of agricultural practices, closely modeled on the earlier surveys done by the agricultural institute. My goal was to study the relationship between technological changes in Indian agriculture and shifts in class relationships. The rapid acceptance of green revolution technology in the countryside had inspired "the mode of production" debate in scholarly journals in India.[30] The question that ran through this controversy was whether a capital-intensive and capitalist technology would lead to increasing class divisions that in turn might create the conditions for revolutionary insurgence. In other words, would the "green" revolution turn red (Gough and Sharma 1973; Sharma 1973)? This was not idle speculation; in the late 1960s, a movement led by landless peasants in Naxalbari had turned into an armed revolutionary struggle in the state of West Bengal, absorbing the national imagination in the manner that Chiapas has more recently done in Mexico.[31] Both supporters and opponents of the green revolution, therefore, watched its effects with bated breath and debated whether the countryside was ready for a revolutionary upheaval.

By the time I went to do fieldwork in 1984, it was clear that the revolution in the making in rural India was not red but, in Daniel Thorner's droll phrase, "steel grey" (cited in Thorner 1982:1963). Capitalist agriculture seemed well ensconced and thriving in the Punjab, Haryana, and, most recently, western Uttar Pradesh. But, although there had been various statistical studies of agriculture, there were very few ethnographies that documented the relationship between the new technologies and the transformations in the manner in which class inequalities were actually lived in rural India. This, then, was what I had hoped to record in my fieldwork. How did the new technologies of production alter the everyday lives of the rural poor? How did it change class relations? Was the introduction of a much more capital-intensive method of agriculture clearly sifting rural society into capitalists on one side and the landless proletariat on the other?[32]

When I came back to Stanford to start writing my dissertation, I realized that the themes that interested me had more to do with the politics of the green revolution than was evident from the painstakingly collected quantitative production data on which I had spent most of my time in Alipur. In doing the survey, however, I had learned much about farmers' beliefs and understandings of agriculture, and I used this knowledge to explain why certain technologies of agriculture had been adopted and had flourished.

I moved away from my dissertation project for a few years (except to collect more data in two rounds of further fieldwork in 1989 and 1991–92). Teaching in social science departments first at the University of Washington and later at Stanford helped me to gain a better appreciation for a range of anthropological concerns and methods and to situate anthropological work within a wider interdisciplinary field. I grew more concerned with the relationship of identities to shifting structural contexts, especially in the light of academic reconceptualizations of culture as a spatialized marker of identity (Gupta and Ferguson 1992, 1997; Gupta 1992). When I returned to this project, I had completely re-thought its analytical frame and had obtained so much more data that I proceeded to write this book anew. It was no longer an extension of the dissertation project but a different project altogether, with different goals and substantially new data. The book came to be centrally con-cerned with the politics of postcolonial identities rather than the green revolution, although the argument crucially hinges on the importance of the latter for questions of identity through a consideration of dis-courses of development.

Because the rest of the book is concerned with explicating this theme, I will not dwell on the topic here; instead, I would like to address my choice of methods and of textual construction. Having taught a gradu-ate seminar on methods for the past two years, I have been surprised at how little most authors say about their methods. When I read an eth-nography, I do not expect to find a lengthy discussion about field methods or even an obligatory discussion thrown into the introductory chapter. But what surprises me is that there is often no statement what-soever about how the data were obtained. I do not naïvely believe that enumeration is an index of quality and that the number of hours of interviews or observation or the length and detail of surveys are neces-sarily fruitful indicators of the quality of the research. But I do think that it is minimally useful to indicate whether the material for a chapter was obtained from participant-observation, surveys, interviews, news re-ports, posters, or literature generated by other ethnographers. One should not have to scan footnotes and keep guessing as to how authors know what they claim to represent. In raising these questions, I take the risk of falling short of these standards; however, I have endeavored to state clearly the methods that I have used at the beginning of each chap-ter. Ethnographers have almost never exclusively employed participant-observation in their monographs, relying on other written sources such as archives, news reports, pamphlets, statistical data collected by states and international agencies, other kinds of audiovisual information, and secondary literature generated by other academics. Despite this fact, participant observation continues to be implicitly coded as the most legitimate source of "real" data.[33] Therefore, part of my interest in seeing a more explicit account of methods is to create room for acknowledging that anthropologists do and should legitimately use a variety of research methods in pursuing their agendas. How important a role ethnography plays in different research projects should depend on the questions that the anthropologist seeks to illuminate. Even within a monograph, some chapters might rely more heavily on observation, others on life narratives, and still others on the analysis of statistical data or textual analysis. Stating *what* they rely on might help readers decide how to interpret the analysis, as well as open up the field of possibilities of what "anthropological analysis" does or should do.

There is then the further question of how one goes about constructing a text. Clearly, methods of fieldwork and techniques of representation are closely linked. Both—the claims made in an ethnography and the presentation of the ethnographer's knowledge—are shaped not only by the kind of data collected but also the manner in which those data were obtained. I should clarify that my use of the term "data" is intended to include different types of information, sense-data, feelings, and memories and is not intended to have solely objectivist connotations. There is, by now, a body of creative work in anthropology that draws attention to diverse questions of representation: how the ethnographer is positioned within the text, questions of polyvocality, the representation of respondents' voices, problems of translation, the "staging" of dialogic encounters, concerns about authorship, the use of photographs and audiovisual techniques, and anthropologists' responsibility to their subjects and respondents. Although I do not intend to deal with each issue here, my positions will be apparent from the choices I make in the text. But I do wish to draw attention to one feature of the manuscript that may help explain my position on other issues of representation.

One of the primary goals guiding the selection of data, the representation of data within the text, and the manner in which I have presented my own commentary and understanding is that I have aspired to write a book that encourages reinterpretation. Of course, all books are open to reinterpretation. But I think that it is reasonable to maintain that some ethnographies allow greater room for rereading than others. It goes without saying that authors carefully select what data to present, how to present these data, whose voices should be included and whose excluded, and what topics are addressed in a text. On any given topic or event described in an ethnography, conflicting and multiple perspectives are usually to be found. Should an ethnographer represent all of them? The most important ones? How does one decide what is important? Once that decision has been made and a few main positions identified, how should the voices of the different people articulating those perspectives be represented? How should the ethnographer's own presence be acknowledged in generating those different perspectives? These are by no means easy questions, and they resist unitary responses: there is simply no formula to determine the "right" approach.

What I have tried to do in this book is to emphasize differences in perspectives on a range of questions. I attempt to include at least some voices representing the different positions that I heard. To do this without undue repetition and to convey the thoughts of different people while keeping the flavor of their own voices has been a real challenge. I have used long quotations wherever possible to impart not only the content of individuals' utterances but also its timbre, texture, and tone. My effort to display contestation and disagreement is not simply a textual device but a choice driven by the argument of the book. If the postcolonial condition is marked by the contradictory juxtaposition of incommensurable discourses in the everyday lives of rural people in northern India, then it behooves me to provide evidence of this fact. Similarly, because my argument is that different discourses are juxtaposed on one another instead of being synthesized into a new, overarching system of meaning, I do not present an analytic frame that unifies the argument. In other words, in my text I do not attempt to demonstrate an analytic mastery over the data, sealing off all the loose ends into one coherent, authoritative explanation. For to do so would edit out all the material that did not fit the explanation, which is indeed the "normal" process by which scholarship proceeds. It is precisely for this reason that the phenomena that I have documented in this book have not received the kind of attention they deserve. In contrast, my effort to embrace what would be considered "the excess" flows out of an analytic concern that the distinctive feature of the material under consideration is that it resists a unifying explanation, that it does not lend itself to that kind of analytic closure. This also makes the text "vulnerable" to reinterpretation and rethinking, and it is precisely this *vulnerability* that I have tried hard to achieve. Odd as such a claim might appear in the face of a model of scholarship in which the attempt to control and to gain mastery is considered a virtue,[34] I think that it is one of the essential qualities of a good ethnography. "Vulnerability" has perhaps an unnecessarily defensive connotation; what I seek to achieve is a text that *invites* rethinking and reanalysis.

There continues to be a fairly large gulf between the humanistic bent of most postcolonial theory and social-scientific scholarship on agricultural issues in disciplines such as anthropology, rural sociology, political science, geography, and agricultural economics.[35] In weaving my way through a complicated set of issues having to do with postcolonial conditions, alternative forms of modernity, development discourses, and the institution of new forms of governmentality, I endeavor to employ postcolonial theory on topics with which it has normally not been associated. Those studying agriculture and political economy are skeptical of the doctors of discourse, who they fear are too entangled in texts and theory that bear little connection to the lives and fears of the subaltern. In turn, those studying representations and discourses are wary of the metaphysics of presence in the descriptions and analyses offered by scholars of agriculture.[36] My objective is to bridge this gap and initiate a critical dialogue between disciplines and, equally important, to present an analysis that could be useful to further the objectives of social movements: I am convinced that a sharpened understanding of the forces that threaten to push the world's poor beyond the edge of survival will help us better resist these forces. If intellectuals are to claim an affiliation with these processes of resistance, then it is surely important to go beyond the territorial claims to topics and methods asserted in disciplinary boundaries.

It is for this reason that I draw on a range of disciplines—development studies, literary theory, feminist theory, cultural geography, political science, sociology, ecology, history, and agricultural economics—to construct this text. My objective is to write an ethnographic text that employs methods considered central to anthropology, as well as methods used more frequently in adjacent disciplines. For this reason, people in different disciplines might find in this book something that speaks to their chief concerns and methods but much that is different or foreign to their way of thinking about these questions.

By now, the call for "interdisciplinary" work is quite old. It is already more than a decade since Geertz declared genres to have blurred (1983:19–35). Yet, the power of institutional procedures being what they are, genuinely interdisciplinary work is still not very common. The recent enthusiasm for cultural studies has seen scholars attempting to emulate its emphasis on combining methodological interdisciplinarity with activist political engagement. In my own case, I started out attempting to understand the class implications of the "green revolution" in northern India. That project led me to an examination of the nature of the development regime in the post–Second World War period and the world food economy, on the one hand, and the detailed ethnographic study of indigenous understandings of agronomy and ecology in one village in northern India, on the other. In showing the tight interweaving of phenomena usually dubbed as global and "macro" and those conceptualized as local and "micro," I have also attempted to bring anthropologists and their concerns into conversation with those in other disciplines.

Any book that covers the range of topics, disciplines, and levels of analysis as does this one will have sections that some readers will find closer to their interests than are others. I have written each chapter so that it can be read independently, and I will now try to indicate which sections of the book might appeal more to which audiences. Those interested in postcoloniality, development, local/global connections, nationalism, agricultural policy, social movements, and South Asia should find the entire book to be of interest. Those primarily concerned with agrarian politics and global food regimes will find Chapters 1, 2, and 5 to be relevant. People who are struggling to come to terms with "the indigenous" might have some sympathy with my own efforts in Chapters 3 and 4. For those interested in the social history of technology, Chapters 1, 3, and 4 will be most useful. Finally, readers whose primary concerns are ecological will find that Chapters 4 and 5 speak most directly to their concerns.

1

Agrarian Populism in the Development
of a Modern Nation

I n this chapter I attempt to delineate what the "postcolonial condition" means for some rural subjects of a "modern" nation-state. Taking Appadurai's insight that there are other histories and modalities of being modern than the one that has characterized "the West" (1991), I endeavor to investigate ethnographically what such "alternative modernities" might consist of by considering the role of development discourses in postcolonial India. To assert that modernity takes different forms, given the specificities of particular historical situations, would perhaps be accurate enough but would remain at the level of a truism. One needs to ask, What makes for a specifically *postcolonial* experience of modernity? And how is that experience shaped by conjunctural relations of inequality that crisscross global, national, regional, and local levels to form particular fields of power?

I argue that the postcolonial period in India is characterized by the distinctive character of the relationship between modernity and development. "Development" has served as the chief legitimating function of ruling regimes and as the most important "reason of state" in independent India. This is quite ironic, for developmentalism, in its evolutionary assumptions, in its essentialization of differences, in its presumption of homogeneity *within* areas considered essentially different, and in its narratives of progress, shares a great deal with colonial, and specifically Orientalist, discourses. Rather than argue that "development" becomes a means to recolonize the Third World, I demonstrate that it enters a series of relationships that institute a new form of government rationality. I borrow the notion of governmentality from Foucault (1991) and extend it to refer to those novel institutional modes for the global regulation of populations, bodies, and things, of which development is a primary example (see also Scott 1995).[1]

Here, I analyze the development of agriculture as a critical link in the forging of a "modern" nation. Global discourses of development and international food regimes play a central role in shaping the evolution of national policies and agricultural practices at the local level. One of the most important ways in which discourses of development have affected the everyday lives of villagers in North India is through populist politics, policies, and programs. Populism not only has been the medium in which the discourses and practices of development are conveyed to villagers but has also provided one of the critical axes along which oppositional groups have organized support for their actions. The failure of development forms the rallying cry for oppositional groups to coalesce. Accordingly, I pay attention both to governmental and oppositional populisms and to their changing relationship over time. If postcolonial modernity is defined by the centrality of "development," then populism, especially agrarian populism, is its most important feature.

Because I have attempted to bring together an unusually ambitious set of scholarly literatures in making the argument here, a word about method is necessary. I have positioned historical changes in national agricultural policy within the broader framework of the global food economy and international discourses of development. Since the latter are intended mainly for contextual purposes, I have resorted to the secondary literature to explain the specificities of populist policies and their reception in India. My explanation of populism concentrates equally on state policies and regional movements. Here, I have used the writings of those who formulated policy, newspaper accounts, and the secondary literature. Finally, to interpret what populist policies meant to rural folk in western Uttar Pradesh, my ethnographic fieldwork proved invaluable. In what follows, therefore, I use a combination of methods derived from anthropology, sociology, policy analysis, and political geography to address the intimate connections between what are sometimes represented, I believe erroneously, as discrete levels of analysis—global, national, regional, and local.

I begin this chapter by attempting to locate the central role played by agriculture in the development of a modern nation. I first analyze development as a modernist discourse and next look at the role of agriculture in colonial and nationalist ideas of "progress" in India during the late nineteenth century and in the two decades immediately preceding independence. These connections between agriculture and modernity were to be transformed by the institutionalization of development and by the structure of the world food economy in the era that followed the Second World War. Postcolonial discourses of development in India reflected a tension between "industry-first" and "agriculture-first" strategies, which was eventually defused by a famine that led to a crisis of sovereignty and the green revolution.

The origins of agrarian populism lay in this crisis of sovereignty, which is the subject of the second section. The green revolution was instituted during the tenure of Indira Gandhi as prime minister, and it was at that very time that she turned to populist programs. To understand why that happened, I first briefly examine the theoretical literature on populism to see the links posited between populism and "underdevelopment." Next, I investigate what it was about Indira Gandhi's rhetoric and policies that qualified them as populist. The section ends with a consideration of how populism was "received" by its audience and what enabled it to succeed among the poor and dispossessed.

The third section concerns the deployment of populism by oppositional groups based in the class of well-to-do owner-cultivators. The first part briefly sketches a history of the most important populist peasant party in North India, the Bharatiya Kranti Dal (BKD). After the demise of the BKD in 1987, a new group called the Bharatiya Kisan Union (BKU) took over and organized a series of successful protests. I closely examine the populist ideology and tactics of the BKU, both the features which have made it so successful and those which have limited its appeal. Because development has played such a central role in the legitimation strategies of postcolonial regimes, the failure to implement development has proved to be an effective strategy for antigovernmental mobilization. Indira Gandhi's own populism relied on an attack on previous regimes for failing to make the fruits of development available to the poor. The BKU, therefore, took the rhetoric of the crisis of development from the ruling Indira Congress and turned it against the regime, making corruption and the government's antirural policies its two main planks. The BKU's success resulted from a clever combination of specific complaints with a broader critique of the industry-first, urban-based vision of a modern nation being pursued by successive governments.

The last section of the chapter situates the struggle over agrarian populism in India in the broader context of changes in the global food economy in the seventies and eighties. Populist struggles within the country took a different turn with the imposition of a structural adjustment program, the signing of the General Agreement on Tariffs and Trade (GATT), the advent of a new kind of plant biotechnology rooted in genetic engineering, and the entry of food-sector multinationals.[2] I consider the reaction of well-to-do peasants to these transformations in greater detail in Chapter 5. This chapter ends by noting that the terrain on which populist struggles in the agricultural sector were based has irrevocably shifted as a result of the transformations in the world food economy in the two decades since the early seventies. A particular strategy of development, in which agricultural subsidies played a central role to ensure *national* food self-sufficiency, is being replaced by an export-oriented, "market-friendly" direction. Because such a path overtly deviates from the history of the "developed" countries, it has thrown into question the possibility of achieving modernity through mimicry. Is it any wonder then that development itself is increasingly being questioned as a desirable goal?[3]

The Place of Agriculture in a Modern Nation

To speak of modernity is less to invoke an empirical referent than a self-representation of the West. In this self-representation, consciously built on a *difference* with another (the "Orient," the "rest"), the West emerges as the "model, the prototype and the measure of social progress" (Hall 1992:313). As Hall (1992:277) points out, "the 'West' is an *historical*, not a geographical, construct." In speaking of "the West," I refer to the effects of hegemonic representations of the Western self rather than its subjugated traditions. Therefore I do not use the term to refer simply to a geographic space but to a particular historical conjugation of place, power, and knowledge. The "modern," the celebration of Western progress, civilization, rationality, and development, came to be instituted as a global phenomenon through colonialism and through multiple and diverse modes of governance and domination in the postcolonial world (Hall 1992). After the formal demise of colonialism, one of the chief mechanisms by which this self-representation has been promulgated has been through the discursive formation known as "development" (Ferguson 1990; Escobar 1995). *Development* is a discourse that rehearses, in a virtually unchanged form, the chief premises of the self-representation of modernity: the belief in teleological narratives; the idea that "progress" occurs along a single path; the conviction that "Western," industrial countries have already arrived at the telos (although it would be more accurate to say that they were always already there); and, finally, the notion that it is nation-states, configured according to a particular logic of territorial exclusion and certain concepts of sovereignty, that constitute the basis of analysis and action. "Development," in other words, is Orientalism transformed into a science for action in the contemporary world.[4]

This self-representation of modernity, as promulgated by the models, doctrines, policies, programs, institutions, and discourses of development, is an inescapable feature of everyday life in contemporary northern India, as in many other parts of the world. To live in the village that I have called Alipur is to confront in many different contexts, shapes, and forms the self-representation of modernity through the discourses, institutions, and practices of "development." When I speak of alternative forms of modernity, I refer in this minimal way to an experience of being, in which the self-representation of modernity is a pervasive and omnipresent fact. At the same time, as will be amply clear in what follows, it does not mean that people in rural India lead, or aspire to lead, "Western" lives.

What, then, does it mean to say that there are other ways of being modern? To the extent that teleological views of history, a belief in progress, a conviction of one's own backwardness compared with the "West," and a naturalization of the spatial imperatives of the nation-state operate to configure the self-understandings of postcolonial subjects, they are indeed profoundly within the space and spell of "the modern." But it is also clear that the state of being modern is not a homogeneous experience, not just across the world, but within the political and geographic space of the nation-state. So what accounts for the difference of "the modern" in India? Clearly, one of the differences lies in the fact that the properties of "the modern" adumbrated above underspecify its contents. Employing a teleological narrative of history, for example, says almost nothing of its contents. This was evident in the deep conflicts between colonial and nationalist interpretations of the past, both of which were committed to teleological narratives.[5]

There is, however, another factor which to my mind is far more critical. What makes Indian modernity different is that the *fact of difference* itself is a constitutive moment that structures the experience of modernity. In other words, what makes the experience of modernity different in India is that, within experience, the self-representation of modernity is never absent. It is found not as an "absent presence" in the way that "the rest" is to conceptions of "European" identity but as an active presence, as present-to-itself. For this reason, the attempt to locate "India" precisely in the narratives of modernity—premodern, anti-modern, just plain modern, or postmodern—is doomed to failure if it refuses to recognize its own complicity with the self-representation of modernity. To search for premodern or antimodern critiques of "development," therefore, as many prominent intellectuals are currently doing, is to occupy a space of opposition created by modernity's representation of itself.[6] This is not to deny the importance of articulating alternatives to "development." To the contrary, it is to argue that the search for alternatives can begin only by rigorously acknowledging the impossibility of transcendence.[7] Modernity's representation of itself is a social fact in the villages of northern India, and not "merely" an analytic choice available to the scholar.[8] That most social science continues to employ modernity's self-representation as well is a separate, if related, question.

The particular form in which self-representations of modernity are deployed most frequently in the Third World is through development discourse. The symptoms of "underdevelopment" are clearly revealed through its agricultural sector. If a high proportion of the net domestic product is dependent on agriculture and if a large proportion of its labor force is employed on farms, then the nation-state is pronounced to be afflicted with the malady of "underdevelopment" (Varshney 1995:200). For this reason, the development of agriculture is an index of the health of the nation. The normalized narratives of development constructed from the "stylized" facts of a few nation-states reveal that agricultural surpluses, extracted by taxation and savings, form the basis on which industrial expansion takes place.[9] Food self-sufficiency, as we shall see, becomes a crucial geopolitical issue. For all these reasons, the agricultural sector is absolutely central to the development of a "modern" nation-state.

In the rest of this chapter, I argue that one cannot understand the project of "developing" the agricultural sector in India without seeing how populism shapes its ideological climate, institutional structures, and the daily practices of different rural subjects. Development practices are crucially shaped by different appropriations of populist policies and the struggles that ensue from those. Understandings of development are largely dependent on the standardized use of certain kinds of aggregate statistics: national income, employment, trade, output, population, and so on. Although no doubt valuable for some purposes, such statistics do not always reveal what the *experience* of everyday life means for people in a particular "development regime."

"Development" as a modernist discourse

Development has thus become one of those words—like security or democracy—which apparently requires no definition, for everyone knows, instinctively, what it is. It is what "we" have.—Kate Manzo, "Modernist Discourse and the Crisis of Development Theory"

Even an archaeologist of "development discourse" would pause to wonder at the remarkable consequences of the apparatus that was put into place at Bretton Woods in 1944, when the World Bank[10] and the International Monetary Fund (IMF) were created (Mason and Asher 1973:11–35; Meier 1984:10–23; Lumsdaine 1993).[11] A regime of development took over where formal colonial rule came to an end.[12] As newly independent nations joined the table at the United Nations (UN), they were put into a prefabricated slot, namely, that of "underdeveloped nations" (Pletsch 1981). Through a small and standardized list of selected indices—gross national product (GNP), savings, investment, population density, production, input/output ratios, and balance of payments—operating on an already chosen division of "sectors"—agriculture, industry, infrastructure, transportation, and energy—countries were deemed to be suffering from the malady of underdevelopment (Escobar 1995:3–4, 23–24). The power of development discourse is evident in the declaration, on President Kennedy's suggestion, of the 1960s as the United Nations "Development Decade" (Lumsdaine 1993:47). A full history of the rise and proliferation of the development apparatus remains to be written.[13] My intention here is to focus on one very specific aspect of this story. I do not, therefore, intend to summarize theories of development but merely to pick up on a few, less-noted aspects that critics of development have pointed out.

The particular aspect of development that I wish to explore becomes evident when we ask who is being referred to when Manzo states that "development" has become a self-evident concept, so that "everyone knows, instinctively, what it is." In other words, what is being proposed here is the formation of a certain kind of subject. This subject position is well captured in the memorable words of Ivan Illich, commenting on the extraordinary effects of the Bretton Woods institutions: "Scarcely twenty years were enough to make two billion people define themselves as underdeveloped."[14] Development discourse makes people subjects in both senses that Foucault emphasizes: subjected to someone else by a relationship of control and dependence, and tied to one's own identity through self-knowledge (1983:212). "Developed" and "underdeveloped" are not just terms that indicate the position of nation-states in an objective matrix defined by quantitative indicators, as the formal operations of the development apparatus—exemplified by the tables of the World Bank's annual reports—would have us believe. They are also, and to my mind far more importantly, forms of identity in the postcolonial world. To be "underdeveloped" is to be a national community that is inferior, backward, subordinate, deficient in capital and resources, an inadequate member of the international order, and (by extension) a shabby imitation of the "developed."

But "underdevelopment" is a condition that reveals something else as well. It displays to the developed a vision of their own past. The reason that it does so is that countries are assumed to follow certain established paths to "development." Sometimes this is conceptualized as a unitary, fixed path with pregiven stages; at other times, there may be an acknowledgment of the possibility of a finite number of multiple routes to the stage of being "developed" (see especially Nandy 1992:264). I realize that such a broad characterization does not do justice to the diversity and subtlety of positions found in the development literature. But it has the virtue of focusing on something which is so basic and obvious that it can easily be overlooked. What I wish to emphasize is that however the paths or strategies to achieve development are described, the means to that end is assumed to be *mimicry*. In all the shifts that development discourse has undergone in the past half century, from an obsession with growth rates to basic needs, poverty alleviation, a focus on the poorest, growth with redistribution, participatory development, sustainable development, and back to "market reform," the constant element has been that the *strategy* of development should be mimicry. To learn, follow, replicate, repeat, improve—these are the incitements of development discourse. And the *subject* that does all this learning and following is the nation-state.

Development thus brings together the phenomenon that Johannes Fabian (1983) has called "allochronism" (the displacement of "others" in the "Third World" to the past) with that feature of colonial discourse that Homi Bhabha (1984) has termed "mimicry." Like colonial mimicry, development discourse produces the less developed countries (LDCs) as a reformed and recognizable Other, "*a subject of difference that is almost the same, but not quite*" (Bhabha 1984:126). Again, as in colonial mimicry, one finds that development discourse is subtly but pervasively racialized, so that underdevelopment connotes not only economic backwardness but also a lower position in the global racial hierarchy.[15] Yet whereas the ambivalence of mimicry produces subjects who at once resemble the colonizers and function as a source of uncertainty in the authoritative discourse, both faithful image and virtual menace, development discourse produces subject nations that present an ambivalent image of the *past* of the "developed."

This temporal displacement has profound consequences for the project of "development" for another reason, namely, that the life stages of personal growth serve as a metonym for the growth of the nation. Many scholars have by now pointed out the superimposition of images of national development on the life stages of humans (Nandy 1987b; Manzo 1991). Nations are "newly born," their economies take time to "grow," and their markets and political systems finally "mature" when they are fully developed. David Ludden, for example, notes that " 'underdevelopment' and 'developing' imply immaturity and unrealized potential; development discourse is replete with the assumption that the realization of potential lies in mature capitalism" (1992:247).[16] The pervasiveness of these figures of speech, I suggest, elevates them from the realm of "mere analogy": here is a discourse that explicitly maps the bourgeois individual subject of the West onto the nation-as-subject. One of the implications of the metonymic relationship between the life cycle of the individual and the nation is that in the "family of nations," the LDCs occupy the role of children vis-à-vis the "developed" nation-states (Manzo 1991:14–16).[17] Therefore, to be a national subject in an "underdeveloped country"—for example, to be a citizen of India—is to occupy an overdetermined subject position interpellated by discourses of the nation *and* by the discourses of development to which that nation is subjected.[18]

There is, however, another consequence of the metonymic association of the nation and the life cycle of the individual subject that serves as a source of uncertainty in the otherwise definitive discourse of development. The allochronism of development, I have argued, presents to the West an image of itself at an earlier stage of its life cycle. In the teleological narrative of development, LDCs represent the "childhood" of the West, the early stages of growth, which one day, given adequate nurture, financial and technical support, and education from their "parents," will join the ranks of adult nations (Nandy 1987b:57; Manzo 1991:14). In development discourse, the narrative of the past of "developed" countries is completely depoliticized, memories of underdevelopment conveyed in the measured tones of the "stylized facts" of economic abstraction. What matters is that they got out of it, moved from then to now, from poverty to wealth, from want to plenty, from "underdevelopment" to "development." It is a tale of triumph in which the overcoming of hardship and poverty, the ability to negotiate a series of experiences successfully, provides the story with an essential coherence which justifies the moral and political leadership of the West and which provides development with an inherent legitimacy. Representations of the past, therefore, are central to development narratives: they prove that progress has, in fact, taken place.

It is because of the importance of narratives of progress that mimicry serves to destabilize development discourse in quite a different way than it does colonial discourse. It does so not only by offering to the powerful an ambivalent image of themselves ("almost the same but not quite") but also by opening up the invisible seams in the Western narrative of progress. Faced with the violence of its effects in the "Third World," development discourse forces the West to confront a version of its own "childhood" in which colonial violence, ecological destruction, the genocide of native peoples, and the repression and displacement of its poor otherwise find no place. The costs of development in Guatemala bring up the genocide of native North Americans at the quincentennial celebrations of Columbus's "discovery" of America; the destruction of rain forests in Brazil's "Amazonian frontier" raises troubling questions about a strategy of growth that mimics the North American frontier experience perhaps all too closely. Within development discourse itself, therefore, lies its shadowy double: not the return of the repressed, not a distorted image of itself, but a virtual presence, inappropriate objects that serve to open up the "developed world" itself as an inappropriate object, that ensure the strategic failure of development not only by the ambivalence of mimicry but by the lack of closure of the self-narrative of progress as well.

Agriculture in colonial and nationalist discourses of progress

Development discourse shares a great deal with notions of "progress" commonly employed during the colonial period. What makes the postwar period distinctive, apart from the founding of institutions whose specific function was to produce and propagate ideas about "development," was the adumbration of a formal comparative theory founded on replicable and largely ahistorical models. By contrast, theories of progress under colonialism, created on the premise of mimicry, remained faithful to the specificity of the historical experience of particular colonizers. The remarkable similarities between discussions of "progress" during the colonial era and those of development today have been emphasized by Bipan Chandra (1991) and Ludden (1992). Ludden, noting that the "cognitive terrain" of development has "remained remarkably stable" since the early nineteenth century, identifies its chief features as "(1) ruling powers that claim progress as a goal, (2) a 'people' whose condition must be improved, (3) an ideology of science that controls principles and techniques to effect and measure progress, and (4) self-declared, enlightened leaders who would use state power for development and compete for power with claims of their ability to effect progress" (1992:251–52). Ludden further argues (260–61) that the institutional structures that were to nurture and sustain this "cognitive terrain" were well in place by 1900. There are thus strong continuities to development discourse between the colonial and postcolonial eras. But just as we need to attend to these enduring patterns, we also need to remember that development discourse was enunciated from multiple positions and that the danger of representing it as a homogeneous formation is that it renders superfluous or epiphenomenal its internal fractures, debates, and discussions.[19]

In the discussions and debates that surrounded "progress" during the colonial era, agriculture, the primary source of employment, occupied a very prominent, if unfavorable, position. In the second half of the nineteenth century, according to Chandra, both colonizers and their native critics agreed on the importance of industrialization. Anticolonial intellectuals argued that the cultivation of arable land was close to its limit and that agriculture was incapable of absorbing a larger number of workers. Therefore, the only solution to easing the pressure of population on the land lay in developing industry, which in any case represented a higher stage of civilization (Chandra 1991:88–89). Although debt relief and tenancy legislation were proposed as short-term measures, there was little discussion of changing agrarian relations, and lower land taxes and the provision of cheap credit were considered important long-term measures necessary to encourage peasants to invest in their lands (127). The progress of agriculture was thought to be dependent on the growth of industry, which represented "the onward march of civilization" (91, 132).

Colonial strategies of economic growth foreshadowed the neoconservative, market-oriented structural adjustment packages prescribed by the Bretton Woods institutions in the past decade, once again drawing our attention to the presence of enduring patterns of social relations in the global economy and to the longevity of the colonial legacy long after the formal demise of colonialism. The main components of the British strategy of economic growth were "(i) the provision of law and order,

(ii) the promotion of private property rights in land, (iii) the development of foreign trade on the basis of the free trade principle, (iv) the promotion of means of transport, and (v) the investment of British capital. The logic of private gain, individual enterprise, and the operation of the market would then take care of development" (Chandra 1991:94). Political stability, unambiguous property rights, opening markets to world trade, development of infrastructure, foreign development aid: this was a list that could very well have come out of a World Bank handbook.[20] Indeed, British writers stressed how well the Indian economy was doing in the second half of the nineteenth century, comparing it favorably with European countries (82–83).[21] It was hoped that permanently fixing the revenue demand from land and eliminating intermediaries between the cultivator and the state would provide incentives to landowners to invest in agriculture. When that failed to happen by the mid–nineteenth century, the colonial state began to expend resources in the building of irrigation infrastructure such as canals (Ludden 1992:269).[22]

The emphasis on industrialization has continued unchanged, with different inflections, unto the present.[23] Among leading anticolonialists, the two main positions on the agrarian question were more similar than their protagonists would have dared to admit. One side argued that industrialization was a precondition for agricultural improvement, and the other, that the application of scientific knowledge to agriculture was the most urgent task, given that the economy would continue to depend mainly on agriculture in the foreseeable future.[24] In 1901, the Indian National Congress pledged its support to agricultural "improvement" in a resolution declaring "that the Government should be pleased to bestow its first and undivided attention upon the department of agriculture and adopt all those measures for its improvement and development which have been made in America, Russia, Holland, Belgium, and several other countries so successfully in that direction" (cited in Ludden 1992:272). The association of progress with science and industrialization proved invincible even in the face of criticism from a person like Gandhi, whose anti-industrial position was well known.[25] In 1928, the Royal Commission on Agriculture in India recommended that the government set up an Imperial Council of Agricultural Research, which would help coordinate agricultural research and policy. There was thus widespread agreement among both colonial officials and nationalists on two issues: the subordinate role to be played by agriculture in India's progress, and the application of scientific knowledge and scientific methods to improve agricultural productivity.[26]

As we shall see in the story that follows, these themes did not disappear but were reinvigorated with the launch of the green revolution in the late 1960s. But some important differences existed between the progressivist narratives of the colonial period and the developmentalist narratives of the postcolonial nation-state. Discussions of agriculture in India were mediated by the wider context of the world food economy, which was to change drastically between 1930 and the development era that followed the Second World War. To understand the transformations in the global food regime so as to set the context for much of what followed, I will first sketch the contours of food aid in the immediate postwar era.

Postwar food aid: Marshall Plan for the free world

Between 1870 and 1929, the world food regime was based largely on exports to Europe from the settler colonies—the United States, Canada, Australia, and Argentina.[27] European imports of wheat went up sixfold in this period, a growing demand that was met largely by increased production in the settler colonies. This food regime collapsed during the Great Depression, and a new system came into place with postwar reconstruction. The postwar food order was to provide a stable backdrop for the era of decolonization and "development." Its origins lay in the price supports given to domestic production in the United States during the New Deal and exports of American agricultural products to rebuild Europe during the years of the Marshall Plan.

Commodity support programs initiated during the New Deal created huge surpluses, the disposal of which became a central problem for the U.S. government. Between 1948 and 1952, 29 percent of Marshall aid was for food and agriculture (Friedmann 1990:17). All told, foreign aid was largely responsible for a ninefold increase in wheat exports between 1945 and 1949. By 1950, subsidized foreign aid constituted 60 percent of all American agricultural exports (Friedmann 1982:S261). The form of aid to Europe—loans in nonconvertible local currencies—was to be later generalized with Public Law (PL) 480 aid to the Third World. There was a critical difference between Marshall Plan aid and PL 480 aid, however, which had to do with the different locations that their recipients occupied in the agro-industrial complex (Friedmann 1990:16–17; 1993:35–39).

Marshall Plan aid avoided the dumping of U.S. surpluses, concentrating on providing food for immediate consumption needs and for feed and fertilizer to rebuild European agriculture (Friedmann 1982:S261; 1993:36). Rebuilding agriculture in Europe, however, implied the adoption of policies of domestic subsidies that mimicked the U.S. model. Despite the negative effects of such policies on European wheat imports, the United States supported European protection of wheat and dairy products in exchange for exempting maize and soy from import controls. The reason for this apparently contradictory move was the growing importance of the livestock sector in the increasingly meat-based diets of the postwar era.[28] Techniques for the factory farming of poultry and cattle had raised the demand for industrially produced feedstock that was heavily dependent on hybrid corn and soybean production. The model of a nationally organized, price-subsidized, import-controlled agricultural sector implicit in the Common Agricultural Policy of the European states, therefore, coexisted with a transnationally organized livestock sector that integrated American corn and soy producers with a transatlantic livestock industry based on factory-farming principles.

It was only after the end of Marshall Plan aid and after the Korean War, which absorbed most U.S. government grain stocks between 1950 and 1953, that the problem of disposing of surpluses came to be solved through sales to Japan and through aid to the newly independent countries of Asia and Africa. Title 1 of PL 480, which accounted for the bulk of food aid (70 percent of all food aid from 1954 to 1977), was directly patterned on the European experience of sales in local currencies. In the two decades from the early 1950s, world wheat exports increased by 2.5 times, of which the U.S. share increased from just over a third to more than half. Most U.S. exports took the form of aid: almost 70 percent in the decade 1956–65 and close to 50 percent from 1966 to 1970. On the receiving side, Third World imports grew from 19 percent of the world's share in the late 1950s to 66 percent a decade later (Friedmann 1982:260–71; 1992:372).[29]

In the process, Third World countries that had been exporters, or insignificant importers, at the end of the Second World War became dependent on wheat imports, primarily those available at subsidized rates from the United States. There were many reasons for this, not least that regimes could keep urban consumers and industrialists happy with low food prices, even though the dumping of American wheat meant that the agricultural sector suffered (Friedmann 1990:18–19; 1992:372).

But the main reason lay perhaps elsewhere: in the models of development that were being employed by the newly independent nation-states of the world. As should be evident from the discussion above regarding debates in colonial India, industrialization signified the status of being developed in these models. Although the archetypical development narrative consisted of the dynamic complementarity of industry and agriculture within a national economy (Friedmann and McMichael 1989:93), it operated with a conviction that the scientific application of development expertise would allow newly independent nation-states to leapfrog the gradualist path to prosperity. Development discourse envisioned applying the Fordist speedup of production to the social engineering of nations.

Significantly, taking the fast road to industrialization meant keeping wages low so that domestic industries could flourish and bypassing the foreign exchange constraints to the purchase of capital equipment. In this equation, subsidized food from the United States was a great boon because it allowed states to save all their foreign exchange for industrial goods. Cheap food for the urban proletariat also enabled industrialists to keep the wage bill low. It was hoped that the growth of industry would enable the absorption of surplus labor from the countryside, thereby raising the average productivity of labor, and that it would also lead to increased demand for agricultural goods, both food and cash crops. The alternative strategy, similar to that being followed by postwar Europe, would have meant high support prices to boost agricultural output and, consequently, high food prices for consumers. Scarce resources would then have had to be diverted from potential industrial ends to agriculture, with high food prices hindering industrial growth by increasing the wage bill. The imperatives to "catch up" for those nation-states that were "behind" were thus very different from those of European nation-states "rebuilding" after the destruction of the Second World War. Postwar food aid, therefore, played a very important role both in Europe and in the Third World, but participated in very different strategies of growth and reconstruction. The model of food aid embodied in PL 480 appeared to be an extension of Marshall Plan aid policies, but food aid to the Third World became part of a completely different set of strategic, international, sectoral, and class relationships. This food regime, dominated by U.S. concessional aid policies, was to last until the early seventies and forms the backdrop against which agricultural policies were to be formulated in postcolonial India.

Agriculture in postcolonial discourses of development

Postcolonial discourses of development in India continued to reflect the tension between those segments among the ruling elites who emphasized industrialization at all costs and those who thought that, because industrial growth depended on adequate and reliable supplies of food, the first task of the new nation-state should be to raise agricultural productivity through the application of scientific knowledge. This tension was evident in the very first Five-Year Plan (1951–56).

The Draft Outline of the First Plan, a discussion document, made agriculture, rural development, irrigation, and power its centerpiece, assigning 43 percent of total expenditure to these concerns (Frankel 1978:86). It stated that "the shortage of food and raw materials is at present the weakest point in the country's economy" (in Frankel 1978:86) and that continuing shortages in this sector would inhibit a faster tempo of development in the future. The Draft Outline stressed the need for increased irrigation and the application of chemical fertilizer to improve yields, as well as the advantages of intensive agrarian development: "Those areas should be selected where, on account of irrigation facilities or assured rainfall, additional effort is likely to produce the more substantial results" (88). As we will see, in its logic and rhetoric, this development path anticipates the green revolution by many years.

There was another, very different, view of agriculture, however, which ultimately prevailed in the final version of the First Plan. In this view, the widespread use of intensive methods of cultivation was not feasible because few farmers could afford expensive inputs such as fertilizers and irrigation. Given the high person-to-land ratios, it was felt that agricultural productivity would be best increased by giving small farmers and agricultural laborers incentives to undertake labor-intensive techniques to raise yields. In the four decades ending in 1946–47, the marginal productivity of labor had declined, as had food production per capita (Blyn 1966:93–126). "Grain yields were low, not only in comparison to advanced countries, but with respect to countries at roughly the same stage of development. Average paddy yields per acre in China were estimated at almost twice the Indian level" (Frankel (1978:96). The plan thus emphasized the productivity-enhancing potential of land reform, cooperatives, community development, and other institutional changes. It aimed to reach a quarter of the rural population through community development programs, with the hope that from the third year (1953) of the plan onward, the government's financial contribution would be negligible, as "people's participation" would ensure the success of the strategy (Frankel 1978:100–106).

This view received further stimulus during the Second Five-Year Plan, which undertook an explicit strategy of rapid industrialization.[30] Since the outlays for the First Plan were constrained by commitments to large infrastructural projects initiated before it was drawn up, it was in the Second Five-Year Plan that a coherent ideology and strategy of development was first articulated by the postcolonial regime. In this strategy, there was an even more marked shift to the path that put industrialization first. New investment in the public sector, chiefly for heavy industry, was allocated at two and one-half times that of the First Plan. By contrast, the proportion of total expenditure allocated to agriculture declined to almost half its previous level (Frankel 1978:131). Because of the plan's almost single-minded commitment to heavy industry, there were precious few resources left for investment in agriculture. At the same time that the planners were redirecting all available savings to the industrial sector, they were keenly aware that growth in agricultural output was of crucial importance. Nehru called agriculture "the keystone of our planning" and pointed out that "inspite of all that we have to do for industry, the fact remains that agriculture is the solid foundation on which we have to build. It is from agriculture and from the increasing production on the land that we can build up our surpluses for future growth" (Nehru 1988:371).[31]

The idea that industrial growth would spur the demand for agricultural goods, combined with a belief that institutional changes in the rural areas would release forces that would boost productivity, led the planners to emphasize changes such as land reform, the rebuilding of institutions of village governance on democratic principles (the *panchayat* system), and tenancy reform, instead of direct investment in agricultural infrastructure and input or output subsidies. It was estimated that food grain requirements would double in the decade covered by the Second and Third Plans; however, the proposed investment in agriculture was enough to ensure only a 15 percent increase in total output (Frankel 1978:136–37). The rest, therefore, was expected to result from the social changes that would alter the relationship between different strata of agriculturists and the land, in particular, the incentives that land reform and tenancy reform would give to the poor to increase output.

In this regard, the example of China loomed large for Indian policymakers. Between 1952 and 1955, various groups of Congress Party officials and Planning Commission members, Nehru and P. C. Mahalanobis (the architect of the Second Plan) most prominent among them, visited China to learn firsthand how the Chinese were going about "developing" their country and came back impressed.[32] For Indian policymakers, China provided both a model and a competitor in the race for development. China was at the "same stage" of development as India, it was pursuing a policy of rapid industrialization along the classic model of squeezing surpluses from the agricultural sector, and it was increasing agricultural production through massive agrarian reforms. Nehru explicitly rejected the comparison of India with the industrially advanced countries of the West because, he argued, they already had 150 years or more of industrial growth and thus faced problems different from those confronting poor countries in Asia. The most important person behind the Second Plan, the statistician Mahalanobis, later commented that "China provided a better model of development for India than the advanced western countries" (in Frankel 1978:125).[33] There were several reasons why this was so: China had embarked on state planning whose object was to *accelerate* the process of development so that it did not take as long as Western countries had historically taken to become "developed"; China was at "the same stage" in the development process as India; both countries had "similar" problems in high population pressures on the land, unemployment, and low levels of productivity; and both countries had to struggle to find sufficient surpluses for industrial growth and to generate foreign exchange reserves to import much-needed capital goods (Frankel 1978:120–41). Nehru articulated Indian policymakers' ambivalent attitude toward China most clearly, eager to profit from China's experience yet expressing a competitive envy toward it: "We know for a fact that some other countries have rapidly increased their food production in the last few years without any tremendous use of fertilizers. How has China done it? China's resources in this respect are not bigger than ours. China is at the same time laying far greater stress on industrial development and heavy industry than we are. Yet, they are succeeding in increasing their agricultural production at a faster pace than we are. *Surely, it should not be beyond our power to do something that China can do*" (Nehru 1988:394; emphasis added). Nehru had previously noted that "we differ, of course, in our political and economic structures, yet the problems we face are *essentially the same*. The future will show which country and which structure of Government yields greater results in every way" (73; emphasis added).[34]

Nehru's statements underline the importance of postcolonial competition among "less developed countries." Competition between the "backward" nation-states adds a twist to the insight that development discourse situated underdeveloped countries in a prior historical stage and gave developed countries the status of models to be emulated. Added to the mix of allochronism and mimicry is an element of competitive learning that flows horizontally in the time-space of nationalism, from one "backward" nation-state to another. Thus, while Nehru completely accepted the central role of industrialization—the model which posited that there were different stages to development and that countries like India and China occupied a lower stage in the narrative of progress than the industrialized West—he also acknowledged the possibility of multiple routes to industrial development. The Western example of "development," with its long gestation period, was clearly unacceptable as a temporal trajectory. At the same time, Indian intellectuals since the 1920s had been keenly aware of the incredibly high growth rates achieved by the industrialization strategy of the Soviet Union. Perhaps more than the Soviet Union, China, with its huge agricultural sector and high person-to-land ratio, appeared to offer a strategy that adhered to the general model prescribed by development orthodoxy while offering a different, faster path that drew, moreover, on the rhetoric of anticolonialism, national sovereignty, and self-sufficiency.[35] China functioned as model, competitor, and alternative, a country with "essentially similar" problems, resources, and goals but (and this was crucial to someone like Nehru) a different—nondemocratic—political system.

The Chinese example of the reorganization of agrarian relations of production, however, ran into insuperable difficulties in India's federal administrative structure.[36] All the institutional changes that the central government wanted to bring about—land reform, tenancy reform, the setting up of cooperatives, reinvigoration of village governance through the panchayat system—were, in fact, dependent on state governments for their implementation, as these were all state "subjects" in the division of powers stipulated by the Indian constitution (Varshney 1995:30–31). The leaders of state governments were mostly men who were beholden to the dominant agrarian classes and to merchants who traded in agricultural products for financial and electoral support.[37] By contrast, the dominant coalition at the national level was more heavily influenced by the monopoly bourgeoisie and bureaucratic and military elites, although agrarian interests were not entirely absent (as the section on Chaudhary Charan Singh in this chapter makes apparent).[38]

Even during the heyday of the Second Plan, at the zenith of an industry-centered development strategy, there were important voices arguing for putting agriculture first. These positions resulted partially from the failure of the Second Plan's agricultural policies. Production fell by 10 percent between 1956–57 and 1957–58, food prices jumped by nearly 50 percent, and the government was forced to import a total of six million tons of food grains in those two years. This led to a severe balance of payments crisis, which nearly derailed the industrialization strategy (Frankel 1978:142–43; Toye 1981:42–44). The food minister, A. P. Jain, warned that measures to force down the price of food grains, such as socialization, forced purchase, or curtailment of interstate movements, would be counterproductive because they would provide disincentives to farmers to increase production. What was needed, instead, was an agricultural strategy that emphasized "scientific" practices and remunerative prices. Greater investments in seeds, pesticides, and fertilizers, not organizational changes, were the preconditions to growth in agricultural output (Frankel 1978:144–47).

Although such arguments were given short shrift during the Nehruvian period because of the single-minded pursuit of industrialization, there were other important reasons why investment in scientific-industrial agriculture was to prove to be much more attractive later.[39] The Indian government could, and did during 1956, draw on heavily subsidized PL 480 wheat.[40] Further, the revolution in corn production following the breeding of hybrid varieties in the United States had not yet been replicated for the main cereal crops of the subcontinent: rice, millet, and wheat. A technological "revolution" in food production was in the works, however, one that was to have enormous consequences for the story of Indian "development."

Food production, nationalism, and the green revolution

The consequences of the technological revolution in food production known as the "green revolution" have been the subject of heated debate.[41] My concern, for now, is not with the immediate consequences of green revolution agriculture in India but with the assumptions it embodied. In this section, I wish to demonstrate that the search for green revolution technology and its subsequent implementation depended on certain taken-for-granted propositions that combined in equal measure a normalization of the U.S. experience, Malthusianism, and nationalism.

The origins of the green revolution lie in the invitation to the Rockefeller Foundation in 1941 extended by the Mexican government to provide technical assistance for raising yields of basic food crops. After a preliminary survey, a team of four scientists, including Norman Borlaug, started work in 1943 on breeding "better" varieties, improving soil management practices, and increasing the productivity of domestic animals. In the course of the next twenty years, the Mexican program was to increase the production of the three basic foods—corn, wheat, and beans—by 300 percent (Stakman, Bradfield, and Mangelsdorf 1967:1–6). More important, it was to serve as an exemplar to Third World countries in Latin America and Asia of what could be achieved by the application of "scientific methods" and a top-down, production-based strategy. Apart from its status as a model, the Mexican program had more concrete effects in that hybrid varieties bred in Mexico were successfully exported to other countries with similar agronomic conditions (216–321).

There is a curious anomaly that lies at the heart of all the narratives about the green revolution, including the story told by the "three ancients" who advised the Rockefeller Foundation on its Mexican strategy, Elvin Stakman, Richard Bradfield, and Paul Mangelsdorf (1967). All three were distinguished agricultural scientists who, by their own reckoning, had seventy-five man-years of professional experience between them, mostly in land grant colleges of the United States (23). Mangelsdorf, in particular, was known for his pioneering work on hybrid corn, which, he had once argued, prevented the spread of communism by ensuring that postwar Western Europe was well fed (Kloppenburg 1988:5). The anomaly is that the association between the story of hybrid corn in the United States and the green revolution in the developing world is seldom made explicit. In fact, the term "green revolution" is, as far as I am aware, never applied to refer to the hybrid corn story and was reserved exclusively for Third World contexts.[42] Stakman, Bradfield, and Mangelsdorf, for example, emphasize the importance of "the contributions of science, technology, and education to the phenomenal progress of agriculture in the United States during the quarter of a century prior to 1941" (1967:23), but they fail to mention *any* of the dislocating social effects of these changes. These include the displacement of millions of the farm population;[43] the growing influence of large corporate interests in agriculture; questions of sustainability raised by the indiscriminate employment of energy-intensive inputs and chemicals; the growth of regional specialization; the enormous increase in the concentration of land and, even more, of output; and the reduction of family farmers ("peasants on tractors") to what is in effect a putting-out system in the giant machinery of capital, plowing a narrow furrow between corporate suppliers of manufactured inputs, on one side, and corporate purchasers of output, mostly intermediate goods, on the other (Busch and Lacy 1983; Kloppenburg 1988).[44] (This is the phenomenon that Marx [1976:1:1019–38] called "the formal subsumption of labor to capital.") However one evaluates the merits of the United States' green revolution—and I recognize that there are a number of sharply divergent positions on this issue—it is baffling that an entire range of consequences appeared invisible to those who pioneered the use of similar techniques in the Third World.[45]

To understand how that could have happened, we need to focus on a series of convergences in those discourses of development explicitly employed by agricultural scientists and those discourses implicit in their actions. The first thread is provided by the complete normalization of the U.S. experience, so that it functions as a model that is absent from deliberation yet instrumental in shaping the strategy to be followed in the Third World. This much is evident from the description of the achievements of science and technology in "the phenomenal progress" of U.S. agriculture provided by Stakman, Bradfield, and Mangelsdorf, in which the geographic extension of crops to colder areas, genetic improvements, yield increases, effectiveness of insecticides, and productivity of industrial dairy and livestock farming are listed to the exclusion of any other consequence (1967:23–24).[46] What is not mentioned anywhere is that since the Morrill Act of 1862, which established the land grant university system, and the Hatch Act of 1887, which established State Agricultural Experiment Stations, agricultural research in the United States was heavily weighted to the largest farmers, to commodity-specific research, and to the search for yield-enhancing varieties that encouraged the heavy use of biochemical inputs supplied by industry. This is entirely consistent with Busch and Lacy's (1983:35) observation that the primacy of increased productivity was not questioned from the mid-1930s to the 1960s.[47] An idealized model of how agricultural research had functioned in the United States thus implicitly shaped the ends to be pursued in the developing world.

Such a productivist emphasis was reinforced by an unabashedly Malthusian view of the Third World. The entire argument for increasing yields was framed by the specter of increasing population.[48] The narrative relies on the motif of a race, which pits food production against population: *In lane 1, the Western scientist, putting his imagination and*

dedication to work in inhospitable conditions; in lane 2, the dark challenger, threatening to undo all the Progress being made by Development.
The outcome of the "race" is always uncertain. It is not until the narrative reaches an electrifying climax that the outcome is announced. Almost any text from the period could be chosen to illustrate this point. *Campaigns against Hunger* (Stakman, Bradfield, and Mangelsdorf 1967) makes the case admirably. After detailing the rapid rise of the Mexican population in the decade of the 1930s, the authors conclude, "*Mexico needed more food; how could she get it?*" (1967:2; emphasis added).[49] Later they announce that "wheat production has won the race with human reproduction. . . . The present population is about 170 percent of what it was in 1943, but wheat production is at least 350 percent of what it was then" (72–73). They set aside the importance of land reform by noting its inadequacy: "Land redistribution was satisfying the hunger of the landless for land, but was it satisfying their hunger for food?" (1).

Several consequences follow from such a stark scenario. The first is an entirely self-serving one, in that it bestows enormous moral and political legitimacy to narrowly defined, technocratic work that, more often than not, disempowers and depoliticizes the poor and leads to increased inequality. No matter what the outcome, one can always spot the angel of progress in this narrative, just as one can locate in the "population bomb" the diabolical, racialized enemy, to whom the thermonuclear anxieties of the cold war had been transferred.[50] After all, who could argue with the lofty goal of eradicating hunger? The death knell of this justification was sounded, perhaps more decisively than ever, by Amartya Sen's elegant treatise on hunger (1981), which drove an ineluctable wedge between the unthinking association of increasing food availability and the eradication or reduction of hunger. Although Sen is careful to delimit his argument to famines, the implications of his position can easily be extended to increases in food production. Stated baldly, Sen's argument leads to the conclusion that whatever *other* positive effects may result from greater food availability, it is by no means certain that one of them will be a reduction in the number of the hungry or the depth of their poverty.[51]

Another consequence of casting the problem in Malthusian terms is that population appears to be an independent and external variable, with its own inexorable logic, unconnected to the distributional and welfare consequences of the techniques and methods of production. The metaphor of a race between production and population puts them into separate and unconnected tracks, the logic being that if one did nothing about production, population would simply zoom away and "win" the race. This leaves no option *but* to join the "race" and "beat" population by increasing production at all costs. And the fastest way to increase production is to approach it in a top-down and technocratic manner: involving ordinary people—farmers and landless laborers, both men and women—would take too long, and the results would be too uncertain. Thus, the commission appointed by the Rockefeller Foundation to chart a direction for Mexican agriculture concluded that the fastest progress would be made by a top-down approach (Stakman, Bradfield, and Mangelsdorf 1967:33). Commission members were not simple-minded, recognizing that education and extension were vital ingredients in a successful strategy. They concluded, however, that research should come first, for without a "great reservoir of potentially useful but unused information" (34), extension would have no scientific knowledge to bring to the farmers. The appeal of such a strategy lay in the assumption that scientific work inherently results in the greater social good. Scientists often make such an argument for basic research on the grounds that the "results" of such research are inherently unpredictable; however, this is too transparent a fiction for those who, like agricultural scientists, do "applied" research, a fact recognized even by scientists themselves. Employing their experience in the U.S. research system, agricultural scientists proceeded to replicate their endeavors with the morally charged mandate of eradicating hunger and "winning the race" against population.[52]

To the normalization of the U.S. experience and Malthusianism was added a third potent ingredient: nationalism. The development of agriculture was conceived entirely in national terms; indeed, the nation constituted the horizon within which all problems were posed and solutions offered. For example, the race between population and food production was conceptualized as occurring *within* each nation and not on a global scale. Thus, growth in national population was pitted against growth in nationally produced food, not taking into account the existence of phenomena such as migration and the world market, which might have profoundly altered food availability and the numbers of people who had to be fed. The ultimate aim of green revolution policies "was to help Mexico toward independence in agricultural production, in agricultural science, and in agricultural education" (Stakman, Bradfield, and Mangelsdorf 1967:33). Similarly, in these discourses, hunger was a problem that afflicted nations rather than particular groups of dispossessed people. Thus, for example, we have statements like the following: "There was hunger in Mexico in 1941. That 'the country has many of the aspects of an overpopulated land' was evident to all who looked below the surface" (31). Notwithstanding theories of comparative advantage, which would have implied specialization in agricultural production to take advantage of natural endowments, the goal of national self-sufficiency in food grains was always paramount in green revolution agriculture.[53] This clearly had to do with the implicit model of agricultural development being employed, namely, that of the United States, rather than with explicit theories of economic development. (It is significant in this regard that no economists were included in the Rockefeller Foundation teams that went first to Mexico and later to India.)

Mimicry and allochronism were inherently contained in the language of "scientific progress," but so was nationalism.[54] All these themes are jointly articulated in metaphors of the life cycle of the subject and its familial interpellation. Stakman, Bradfield, and Mangelsdorf provide a wealth of examples that demonstrate this all too clearly:

> In 1941, agriculture was traditional; now it is progressive. And it will continue to progress because it is continually becoming more scientific. . . . Research and education are *growing* together. . . . Mexico has reached its *majority*. . . . In 1943 Mexico was national in scientific outlook; the exigencies of the time demanded it. Now she is both national and international in outlook. . . . Mexico has shown many retarded countries a road to progress if they have the will to follow it. . . . Mexico is indeed rapidly approaching the *upper echelons* in the world's *family of nations*. As President López Mateos said in speaking to the Mexican Union of Associations of Engineers, "We are no longer an underdeveloped country, but a nation in course of full development, which requires the professional competence and human qualities of all its *sons*." (1967:9, 15, 16, 19, 178; emphases added)

When teleological premises are embedded in the life narrative of the nation-as-subject, can the patriarchal family be far behind? The "family of nations" reconstituted an orderly and hierarchical world community in the aftermath of decolonization, in which the young, the "retarded," the "underdeveloped," and those who had not yet reached their "majority" were to grow, with the help of scientific knowledge, until they reached the "upper echelons" of the family and became adults through the realization of the full potential of their sons. This is by no means an extraordinary document; in fact, it is precisely the ordinariness of these phrases, the unselfconscious manner in which they are deployed, that makes it clear that these associations have been neither incidental nor extraneous to discourses of development in the postwar era.[55]

Between 1952 and 1955, several teams of Rockefeller Foundation experts visited India to assess the situation of agriculture with a view toward replicating the Mexican success story. The "problem with Indian agriculture" was, once again, theorized in terms of food production keeping up with population growth.[56] Proof that population had outpaced food supply was found in the fact that "during the past 400 years the country has suffered 45 famines. . . . In the Bengal famine of 1943, between one and three million people died" (Stakman, Bradfield, and Mangelsdorf 1967:238). The use of the Bengal famine to make the authors' point is highly ironic, because it has been confirmed subsequently by a good deal of scholarly analysis that if the Bengal famine demonstrated anything, it was that great human misery could exist *despite* above-normal years of food production.[57] In April 1956, the Rockefeller Foundation entered an agreement with the Indian government to "cooperate in the improvement of maize, sorghum, and millet production and in the development of a modern postgraduate school of agriculture at the Indian Agricultural Research Institute at New Delhi" (241). The big breakthroughs occurred not in these crops, however, but in wheat, in which a breeding program began in the early sixties at approximately the same time as the continued failure of agricultural policy became evident after the first year of the Third Plan (Frankel 1978:276; Stakman, Bradfield, and Mangelsdorf 1967:235–66). Progress in breeding wheats appropriate to Indian conditions was much more rapid than in Mexico because many of the varieties bred there could be relatively easily adapted in the subcontinent.

At the same time that the teams of agricultural scientists were making breakthroughs in breeding new varieties of wheat and maize in India, the newly founded International Rice Research Institute (IRRI) in the Philippines, the second Rockefeller-funded center after the International Maize and Wheat Improvement Center, CIM-MYT, was reporting results with high-yielding varieties of rice (Plucknett and Smith 1982:215). Subsequently, two other centers for tropical agriculture were set up in Colombia and Nigeria, jointly funded by the Rockefeller and Ford Foundations, respectively. In 1971, the whole program was institutionalized in a massive way by the formation of the Consultative Group on International Agricultural Research (CGIAR), sponsored by the Food and Agriculture Organization (FAO), the United Nations Development Program (UNDP), and the World Bank. Nine new institutions were set up in quick succession, the most interesting for our purposes being the International Board for Plant Genetic Resources (IBPGR), founded in 1974 for the purpose of promoting "the conservation of crop diversity by sponsoring an international network of germplasm collections," and the International Service for National Agricultural Research (ISNAR), founded in 1979 "to help strengthen national agricultural programs so that research results benefit the inhabitants of developing countries" (Plucknett and Smith 1982:215, 216). There is not a little irony in the founding of an international agency whose goal is to strengthen national agricultural programs. An ideology of national self-sufficiency continued to lead the Rockefeller Foundation's programs. Improving agricultural methods, developing national scientists and institutions, disseminating the results of research nationally and internationally, and "helping each *country* toward independence in the various phases of agricultural improvement" were the foundation's guiding principles (Stakman, Bradfield, and Mangelsdorf 1967:305; emphasis added). On the other hand, germ plasm collections are important because they were to become a key to the debates regarding ecological imperialism. One of the arguments in this vein is presented by Jack Kloppenburg (1988:15):[58] "The creation of the Green Revolution research centers (e.g., the International Rice Research Institute, the International Center for the Improvement of Maize and Wheat) was the product not only of an effort to introduce capitalism into the countryside but also of the need to collect systematically the exotic germplasm required by the breeding programs of the developed nations." Once in place, germ plasm banks are available to universities, national research programs, and private companies (Plucknett and Smith 1982:217). It is precisely this issue—that is, the access enjoyed by multinational seed corporations to germ plasm banks—that has drawn the most controversy in recent years.[59]

Conjunctures: The Indian Food Crisis and the Origins of Populism

The "development regime" that has informed the character of Indian agriculture in the postindependence period has been shaped most of all by considerations of sovereignty and redistribution. Questions of sovereignty loomed large in the emphasis given to rapid, state-sponsored industrialization. But it was a crisis in the agricultural sector that truly challenged the sovereignty of the nation-state.

By the middle of the Third Plan, it became progressively evident that increases in agricultural output were not occurring and certainly would not even approach the rapid increases hoped for by the planners. At the same time, Nehru's death brought to power a new prime minister, Lal Bahadur Shastri, who was far more favorably inclined to the agricultural sector. The new agriculture minister, C. Subramaniam, was in favor of a policy based on price incentives, biochemical agriculture, and "betting on the strong"—that is, cultivators already favorably positioned in terms of land and water resources. Beginning with the 1965–66 season, when two hundred metric tons of wheat were imported from Mexico and planted on a thousand plots, the demand for HYV seeds went through the roof. Total grain output rose rapidly, from 72.3 million tons in 1965–66 (a drought year) to 108.4 million tons in 1970–71, with increases in wheat output, which more than doubled from 1965–66 to 1971–72, leading the way (Frankel 1978:510; Plucknett and Smith 1982:216; Varshney 1989). In implementing this strategy, foreign exchange was a crucial bottleneck; in that regard, aid from the World Bank and the U.S. government was absolutely critical (Varshney 1989:314).

The success of green revolution policies depended on the conjuncture of a number of different events. The monsoons failed for two consecutive years, in 1965–66 and in 1966–67, sharply bringing down the total output of food grains. This, in turn, led to significant increases in food imports, which rose steadily from 3.1 million tons of wheat in 1956–57 to a peak of 10 million tons in 1965–66. Although imports from the United States never reached more than 15 percent of domestic output, the public distribution system became almost entirely dependent on PL 480 wheat. President Johnson further complicated the political situation by putting wheat supplies on a "short tether." India was required to submit its food needs every month, and the president himself cleared the shipment of food aid, depending on India's "progress" in implementing "reforms" in agricultural and fiscal policy. Ashutosh Varshney's (1989) careful research has demonstrated that the Indian government was already moving in the direction of Johnson's "reforms," so that pressure from the United States did not alter the direction of agricultural policy. After the war with Pakistan in October 1965, food aid was suspended until Indira Gandhi made the politically fraught decision of devaluing the currency in June 1966. The *manner* in which Johnson treated Indian leaders and policymakers was to hasten the drive to food self-sufficiency to no small extent. Finally, there was the significant factor that institutions where agricultural scientists could breed hybrid seeds and where these seeds could be duplicated and commercially produced had been operating for almost a decade by that time. In addition to the postgraduate program, set up with Rockefeller help, at Pusa, New Delhi, at least two other universities, one at Pantnagar in Uttar Pradesh (UP) (started with the assistance of the University of Illinois and the United States Agency for International Development [USAID]) and the Punjab Agricultural University (set up in Ludhiana with the help of Ohio State University), were involved in training, seed production, and agricultural extension.

Questions of sovereignty always loomed large in the promotion of the green revolution. The agriculture minister, Subramaniam, criticized the strategy of institutional reforms pursued by the Nehru government as "mere slogan shouting" and argued for a more "pragmatic" approach, stressing that the choice faced was the following: "Would you like to have . . . high production and attain self-sufficiency within the country . . . or would you prefer to continue dependence upon foreign imports indefinitely?" (Subramaniam 1979:28).[60] Nationalism was a vital ingredient in the discourse of development pursued by the postcolonial state. Those who disagreed over whether industry or agriculture should be given top priority in development plans were expressing differences about the quickest path to self-sufficiency and sovereignty. However large the differences in approach, the *goal* of a powerful, sovereign nation was widely shared. The perception of Indian leaders and policymakers that Johnson had humiliated them only strengthened their desire to see rapid increases in food output, so that the nation would no longer be dependent on food aid. National food self-sufficiency was also the explicit goal of green revolution agricultural science, although Malthusianism, rather than anticolonialism, was the chief motivating factor there.

When the monsoons failed for two successive years, agricultural output, which had increased at a steady rate until then, mostly owing to bringing new areas into cultivation, fell precipitously.[61] Obtaining aid in an international food regime dominated by the dumping of U.S. surpluses would have meant acquiescing to American pressure to change agricultural policy, curb population growth, and depreciate the currency (Frankel 1978:246–92).[62] It was in this context that the Indian government hit on the policy of promoting the green revolution, the high-yielding varieties (HYVs) of hybrid seed. But because it concentrated on areas already well endowed with water resources and low person-to-land ratios, the green revolution further exacerbated interregional inequalities. It also increased inequalities within regions because larger farmers were better positioned to take advantage of the new technology.[63] The next chapter demonstrates how the spur given to agrarian capitalism loosened the densely interlinked ties between landowners and landless laborers in the countryside. Together, the rise of a class of surplus-producing farmers, growing inequalities between and within regions, and the relaxation of ties of patronage created the structural conditions favorable for populist appeals to succeed. Thus, any consideration of the rise of "peasant movements," led largely by and in the interest of the better-off sectors of the agrarian population, has to take into account the powers of accumulation unleashed by the green revolution.[64]

By now, analyses of parties, interest group politics, and the intent of government policies and their implementation are topics that have been well traversed in the study of Indian agriculture. I will concentrate, therefore, on an extended analysis of discourses, ideologies, and actions pertaining to the green revolution by focusing not merely on what was done but also on what it meant, both to the leaders and, more important, to the people who were the objects and subjects of their discourse. How did these pronouncements and policies find their way into the everyday lives of village people? What did these discourses and programs mean to them? How were they interpreted?

It is for this reason that, in the next section, I will concentrate on the phenomenon of *populism*. Populism is the form in which discourses of "development" and hence of modernity infiltrated the crevices of daily life in rural northern India. While many analysts have pointed to the phenomenon, few have analyzed it in any detail. Under what circumstances was it deployed? What difference did it make? Why was it successful? What kinds of resistance did it enable? What were its silences, exclusions, and erasures? How do we understand populism theoretically?

Redistributive politics and populism: "Garibi Hatao" and the Indira Congress

Most scholars of Indian politics agree that the 1971 national elections signified a change in the style and content of political mobilization in a direction often termed "populist." For example, in her influential book, Francine Frankel attributes the two-thirds majority obtained by Indira Gandhi's party to a political gamble that employed the language of class through the promise of radical, but democratic, economic reform. She stresses that the campaign capitalized on Indira Gandhi's image as a leader committed to economic and social reform (1978:454–55). Similarly, Lloyd Rudolph and Susanne Hoeber Rudolph argue that the unexpected success of her party owed mostly to Indira Gandhi's "comparative advantage as India's only national political personality" and the decision to match her personality to one simple and appealing slogan, "Remove poverty" [*Garibi hatao*] (1987:135). The strategy of incorporating the popular classes by appealing to distributive goals and social justice has been seen as the distinctive feature of populist politics. Therefore, a consideration of "populism" may help us shed some light on the peculiar ideological formation forged by Indira Gandhi in the wake of the demise of traditional Congress politics, which was based on distributing favors to supporters in the classic pattern of pyramidal machine politics.

Populism may have signified a change in the style and content of political mobilization, but what did such a change imply for the development of the nation-state? The significance of Indira Gandhi's populism, I wish to argue, lay in that it represented a quantum leap in the dissemination of discourses of development. This resulted not only from better use of the mass media but also from finding new audiences who were receptive to populist messages. Populist politics altered both the content of development and the degree to which development discourses entered the everyday life of the rural poor.

Populism and "Underdevelopment." Before going on to examine how populism has functioned in the Indian context to shape the experience of modernity for people in rural areas, I will briefly dwell on theories of populism. The study of populism has taken Latin America as the exemplary case. Among the larger countries, the thirties and forties witnessed the phenomena of Peronism in Argentina, Varguism in Brazil, and Cardenism in Mexico (Collier 1987; Davis 1992; Torre 1992:388; Laclau 1977; Adelman 1994).[65] Populist politics arose in a period when large-scale urbanization and import-substituting industrialization accompanied mass mobilization.[66]

Apart from making connections to urbanism and to a particular phase of economic "development," theories of populism usually imply that "the masses" are manipulated by charismatic leaders, that populist coalitions typically consist of vertical, multiclass alliances, that redistributive policies and programs are central, and that populist rhetoric aims not at linking lower classes to a unified ruling class through democratic processes but at creating an antagonistic ideological field in which "the people" are pitted against "the oligarchy" or, put more generally, against historically privileged social groups (Torre 1992:386; Laclau 1977).[67] Populism, therefore, is the name given to a singular sociopolitical formation, a particular type of hegemonic bloc, which can be distinctively identified. An enumeration of its characteristics, however, is not sufficient to tell us why and under what circumstances it arises.

Explanations of populism arising from modernization theory offered an understanding of distinctiveness in terms of the failure of Latin American politics to replicate the European experience. Ironically, although modernization theorists in Latin America quite effectively described an experience of modernity that differed strikingly from an archetypical (and largely mythical) European one, their explanation for this difference was circumscribed by a teleological view of history. Thus, Germani (1978) and Di Tella (1965), in different ways, attribute the rise of populism to a lack of synchronicity between economic, social, and political development. The "demonstration effect" of Western consumption practices translates into a "revolution of rising expectations" that the slowly developing economy is unable to satisfy. There develops a chasm between rapidly growing social and political demands and the slow pace of economic development. Demographic expansion; infrastructural incapacity; dependence on foreign capital, technology, and markets; and fiscally irresponsible redistribution: these further underline the gap that separates rising political demands from economic resources (Di Tella 1965:49). Unable to bridge this gap through channels of incorporation that, in the "Western" experience, integrated workers gradually, the phenomenon of populism arises in response to what modernization theorists have called "the crisis of governability." Populism is a device to suture recently mobilized groups, often newly urbanized working classes and lumpenproletariat, to elite projects of import-substituting industrialization and nationalism. It becomes, therefore, a practice of constructing hegemonic blocs that is, by definition, restricted to the Third World.

According to this perspective, economic development would automatically restore "normal" politics—that is, a politics of incorporation in which the demands of the subaltern would not exceed the capabilities of the economic system. In other words, economic development would restore the synchronicity that had been lost because modern technologies of communication had prematurely raised the expectations of the Third World's poor. By definition, populism was a phenomenon that characterized "transitional" societies and exemplified the uneasy and unstable balance between modernization and tradition. In the teleological narrative of modernization theory, the eventual arrival of Third World peoples into consumer heaven was never in doubt: the concern was that the process not be disrupted by the uneven pace of change in different functional domains. In acknowledging that the "demonstration effects" of consumerism on poor economies was potentially dysfunctional, modernization theorists openly acknowledged that the experience of modernity in the Third World could not possibly mimic the mythic narrative of European development because "intellectuals of eighteenth- or nineteenth-century Europe or the United States . . . did not have the opportunity to imitate more advanced nations" (Di Tella 1965:48). However, unlike the *dependistas*, who insisted that asynchronous development was a structural feature of capitalism and not an accident that had befallen poor countries, modernization theory maintained its steadfast faith in the Enlightenment narrative of progress. Modernity was its telos, and mimicry its method.

The influential work of Ernesto Laclau (1977) stands in sharp contrast to the explanation of populism offered by modernization theory. Laclau argues that populism is connected not as much to a determinate stage of development as to a crisis "of the dominant ideological discourse which is in turn part of a more general social crisis." In such a crisis, a fraction within the dominant bloc seeks to impose its hegemony through a direct appeal to the masses. Although all populist discourses have in common the feature that they speak in the name of "the people," not all discourses that speak for "the people" are populist (Laclau 1977:172–75). In particular, there is a difference between dominant blocs that consolidate their hegemony by incorporating "the people" as an order of difference and populist blocs that incorporate them as an antithetical force. In the former, "the people" form part of a stratified, multiclass alliance that seeks to diffuse or dislocate the tensions between the different structural locations represented in the alliance. Laclau puts it very well when he writes (1977:161), "A class is hegemonic not so much to the extent that it is able to impose a uniform conception of the world on the rest of society, but to the extent that it can articulate different visions of the world in such a way that their potential antagonism is neutralized." Examples of such political coalitions are the Congress Party before the 1969 split and the Institutional Revolutionary Party (Partido Revolucionario Institucional, or PRI) in Mexico.

Populist coalitions, by contrast, depend on Manichaean discourses that divide society into antagonistic fields: the people versus the oligarchy, Bharat (one of the "traditional" Hindu names for India) versus India. One pole is authentic, good, moral, just, true, responsible; the other is inauthentic, foreign, evil, unjust, immoral, false, and irresponsible. Such a discourse leaves no room for compromise or dialogue because exclusion is its founding principle (Torre 1992:399–406). It is a polarizing discourse that seeks not to attenuate or soften the hard edges of conflict between classes, races, ethnic groups, linguistic communities, and religious groups but to build on these conflicts by defining a common enemy. Contained within the (usually) disparaging references to populism as a political phenomena is the recognition that such a discourse of opposition, wielded in the name of large majorities (especially historically underprivileged majorities), unleashes, or has the potential to unleash, powerful social forces. The suggestion of danger thus always lurks around discussions of populism, the danger that leaders who stoke destructive, mass anger may be unable to control it. This has sometimes been the way in which that exemplar of populist politics, Peronism, has been understood.[68]

Populism as a Direct Link with "the Masses." In this section, I will first attempt to delineate in what respects Indira Gandhi's campaign of 1971 represented a shift toward populism. My goal is to understand whether and how Indira Gandhi managed to create a populist coalition.[69] The reason why this is important is that in the shift to populism, "development" and, by extension, poverty were the central terms of reference. Indira Gandhi's populist policies also mark an important change in the discourses and programs of "development." I then go on to assess how the pronouncements of political leaders were being received by those who were the objects of that discourse.

The standard narrative of Indira Gandhi's tilt toward populism begins with the crisis in the country in the late sixties and with the bitter infighting within the Congress.[70] The 1967 elections saw the Congress poll less votes (41 percent) and less seats (55 percent) for the lower house of Parliament (Lok Sabha) than ever before. On the national level, the food crisis of 1966–67, precipitated by two disastrous monsoons, a war with Pakistan, and an unsuccessful devaluation, had steadily undermined the Congress's position (Rudolph and Rudolph 1987:133). Polling data analysis suggested that young and low-income groups were deserting the Congress.[71] Moreover, the Congress performed even worse at the state level, losing a majority in eight important states. Regional parties emerged as an important force and had, in common, the strategy of employing populist rhetoric to attract electoral support (Frankel 1978:385).

After the debacle at the polls in 1967, the Congress decided that it needed to improve implementation of the "socialist" policies for which the party had long stood. A growing struggle between the well-established leaders of the party, on the one side, and the prime minister and young radicals in the party, on the other, culminated in the resignation of Morarji Desai as deputy prime minister. In the immediate aftermath of Desai's resignation, on July 21, 1969, the government announced that it had nationalized the largest fourteen banks in India by presidential decree. This proved to be an unexpectedly popular step as it identified Indira Gandhi with a new direction in economic policy. Indira Gandhi abandoned the old Congress principle of accommodation and mediation. By late November 1969, the Congress had divided into two: Congress (O) for Organization, popularly known as "Old Congress," and Congress (R) for Requisition, popularly known as Indira Congress. One side consisted of the traditional leaders of the party, men who had risen from their primary political base in various states to politics at the center. On the other side stood Indira Gandhi, a few veteran leaders, and a large contingent of younger, more radical politicians.[72] Three months later, Indira Gandhi dissolved Parliament and called for fresh elections, a year before they were normally scheduled to occur. This "delinked" the elections for Parliament from the elections to state legislatures, thereby separating national issues from regional ones for the first time.

Most of the lower-level organization of the old Congress Party had gone to the Congress (O), since it was those leaders who had institutionalized bases of support at the grass roots. Therefore, not many seasoned observers forecast that Indira Gandhi's Congress would obtain a majority in the new Parliament (Frankel 1978:452; Rudolph and Rudolph 1987:135).

Indira Gandhi went on an unprecedented, forty-one-day campaign tour, addressing over 250 large rallies and many small ones (Frankel 1978:454). She underlined the impression that she was conducting a personal struggle on behalf of the poor against entrenched interests. Her campaign emphasized that whereas her opponents were interested mainly in her removal, she had no interest other than the removal of poverty.[73] Rather than rely on state party bosses to deliver the vote, as the Congress historically did, she went over their heads to make a direct appeal to "the people."

The appeal succeeded beyond anyone's imagination. Her party swept to power with 350 seats in the 518-member Lok Sabha, more than the two-thirds required for amending the constitution. The old Congress bosses were routed, obtaining only sixteen seats in Parliament (Frankel 1978:455). Indira Gandhi's populist, personalist, and plebiscitary politics had won the battle (Rudolph and Rudolph 1987:132–40). The (Indira) Congress Working Committee observed the dawn of a "new historic situation which brought into the national mainstream vast masses of the weaker sections of society" (Frankel 1978:459).[74] Why did the old Congress machine fail to deliver the votes this time? What were the implications of this fact for the emergence of a different model of peasant politics, one not so strongly dependent on existing rural elites but on the emerging, upwardly mobile middle castes?

With a clear popular mandate and a two-thirds majority in Parliament, Indira Gandhi moved to amend the constitutional guarantees of property as a fundamental right as a prelude to the removal of privy purses in December 1971. In the same month, a war with Pakistan resulted in its partition and the establishment of the new nation-state of Bangladesh.[75] Even more so than the general elections, the state vote highlighted the complete breakdown of clientistic politics as the leaders and representatives at the state level historically consisted of rural elites. Frankel (1978:478) takes the results as demonstrating that "the awakening of large numbers of the rural poor to a desire for the implementation of new principles of equality and participation had taken political form." Rudolph and Rudolph (1987:137), however, see it mainly as evidence of the success of "plebiscitary politics" rather than class-based mobilization. Victory at the polls did little to transform the Indira Congress into a party that was institutionally capable of effectively implementing its promises to help the poor (Kohli 1987).[76]

It would be a mistake to infer from this, however, that the populist promises made by Indira Gandhi were just cynical postures intended to deliver the vote. If one looks at specific policy measures, many new programs were started in this period. In the next chapter, I argue that it is not enough to judge these programs as "failures" according to standard criteria of "program management." Such an evaluation does not do justice to the remarkable political effects of these purportedly "failed" programs. Frankel (1978:491) points out that instead of embarking on a strategy that would achieve the objective of growth *with* redistribution, the government essentially decoupled the two goals, pursuing standard policies of providing incentives for industrial growth, on the one hand, and thinly disguised welfare programs whose main goal was redistribution, on the other. Populist programs, therefore, signaled a shift in the dominant conception of "development," which had been defined largely in terms of canalizing savings for productive investments into primary goods and infrastructure. Not only did populism give welfare programs legitimacy in a model of development, it made them politically essential.

As early as July 1970, a few months before the elections, Indira Gandhi extended the pilot program for the Small Farmers Development Agency (SFDA) to almost twice the number of districts and approved an additional forty projects for the agency for Marginal Farmers and Agricultural Laborers (MFAL). Soon after the elections, a Crash Scheme for Rural Employment (CSRE) was inaugurated in April 1971 to generate employment for one thousand people in each district in the country. In December 1971, just before the state elections, a Drought-Prone Areas Programme (DPAP) was started in seventy-four districts. The net effect of these programs on rural poverty was probably not significant. Frankel's assessment of these schemes puts the emphasis in the right place: "On the whole, the central sector SFDA/MFAL projects could not be distinguished from social welfare programs that temporarily—for the duration of the subsidy scheme—increased the consumption of impoverished participants, but could not create additional opportunities for productive employment to raise their income permanently" (1978:499). In the next couple of years, at least some of these welfare schemes had found their way to small farmers and landless laborers.[77]

From the discussion so far, certain themes that link populism with the reformulation of development goals and priorities emerge with particular clarity. The Congress was historically a dominant bloc in which the "masses" had been incorporated within an order of difference. In other words, the needs and aspirations of lower castes and classes were acknowledged within an overarching framework of compromise, such that "their potential antagonism was neutralized." Indira Gandhi introduced a "conflict idiom" that explicitly rejected compromise with those who disagreed with her policies and ideology. Enacting measures like the nationalization of banks and the abolishment of privy purses signaled her determination to fight for the poor against the urban rich. Similarly, her vow to abolish poverty signaled an end to the class compromise implicit in the machine politics of the old Congress, which was dominated by locally powerful upper castes and classes. In its emphasis on exclusion, the incorporation of "the poor" as an antithetical force, its Manichaean characterizations of certain fractions of the former ruling classes and urban moneyed interests, and its personalistic and messianic self-portrait, Indira Gandhi's discourse had all the features usually attributed to populism. Unlike populist movements, however, the Indira Congress made no effort to institutionalize its ideology in organizations within the party, except by way of introducing new programs whose primary orientation was toward social welfare. However, whereas other scholars have seen this failure to build institutions as proof that Indira Gandhi used populist slogans merely to forge a winning electoral coalition in the short run, I think it is more useful to think of it as shaping the kind of development regime that was eventually put into place. The redistributive programs that were implemented as part of her populist platform, such as the Small Farmers Development Agency and the Drought-Prone Areas Programme, were, despite their small size, to have profound and unforeseen consequences for social relations at the grass roots. As will soon become evident, the transformations of social relations brought about by populist programs were linked to the appropriation and redeployment of development discourses by farmers groups led, in turn, by well-to-do owner-cultivators.

Contemporary observers, journalists as well as scholars, interpreted Indira Gandhi's move toward populism in the 1971 elections as a stroke of genius, thereby further embellishing her image of political astuteness. Most accounts emphasized struggles within the realm of high politics to explain why a switch to such a strategy became a matter of political survival. Left without the organizational base of the Old Congress, Indira Gandhi, aided by the intensive use of mass media in the form of posters, film slides, radio news, and so forth, made direct appeals to rural voters. The unexpected enthusiasm with which the news about bank nationalization had been received seemed to indicate that the support of the "popular classes" had not already been "captured" by the policies and organizations of existing parties. Development discourse, which had hitherto been mainly an elite preoccupation, revealed a surprising potential for radical democratic mobilization. Populism unleashed a specifically postcolonial appropriation of development in which the "premature" incorporation of "the masses" threatened to derail the engine of progress on its route to modernity.

The analysis offered so far of the extension of development discourse in a populist direction leaves an important question unanswered. Although it accounts for the actions of a specific leader, Indira Gandhi, it does not shed much light on why populist appeals succeeded. In other words, if we are to understand what makes populist appeals successful and what they mean to "the people" who are being appealed to in these discourses of development, we have to go beyond the realm of elite politics and policy statements. The next section is devoted to what "Indira Raj" meant to the subaltern in a north Indian village.

Understanding Populism through "Reception Theory" and Beyond. The statements and actions of a charismatic leader explain what kinds of appeals were made and how they were articulated and put into practice. What remains to be understood is how they were interpreted and employed by those who were the objects of this discourse. A "reception theory" approach emphasizes the structural location of particular groups as an explanation for why they are predisposed to receive populist appeals favorably. Although such an approach is useful, one has to go beyond an invocation of subject positions to ethnographically investigate the particular conjunctures to understand the favorable reception of populist discourses.

If populism is, by definition, based on the recognition or creation of antagonistic fields, then it certainly left its mark on the life of villagers in Alipur. It mobilized lower-caste (and usually lower-class) people against those landowning groups that exercised control over them and had "delivered" their votes to the Congress in previous elections. The residents of Alipur, especially lower-caste people, routinely pointed to Indira Gandhi's reign as introducing very significant changes in social relations at the grass roots.

Their anger was directed, most of all, at the *thakurs,* who were traditionally the landlords [zamindars] of Alipur. Shortly after I reached Alipur in 1984–85, Indira Gandhi was assassinated and, thus, was even more readily a topic of conversation. When I talked to groups of lower-caste men, they would often criticize the thakurs but rarely did so to their face. During my last research trip in 1991–92, although the younger generation was considerably less inhibited, this was still largely true of the older generation. Many lower-caste people told me that their lives improved considerably during the tenure of Indira Gandhi.

During a windswept and overcast monsoon afternoon toward the end of July 1992, I was sitting outside the cattleshed owned by four jatav brothers and their families.[78] Two of the older generation were there, along with an assortment of their sons, grandsons, and neighbors. One

Monsoon clouds

of the brothers, Chotu, put it this way: "Most of all [the thakurs'] power has been slashed since the raj of Indira—Indira hung them up to dry [sab taang deeay], got rid of untouchability, abolished unpaid labor, increased the wages of laborers, and introduced subsidies for the Scheduled Castes in all programs." Attributing this impressive list of accomplishments to Indira Gandhi struck me as implausible. Nevertheless, it was significant that laws abolishing untouchability and unpaid labor, long on the books, as well as the introduction of subsidies for lower castes and higher wages for laborers, were being credited to her. What was it about Indira Raj that made it appear the source of these changes? In response to this question, Chotu answered: "[The administration] kept writing reports. If there was tension in the village, there was a greater chance of it being heard [by the authorities]. The news started appearing in the newspapers and on the radio [as if to say]: 'Don't harass laborers; give them a proper wage; don't persecute them; eradicate untouchability; work together.'" That the administration would, in an unprecedented step, sometimes intervene on behalf of the lower castes was borne out by the experience of some harijans in the village. In one instance, facing threats from a powerful landlord, the harijans complained to the district administration. Following orders from above to investigate and promptly and actively respond to complaints filed by

Scheduled Caste people, the district administration sent a contingent of policemen who camped out near the harijan houses. They stayed long enough to ensure that the thakur got the message that he could not intimidate the harijans except at his own peril. This incident caused waves in the whole area and indicated how far things had changed for all concerned. Its value lay less in the immediate goal of protecting the harijan households than in the fact that it symbolized a drastic change in the regime's commitment to laws that had long been on the books but rarely enforced.

Apart from concrete changes in administration, the government also employed the radio to symbolize a change in its willingness to enforce the law. As Chotu pointed out, the mass media was used to convey the message, "Don't harass laborers; give them a proper wage; don't persecute them; eradicate untouchability; work together."

"But the same laws were in effect before Indira Gandhi," I reminded him. "Haven't these been the stated policies of the Congress ever since independence?"

The answer was that such may have been so, but before Indira, the effect of these statements was minimal. During Indira's raj, everything was done satisfactorily. I was then provided with the following example: "Earlier, [the thakurs] used to command people to do unpaid labor [begaar]. We had to go and work there even while our own fields were neglected. If we didn't go, they insulted us. Now, they do the same thing but it doesn't work. Now the society is literate. Everyone knows the law. Just as they read what is in the newspapers, so do our children. So now everyone knows everything, and [we know] there's no such thing [as begaar]. We may help them voluntarily, but it is no longer a question of compulsion and threat." Many different lower-caste men related similar stories when they recounted how things had changed within their own lifetime.[79] It was a measure of the success of Indira Gandhi's populist pronouncements and policies that such an astonishing degree of credit for that change was attributed to her. Whereas social justice was previously seen as an ancillary to development, it was identified as a central component of the project of national development in Indira Gandhi's populism.

On the other side were the statements of the upper castes, which inverted the evaluations of the lower-caste men. I was frequently told that the country had gone downhill ever since the Scheduled Castes had been inducted into the bureaucracy.[80] Often, discussions of corruption among upper-caste men would conclude that the problem took root when large numbers of lower-caste officers were inducted into the administrative services. An upper-caste informant blamed the government for changing a system of orderly hierarchy that "even the Muslim kings and the English did not disturb," thereby increasing corruption. He emphasized the point with a couplet, "Bringing untouchables into the state/Is to increase corruption by spates" [*Shaasan main shudron ko laanaa/Hain bhrashtaachaar ko badhaana*]. Another upper-caste (thakur) informant, who attributed the origins of government policies on behalf of Scheduled Castes to the preoccupations of Mahatma Gandhi, went on to argue that Indira Gandhi's death was directly tied to her promotion of the lower castes. He claimed that her assassins, Beant Singh and Satwant Singh, were hired by the government because they were Scheduled Caste and Backward Caste, respectively.[81] Just as Beant Singh and Satwant Singh had turned out to be untrustworthy, he implied that other lower-caste people would bite the government's hand in return for what it was doing for them. Particularly among the thakurs, there was an unmistakable tone of bitterness toward policies perceived to be responsible for the erosion of their power. And, once again, the person held most responsible for this was Indira Gandhi.

Yet if Indira Gandhi was the first national leader to seize upon populist politics as a means to consolidate power, there soon developed oppositional movements that sought to do the same thing. In the decade after Indira Gandhi first introduced "Garibi hatao," the most important social movements in India were led by well-to-do farmers, articulating the interests of the countryside against the cities (see T. Brass ed. 1994). Whereas Indira Gandhi's populism mounted an attack on the failure of "national development" to reach the poor, the farmers movement would target the failure of development to reach the countryside and, in particular, farmers, who were thus represented as an unitary category.

Peasant Movements and Agrarian Populism

Struggles over the meaning and direction of development exhibited in populist politics demonstrate the degree to which "development" was the outcome of strategic political choices, and not a technocratic solution to national problems of poverty and sovereignty. Indira Gandhi attempted to consolidate a hegemonic bloc by incorporating the poor into a regime of development based on policies of import-substituting industrialization and state control over the economy. These efforts, however, did not go without challenge. In rural areas, particularly in the surplus-producing states of Punjab, Haryana, and western UP, this challenge came in the form of farmers' efforts to construct a counter-hegemonic bloc that employed populist discourses of development. This was manifest in various farmers movements that identified the chief contradiction as that between Bharat and India, the country and the city. Populism was, thus, not just a project of the ruling regime but also deployed by oppositional groups to construct alternatives to the ruling coalition. As we shall see, it is oppositional populism, rather than the appeals to the poor initiated by Indira Gandhi, that have gathered strength since the early seventies.

There are two parts in this section. In the first I chronicle the rise of "peasant" politics by concentrating on the ideological and intellectual direction given to it by its chief proponent, Chaudhary Charan Singh. I explore Charan Singh's actions and pronouncements in some detail to explain the events that led to the dominance in "peasant" politics of substantial owner-cultivators belonging to the middle castes. Significantly, Charan Singh articulated a critique of dominant models of development and even managed to found a political party based on that critique. It was not until after his death, however, that the ideological ground that he had helped prepare could be utilized successfully to mobilize a coalition of rural groups. The success of antigovernmental populism depended not only on the wealth created by the green revolution but also on the legitimacy provided to a conflictual reconfiguration of the nation by Indira Gandhi's attack on regnant models of development.

The second part picks up the story in the late eighties, when the BKU became a major presence in northern India. It demonstrates how the Kisan Union effectively marshaled a populist position that focused attention on the "urban bias" of development policies. The elements of this populist discourse are the positing of a sharp and irrevocable divide between rural Bharat and urban India, which, in turn, is built on a critique of the strategy and implementation of "development." But this construction of a unitary "Bharat" is strafed with the tensions that pervade rural northern India and is built on powerful exclusions based on the intersection of gender domination with caste and class rule.

Oppositional populism: the BKD and its descendants

The first organized political party to articulate a rural critique of development and represent itself exclusively as a party of peasants [kisans] was the Bharatiya Kranti Dal, or BKD, founded by Chaudhary Charan Singh in 1967 (Brass 1993; Byres 1988:145; Duncan 1988:40).[82] Charan

Singh, a veteran Congress leader, left the Congress Party shortly after the elections of 1967, bringing down the government in the state of Uttar Pradesh. Long a champion of the interests of the landowning peasantry, Charan Singh's personal ambition, as well as his advocacy of "peasant" causes, was consistently foiled by opposing interest groups within the UP Congress. In the elections of 1969, the BKD emerged within just two years as the largest opposition party in the UP legislature, with more than a fifth of the popular vote. Its support was particularly strong in the western part of the state, where it polled over one-third of the votes (Duncan 1988:40–41; Brass 1980:411–12; 1993).[83]

Charan Singh's credentials as a "peasant leader" were forged through a lifetime of political work and intellectual production that consistently articulated the viewpoint of the landowning peasantry.[84] It would be no exaggeration to say that he, more than anyone else, was responsible for laying the ground for the later emergence of "peasant" politics. As early as 1937, he introduced the Agricultural Produce Markets Bill to protect the direct producer from "the rapacity of the trader" (Byres 1988:148).[85] His crowning achievement, however, was to sound the death knell of the large, especially absentee, landlord by steering the UP Zamindari Abolition Act of 1952 through the legislature. More than anything else, the Zamindari Abolition Act signaled the Congress's willingness to oppose the large landlords, who had dominated village life, in favor of the class of small landlords and well-to-do occupancy tenants who provided the party with the backbone of its support in the rural areas.[86] Although the act did little in the way of providing land to the landless, it did transfer small but significant amounts of property from noncultivating owners to hereditary tenants. These were the groups that would later form the main basis of the BKD, traditionally agricultural middle or "backward" castes like the Jats, Ahirs, Kurmis, Yadavs, and Gujars (Duncan 1988:44). The Zamindari Abolition Act was consistent with Charan Singh's conviction that agriculture had a central role to play in the development of the nation and that agricultural growth depended on providing incentives to the actual cultivator and protecting him from usurious landlords and traders.[87]

As UP minister for revenue and agriculture in 1953, Charan Singh seized the opportunity offered by a strike of village land record keepers [patwaris], who were considered an impediment to dispossessing large landowners, to dismiss thousands of them.[88] He also engineered the UP Consolidation of Holdings Act of 1953, which enabled the consolidation of hopelessly fragmented landholdings into a single farm for each family.[89] Land consolidation was a precondition to such capital-intensive investments in agriculture as the sinking of tube wells.[90] Finally, during the food crisis of 1967, he reluctantly enforced the Government of India's food procurement scheme, but he did so in such a way that it paid producers a price for their output that was comparable with what they might have been able to obtain on the market.[91]

The transfer of land to owner-cultivators, the consolidation of holdings, decreases in the land revenue in real terms, and support prices were the preconditions that enabled the adoption of green revolution technology by rich and middle peasants. As I shall presently contend, the "package" of policies introduced with the high-yielding varieties enabled this segment of the peasantry to "take off" as a potent political force. However, the elements for the consolidation of what is sometimes disparagingly referred to as a "kulak" populism were already in place. Charan Singh was its chief ideologue and architect. He consistently argued that his actions were on behalf of *all* members of the "farming community." Although it was abundantly clear that his policies would disproportionately benefit the rich peasantry, his discourse steadfastly refused to acknowledge any such differentiation (Byres 1988).

The populist elements in Charan Singh's politics arose out of a careful delineation of the forces "opposed" to "the farming community." These forces included landlords, patwaris, traders, and moneylenders, all of whom managed to extract, through a variety of morally or legally dubious means, the surplus that legitimately belonged to the farmer. There is no doubt that his positions against these groups found resonance among a broad spectrum of the rural population, including the rural poor. Charan Singh strongly opposed the reorganization of agriculture along industrial lines through, for example, the extensive use of wage labor and the development of large mechanized farms (Byres 1988:175–76).[92] He also opposed collectivization, by which he meant the establishment of farming cooperatives based on the Soviet model, with large farms collectively worked by a commune. Against both these models, he used arguments about the greater productivity of small holdings (the famous "inverse" relationship between farm size and yield per unit of land) and the failure of tractorization to increase productivity. Capitalism and collectivization, with their presumption of state control, were represented as furthering urban interests against all the rural people (Byres 1988:179). Charan Singh thus implicitly articulated the sectoral interests of agriculture through a series of oppositions to others who were seen as advancing (urban-based) industrial or state interests.

Hence he forged a discourse that represented an urban and industrial model of national development as inimical to the interests of the vast majority of the population that lived in rural India.[93]

The BKD's success in gathering more than a fifth of the popular vote in UP in its very first election in 1969, the highest of any non-Congress Party since independence was gained, signaled the emergence of a major new political bloc rooted in agrarian interests. The next elections in 1974 made it clear that the BKD's initial success was not a flash in the pan. Once again, the BKD polled more than a fifth of the popular vote, despite strenuous electoral efforts by Indira Gandhi and the central leadership of the Congress (Brass 1980:415–16). The BKD merged with the Janata Party in the historic winning coalition of 1977, the first non-Congress government to rule the country, but then split off from the Janata Party and contested the 1980 elections as the Lok Dal, once again gathering almost 30 percent of the popular vote.[94]

When the BKD was founded in 1967, the technological revolution known as the green revolution was yet to be widely promulgated in western Uttar Pradesh. The strata of the peasantry that owned between 2.5 and 27.5 acres of land, the backbone of the BKD, were also those most favorably positioned to employ the new technology. Because the capital investment required to sink a tube well, essential for a steady and reliable source of irrigation, was quite large, those who had land to offer as collateral had less difficulty in obtaining loans. On the other hand, a tube well became a profitable investment only because holdings had been consolidated: the more land that could be reliably irrigated with one well, the less its fixed cost per unit of output. The aggregate output of wheat jumped because of the new technology, and food grain production quickly reached levels which ensured that the shortfall of 1966–67 would never be repeated.[95]

For the better-off peasants, the new technology was a great boon. The "package" of policies introduced by the government included not only price guarantees for output, thus ensuring that great increases in output would not result in price depression, but also subsidies for inputs such as chemical fertilizers. At the same time that this new technology enabled rich farmers to obtain larger net surpluses, it also made them more dependent on government policies and programs. Suddenly, the support price announced before the growing season was not merely the concern of an elite stationed in Delhi but of the entire class of farmers with marketable surpluses. Changes in the support price, as compared with input prices, in effect indexed the terms of trade for the agricultural sector. If the support price rose faster than the cost of inputs, it resulted in a distribution of income in favor of agriculture. If it rose more slowly, it amounted to a de facto tax. Thus, not just farm incomes but also intersectoral distribution effects came to hinge on the level of support prices.

It is in this context of the development of different sectors of the economy that we have to understand the growing organizational ability and militancy of "peasant" groups. That the better-off segments of the rural population were a powerful political presence[96] becomes clear from an incident surrounding discussions in the Planning Commission to tax agricultural incomes as a means to raise government intakes, which was unequivocally rejected by the prime minister.[97]

Charan Singh himself employed the growing power of the peasant lobby to great effect in struggles within the Janata coalition after it came to power in 1977.[98] Forced to resign from his post as minister of home affairs in 1978, Charan Singh sought to demonstrate his popular support by organizing an enormous rally of "peasants." On his seventy-sixth birthday on December 23, 1978, a farmers rally was held in New Delhi, which was attended by an estimated one million farmers, mostly from neighboring states, in what was perhaps the largest such gathering in the history of the capital. The speeches at the rally portrayed India's villages as the "colonies" of its cities. In its aftermath, Charan Singh was hastily reinducted into the cabinet, as minister of finance and deputy prime minister.[99] In the budget that he presented to Parliament shortly thereafter, a budget that an associate described as possessing "the breath of the people and the smell of the soil," he cut the duty on chemical fertilizers by half, reduced taxes on agricultural equipment, and increased government expenditure on rural electrification and dairy farms (Byres 1988:163).

Peasant politics and developmentalism

Shortly after Charan Singh passed away in 1987, several people, including his son, Ajit Singh, staked their claim to the party that he had helped found and had raised to such prominence. Fights over who would inherit the Lok Dal legacy led to a split within the party. But it was not in the realm of parliamentary maneuvering that "peasant" politics in northern India was to find its resurgence. That came with the founding of the Bharatiya Kisan Union, or BKU, a nonparty organization led by Mahendra Singh Tikait, a rural jat leader from the prosperous cane- and wheat-growing district of Muzaffarnagar in western Uttar Pradesh.[100] At the same time that the Kisan Union (as the BKU is often called) was gathering strength in UP, very similar movements based in the rich peasantry were making their presence felt in other states. The most important of these in the last few years have been the Shetkari Sangathana led by Sharad Joshi in Maharashtra and the Karnataka Rajya Ryota Sangha led by Dr. Nanjundaswamy.[101] In 1989 a meeting to convene a unified national peasant association drew thirty farmer organizations from twelve different states.[102] All these organizations relied heavily on the stratum of owner-cultivators with substantial holdings for their core support, a fact reflected in their consistent demand to raise output prices and reduce the cost of inputs.

Of the various features of Charan Singh's "peasant" discourse, the one most emphasized by successor movements points to the dual nature of the country's development. The leader of the influential farmers movement in Maharashtra, Sharad Joshi, very clearly articulated the division between "Bharat" and "India." Perhaps taking a cue from dual-economy models, he argued that rural Bharat and urban India were two different countries.[103] The intent was to contrast the vernacular name denoting the ordinary, the rural, the little tradition, the "real" country of small peasants and agricultural laborers, with the Western, urban, industrial, internationally oriented, modern nation-state. This division was intended to highlight the "urban bias" of development policies that have resulted in a widening gap between urban dwellers who work for the state and industrial sectors and rural folk who work in the agricultural sector. This duality between Bharat and India, as we shall see, managed to coalesce a variety of dissatisfactions experienced by different classes and segments of the rural population into a unitary framework. In its ability to map different grievances into a singular antithesis, it functioned as a truly powerful oppositional populism. It was oppositional in that its chief target was the government, which it accused of failing to deliver on its developmental promises. Peasant populism insisted that the interests of "India" systematically undermined the well-being of "Bharat" (see especially T. Brass ed. 1994, 1994b).

Implicit in the division between Bharat and India was a more wide-ranging critique of the model of a modern nation being pursued by successive postcolonial regimes. The envious disdain for "India" shown by the proponents of "Bharat" often included an explicit critique of the lifestyles of the denationalized, decultured, urban elite who sought to mimic "the West." The implication, by extension, was that a plan for national development built on the mimicry of the West was guaranteed to fail, since it would adversely affect the rural population. The agrarian populism espoused by peasant groups, therefore, attempted a far-reaching critique of development models, one that quite consciously sought to build a "modern" nation that was not a pale imitation of "the West." I now take a closer look at peasant populism and its relation to the actions of the Kisan Union at the ground level. My sources for this analysis are interviews with the residents of the village in western UP where I did fieldwork and reports in vernacular newspapers in the area.

Bharat versus India. The contrast between Bharat and India finds one powerful axis in the critique of "urban bias," in pitting the countryside against the city. Under the leadership of the Kisan Union, this critique has been expressed in many ways and sometimes leads to overt violence between villagers and urban groups. One such incident occurred in the small town of Khair in Aligarh District in June 1989. Although the reports state that there was no organized Kisan Union leadership in the district, the conflict involved people who claimed to be members of the BKU. According to the account given by the chairman of the town municipality, there was a legal dispute between the township and the owner of a shop in the main market. Just as the owner of the shop and the municipality were about to reach a compromise, some Kisan Union activists approached the owner and offered to settle the matter to his monetary advantage. When he agreed, they demolished the shop at night and attempted to carry off the debris. This prompted the police to intervene and arrest five BKU activists. A confrontation then arose between the Kisan Union and the police in which six activists were killed. Because this incident occurred just a few months before the national elections of December 1989, it was at once seized upon by leaders of the opposition, who made it a "pilgrimage" site.[104]

This incident occurred after several months of tension between the administration and union activists. Farmers stopped paying taxes whenever any one of them was punished for failing to pay back loans or taxes, "rescued" arrested Kisan Union volunteers from police custody, closed government wheat purchase centers if they considered the purchase price to be too low, stripped and "arrested" a police inspector for eight hours, and held another district official captive for twelve hours. But what is most interesting, from my perspective, is how the death of the Kisan Union activists was construed as a "confrontation between the farmers and 'the rest' of the population." The president of the town's chamber of commerce stated: "BKU volunteers in the surrounding villages are ready to confront anyone belonging to Khair town. Today this campaign is directed against the urban population of Khair, tomorrow this is going to spread all over western Uttar Pradesh."[105]

Of course, market towns were especially offensive to peasant activists because they housed merchants, long considered people who used their guile and knowledge of the market to shortchange farmers. Ranbir, a jat "middle farmer" living in Alipur, was an enthusiastic supporter of the Kisan Union. In a conversation that took place in late July 1989, he talked of the importance of obtaining a good support price for wheat from the government. He felt that by uniting, farmers could have a say in fixing the selling price of their produce. He contrasted such a situation favorably with the prevalent context in which merchants fixed prices. "If you take your wheat to the market," he told me, "one trader will negotiate the price with another while you sit on a side. Then, he will come to you and say, 'I've managed to get you a good price, but it wasn't easy.'" Ranbir felt that the farmer was powerless in the entire negotiation. Suresh, a brahmin who owned a small plot of about two acres, gave me a similar reason for why farmers were opposed to merchants. Like others in Alipur, Suresh was not an active supporter of the Kisan Union. In fact, unlike Ranbir, he was not even inclined to view the Kisan Union favorably. Nevertheless, he admitted that the organization was doing much good work. He explained that the conflict with merchants arose from the question of who should benefit from the proceeds of farming. The Kisan Union merely maintained that the merchants were reaping "unnecessary" profits, and wanted to ensure that proceeds from the sale of farm commodities went into the hands of farmers themselves and not of middlemen. The merchants of the nearby town, he added, had tried to split the Kisan Union in their region by creating divisions between leaders within the organization. The ploy backfired, however, and the union had now organized against the merchants as well as the state.

Not everyone shared the perception held by Suresh and Ranbir regarding the efficacy of the Kisan Union. A group of thakur men in Alipur told me that the Kisan Union could not face up to the government. They said that hundreds had been killed in the firing at Khair, even though official reports and news bulletins claimed that only six had died: the police took all the bodies and dumped them somewhere; they had never been found. The Kisan Union was no match for the government. The thakurs, long the dominant landlords and political force in Alipur, had been hostile to the Kisan Union because they saw it as an expression of jat assertion.

The presence of merchants was not the sole reason for the peasants' wrath against urban centers. Other resentments harbored by peasants focused on the better infrastructure available in cities. The vast differences in educational and medical facilities, as well as the unavailability of electricity, telephones, and tap water outside the city, were often commented upon. For example, in a meeting called by the Kisan Union in the town of Danpur in Bulandshahr District, several speakers seized on this theme of the disparities between their lives and those of urban residents. The chair of the district unit, Gangaprasad, blamed the government for corruption in the schools. He said it was not just the teachers who were responsible but the poor condition of schools in the villages. This despite the fact that the farmer was the "true owner" of this country. Gangaprasad added: "A farmer who spends his day weeding is as intelligent as the Chief Minister. He is not a fool. Our village children should receive exactly the same education as that available to the children of ministers and industrialists in Delhi. We cannot tolerate this stepdaughterly treatment."[106] An Op-Ed piece in another vernacular newspaper, the *Bijnor Times*, advanced a similar complaint: "As far as the question of opening the gates of education, health, civic amenities, and knowledge, and of the ability to take advantage of these, the farmer is at a disadvantage."[107]

There were also grievances that centered on the supply of electricity and the government's perceived enthusiasm for debt collection. Gangaprasad went on to say, "We want to tell the government that the villages should be supplied electricity twenty-four hours a day, just as Delhi is." He highlighted the inequalities in the government's loan collection policies: "Rich and famous people owe the government millions of rupees but we have never seen them go to jail for it. But if the farmer owes a little bit, he is promptly hauled off to jail."[108] This statement has to be understood in the context of the Kisan Union's long-standing demand that the farmers' debts should be "forgiven" or written off, a position also adopted by almost all other farmers organizations. For example, Sharad Joshi led *karjmukti* (liberation from debt) agitations to do the same in Maharashtra. Since a disproportionate amount of loans were made to those farmers who had some land as collateral, the class implications of these agitations are clear.

Another major argument that fed into the "urban bias" thesis was that the terms of trade were set against agriculture. In fact, a central demand of the farmers organizations was that agricultural prices be restored to pre–green revolution levels. Peasant leaders demanded that the price of agricultural output relative to inputs be restored to 1967 levels.[109] This also tied into the perception that the discrepancy between those working in the industrial and government sectors and those in agriculture had actually widened. It was pointed out, for example, that government outlays for mining and industry were 50 percent greater than for farming and irrigation in the first six five-year plans.[110] The same article indicated that the gap in income per worker between nonagricultural and agricultural sectors had widened from a ratio of 1.5 in 1951 to approximately 3 in 1983. In other words, instead of a decrease in the inequality of workers' incomes between sectors, there had been an increase in the thirty years following the First Plan.

Yet it was not just in critiques of "urban bias" that the dualistic view of and identification with "Bharat," as against "India," found expression. Apart from expressing a range of grievances, these discourses also created a particular kind of subject position, one whose moral bearings were quite different from those found in "India." This was the virtue of those who were poor, politically helpless, exploited, but who, on gaining power, refuse to exploit it. The implicit contrast was with the high-handedness, arrogance, and corruption of the powerful, both government officials (a favorite target) and the urban bourgeoisie.[111] Poverty—and the lack of political power—was a constant theme in the discourse of Tikait, the leader of the Kisan Union. When asked about the role that the Kisan Union would play in the elections in 1989, he replied: "What can the farmer do to change electoral fortunes? Look at them—they are so poor, they can only listen when we speak, no more. We have no power."[112] It is as if the poverty of the farmers, iconicized by their clothes ("look at them—they are so poor"), is also what renders them mute—unable to represent their interests or desires ("they can only listen"). Their appearance, therefore, represents both their poverty and the lack of a political voice. But then there is a subtle transference from the poverty that renders the peasantry mute to its leader ("they can only listen when we speak. . . . We have no power"). By a series of transpositions, the iconicized poverty of the peasants becomes a generalized signifier of peasant powerlessness.

The employment of sartorial signifiers was absolutely crucial to everyday life in Alipur. The enterprising son of the wealthiest household in the village deliberately wore torn clothes as he went about his work.

When, in the course of conversations with others, he was accused of being "greedy," he loudly pointed out that if he was indeed as wealthy as they claimed, why did he continue to wear the kind of clothes that no self-respecting person, who could afford better, would want to? Those village men who had obtained jobs in the city signified their status by wearing trousers and a shirt rather than the pajama-kurta or dhoti worn in the village. Clothes made the man a villager or a city slicker. What a person wore signified not merely how wealthy he was but where he belonged as well. Clothes thus possessed great representational efficacy, and it was this that Tikait deployed in his discourse.[113]

Those who lived in the village and continued to think of themselves as farmers therefore went to great trouble *not* to stand out in the way they dressed.[114] In fact, they went to considerable lengths not to incur the envy of their neighbors. One of the most dynamic men in the village was Naresh. Although he worked full-time as a government employee on a farm run by the state and was, therefore, quite well paid by local standards, he had, in addition, rented some farmland as a sharecropper. He devoted most of his time and energy to his farming but somehow also managed to fulfill the sometimes strenuous obligations of his formal job. He told me that he deposited his government income and most of the money he obtained from sharecropping in a bank as quickly as possible. He did not keep any utensils or objects in the house that would make his wealth visible. In fact, he preferred to stay in debt for nominal amounts so that people would continue to regard him as poor. "That is the only way not to arouse jealousy in this place," he said. Therefore, when Tikait pointed to his followers, saying "Look at them," he was pointing to a highly charged signifier whose encoding was probably interpreted quite differently by a casual observer such as an urban reporter than by someone more intimately familiar with village life in western Uttar Pradesh.

The poverty and helplessness of the "farmer" was connected to the effort to recuperate his self-respect [swaabhimaan].[115] Through its activities of mass protest and noncompliance with government regulations, the Kisan Union was attempting to "reawaken the pride of the peasant." In another incident between Kisan Union activists and the police over the kidnapping of a young Muslim woman, Naiyma, the police had reportedly pushed three tractors belonging to peasant activists into a canal near the town of Bhopa in Muzaffarnagar District. Tikait reached the scene by the side of the canal shortly thereafter and, along with thousands of farmers who joined him, proceeded to lay camp for the "recovery of Naiyma." Pointing to the submerged tractors periodically burping oil to the surface, Tikait announced dramatically, "See, there lies the self-respect of the kisan—immersed in that canal."[116] The self-respect of the peasants was identified with the tractors, whereas the ostensible reason for the gathering was to address the kidnapping of Naiyma. Taking up the cause of an unknown Muslim woman may have had the strategic intent of consolidating the Kisan Union's position as an organization of farmers that crossed religious lines. But it was also related to dominant discourses about male honor being tied to the successful control of female sexuality. It was widely rumored that Naiyma's "abductor" was the relative of a powerful minister in the UP cabinet. Hence, the Kisan Union was protesting the inability of male peasants to "protect" their women against representatives of the state.

Naiyma became the means to mobilize people, but her misfortune was displaced by the sunken tractors, which were obviously more potent icons of the "self-respect" of (male) peasants.[117] Tikait demanded that the chief minister of UP or the prime minister come to Bhopa to see the peasant's fate "with his own eyes." He said that farmers could not really expect justice from these higher officials. But, he wanted them to "come and see what their minions had done to the peasant's self-respect."[118] Tikait repeatedly emphasized the powerlessness of the peasantry and their suffering at the hands of urban rulers. He told the gathered farmers that the city-based government [sarkaar] would never provide real justice for the farmer.[119] After the body of the abducted Naiyma was found, Tikait vowed that the struggle for the farmer's self-respect would continue. He claimed that because the government was dishonest, theirs would be a protracted struggle, but one in which he was confident they would eventually triumph.[120]

Urban commentators noted how these themes of poverty and helplessness, along with the perception of injured pride, lent a "moral" character to the evocation of "Bharat" struggling against an all-powerful "India."[121] The legal system was itself seen as complicit in this project of domination. Thus, Tikait rejected a priori the government's efforts at adjudication by saying, "No dispute can ever be resolved satisfactorily by legality; it can be settled only through a search for the truth [sachchaai]."[122] One commentator, Chandan Mitra, wrote that, unlike a trade union leader whose success would be judged by "materialistic" criteria of winning a majority of a charter of demands, Tikait's success depended on his ability to invoke and reinscribe a "rural" moral code. Thus, an evaluation of the agitations led by Tikait would be incorrectly interpreted in a straightforward means-end calculus. Drawing from the Kisan Union's rhetoric and from modernization theory to invert Marx, Mitra concluded: "A modernizing state can ignore this kind of rural backlash only at its own peril. But before it devises a strategy to combat the resurgent peasant, it needs to understand the peasant mind, dispassionately, but not without empathy. Analysts of 'India' have so far tried to change 'Bharat.' The point, right now, is to interpret it."[123] The analytic force of such statements depended on their reliance of "the peasantry" as a *singular* category: "the resurgent peasant," "the peasant mind," "a rural moral code," "rural backlash," and so on. This is indeed exactly what the Kisan Union attempted to do in its depiction of "Bharat."

The emphasis on the poverty and helplessness of the peasant and the mistreatment of "Bharat" at the hands of "India" formed the ground on which the Kisan Union made its appeals for peasant unity. This point was forcefully emphasized to me by Ranbir, the jat farmer introduced earlier, who was a sympathizer of the Kisan Union. He said that the union of bus conductors and the union of traders could stop work when they wanted to, but farmers did not have that luxury. For that reason, the government did not do much to help the peasants. If the Kisan Union was successful, he claimed, it would become so strong that it would overturn the government. The Kisan Union had created a sense of togetherness among peasants, and unity was the only way in which peasants could gain some power. If you desired to get something done on your own, he inquired, how likely were you to be successful? But if you were part of a professors union that had fifty local members, then those fifty people would stand behind you to ensure your success. That was exactly what the Kisan Union was doing. In the vocabulary of villagers, "getting your work done" invariably referred to matters pertaining to government departments.

Members of the Kisan Union pointed out that they were careful not to abuse the strength gained through collective action and that this was how peasants differed from government officials. For example, when the Naiyma agitation was almost at its end, the government sent a crane to Bhopa to fish out the sunken tractors from their watery graves. Because removal of the tractors would have deprived them of the most powerful symbol of the administration's contempt for the peasantry, however, Kisan Union activists surrounded the crane and prevented it from taking out the tractors. Speaking at the end of the campaign near the Bhopa canal, Tikait talked about how the Kisan Union had brought the administration to its knees. Although they had stopped the administration from doing what it pleased, Tikait emphasized that the Kisan Union did not wish to be arrogant about its own strength. He thereby underlined one big difference between the collective strength of peasants and the bureaucratic power of the state. Once again, the demonstrable difference between "Bharat" and "India" was made apparent.

The Failure of "Development." Development has served as the cornerstone of the legitimation efforts of the postindependence Indian state. The success of Indira Gandhi's populism lay precisely in its attack on the failure of the previous regime's development efforts to go far enough in improving the lives of those in whose name they were being launched, namely, the poor. But she did not put into place an effective mechanism by which to implement new populist policies explicitly targeted at the poor. Therefore, it was only a matter of time before oppositional groups would take up the battle cry of the "failure of development" to attack her regime. And this is precisely what the Kisan Union did in the late eighties. Although much of the Kisan Union's rhetoric was aimed at protecting the interest of peasants and consolidating them into a unitary force, in practice this most often translated into attacks on the state for its failure to implement development policies properly. A large proportion of the Kisan Union's local-level organizing was around issues of corruption and the failure of the government to implement rural development programs to the benefit of farmers. However, members of the Kisan Union sometimes articulated a broader critique of those development strategies which put industry first and which deliberately keep agriculture backward. Although both critiques built on the modernist premises of the discourse of "development," they had quite different implications for how those premises became lived realities. Different formulations of development, thus, speak of *alternative* modernities and do not just index non-Western modernities. Notions of "alternative modernities" indicate that modernity is a contested field of possibilities whose shape and form is inherently unpredictable. This helps us qualify the theoretical discussion that often posits "modernity" in the singular, as if it were a unitary phenomenon.

In my conversations with peasants in Alipur, it became evident that the appeal of the Kisan Union at the local level owed much to its stand against corruption and government mismanagement. Although no one from Alipur actively participated in its rallies, many were extremely sympathetic to the union. For example, Suresh, the brahmin farmer described above, told me that the main achievement of the Kisan Union had been to oppose government officials. He said that when officers of the Electricity Board "needlessly" harassed farmers by threatening to cut off their electric connections for nonpayment of dues, the Kisan Union intervened effectively to prevent that from happening. He felt that the "main purpose" of the Kisan Union had been the elimination of bribery. Naresh, the government employee we met earlier who maintained a second job as a sharecropper and deliberately stayed in debt so as to give the impression of being poor, felt that the main purpose of the Kisan Union was to fight injustice. As a jat, he was particularly supportive of the Kisan Union and felt that its message of farmers uniting to act in their common interest made a great deal of sense. He appreciated the fact that the Kisan Union did not interfere in village life and did not affiliate itself with any political party. "They swing into action only when some injustice has been done," he claimed. When Ranbir, a more prosperous jat farmer, told me why he supported the Kisan Union, he too pointed to its ability to fight corruption among government officials: "If I go to officials of the Electricity Board, they won't listen to me. They will ask me to give them Rs 100 or even Rs 200 to get my work done. Even after I pay them, they won't do the work. I will have to run after them for a few days, go there at the very least a couple of times, before anything will be done. With the union, why will I go alone? We will all go in strength, forty or fifty of us, then the electricity officials will automatically do our work." He recounted how soon after a Kisan Union rally had encouraged farmers not to pay their electric dues and land taxes, electricity officials had come to a neighboring village and attempted to cut off some connections. Someone got wind of the officials' actions and informed Kisan Union activists. They rushed with a large group to the spot where the connections had been cut, caught the officials, forced them to reconnect the lines, took them back to the village, and locked them up for good measure! Ranbir pointed out that if one went to districts where the Kisan Union was really strong, such as Muzaffarnagar or Meerut, one would see that the villages there enjoyed an uninterrupted supply of electricity. No government official dared touch the connections in those areas. For their part, government officials did not like to work in Mandi, the district where Alipur was located. Kishan Chand, an official who had recently been transferred from another district, told me that Mandi was an "undesirable post" because of peasant activism. He claimed that they got their way by employing the tactics of hooligans [*gundagardi*]. No government official would willingly place himself in a position where he would be subjected to such "hooliganism."

Yet corruption, conceptualized as a failure of the government's ability to implement its policies, was not the only source of dissatisfaction with "development." Explicit criticisms of the *model* of development followed by successive regimes in independent India expressed doubt about the value of concentrating on industrialization. The following critique appeared in a local vernacular newspaper:

> The question remains why the condition of the peasant is what it is despite 38 years of planning in which so much of the discussion has focused on the progress of agriculture and the development of villages. Have the benefits of development been unable to reach them? What happened to those resources that were spent in the name of agriculture and farmers? . . . [I]t is evident that the concern for agriculture has been a sham, whereas the truth is that from every viewpoint the farmer has been discriminated against and agriculture has been deliberately kept backward compared with industry and other sectors. There is no need to deny the fact that the price of grain was deliberately kept low right from the beginning so that the urban population and industrial workers could be protected from the burden of expensive food. The results have been predictable: the price of other goods has risen sharply compared with agricultural products. This has meant that farmers' incomes have risen more slowly than [have those in] other sectors. Their dissatisfaction is therefore entirely understandable.[124]

"Despite 38 years of planning"—here is a sentence whose parallels are encountered with numbing regularity in conversation and reportage. If one needed an example of how thoroughly teleological and developmentalist discourses were imbricated in everyday life, one need not look beyond such formulations. The expectation of change inherent in such narratives in fact enables the author to formulate his well-articulated critique of the model of development followed in India since independence. The question was not one of implementing existing policies better but of completely changing course because the entire model of development discriminated against the agricultural sector. This critique found tangible expression through demands that the support price of wheat, the chief cash crop in the area, be raised and that subsidies for fertilizer, water, and electricity be increased. This was seen as a tactic at least to stem, if not reverse, the discriminatory treatment of agriculture.

The agitation for higher output prices was, in fact, one of the most successful strategies of the Kisan Union in western UP. When the government fixed the purchase price of wheat at Rs 183 per quintal in 1989, the Kisan Union forced the shutdown of government scales in the area around Alipur.[125] The open market price for wheat was actually higher than the price set by the government, about Rs 200 per quintal. The Kisan Union seemed to have set out to violate consciously the government's ban on interstate trading of food grains. They took trolley loads of wheat to the neighboring state of Haryana, where it fetched as much as Rs 250 per quintal. Instead of leaving this to merchants, farmers carried the wheat across the state border themselves and sold it on the other side, earning a handsome profit in the process.

The Kisan Union's use of the very discourse of development that had been employed as a legitimizing strategy by the postcolonial state demonstrates that the meanings of hegemonic ideologies are never stable. The ability to rearticulate development into an oppositional discourse that challenges the coherence and stability of the ruling bloc relies on a successful inversion of its claims. Indira Gandhi's populist appeals had already demonstrated that the stable order constructed by the Congress was falling apart. But there was no reason why the same discontent, that had so successfully been nurtured into electoral success, could not be rearticulated to an oppositional ideology. The Kisan Union did this not only by judging the project of development to have failed by its own standards, especially in its effects on the majority of the Indian population living in rural areas, but also by a thoroughgoing critique of the industry-centered model of development itself. It is for this reason that, despite the fact that analysts repeatedly emphasized its "kulak" nature, the Kisan Union was so successful in constructing a genuinely multi-class alliance (but see T. Brass 1994b:252). If, as Antonio Gramsci has argued, the success of a hegemonic bloc depends on the simultaneous mastery of a whole series of positions on different fronts, then the Kisan Union did manage to cohere a remarkably disparate set of concerns and subject positions.

Divisions within Bharat—a Split Subject? Although the Kisan Union was remarkably successful in forging a multiclass, multicaste alliance that simultaneously managed to cross the religious divide between Hindus and Muslims, there were other fault lines in rural society that it was unable to paper over. In fact, the very source of the Kisan Union's strength—its rootedness in the concerns, ideologies, and idioms of the owner-cultivators of western UP—was also its chief limitation. The Kisan Union was unable to work constructively with (potentially competing) farmers movements in other states. Tikait's ability as an "organic" leader to articulate the grievances of the cultivators relied on a discourse that reflects the class, caste, and gender divisions of rural society. Moreover, it was not a strategy that necessarily attempted to encompass *all* sections of rural society. In this section, I concentrate on some of these divisions, attempting to demonstrate why the Kisan Union succeeded or failed to overcome the fractures that run through the rural areas of western Uttar Pradesh. Understanding the nature of these splits within Bharat may help us understand whether the Kisan Union's critiques of development were aimed at bridging these fissures or at consolidating the dominance of a particular group. Despite its universalizing claims, development had very different consequences for different groups within rural areas. Therefore, *which* vision of development prevailed was not inconsequential. The politics of caste, class, and gender circumscribed and refracted the ability of the Kisan Union to construct a hegemonic bloc.

Perhaps the most remarkable aspect of the Kisan Union's activities was its ability to straddle the divide between Muslims and Hindus.[126] It did so not by denying religious differences but by aggressively emphasizing their solidarity and joint interests. For example, Kisan Union meetings brought together key leaders of the BKU such as Swami Omvesh, the district president of the Bijnor unit, who favored the saffron garb of Hindu holy men, and Ghulam Mohammed, the Muslim district president of the Muzaffarnagar unit. A *maulana* was invariably present on the dais at public meetings.[127] The slogan consistently employed at Kisan Union rallies daringly combined the religious slogans of Muslims and Hindus. From the dais, someone would shout "Allah-O-Akbar," to which the gathered crowd would respond with "Har Har Mahadev." These slogans were used in all public meetings and in the BKU's monthly meeting [*panchayat*] in Sisauli. Ghulam Mohammed, who conducted the monthly meetings, joked about the stereotypes and beliefs of Hindus and Muslims, something that no major political leader would ever dare do in public.[128] Instead of attempting to deny the importance of religion or proclaim its irrelevance for its purposes, the Kisan Union stressed that only by being a *good* Hindu or a *good* Muslim could one also be a good human being.[129]

To achieve Hindu-Muslim amity, however, one has to go beyond public pronouncements, a fact not lost on the Kisan Union. Apart from ensuring that Muslims occupied leadership positions within the organization, the Kisan Union also played an active role in mediating disputes between groups. Sometimes these disputes spilled over into interclass conflict. In Modh Kurd village in Meerut, there arose a dispute between Muslim jats and harijans when the latter installed a statue of late *dalit* leader Dr. B. R. Ambedkar in the village square.[130] The houses of Muslim jats faced the square, and they did not want the statue to be placed there. The dispute soon escalated, with the main road being blocked in protest against the installation of the statue, the arrival of senior police officials, and the interference of local politicians. When the Kisan Union was asked for help, Ghulam Mohammed was dispatched to mediate the dispute. He called a meeting and decided that the statue would remain in its present place. Despite being a Muslim leader, he ended up ruling in favor of the lower castes. Had this decision been taken by an administration official, it is highly unlikely that the Muslim jats would have consented to abide by it.[131]

Not all conflicts between the cultivating classes, who formed the backbone of the BKU, and lower classes were amicably resolved. In fact, there was an irrevocable structural tension between them that often proved unbridgeable. In Chaprauli village in Meerut, the village council [*panchayat*] dominated by jat farmers attempted to fix the wages of harijan laborers at a rate that was two-thirds to four-fifths of the going market wage. They threatened to punish any farmer who violated the agreement. In addition, they refused to allow laborers who did not consent to work for the lower wages to gather free grass from their fields. In response, the harijans called their own panchayat and announced a list of wage rates for different kinds of work, all of which were higher than the going market wages. They also threatened any laborer violating the agreement with fines and punishments and sent a letter to the prime minister requesting his intervention in having the ban on the cutting of grass lifted.

The tension between owner-cultivators and laborers coincided, to a large extent, with the conflict between the "backward" cultivating castes and harijans. The difficulty of containing this conflict can be discerned from the defensive tone adopted by Kisan Union leaders and sympathizers when faced with this question. When asked whether the Kisan Union also represented landless laborers, Tikait attempted to sidestep the question by saying, "There is no *mazdoor* (laborer) as such. We are all laborers. Some are big laborers, some are small."[132] Similarly, when asked whether his organization represented the interests of all farmers or just the richer ones, he replied: "Who is the rich farmer? There is no rich farmer. This house we're sitting in belongs to a farmer who is considered the third richest in this village of 20,000 people. And yet he doesn't even have 18 acres of land—the ceiling."[133] Tikait therefore denied that there were structural antagonisms among the rural population by pointing to their common need to expend family labor in farming activities, to work with their own hands. Owner-cultivators were, by definition, more like landless laborers and marginal farmers by virtue of the fact that they did their own work.

I put the same questions to Ranbir when he was telling me about all the wonderful things that the Kisan Union had done. First, Ranbir challenged the suggestion that the Kisan Union may have been pitting agriculturists and nonagriculturists against each other. Ranbir told me that everyone was a farmer these days, "even the merchant [baniya] who owns one hundred bighas [approximately sixteen acres] is a farmer." When land consolidation took place, some land was taken away from each plot and later distributed to the landless, mostly lower-caste, population. "So now even they are farmers. Everyone, therefore, is eligible to join the Kisan Union." If the Kisan Union does not help all farmers, he inquired, how will it forge ahead? But my skepticism was not dimmed. Does it benefit small farmers as much as big ones? I asked. Ranbir replied: "There is no difference between small and large farmers. The small farmer uses water for irrigation; so does the large one. The small farmer puts chemical fertilizer on his fields; so does the bigger farmer. The small farmer has to plow his field; so does the large farmer. The only difference is that the small farmer has a small income and the large farmer a large one. Even if the small farmer does not sell his output, he is still a peasant." Ranbir's point was that all classes of peasants had a common interest in such policies as input subsidies. If irrigation water was cheaper, chemical fertilizer inexpensive and plentiful, and tractors to plow fields readily available, then it would benefit all farmers, not just rich ones. Unlike Tikait, however, Ranbir did not pretend that the Kisan Union supported landless laborers as well. He said that if laborers did not own any land, they had little reason to participate in Kisan Union activities. He pointed to the fact that in a neighboring village, which was dominated by jats, all the village commons (land belonging to the gram panchayat) had been given to schools and colleges instead of the landless. There are seven schools and colleges there, he noted, and they have managed to take away all the land from redistributive ends ["*saari za-meen khainch lee*"].

Although Ranbir felt that it was "not surprising" that an organization of farmers had no place for landless laborers, he did not believe that the positions of farmers and landless laborers were necessarily antagonistic. He told me that the government was doing its best to improve the living conditions of laborers ["*sarkaar mazdooron ko upar khainch rahee hain*"]. Nowadays, he said, if a laborer is offered less than the minimum wage, he refuses to work. Even if he has no other employment opportunity, he would rather sit at home than work for a lower wage.[134] Thus, Ranbir implied that the Kisan Union didn't need to look out for wage laborers because they already had the government in their corner. Given the Kisan Union's fervent antigovernmentalism, this was in itself a revealing statement. Ranbir at least acknowledged that laborers needed help to improve their condition.

Other supporters of the Kisan Union denied even that. Birendra, a young jat man from a village whose lands adjoined Alipur, was typical of the younger generation of Kisan Union advocates. He was studying toward an undergraduate degree at the once prestigious college in Mandi, the nearest large town in the area. He strenuously argued that agricultural laborers were, in fact, better off than owner-cultivators. "At least the laborer's child is free to go to school," he said, "whereas the farmer needs two hands if he is sowing, two hands if he is preparing [irrigation] ridges in his field or if he is doing almost anything else." The farmer's children had to help him because no one else was going to do their farmwork for them. Thus it was that peasant children were deprived of an education. In Birendra's eyes, there could be nothing worse. Of course, such a view completely overlooked the discrepancies in capital and income between what were, in fact, disparate class positions. Birendra inverted the normal hierarchy to paint a picture of peasants as the most exploited class, one occupying the lowest rung of the rural socioeconomic hierarchy. If not true today, he implied, it would be true tomorrow, because the owner-cultivator's condition makes him underinvest in the cultural capital that would guarantee his children a bright future.

It was not just the divide between owner-cultivators and agricultural laborers that was fraught with tension. Even within the category of landowning peasants there were differences between large farmers, on one side, and small and medium ones, on the other. Although all peasants with a marketable surplus had a common interest in higher output prices and all those who farmed benefited from lower prices for inputs, peasants with larger landholdings stood to gain relatively more from the Kisan Union's demands (Hasan and Patnaik 1992). Local officials of the Kisan Union were sensitive to these differentials. For example, the Kisan Union branch in Jatpura, Bulandshahr District, had organized a meeting during which they decided to launch a campaign against dowry. The leader of the branch appealed to Tikait to ban the "demon of dowry." This, he claimed, would prevent the lives of poor and medium peasants from being ruined (*Aaj*, July 18, 1989). This was an acknowledgment that the increasing commercialization of agriculture and the corresponding acceleration in the demand for consumer durables had squeezed poor and middle peasants especially hard. With the availability of an increasing number of gifts that could or had to be purchased as part of a dowry, pressures to spend increased at a faster clip than earnings.

Not just differences between richer and poorer segments of the peasantry were at issue, however. The Kisan Union encountered its greatest resistance from other sections of the rich peasantry. This was partly due to the fact that the Kisan Union had a strong base among the jats, the better-off segments of the Backward Castes. The established, landowning, upper castes interpreted the rise of the Kisan Union as a threat. Specifically, they saw it, quite correctly, as a means by which the Backward Castes, such as the jats, were asserting their own power in the countryside. One of the reasons why there was not more overt support for the Kisan Union in Alipur may have been that the thakurs, who were once the landlords of the entire village and continued to be the most powerful political force, were strongly opposed to it. Naresh, the jat employee of the government farm, told me that "the reason that our village does not have a Kisan Union is that the thakurs feel that they will lose control if the Kisan Union is formed. The union says everyone is equal, but the thakurs feel that they are superior."

I was given a somewhat different view by an elderly thakur, a former headman of the village and its most eminent (or powerful) elder.[135] The man said that Tikait had stopped at his house for breakfast on the way back from a nearby jat village. The thakur felt that, like many other jats, Tikait was an illiterate man, denoting by that term not merely his educational achievements but his manners and refinement. It turned out that his opinion of the Kisan Union leader was so low because Tikait had told him—a thakur—that "the thakurs spend all their money on weddings instead of investing it in farming." The elderly man had responded by saying that the thakurs didn't have any money to invest in anything because the only people who had money these days seemed to be jats. Another reason why the thakurs were against Tikait was that he had deliberately snubbed the thakur chief minister by not allowing him to address a Kisan Union rally in Muzaffarnagar. "Even if your enemy were to come to your door, you are obliged to ask him to sit down and to offer him something to eat," offered Virendra, one of the more opinionated of Alipur's residents.[136] It was completely unacceptable for Tikait to have treated a distinguished person in such a rude manner. "This is where he showed his *jatness*."[137]

It is therefore evident that the Kisan Union followed a two-pronged strategy to deal with the multifarious conflicts that afflicted Bharat. The first was to downplay structural contradictions by denying their salience: thus everyone was a laborer, those who used caste were enemies of the nation, there were no rich farmers, and so forth. The other aspect of the union's strategy was to take up different causes that affected various segments of its supporters. The campaigns against corruption, the amelioration of conflict between the Backward Castes and lower castes, and action against "social ills" such as dowry all fell within this category. Despite these efforts, the tensions and conflicts among groups that the Kisan Union wished to unify always threatened to rend the fabric that held the organization together. Oppositional populism such as that promulgated by the Kisan Union, which deployed a Manichaean discourse of "Bharat" against "India," itself constructed a certain kind of location to be occupied by its followers. What united those included in Bharat was not a singular subject position as much as a shared space of opposition. For, although Bharat represented a contradictory unity that allowed the articulation of different interests and positions, it was also built on particular exclusions.

The Place of Patriarchy. I have already dealt with those exclusions having to do with landless laborers, lower castes, and the poor. Now I come to one that was so deeply embedded in the discourses of the Kisan Union that it escaped reflexive commentary altogether. This was the conjugation of discourses of place and patriarchy, self-evidently "rooted" in the ideology of the upwardly mobile Backward Caste groups that formed the backbone of the Kisan Union.

In the summer of 1989, Rajiv Gandhi, still prime minister, instituted a policy to reinvigorate village governance [*panchayati raj*] through new laws and through changes in the manner in which development programs were implemented. Instead of relying on those state bureau-cracies that had been set up to implement "rural development," he proposed that all the money in a new scheme called the Jawahar Rojgaar Yojana (Jawahar Employment Scheme) be allocated directly to village headman [*pradhan*]. In this manner, the money intended for villages would not be siphoned off by corrupt officials. When Tikait was asked for his opinion on Rajiv Gandhi's panchayati raj scheme, he replied: "Only a man whose line of succession is clear, who can reel off his paternal grandfather and great grandfather's name without a slip, can suggest panchayati raj. A panchayat is run on patriarchal lines, not matriarchal. Rajiv Gandhi has come to power through his mother—even a harijan whose gotra [subcaste or lineage] line is quite clear is better than such a man. . . . What right then does the prime minister have to announce panchayati raj?"[138] In Tikait's formulation, Rajiv Gandhi lacked legitimacy as a leader because he had "come to power through his mother." Since it was self-evident that legitimate succession could only be through males, Rajiv Gandhi was worse than an untouchable, who at least had a clear line of patriarchal descent. According to Tikait, any person who did not understand this (self-evident) principle was inherently unqualified to talk about, or institute, panchayati raj. Signifi-cantly, Tikait's own power base as the head of the Balian Khap, a pan-chayat of eighty-four villages in Muzaffarnagar District, was obtained after an intense struggle in which he displaced his own father-in-law.

Tikait elaborated these concerns in a letter to Rajiv Gandhi just before Independence Day, August 15, 1989. Traditionally, the prime minister unfurls the national flag from the Red Fort and addresses the nation on that day. Tikait wrote:

> Those who have no lineage [*hot-khot*] have no right to fly the national flag. If Rajiv Gandhi does not announce his lineage by August 15, then he too should not touch the national flag. . . . I do not want to sling mud at anyone. I do not hold any grudge against you [Rajiv Gandhi,] but we must have a record of the lineage [*pataa*] of the country's prime minister. Therefore, Rajiv Gandhi should announce which village he comes from, in which state that village is located, and what the names of his father and grandfather are. . . . The fact that you do not talk about your father, this must be your mother's fault, not yours. . . . He who has no lineage should not attempt to besmirch this spiritual nation [*rishiyon kay desh ko bigaadnay ki koshish na karay*].[139]

What I have loosely translated as "lineage" also connotes "a sense of place" or "belonging." The lack of rootedness which Rajiv Gandhi exemplified and which, by extension, afflicted others who live in "India" was revealed by his failure to claim descent in terms of a patriarchal lineage. In this discourse, place and patriarchy are completely interchangeable: to have one is to have the other. That is why the shift from "which village he comes from [and] in which state that village is located" to "what the names of his father and grandfather are" is completely transparent. To know your village and to know the name of your grandfather are the same thing.

There were several reasons why social and geographic location come together. Almost all marriages in this part of western UP were exogamous. Most married couples also resided virilocally. The system of inheritance was patriarchal and coparcenary: only the son received an equal share in his parents' property. Thus, a daughter was given dowry, married outside the village, and usually moved to her husband's village. A son, by contrast, inherited an equal share of the land along with his brothers, stayed in his father's village, and brought a wife from another place.[140] Therefore, to know your village and to know the names of your male ancestors was to be a man whose antecedents and social position were knowable. Not to know these things was to be rootless, one not fit even to "touch the national flag."[141]

That this was neither an isolated incident nor one of Tikait's idiosyncratic views is clear from statements made by other "peasant" leaders. Sharad Joshi, addressing the farmers who had gathered to grieve the death of the abducted woman, Naiyma, said: "It is deplorable that even today in our country the poor cannot protect the honor of their wives and daughters. To stop the recurrence of these shameful incidents, we have to fight poverty with renewed vigor."[142] Joshi's discourse combined "developmentalism" with patriarchy. His concern was to rescue the manly virtue that "protects the honor of women," rather than with the more direct issue of patriarchal violence against women themselves. He linked the failure of the fight against poverty with the failure of poor men to protect their women. Thus, his concern was with poor men rather than with violence against women. Although he was correct in suggesting that poor women were more vulnerable to acts of violence by strangers, he did not entertain the thought that domestic or familial violence could be equally devastating for women.

At the same rally, Maniram Bagdi, another "peasant" leader, urged the attending farmers to step up their struggle to such an extent that the following year "a farmer's son" would hoist the flag over the Red Fort. He was no doubt referring to the impending election. Almost identical language is found among local-level leaders of the Kisan Union. At a meeting of the Danpur branch in Bulandshahr, one of the local leaders said, "On the day that a farmer's son unfurls the flag over the Red Fort, that is the day when our souls will sing."[143] Once again, that it should be a farmer's son is not even an issue. Both the farmer and the politically ascendant offspring are assumed to be male.

Male descent is part of a larger discourse about the gender specificity of lineage, in which boys inherit the qualities of their fathers and girls those of their mothers. Explaining why he chose to stay apart from, but not oppose, Ajit Singh, the son of Charan Singh, who originally founded the BKD, Tikait said that he had nothing against Ajit Singh. He did not like Ajit Singh's confidants and associates, however. He pointed out that he couldn't possibly oppose Ajit Singh because of his descent, emphasizing the point with a saying:

> A girl's like her mother;
> A son his father.
> If not much,
> At least a touch.[144]

Tikait's concern with Rajiv Gandhi's paternal line was therefore entirely consistent with this view of a gendered genealogy.

Another way in which to view how discourses of gender were completely naturalized is to consider their use in dealing with subordinate groups. When asked what his organization had done to help harijans, Tikait responded with a telling analogy: "Show me one instance in this village of any harijan being harassed and the aggressor going unpunished. We are compassionate toward harijans. As far as petty quarrels go, even husband and wife are entitled to them. People merely exaggerate discord because they want to politicize everything."[145] Here is a transposition that explicitly equates social domination to gender inequalities. There is no doubt who is positioned as the "wife" in the "petty quarrels" between supporters of the Kisan Union and harijans.

What I have attempted to demonstrate in this section is that the very rhetoric which helps consolidate Bharat as a counterhegemonic populism and which makes its opposition to "India" evident is built on certain powerful exclusions. Whereas in the last section I explored the limits of unity in the face of existing tensions, in this one I focus on the silences and evasions of "peasantist" discourse. The completely taken-for-granted, commonsensical elision of place with patriarchy in the construction of Bharat has serious implications for gender inequalities. These inequalities are in turn conjugated to caste and class domination to constitute a naturalized discourse in which the fact of domination remains eternally below the threshold of reflexivity.

More generally, the discussion of populism and agrarian politics pursued above demonstrates that populism is not merely an electoral strategy of ruling regimes.[146] It comes to be employed rather forcefully *against* the governing regime by peasant movements that seek to consolidate a hegemonic bloc by pitting Bharat against India. The discourse of "Bharat versus India" shares all the trademarks of populism outlined earlier: exclusion, a Manichaean characterization of the "other," the articulation of diverse interests through negation, and a claim to speak in the name of "the popular."

It is important to contextualize the emergence of populism, employed first by the ruling regime and then by oppositional groups, within the changing contours of the global food economy. The story of agrarian populism was inseparably intertwined with that of the green revolution. But what effects did the green revolution have on India's location in the international food economy? Clearly, one influence was that a period of national self-sufficiency followed the implementation of a green revolution strategy that lasted roughly two decades after the bumper crop of 1970–71. During this period, ruling regimes were protected from the kind of pressure that had been exerted by the United States' manipulation of food aid during the Johnson years. However, fundamental shifts in global political economy, characterized as a period of "late capitalism" by Mandel (1975) or as a regime of flexible accumulation by the regulationists (Harvey 1989), articulated with the world food economy to create new kinds of pressures on domestic agricultural policy. I will now briefly sketch the contours of this global context.

The World Food Economy in the Seventies and Eighties

The relatively stable food regime that operated in the aftermath of the Second World War, which had been dominated by the export of American farm surpluses to the Third World at subsidized prices paid in local currencies, unraveled in the early seventies with grain sales to the Soviet Union.[147] The scale of these transactions (three-quarters of all commercially traded grain in the world in 1972–73, for example) created sudden shortages and inflationary prices. This gave other countries such as Brazil, which had carefully nurtured surpluses with a policy that mixed protection and subsidies, a chance to win a significant market share in high value-added exports such as soymeal. As a result, the U.S. share of world exports fell rapidly in the most important agricultural products.

The sudden jump in world food prices and the resulting shortages had two important consequences. First, Third World economies split into two groups. One group, which had until then depended on imports of subsidized American wheat, found itself forced to purchase expensive grain with hard currency. Apart from a few countries that had petroleum, this group of countries experienced a deep debt crisis from the twin shocks of skyrocketing grain and petroleum prices. (Meanwhile, to meet the Soviet demand, American farmers borrowed to expand operations, tripling the farm debt in the 1970s alone [Friedmann 1993:40].) The second group consisted of countries such as Brazil and India, which had successfully "developed" a national agriculture based on subsidies, biochemical inputs, tariff barriers, and price supports. These countries were relatively unaffected by the jump in world grain prices and even joined the group of nations exporting agricultural products. The same events, therefore, had widely discrepant outcomes in different nation-states, depending on the path taken with domestic policies in the past.

The second consequence of the disruption caused by the Soviet grain deals was that nation-states such as Japan, which had come to depend on supplies from the United States, started looking elsewhere to diversify their purchases. At the same time, surpluses were being produced by protected agricultural sectors in many different parts of the world—Western Europe, North America, Australia, the larger economies of South America, South Africa, Thailand, and so forth. In the absence of highly subsidized aid from the United States, countries purchasing on the open market could choose from a variety of suppliers. The collapse of the Soviet market in the 1980s not only drove highly indebted U.S. farmers into bankruptcy in record numbers but also left a world market in which there was both greater competition among national agricultures and tighter interconnections forged by multinational capital (Friedmann 1993:42).[148]

For the Third World, these conditions were fundamentally transformed from two directions. First, the debt crisis that swept the Third World in the eighties allowed the IMF and the World Bank to impose structural adjustment policies on the great majority of nation-states.

These "market-friendly" reforms that sought to "get prices right" in effect opened up for multinational capital those remaining economies which had insulated domestic agriculture by protective tariffs. Furthermore, as in the case of India, pressure to reduce the fiscal deficit has meant that agricultural subsidies, which are by now the largest single component of government expenditure, have been put in serious jeopardy and will almost certainly be dismantled in the near future. Structural adjustment, therefore, threatens to overturn a national agricultural program that, through price supports and input subsidies, explicitly modeled itself on the "successful" agricultural policies of "developed" countries.

The second direction from which changes were forced on the Third World was the General Agreement on Tariffs and Trade. Agricultural issues played a surprisingly large role in the GATT negotiations. Conflicts over agricultural policy between the United States and the European Community threatened to bring down the entire treaty at one stage and completely dominated Western debate and discussion. Although this feature attracted relatively little comment in the West, however, the treaty displays disproportionate zeal in subjecting Third World farmers to the "discipline" of the market, while protecting farmers in Western Europe, Japan, and the United States from the trauma of unduly rapid market reforms (Goodman and Watts 1994:27). Those aspects of the treaty that have drawn the sharpest protest from Third World nation-states deal with biogenetic resources.[149]

The combined effect of these two changes has been that in such nation-states as India, where agricultural policy for over two decades has steadily pursued the goal of national self-sufficiency, the agrarian sector has been thrown into turmoil. Structural adjustment and the GATT have split the populist farmer groups described above into factions which support the free market and those which oppose it in the name of nationalism, respectively. Biotechnology and the harvesting of biogenetic resources have introduced further uncertainties into the picture. Finally, the incorporation of Indian agriculture into global markets through multinational capital has just begun in earnest, with the entry of Pepsico and the giant trading company, Cargill, into the picture. The agrarian sector in India stands on the brink of a major structural transformation, in which the conflicts and confrontations described above will be transformed by the introduction of new issues and new players. However, to understand the direction likely to be taken by these conflicts, the shifts of policy, the pressures exerted from below, and the implications of policy shifts for the everyday lives of rural peoples, we have to begin with the kind of map of the complex ideological field that I have attempted to draw here.

Conclusion

In this chapter, I have demonstrated the complex interactions between global transformations, governmental ideologies and actions, and the everyday lives of a particular set of rural people by focusing on the agricultural sector. Agriculture occupies a central place in development discourse. Underdevelopment afflicts those nation-states in which a high percentage of the national product comes from agriculture and where a high percentage of the labor force is employed on farms. Therefore, to move "out of agriculture," preferably as fast as possible, is a most desirable goal for a modern nation. These desires are inscribed within plans to "modernize" or "develop" the agricultural sector by appropriate doses of capital and technology. Agriculture, however, is not just a sector in an input-output table. It is a field of power with its own discourses and regimes of truth. It is in these discursive fields that "becoming modern" can be articulated, where institutions can be changed and practices altered. In this chapter I have attempted to trace the changing contours of this discursive field, its ideological struggles, idioms, alliances, interests, and organizations. Although I have concentrated on some people in western Uttar Pradesh that I grew to know particularly well, my goal has been to convey a broader sense of what the lived experience of modernity might be like in a postcolonial setting.

What, specifically, is it about postcolonial conditions that enables us to speak of "alternative modernities"? I have argued that any answer to that question must begin by keeping the relationship between modernity and development in the foreground. The purpose of this chapter has been to establish that one of the dimensions in which the experience of modernity in the Third World is significantly different than in the West is that a sense of underdevelopment, of being "behind," of being "not like" powerful Others, is a constitutive feature of social and political life. I have explored how particular representations of modernity embedded in narratives of development circulate in agrarian populism. Rather than seeing "developmentalism" as a hegemonic ideology straightforwardly employed by a coalition of ruling classes, I demonstrate its internal fissures and its contentious redeployment in the discourses of antiurban, rich peasant groups. Therefore, one has to be careful in asserting that there is something about development that is inherently legitimating of certain classes and sectors.

In bringing together analyses of changes in the world food economy, national agricultural policies and programs, and the actions of "peasant" groups, I have tried to show that complex ideological and institutional determinations have shaped the agricultural sector. An understanding of the broader discursive field of development discourse and the role of "scientific" agriculture within it, for example, qualifies the debate about whether the green revolution was imposed on India by external actors for geostrategic reasons and to promote the interests of capital or whether it was independently arrived at by the Indian government. Although there is much to be learned from an exact determination of the latter alternative, it is important to keep in mind that *both* strategies are compatible with a broader vision of what constitutes development, what it means to be a "modern" nation, and, very important, what the order of nation-states should look like.

It is these considerations that lead me to believe that just as the reorganization of national agricultural policy in India in the sixties prompted a shift in the institution and tactics of peasant politics, global changes in the recent past have created and will continue to create new transnational alliances of peasant groups and others who are affected by these changes. And just as populism has been appropriated and turned against ruling regimes, so will contestations of the "market-friendly" ideologies of multilateral institutions and multinational corporations shape the nature of the emerging world system. I have merely hinted at these themes here; their theoretical importance is drawn out in Chapter 5.

2

Developmentalism, State Power, and

Local Politics in Alipur

━━━━⋙

Having overshot the village, I got off the bus at the next stop and walked back toward Alipur. An older woman heading in the same direction asked me whose house I was going to. For want of a better answer, I said, "The headman's." "Which one?" she demanded, "we have two headmen in our village—the headman of the thakurs and the headman of the brahmins." In this manner, even before entering Alipur, I had been introduced to its political divisions. A small village in western Uttar Pradesh whose population was approximately seven hundred people in 1984 (see Table 1), Alipur had seen major changes not only in farming practices and techniques but also in the entire pattern of village life, including local politics as a consequence of the widespread adoption of high-yielding varieties of wheat.

In this chapter I attempt to trace the relationship between these political divisions and the high-yielding varieties of wheat that had drastically altered forms of agriculture in Alipur. I argued in Chapter 1 that the postcolonial condition for rural people in India needs to be conceptualized within three macrological frames—development, global capitalism, and technologies of food production. These macrologies intersected in the green revolution and in agrarian populism. Earlier, I demonstrate how, shaped by considerations of national sovereignty and competitive electoral politics, the green revolution and agrarian politics articulated at the national level. Although that analysis helps us understand the success of the green revolution and of peasant politics, it does not tell us how these changes were experienced by villagers in their everyday lives. How did the green revolution change relations and practices of production? What did populism mean in the lives of poor and lower-caste people? What difference did these phenomena make to the

lived relations of dominance and subordination in rural India? By looking closely at social relations and ideologies of domination in one village, we can gain a good understanding of the conjunctures that gave
the green revolution and agrarian populism their particular shape in
villages such as Alipur.

What was the relationship between the political divisions that I observed in Alipur, changing class divisions that accompanied the new
agricultural technology, and the policies of the state that had redistributive as well as productivist emphases? At the same time that the government was pursuing a policy of subsidies for electricity and fertilizer that
largely benefited well-to-do farmers, it was also prescribing that small
parcels of "wasteland" be allocated to lower-caste, lower-class people
who had previously been landless. How were these policies implemented, and to what political effect? Did the state's development policies have contradictory effects, exacerbating class tensions while seeking to diminish them? In this chapter I will explore the contradictory
effects of "development," particularly in examining how policies intended to create a modern agricultural sector articulated with caste and
class ideologies. If, as I contend previously, understanding the postcolonial conditions of farmers entails attending to the specificities of particular conjunctures of development, global capitalism, and agricultural
technology, then my task here is to delineate the manner in which the
developmental discourses of a modern nation relate to the differentiat-
ing practices of a village in northern India.

Questions of postcoloniality become especially pronounced in looking at the implications of developmentalism for relations of class and
caste in Alipur. Nationalists charged that the drain of surplus and colonial indifference to the welfare of the population were responsible for
India's underdevelopment. Therefore, the end of colonial rule would
initiate an era of development; indeed, development became the chief
"reason of state" in independent India. As a state project, developmentalism was never conceptualized in narrow economic terms. Rather, in
the progressivist ideology of national development, economic changes
were seen as triggering social and cultural transformations. For instance, it was believed that economic development would rid the country of social "evils" such as untouchability. Developmentalism had
become so much a part of the collective unconscious of nationalist
planners and elites that no justification was needed to argue that raising
the living standards of lower-caste people would eventually result in the
elimination of caste discrimination. And, indeed, given the high cor-

relation between class and caste in rural India, a strategy that visualized class mobility as a *necessary* feature in combating casteism made eminent sense. But how enthusiastically would such a "progressive" agenda be embraced by primarily upper-caste rural elites? And if they did support it, what reasons would they have for doing so?

Examining the political history of Alipur gives us some idea as to why upper-caste rural elites may have thrown their weight behind development programs targeted especially at lower-caste and poor people. But to speak about "the political history" of the village is to presume that there exists a coherent and widely-shared narrative of Alipur's past. Nothing could be further from the truth. It is precisely in the contested narratives of the past that we find different visions of development and varying evaluations of the degree to which "development" has proved successful. Even the end of zamindari, which so clearly marked an era associated with colonial rule, was not considered in an unambiguously positive light by all villagers. Many people who belonged to the dominant, landowning lineage of thakurs interpreted postcolonial efforts at nation building through development projects and quotas in government jobs for scheduled castes as initiating a period leading to corruption in public life and the debasement of social life. Despite their participation in development projects, many thakurs were openly critical of the postcolonial state's development efforts.

In contrast to the views of some thakurs stood the large majority of people in Alipur, whose narratives of the past were significantly configured by developmentalism. Previous village headmen were evaluated in terms of whether they brought "progress" to the village and whether people lived together harmoniously: in this manner, the past was assessed in terms of development discourse. Some villagers appropriated the rhetoric of "development" and its claims of improving the living conditions of people in the village in order to criticize severely the unequal and partial distribution of the benefits of development programs.

The structural positions of people in Alipur refracted their assessment of the developmental efforts of the state and their narratives of the history of the village. The thakurs' negative evaluation of the developmental efforts of the postcolonial state did not result from its programs for economic growth, which they, like other well-to-do farmers in Alipur, welcomed. Rather, what upset these upper-caste men were the social changes being promoted by the state that disturbed an orderly hierarchy of deference in which control over lower-caste labor was central.[1] Not surprisingly, it was precisely this ability to refuse the arbitrary exaction of labor and the capacity to assert their equality that lower-caste people identified as the greatest "benefits" of development (Wadley 1994:5).

A thorough understanding of the most important relations of power and inequality in Alipur is necessary to explain the far-reaching transformations in discourses of caste and class that were an integral part of the development efforts of the state. This chapter outlines the relationship between the specific conjunctures of capitalism, developmentalism, and technological change presented in the previous chapter and the agronomical and ecological practices detailed in the following two chapters. I begin with the conflicting narratives of the political history of Alipur. Villagers' narratives of their own histories and the history of the village community were shaped by their positions and perspectives on the development discourses and policies of the postcolonial state. It is this relation of the conflicting narratives of the political history of the village to the larger structural transformations that I will specify in the remaining sections of this chapter. In the second section of the chapter, I tie conflicting narratives of politics in Alipur to changing relations of production. My concern throughout is to understand how these changes were being experienced and understood by different classes and caste groups. I then outline how changing relations of production articulated with state redistributive programs.

Contested Narratives of the Past

In this section I present different narratives of politics in Alipur to explore the contested history of "development" as well as to trace changes in the nature of class and caste domination in one area of rural Uttar Pradesh. When I first arrived there in 1984, social life in Alipur was shaped by political conflicts between two factions. The officially elected headman of the village, Prasad, was a brahmin whose family owned a fairly substantial plot of fertile land (approximately thirteen acres). His opponent, the thakur Sher Singh, was even wealthier and owned approximately twenty-one acres.[2] The thakurs had historically been the village landlords. Although forced to relinquish much of the village land to their hereditary tenants under the Zamindari Abolition Act, they were as a caste group still the largest landowners in the village.[3]

While there was considerable agreement regarding thakur dominance in the stories that different informants crafted about the history of Alipur, varying class and caste position did lead to a change in emphasis in narratives about the time of zamindari. The Subedar and the Old Thakur, who belonged to two of the dominant thakur lineages of the village, narrated a story of lost glory. The Subedar said that the area had originally been a "big jungle" where Englishmen came to hunt. The first inhabitants were the *banjaras* (Gypsies) who settled in the village when they dug the ground and found water at the site that became the main village well. Despite acknowledging the banjaras as the first settlers of Alipur, however, the Subedar proceeded to claim that the rajputs had been its founding inhabitants. They brought along some brahmins and the service castes, who came initially as one or two households and were subsequently followed by others. The most recent inhabitants of the village were the jats. According to the Subedar, when he was young, there had only been one or two jat families in the village, and they had no land of their own. They used to cultivate the zamindar's lands. It was in the last twenty to thirty years that the migration of the jats had increased and they had become a significant caste in the village.

According to the Subedar, the will or command [*hukum*] of the elder brother was always followed in previous generations of thakurs. Even when the land had been divided equally among all the brothers of a lineage, in effect, following the father's death, the eldest made decisions for the entire clan. The oldest brother was the zamindar of the village, and he was like a king. Our ancestors, the Subedar proudly recounted, never had to work in the fields; now, we have no choice but to do our farming ourselves. It used to be that the *lambardar* (landlord) went to inspect his fields on his horse. Pointing out that the landlord did not even dismount to inspect his fields, let alone tend them himself, the Subedar emphasized the zamindar's distance from manual labor.

The zamindar could order people to work for him but, the Subedar claimed, it was a reciprocal relationship. "Not like the present," he added, "when one has to pay the headman for everything, and the relationship is entirely one-way." He felt that while it was true that the zamindar had taken advantage of the peasant [*raiyat*], the peasant benefited from his relationship with the zamindar as well. Service castes like the *nais* (barbers, who also played an important role as ritual specialists) and the *chamaars* (leatherworkers) had been brought to the village by the thakurs and settled in Alipur. The Subedar wistfully recalled that they earlier had to work for free on the zamindar's land. "Now, even if we plead with them, they don't want to work for us," he said.

The Old Thakur, a former headman, village elder, and relative of the Subedar, told me a similar story about his ancestors, emphasizing their martial prowess in struggling to control the territory against the Moguls. Curiously, the Old Thakur had little to say about the period under British dominion; instead, he skipped to an earlier history of resistance against "Muslim rule." He claimed that when they first settled in Alipur, the thakurs brought along with them some brahmin and harijan families. "Most of the people in the village now are the direct descendants of the original families. Only some brahmins and jats have come later." The Old Thakur recounted the glorious days of thakur rule: "At the time of zamindari abolition, my father and his brother were the big men in the village. All the land belonged to us but we used to give it out to various castes on sharecropping for cultivation." Almost all the castes cultivated land; one or two families of service castes such as *badhais* (carpenters), *lohars* (ironsmiths), nais, and *dhobis* (washermen) were given a fixed share of the harvest in exchange for their specialized services.

According to the Old Thakur, some of the service castes were given fields free of charge as a gift from the zamindar. Others were leased land on plots whose location varied from year to year. "Sometimes a person would be given one plot, and given another the following year. In 1950, people obtained title to whatever land they happened to be cultivating that year. Some people only got a few bighas, others got a lot. It was not distributed very equally. They got the land almost free."[4] In the Old Thakur's narrative, the passage of laws abolishing zamindari signaled the decline of thakur rule.

Although they corroborated the story told by the thakurs in other respects, people from less powerful castes perceived the end of zamindari in a much more positive light. I was speaking to two men who were of the same age set as the Old Thakur and the Subedar (that is, in their sixties) but who belonged to lower castes. One of them was a jat, perhaps the most prosperous agricultural caste in Alipur, and the other was a *kayasth,* who had served the zamindars as a clerk and keeper of village land records. Supplementing what the other had to say, or interrupting him to add further details, they spoke as if one person:

In those days, the zamindar called you and said, "You cultivate that plot and you cultivate this other one." The tenant didn't have to pay much by way of rent. When the rains came in *ashad* [in the monsoon season], we went to the zamindar and asked for some fields. He gave some to one man and some to another. If we were unable to pay rent, he seized the fields the next season and rented them out to someone else. When zamindari abolition became law, the zamindar called all the tenants and distributed twenty to thirty bighas to each of them. They had to pay him for the property, of course, but in those days one didn't have to pay that much for it. Once the plots were allocated to independent cultivators, people started investing in the land. Before that, no one had the incentive to improve the land. Why should they when it could be taken away from them the next year? After getting their own plots, people started digging wells; then they installed waterwheels; after that, tube wells.

Rather than see the end of zamindari as signaling a decline, people from intermediate cultivating castes thought that it precipitated a new relationship between cultivators and the land. Since those who received land after zamindari abolition were also its cultivators, they invested in irrigating the land. Thus, the end of zamindari enabled the land to become more productive and, by implication, allowed people who obtained that land to become more prosperous.

When I asked Suresh, a brahmin in his thirties who owned a small piece of land, about the history of the village, he narrated a remarkably similar story to the one told by the older men from the other intermediate castes. The zamindar transferred his tenants from plot to plot every year and collected his payment at the end of the winter, or *rabi*, crop. He did not necessarily favor upper castes in the allocation of land for tenancy. If he felt that a particular tenant might have difficulty in paying his share [the *lagaan*], he sent a man armed with a big staff [*lath*] to the threshing floor. After the grain had been threshed, the zamindar's share was first loaded onto a cart and delivered to his home. The tenant was allowed to remove his share only after the zamindar had received his. It did not matter how little was left for the tenant, said Suresh, the zamindar's share had to be paid first. Suresh thus underlined the extent to which the zamindar's authority rested on his ability to use threats and physical violence to extract the surplus.

Suresh informed me that when the zamindars sold off their land, it was mainly bought by the brahmins living in the village. The rest of it was purchased by the first jat families to move into the village and by *khatiks* (low caste whose principal occupation in Alipur was horsecart driving), *kumhars* (potters), and chamaars. In Suresh's narrative, the end of zamindari brought about major changes in the power of the thakurs. People who obtained land after zamindari abolition no longer had to pay land revenues to the thakurs but paid the government directly. Paying land revenues directly to the government, along with the end of the practice of coerced labor called begaar, greatly diminished the thakur's dominance in the political life of the village. The following narrative of the past was constructed by Suresh:

> Earlier, the thakurs would come in the morning and take whatever bullocks and plows they needed for their own fields. They would say, "We're having a well built today, come and help us dig it." And people would have to go out of compulsion. Since then, begaar has ended. Some people, out of respect for the thakurs, continue to honor them, and that is why they have now become the headman, manager [of the village school], etc. The thakurs think that by occupying these positions, they can continue receiving begaar. That is why they are unused to working. You will not find a pair of bulls today in any of the thakur households. All of them give out their land on *bataai* [sharecropping] and get free grain at the end of the year.

Suresh's implication was that because no farmer could survive without a pair of bulls or a tractor, the thakurs still expected to live off the labor of others rather than do their own work. The "laziness" of the thakurs was commented on frequently by people of all other castes in Alipur, and Suresh's statement fit that pattern. The thakurs were often criticized for living off the prestige that they had enjoyed in the past instead of behaving like equals in the present. Suresh reiterated statements made by the other men that investments in land began only after zamindari ended because owners now had some stake in the improvement of their property.

After the end of zamindari, the thakurs continued to dominate village politics for some time. Like Suresh, most people in the village remembered that Sukhi Singh, a thakur from the dominant lineage whose father Savera Singh had been the zamindar of the village, became the headman in the period after zamindari abolition and that during his tenure, "the village was one." But the Old Thakur recalled a slightly different, and more complicated, history: "Before 1960, Jahangirpur and Alipur were considered one village for electoral purposes, and so we had one headman who was from Jahangirpur. Then I became the next headman, followed by Sukhi Singh, Harisaran, Om Pandey, Prasad, and now Sher Singh. Until Sukhi Singh's time, elections were held by raising hands. The police [*thanedar*] or some other local official used to come, gather everyone in a central place, the men on one side and the women on another, and ask them to raise hands."

The Old Thakur's order of successive headmen is important in tracing the contested genealogies of factionalism in the village. In referring to the tenure of Sukhi Singh as a period when the village was united, Suresh in the quote above intended to contrast Sukhi Singh's term with the subsequent history of factionalism [*party-baazi*] in Alipur. And the person most people held responsible for the origins of factionalism in Alipur was Om Pandey. The Old Thakur told me that Om's father used to be the thakurs' priest [*purohit*], and so they had donated seventy bighas of land to him. From his earliest years, Om was interested only in politics, no matter where he went. He was kicked out of numerous institutions, including a college where he used to teach, for starting cliques and creating trouble. He came back to the village to found a school in the memory of his brother, who had died accidently, with seed money donated by his father. According to the Old Thakur, Om managed to obtain substantial sums from the government to operate the school but embezzled all the funds.

No sooner had Om settled down in the village than he started his own faction. He formed a coalition with the other two thakur lineages in the village and with Sukhi Singh's half brothers. The opposite camp was left with just Sukhi Singh and his three brothers from the dominant lineage. But, because he was a brahmin, Om also managed to obtain the support of other brahmins. The Odhs, who live on the brahmin side of the village, threw their weight behind him too. In this manner, Om managed to become the headman of Alipur.

Although Suresh was very critical of Om's role in creating factions in the village, he also traced the decline of thakur control [*thakur ki rutvaa kuch kam ho gayee*] to the fact that Om had wrested the headmanship away from them. "Until then, coerced labor still continued, more or less unchecked. When the thakurs were unsuccessful in intimidating people, they tried to get them in trouble with the law on some pretext or the other. This was easy to do since the thakurs were well connected to the police [and still are]."

Although the role of Om Pandey loomed large in many villagers' narratives about the origins of infighting and party-baazi, not everyone agreed that factionalism in the village had begun with Om Pandey. Sompal and his spouse, Santoshi Devi, traced the origins of villagewide conflicts to fights among the thakurs that preceded the arrival of Om Pandey in the village by several years. According to Sompal, the conflict first arose in struggles over property in the dominant thakur lineage. Savera Singh, the eldest of three brothers of the dominant lineage of thakurs, was the zamindar before it was abolished. He had four sons by his first wife—Sukhi Singh, the Old Thakur, and their two younger brothers. As the zamindar, Savera Singh had to collect land rent from his tenants. One household renting land from him in an adjoining village was having difficulty in paying its rent. When he went to collect the rent, a girl in the household, much younger than he was, caught his eye. He brought her to Alipur with him in lieu of the land rent and kept her as his common-law wife. She bore him three sons, Hardeep, Baldaan, and Chotu. With Savera Singh aging, the four sons from his first wife went to court to block the three "illegal" heirs from inheriting a share of the property.[5] They lost the case because their uncle (father's younger brother, or FYB) gave testimony that a wedding procession had gone to the woman's house and that a "regular" marriage had actually taken place. Savera Singh had even produced a brahmin priest to testify that he had performed the wedding. Sompal, however, claimed that no such thing had ever happened: Savera Singh had simply brought the woman from the other village to his home and kept her. Since then, there had been intense conflict between the two branches of the family.

Sompal's description of conflict among the thakurs was confirmed by others, who clarified that even in the formal political arena of elections for headman, factionalism predated Om Pandey's return to the village. The previous headman, Sukhi Singh, who was from the dominant lineage of thakurs, was challenged in the election for headman by his half brother, Baldaan Singh. My inquiries as to what prompted that challenge were answered by Suresh, who claimed that the reason why Baldaan Singh opposed Sukhi was that, despite having an equal share in their father's property, the younger, "illegitimate" brothers had been kept under the control of the older ones. Sukhi Singh would not allow them to farm their own lands or allow their fields to be leased to tenants. When Baldaan Singh attempted to gain popularity in the village by organizing musical evenings [naach-gaana] at his house, the older brothers called the police to prevent these events.[6]

According to Suresh, there was some land (approximately seventy-five bighas) that was to be inherited equally among the seven sons of Savera Singh. But Sukhi Singh confiscated the entire area, thus preventing Baldaan Singh from getting his share. Contesting the elections for headman was Baldaan's central strategy for getting the land back. Had Baldaan won the election, the additional power conferred on him as headman might have enabled him to recover his share of the lost land. After one term in office, however, Sukhi Singh had alienated enough people in the village that public sentiment was running against him. It was then, Suresh continued, that Sukhi decided to have one of his men stand in his place so that he could continue to control the show without having to face possible public humiliation at the polls. So Harisaran, the keeper of village land records, was elected headman. Harisaran was completely under the thumb of the thakurs. Once, when he mustered the courage to disagree with Sukhi openly, he was "brought to his senses" by a ferocious slap from Sukhi Singh. Thus Sukhi continued to be the de facto headman until Om Pandey unseated him.

Once he was made headman, Om Pandey stayed in the village for only a short period, moving to the district headquarters to pursue grander political ambitions. While Om Pandey lived in town, he delegated the day-to-day affairs of the headman's post to Prasad. It was during this period that Prasad acquired the skills to function as the village headman. When I reached Alipur in 1984, Prasad had already been headman for several years, having defeated Sukhi's nephew, the thakur Sher Singh, in a two-way contest. Yet the impact of the election could still be felt. For one thing, the election seemed to have crystallized lines of conflict, forcing people to take sides and subsequently implicating them in new enmities.[7]

Prasad won the election by carefully marshaling support from different castes. For example, his assistant and vice-headman, whose position was largely symbolic, was a low-caste (khatik) horsecart driver. To his lower-caste supporters, Prasad promised and delivered benefits flowing from the various development schemes targeted at them. For instance, he assisted some of his landless, low-caste supporters in obtaining titles to small pieces of wasteland owned by the village council. As headman, he was officially responsible for identifying the landless families who qualified for this program. Predictably, families unfortunate enough to have opposed Prasad in the elections had to wait much longer for land even though some of them were more indigent and lower in caste status than those who benefited.[8] According to Sompal, Prasad, following the rules laid out by the government, had demarcated some village council land for a "harijan colony," but he had not distributed land titles for those plots to individuals because in the election the harijans had supported Sher Singh's unsuccessful bid to become headman. Sher Singh made the most of this opportunity to demonstrate his leadership skills by taking the land that Prasad had kept aside for

Table 1. Caste and Household Structure, Alipur, 1984–1985

Caste	Number of people	Percentage of population	Number of households
Brahmin	147	23	21
Thakur	82	13	14
Jat	106	16	16
Odh	42	6	9
Badhai	21	3	3
Kayasth	15	2	3
Dhimar	6	1	1
Kumhar	10	2	2
Teli	53	8	10
Khatik	64	10	10
Jatav	72	11	14
Harijan	28	4	5
Total	646	100	108

Notes: There were 118 households in the village. The Mali caste, which consisted of just one household, is not given in this table. Percentages do not add up to 100 because of rounding.

harijan housing, parceling it out, and getting houses constructed. All this was done in exchange for "payment" from the harijans in the form of money and liquor, which Sher Singh no doubt shared with the relevant government officials. Thus, even when Prasad was headman, struggles between him and his defeated opponent continued through their competition to deliver benefits from development programs to their lower-caste supporters.

The brahmin Prasad's carefully calibrated pursuit of lower-caste votes had been dictated by the demographics of Alipur. Brahmins and thakurs were a minority and thus needed to seek support from members of the other eleven castes, who were all lower in the ritual hierarchy. The brahmins, the most populous caste in the village, made up less than a quarter of the total population. Numerically, the thakurs were an even smaller group, constituting about one-sixth of the total numbers in Alipur (Table 1).[9] Even if a candidate had been sure of getting all his caste votes (and Sher Singh most certainly was not), he would still have needed to obtain a large proportion of lower-caste votes to win the election. Thus, upper-caste aspirants to leadership competed with one another to obtain the support of lower-caste villagers. And one of the most effective ways of obtaining lower-caste backing was for candidates to promise that they would deliver the fruits of development to their supporters.

One factor that may have contributed to Prasad's success in the elections was the deep-seated antipathy felt by many villagers toward Sher Singh. The tenure of the previous headman, Sukhi Singh, Sher Singh's uncle (father's elder brother, or FEB), had been marred by what most people in the village saw as unmitigated greed. Sher Singh himself had an unfortunate reputation in this and other regards, and his support derived mainly from his ability to browbeat less powerful people. In 1985, a close kinsman and supporter of Sher Singh told me that if any thakur other than Sher Singh had contested the election, he would easily have won, a claim that I regarded with some skepticism. The same person told me that people deliberately called Sher Singh "headman" [pradhan] to taunt him. Whatever their intentions, it was clear that Sher Singh thought he still had a legitimate claim to the post despite having lost the election. Sher Singh continued to wield considerable influence within the village, derived in no small part from his connections with the police and bureaucracy.

Santoshi Devi told me that even during Prasad's tenure as headman, many people went to Sher Singh when they needed help with bureaucratic matters. They preferred to ask Sher Singh for help because, even if he skimmed some money for himself, he knew how to pay bribes and get the job done. Santoshi Devi claimed that Sher Singh's lack of success at the polls did not prevent him from functioning as if he were the headman. When fights broke out, for instance, Sher Singh was often called on to settle the dispute. The reason, according to some, was that Sher Singh had good relations with the local police. He fed them, bought them liquor and drank with them, and functioned as their snitch [guftgoo] in the village, supplying them with information that enabled them to extract bribes. Much of his power in the village derived from his relationship with the police. When I inquired why other people in the village did not bother to cultivate good relations with the police, I was told that very few people wished to get mixed up with "bad elements" and hoodlums like the police.[10]

When I returned to Alipur in 1989 for a second round of fieldwork, new elections for the headman had taken place in which Sher Singh had defeated a lower-caste candidate, Ram Singh. Although I reached there several months after the elections, the village was still buzzing with election gossip. Prasad had chosen to step down instead of mounting another bid for the headmanship. One of his supporters informed me that Prasad had opted not to contest the elections because he had accepted too many bribes; had he been elected again, there were sure to be some court cases filed against him. So he strategically stepped aside and, instead, threw his weight behind Ram Singh.

Ram Singh was an older jatav man who lived on his farm on the outskirts of the village in a little hamlet founded by his grandfather and inhabited exclusively by his extended kin. When I spoke with Ram Singh, he expressed extreme bitterness about what had transpired in the elections. He told me that he had been hoodwinked into contesting the elections, for the people who encouraged him to run knew that he did not stand a chance of winning. Some time before the elections, a panchayat (village meeting) was called to arrive at a decision about the next headman. According to Ram Singh, all the castes [*saat jaat*] were present, including the thakurs, brahmins, and jats. There, Ram Singh was unanimously chosen headman. He was elected unopposed. It was only after that meeting that Sher Singh and the other thakurs demanded a "proper" election, saying that they would not accept the outcome of the meeting.

At that point, Prasad and others encouraged Ram Singh to contest the election. They told him that the village was tired of Sher Singh's antics. They reasoned that matters would become that much worse if Sher Singh was elected headman. They convinced him that no one would vote for Sher Singh and that he would easily win the election. Ram Singh claimed that had the people of the settlement [*basti kay log*] not persuaded him that he would easily be elected, he would not have sought the headmanship. He was not interested in creating factions. Had he not been misled and had he been told the full story, he would have opted out of the competition even after declaring his candidacy.

Ram Singh felt that, initially, people in the village were on his side. "Then, God knows why, they began to oppose me almost overnight." His explanation was that many people did not perceive him to be a resident of Alipur: "Although we live in Alipur, although we vote here, although our fields are here, we are still considered outsiders. People say that we are just like anyone else, but in their hearts they still think of us as outsiders. We used to live in Shadipur but have settled here for a long time." There was indeed something to the fact that Ram Singh did not reside in the nucleated settlement that constituted "the village" but in an outlying hamlet. In a discussion about the relationship of Alipur to its hamlets, Suresh elaborated on Ram Singh's ambivalent location:

They are now considered part of the village because they started living within its boundaries [*gaon ki hadd*], and bought their land from a thakur of the village. Before that, they were considered residents of Shadipur. They used to vote there but they now vote in Alipur. They have extensive social relations with people in Alipur. They call all the chamaars of the village for their feasts and are in turn invited by the chamaars in the village on all social occasions. By contrast, only a select few are invited from Shadipur, only those who are particularly close. They don't intermarry either here or in Shadipur. When a girl from Ram Singh's hamlet gets married, our villagers are unlikely to say, "A girl from our village is getting married [*hamaare gaon ki ladki ki shaadi hain*]." Since the hamlet is far away and stands independently as its own village, it has some relations with Alipur, but they are not terribly dense. For example, if a fight breaks out between them and a resident of Alipur, I would be inclined to take the side of our villager.

Despite living and voting in Alipur, routinely attending social events of their caste, and observing the rule against endogamy vis-à-vis Alipur, villagers did not necessarily treat Ram Singh's hamlet as their own, as was evident from Suresh's remarks about whom he would side with in a conflict and about not claiming women of the hamlet as "daughters of the village." It is significant that membership in the village community should have been indexed by claims to the ownership of women's bodies and specifically to a patriarchal relationship embedded in the notion that a marriageable young woman was "a daughter" of the village (men). The boundaries of the village, the space of the community, depended centrally on gender relations. Ram Singh may have been securely positioned as a member of the village by the political and developmental apparatuses of the state, but his status as a member of the village community was far more ambiguous. Suresh clearly thought that Ram Singh would have obtained more votes had he been a resident of the main settlement.

Ram Singh was silent on the role of caste in the explanation he offered for his electoral loss. Perhaps he did not wish to voice his frustrations in that regard. Everyone else I spoke with emphasized the role played by Ram Singh's lower-caste status. His opponents clearly exploited that fact to the hilt. One thakur told me that in the last two days before the election, Sher Singh's supporters had managed to make real headway by playing up Ram Singh's lower-caste status. They were especially successful in persuading older brahmins that they would regret making a chamaar the headman. They were told that whenever they needed the headman's assistance or intervention, they would have to trudge the long distance to his hamlet. In turn, when he visited them, they would have to welcome him and offer to seat him at the upper end of the cot.[11] They would have to behave in a deferential manner toward him and say, "Please, sir, do take a seat" [Aao ji, pradhanji, baitho]. This tactic made its impact and managed to swing a number of voters toward Sher Singh, despite his generally poor reputation among the brahmins. One such brahmin told me that he had not voted for Ram Singh because he thought that a lower-caste person [neech jati] would act in a degraded way.

Apart from raising doubts about Ram Singh's affiliation to the village and attacking his lower-caste status, Sher Singh also resorted to intimidation and force to win the election. In this light, the margin of victory—the difference between the two candidates in the number of votes received—was a highly contested "fact," as various people attempted to guess what the difference was between the "official" count and the "actual" one. Sher Singh's opponents either deliberately exaggerated the size of the margin of victory to highlight the extent of cheating or reduced the official margin to suggest how close the election had in fact been. A brahmin who repeatedly claimed "We elected Sher Singh" nevertheless insisted that Sher Singh had won by a very narrow margin of less than 45 votes. On the other hand, Ram Singh himself maintained that as a result of the intimidation tactics, he received only 90 to 100 votes out of 475 on Alipur's voter list. Yet another thakur man told me that Sher Singh had won by a substantial majority of approximately 125 votes.

All the people I spoke with, whether supporters or opponents of Sher Singh, agreed that cheating had occurred during the elections. And all attributed the cheating to the fact that some women who supported Sher Singh managed to cast multiple votes. My reconstruction of what happened in the elections is based on accounts offered by several people who described, in almost identical terms, the exact mechanism by which cheating had taken place. Each candidate was allowed to have an "agent" inside the polling site. Voters filed into the site, had their names ticked off on the voter list, and were handed the ballot paper. Unlike the parliamentary election, voters' hands were not marked with indelible ink after they had voted. If either of the agents of the candidates were unsure of the eligibility of a potential voter, they could challenge him or her, depositing a small sum of money for every voter that they challenged. Election officials, who were appointed by the government, then had to verify the identity of the voter by taking that person outside and asking the people standing around to identify him or her.

Given that all these precautions were in place to prevent cheating, the two main methods of cheating were to have people cast votes several times, once in their own name and a second time in someone else's, and to pad the voter registration list with extra names. Both these techniques were fully used in the election. Some people claimed that Ram Singh's biggest mistake lay in choosing an agent who did not recognize the women from the village. The reason why it was harder to identify women was that it was customary for women, especially those from the upper castes, to cover their faces when talking to or passing by men, particularly older men and outsiders. A man who had grown up in the village could perhaps identify all the women by sight, but one from outside had no hope of doing so.[12] Thus, although women were not represented as candidates in the election, village politics hinged crucially on women, and it was precisely their lack of visibility that enabled them to become so politically significant. Once again, women functioned to indicate membership in the village community. A man's ability to identify a woman voter successfully depended heavily on whether he had grown up in the village or was an outsider. Women, therefore, were positioned at the very center of a contest in the overtly masculine sphere of village politics.

Ram Singh himself identified this to be the major difficulty in his election tactics: "Our problem was that no one from here [his settlement] could recognize the women from that side of the village. When I asked someone from the village to be our agent, no one agreed. They were all afraid [*dhaisat khaa gaye*]. Finally, Mirpal [a younger, lower-caste man] agreed." "So you did have someone from the village?" I countered. He dismissed the significance of this fact: "What good did it do? He [Mirpal] was so afraid that he didn't challenge anyone. The night before, Sher Singh went to Mirpal's house and threatened to kill him if he created any problems. His wife and family were so afraid that they all voted for Sher Singh. He did not dare to challenge anyone who was voting for the second or third time. It all goes to show that the weapons that rest on another's shoulder are useless [*doosrey ki kandhe pey hatyaar kisi kaam key nahin*]." I heard a similar story from others, but an additional piece of information was added, which was subsequently verified by the man who served as Sher Singh's agent. It appears that early in the process of voting, Mirpal had in fact challenged the credentials of one woman. Sher Singh's agent was his paternal cousin, a burly and aggressive man, who started quarreling with Mirpal and then slapped him hard two or three times. After that, Mirpal did not dare to challenge anyone, and many women voted several times. In this way, the voter turnout was recorded to be a fantastic 90 percent, although a great many people on the list of registered voters were not even present in the village at that time. If Sher Singh had not been sure of victory by then, I was told jokingly, the voter turnout might well have exceeded 100 percent.

When I spoke to Ram Singh, he appeared disgusted with the whole process: "The thakurs intimidated the 'small' [lower-caste] people [*chotey logon ko daraa diya*]. I have never seen a place where people were such cowards as in this village. And it wasn't just the lower-caste people; the whole village was intimidated by him [Sher Singh]. Even the lower castes did not support me fully. They were all afraid of Sher Singh. Elections these days are fought on the strength of one's arm." Others in the village repeated this sentiment in almost identical language. I was told that apart from garnering the votes of those lower-caste people who lived on the side of the village closest to the thakurs, Sher Singh managed to split the votes of jats and brahmins. These caste groups had supported Prasad in the previous election. Ram Singh had difficulty in gathering the votes of people from his own caste in the village because he was seen as Prasad's candidate. And during Prasad's tenure as headman, the jatavs did not receive any benefits because they were perceived to be in Sher Singh's camp. The history of factional politics, therefore, determined who the beneficiaries of development programs were; in turn, the pattern of distribution of benefits affected future support. Yet, a straightforward determination of interests would be insufficient to explain why some brahmins and jats voted against Ram Singh, just as an explanation based on caste vote-banks could not account for why jatavs failed to rally around Ram Singh.[13]

Several people gave me a detailed breakdown of who voted for one candidate and who for the other. "This time, families were split," confided Sompal. "How do you know?" I asked. "Isn't the voting by secret ballot?" He replied: "The truth comes out because people tell their closest friends and then everyone comes to know. For example, people would come to me and say, 'I'll take an oath to vote for the candidate that you have decided to support.'" In this way, Sompal maintained, although no one could tell for sure, everyone had "a good idea" of how individuals voted.

From the description of village politics given so far, several themes emerge clearly. The elections for headmen were keenly contested affairs, in which the successful candidate had to make a concerted effort to obtain the support of lower-caste voters. No lower-caste person had ever been elected headman, and Ram Singh was in fact the first such person even to aspire to that position. Ram Singh's defeat indicated the extent to which village politics was predicated on gender, since everyone acknowledged that Sher Singh won the election because women who supported him voted multiple times. Gender was also critical to assessments of who belonged to the village community and who did not, a fact that also hurt Ram Singh. The winners of village elections rewarded their supporters by making them the beneficiaries of development programs. In turn, voters' decisions depended on whether they had gained from development programs or had been excluded from them. One of the chief benefits that headmen could dispense to lower-caste supporters was ownership rights to village council land. Caste, community, land, gender, and development were thus closely tied together in village politics.

In addition to the headman, voters also chose a nine-member village council [*gram panchayat*]. Village governance was supposed to be in the hands of this council and not vested in the headman alone. The village was divided into "wards," with a member of the village council chosen from each one such that people from different castes and factions ideally found some representation on the village council. Two of the elected members of Alipur's council, for example, told Sher Singh explicitly that they would never sign any proposal that he put forth as the headman. Although women were supposed to be guaranteed 30 percent of the seats on the village council by government decree, there were no women on the ballot. After his election, Sher Singh added the name of Santoshi Devi, Sompal's spouse, to the list of representatives. She told me that, as a token representative, she signed anything that Sher Singh brought to her. Sher Singh never did consult the village council, preferring to make all decisions by himself. But because he needed written proof that at least five of the nine members of the council supported him, after he had decided to undertake a particular course of action, he would go round individually to the members of the council who were his friends and clients and ask them to sign the register.

Unlike Prasad, Sher Singh did not appear to be interested in rewarding supporters. One person, who was eventually elected to the village council, had openly announced that he would *not* vote for Sher Singh under any circumstance. Instead of punishing this man for his opposition, one of the first things that Sher Singh did after the election was to arrange to have the government-sponsored crèche [*anganwadi*] moved to the man's house. There was speculation that Sher Singh had arranged the move of the crèche to win that person's support for decisions that needed the village council's endorsement.

Several people told me that Sher Singh's concern with village governance extended only as far as the next bottle of liquor. One of his relatives confided: "He drinks a bottle [of country liquor] practically every day. Sometimes, he misses a day. Then he announces the next morning, 'I've given up drinking.' If someone asks him how long its been, he says he hasn't had any liquor for a whole day!" Another man joined in, saying: "Sher Singh does nothing but drink liquor and eat buffalo [*katra*] and goat [*bakra*]. The only thing lacking are dancing girls, and that too shouldn't prove too difficult to arrange."[14]

The significance of these remarks lay in the fact that money for liquor had to be obtained from bribes and payoffs, and Sher Singh extracted it with a practiced ease. During Prasad's tenure as headman, Sher Singh had helped some harijan families circumvent the headman's authority and build homes on land designated for that purpose by the village council. After being elected headman, Sher Singh threatened to tear down the "illegal" construction that he himself had earlier sponsored. It took a payoff to keep him quiet. After that, he approached those households again and told them that, as headman, he would have the house sites officially registered in their names in exchange for some cash. They paid up, but he just pocketed the money and took no action. It was unlikely that the harijans would ever get deeds to their property.

Although Sher Singh's election as headman might well be interpreted as the "return" of thakur dominance in village politics, such an interpretation would seriously miss the underlying structural changes that made Sher Singh's tenure as headman so different from that of his uncle. Since Sher Singh's time, development programs and the green revolution had fundamentally altered the nature of village society. Sher Singh, like any other candidate for the headmanship, had to promise that he would deliver development programs to his lower-caste and landless supporters. This role in fact enabled him to earn substantial sums of money through kickbacks and bribes, which outweighed his earnings from farming, and took up most of his time. But exactly how important did landownership and landlessness continue to be for politics in Alipur?

One of the first major policies of the postcolonial era was the abolition of zamindari, which severed the hold that large, mostly absentee land-lords had on the rural population. Because these landlords were also the closest allies of the colonial government in rural areas, there was a nationalist edge to zamindari abolition. But what did the elimination of zamindari do for class privilege? How did it change relations between landowners and landless people? What can we deduce about relations of power from patterns of landownership in Alipur today?

We can learn a great deal about relations of power in Alipur by tracing the interaction of caste and class within the changes occurring in the system of patronage. A system of patronage and dependence built on landownership and tenancy declined, but development programs and populism created new mechanisms of patronage. How were these processes experienced by people belonging to different classes and castes? Zamindari abolition had a dramatic impact not only on the lives of the landlords but also on the middle peasant groups, who gained ownership of land, and on landless people, who gained freedom from forced labor. Other important changes occurred after the abolition of zamindari. The green revolution had been introduced into western Uttar Pradesh, drastically altering cropping patterns, land use, and demand for labor. And accompanying the green revolution were other kinds of government programs aimed at alleviating poverty and raising the living standards of lower-caste and poor people. In the previous section I charted the history of village political alliances; in this section I attempt to provide an explanation for the changing nature of factionalism in Alipur by relating it to developmentalism and agrarian capitalism. How did the changing nature of local politics articulate with state-sponsored development strategies—in particular, the introduction of an intensive, capitalist agriculture?

Although the abolition of zamindari took village land out of the exclusive control of one extended family and distributed it more widely, it did not fundamentally alter a system in which land provided the means to bind clients and dependents to powerful patrons. Patronage is essentially a relationship that locks land, labor, and credit markets either in combinations of two or all together (Bardhan 1980; Srivastava 1989a). For example, a patron might extend consumption credit to a client in the lean season in exchange for guaranteed labor, either unpaid or underpaid, in the peak season.[15]

In Alipur, tenancy was the main kind of patron-client relationship (Srivastava 1989b). An examination of the different kinds of tenancy found in the village showed that it combined land and credit markets, land and labor markets, or all three. There were four chief forms of tenancy, which varied in their duration and terms (see Table 2). The most common form was the pure sharecropping [*bataai*] model. In this arrangement, the landlord rented the land to the tenant for the entire agricultural cycle. The costs of all inputs, including purchased inputs such as fertilizer, irrigation water, pesticides, and hired labor, were evenly shared between owner and tenant. The tenant was responsible for field preparation, sowing, and weeding. The costs of harvesting with hired labor were split, and the resulting grain was equally divided between landlord and tenant. The cost of threshing was borne individually. Sharecropping had the disadvantage that it required close consultation between landlord and tenant, as decisions to purchase inputs and hire labor depended on both parties. Landlords who either lived outside the village or did not wish to work as closely with tenants employed other options in leasing out their land.

One of their options consisted of leasing out land for cash (*peshagi*). By the time I first reached Alipur in 1984, this form of tenancy had, according to villagers, declined in importance. Cash rentals had the hallmark of simplicity: the tenant paid a fixed sum at the beginning of the agricultural year and then had to bear all responsibility for the crop. A similar and more widely used arrangement consisted of payment in kind [*jins*]. The big difference between jins and peshagi was that jins required payment in kind at the end of the agricultural year, whereas peshagi mandated payment in cash at its beginning. In 1984–85, jins payments were usually fixed at 2–2½ man/bigha (approximately 5–6.5 quintals/acre). Although the contract was for the entire agricultural year, the tenant could decide whether to pay none, half, or all the rent at the end of the first season [*kharif*]. It was the usual practice for tenants to pay half the rent at the end of the kharif season and the remaining half at the end of the rabi season. Since maize, the usual crop grown in the kharif, sold for far less than wheat, the main crop in the rabi season, it made sense for tenants to pay at least some portion of the annual rent in maize rather than wait to pay the entire quantity in wheat. If there was an especially bad year, a landlord might agree to a share of the crop rather than demanding the agreed-upon quantity specified in the jins contract; this, however, was entirely the landlord's prerogative.

In addition to these annual leases, a type of tenancy contract used

Table 2. Types of Tenancy Contracts, Alipur, 1984–1985

Name of Sharecropping Contract	Seed (T/L)	Fertilizer (T:L)	Water (T:L)
Bataai (sharecropping)	T	1:1	1:1
Peshagi (cash rental)	T	T	T
Jins (in-kind rental)	T	T	T
Chauthaai (quarter share)	L	1:3	1:3

Notes: T = tenant's responsibility; L = landlord's responsibility; Own = each responsible for own share; T:L = ratio of tenant's share to landlord's share.

frequently in the monsoon or kharif harvest was the *chauthaai* (literally, "a quarter"). This was an arrangement of task-specific contract work akin to wage labor. In this contract, the landlord was responsible for field preparation and sowing. Once the field had been tilled and the crop planted, responsibility passed over to the tenant, who did the weeding, supplied the labor for irrigation, protected the crop from birds and pests, and harvested the cobs. The costs of irrigation water were split between the landlord and tenant so that the latter paid a quarter of the total. The output was split in the same ratio: the landlord got three shares to one for the tenant. The main costs of harvesting corn consisted in husking, but that was done after the output had already been split.

Production loans were not uncommon but, in most cases, were made in the context of tenancy: the landlord gave seed to the tenant, receiving in exchange 25 percent more as interest at harvest time.[16] Another, minor form of tenancy was found in raising cattle on a share basis. Typically, an owner would "loan" a calf to another villager who would feed and care for it until maturity. When it was sold, the returns would be evenly split: if either the original owner or the "tenant" wanted to retain the animal, they would pay the other party half the market price.

The bond formed through relationships of tenancy was not an enduring or stable one because of two features. The first of these was the phenomenon of tenant rotation or tenant switching. Landlords in Alipur were well aware of the law that stipulated that tenants who cultivated the same plot for three consecutive years could claim ownership rights to it. Consequently, they were careful to switch tenants every year or every

Field Preparation Labor (T/L)	Weeding Labor (T/L)	Harvesting Labor (T:L)	Threshing Labor (T/L)	Division of Product (T:L)
T	T	1:1	Own	1:1
T	T	T	T	None
T	T	T	T	Prefixed amount to landlord
L	T	1:3	Own	1:3

Length of contract for first three types: kharif and rabi crops. Length of contract for chauthaai just kharif crop.

two years. Or, if they owned more land than they could cultivate themselves, landlords sometimes switched plots while retaining the same tenant, although this was relatively uncommon.[17] The second noteworthy feature in tenancy contracts was the limited length of the lease period. Even tenants who were given plots for two years had to renew the lease at the end of the first agricultural cycle (usually defined as covering the kharif and rabi harvests). The yearly lease was the reason most often cited by tenants for not applying such productivity-enhancing inputs as organic or green manure, for in the "indigenous" system of agronomy manure was considered efficacious for as long as three years.[18]

The qualitative changes that made tenancy less important as a form of patronage in Alipur were complemented by a decline in the frequency of tenancy itself.[19] During the main harvest season (the winter rabi crop) of 1984, I observed that only 49 of 303 plots cultivated were rented out. Of these, 33 (or about 10 percent) were rented within the village, amounting to just 3 percent of the total cultivated area. A closer analysis reveals that only 2 of these 33 plots were rented by higher-caste owners to lower-caste tenants (Table 3).[20] The figures for the kharif harvest were not very different. It is thus obvious that tenancy was not an important means by which to recruit clients.[21] As opposed to the time of zamindari, by 1984 landownership had quite clearly ceased to be the central means of extending patronage to landless clients. This had important implications for village politics, as it made evident that the labor of lower-caste, lower-class households was no longer tied to the land owned by upper-caste, upper-class landowners.[22]

Table 3. Land Rented Out by Villagers, Number of Cases, Rabi Crop, Alipur, 1984–1985

	Caste of Tenant				
	Brahmin	Thakur	Jat	Other Lower Castes	Total
Caste of Landlord					
Brahmin	0	0	0	1	1
Thakur	2	2	2	0	6
Jat	1	0	5	1	7
Other lower castes	0	0	2	17	19
Total	3	2	9	19	33

Landownership in the village continued to be highly unequal and stratified. Figure 1 shows that the three upper castes—brahmins, thakurs, and jats—controlled 90 percent of agricultural land owned by all villagers.[23] Superimposing Figure 2 on the first map demonstrates that the largest plots in the village belonged to these three castes, and particularly to the thakurs. The mean size of thakur landholdings was twice as high as that for brahmins and jats (13.6 acres per household as opposed to less than 7 acres for the other two castes). Taking land quality into consideration would have demonstrated an even sharper divergence between the (on average) large plots of high-quality land owned by upper-caste groups and the small, fragmented plots of marginal land held by the lower castes. For example, yields of the main crop, wheat (see Figure 3), on land owned by brahmins was twice as high as yields on plots owned by lower castes (216 kg/bigha as opposed to 108 kg/bigha for the lower castes). Figures 4, 5, and 6 demonstrate that yields per acre were rising, that annual wheat production had trebled in the district between 1961 and 1982, and that the area devoted to wheat in the rabi crop had doubled in the same period. In contrast to the good-quality land owned by the upper castes, just a few lower-caste, mostly jatav, families owned substantial pieces of good-quality land.

Despite the continuing inequalities in landownership, the decline of tenancy and the system of patronage that depended on tenancy had tremendous repercussions for relations within the village. For instance, I once walked into a particularly ferocious argument involving a lower-caste laborer and one of the thakurs from the dominant lineage. The dispute arose because the laborer helped himself to a cucumber growing on the thakur's plot while walking past. The thakur angrily denounced him, saying that lower-caste people behaved as if they had the same rights as during the time of zamindari but were unwilling to reciprocate in the expected manner—that is, by providing free labor and by showing "due" respect to upper-caste people. The laborer, on the other hand, complained that the thakurs had become stingy and petty and gave as evidence the fact that such a fuss had been made over one cucumber. He added that the thakurs failed to pay their workers adequately or on time and in the requisite amounts and that they behaved as if they could continue to exploit "small" people as they had done historically. What is significant about this episode was not merely that the thakur's and the lower-caste laborer's assessments of each other's "proper" behavior diverged so much but also that the laborer could voice his criticism so freely.[24]

Other upper-caste people in Alipur, who did not experience to the same degree the thakurs' perception of lost privilege, nevertheless positioned lower-caste self-assertion as part of the breakdown of a nostal-

Figure 1. Ownership of Land by Caste, Alipur, 1984–1985

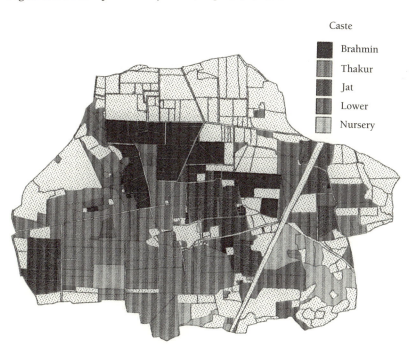

Caste

■ Brahmin
▨ Thakur
▨ Jat
▨ Lower
▨ Nursery

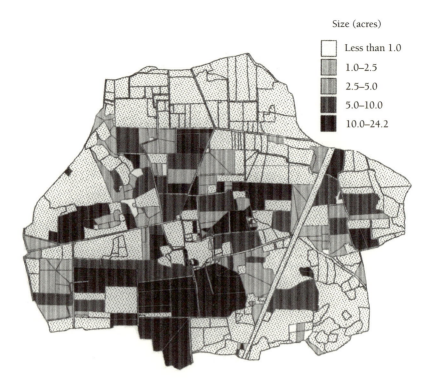

Size (acres)

☐ Less than 1.0
▨ 1.0–2.5
▦ 2.5–5.0
▩ 5.0–10.0
■ 10.0–24.2

Figure 2. Size Distribution of Holdings, Alipur, 1984–1985

gically invoked period of village harmony. It is interesting that this period of village harmony was seen as occurring before massive state interventions in the form of the green revolution and development programs had made their impact on village life. In contrast to the usual glowing self-assessments of their own village, people in Alipur repeatedly asked me: "Why have you come here? This is one of the most useless villages in India. There was a time when everyone lived together harmoniously. Now men do not trust their own brothers."[25] Significantly, village harmony was measured entirely in terms of male relationships—of how men dealt with one another—and not at all in terms of relationships between women.

These themes were elaborated and qualified by Ranbir Singh, a well-to-do jat farmer who had inherited a fair amount of very high-quality land from his uncle. Before Ranbir Singh took over the day-to-day oversight of the farm, his uncle employed two lower-caste servants and two sharecroppers to look after the farm. Ranbir's views of a more harmonious time in the past, when people knew their proper place, may have been tinged with nostalgia, but they were also shaped by a shrewd appreciation of the changes in social relations wrought by new technologies. Ranbir maintained that when the village barber [*nai*], sweeper [*bhangi*], smith [*lohar*], water carrier [*dhimar*], tailor, and so on were paid a fixed amount every agricultural season [*chamai*, literally, "six months"], "Everyone worked in their own place, and worked willingly and with enthusiasm." In saying this, Ranbir was implicitly contrasting the present to a time when people "willingly" accepted social inequalities (Wadley 1994:81–92). These people left their traditional occupations, he maintained, because they became concerned about their status: "Earlier, all these chamaars, and so forth, would be working for the farmer. Now their children, having been educated, became teachers or judges. If the child has the position of a judge, will the parent want to work in the field? He will want to be respected once his child is a judge!" According to Ranbir, this was the difference between the past and the present. It was not that hereditary occupations could no longer be followed but that younger people in the service castes no longer wanted to do low-status work. Unlike many upper-caste men, Ranbir's perspective

Figure 3. Winter (Rabi) Crop

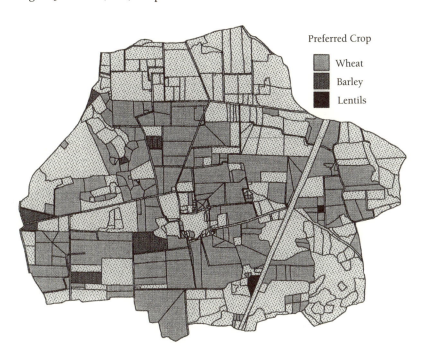

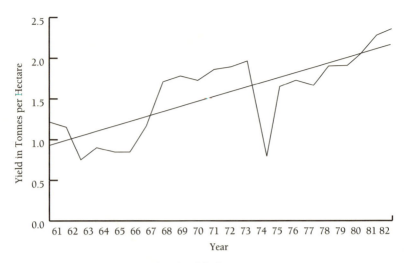

Figure 4. Annual Wheat Yield, Bulandshahr District

on the abandonment of "traditional" occupations was not simply one of loss. He maintained that "when they stopped practicing their occupations, the question of good or bad doesn't arise." He felt that service castes had improved their position in society because their children had been able to go to school and obtain decent jobs. Ranbir's example of lower-caste children becoming teachers and judges commented on the new opportunities that had opened up owing to state programs specifically targeted at providing schooling and jobs to lower-caste people. But it was also a comment on the displacement of traditional occupations by state policies to promote the green revolution.

Ranbir felt that the bonds between people had weakened because farmers and service castes were no longer dependent on each other:

> [Traditional occupations] used to maintain village society. Suppose I want to have a plow made by the carpenter. Now that the impact of tractors has increased, I figure why keep these two oxen? There is the expense of fodder, giving them water, green fodder, all these expenses have to be incurred. But when I don't have any work to give to the carpenter, when I don't need to get a plow made at all, then I approach the tractor person and do the plowing with a tractor.

Replacing the oxen and the plow with a tractor thus not only reduces the demand for the carpenter's labor but also weakens the relationship of the farmer with the carpenter:

There is a definite difference in our relationships. When we have no business with someone, then we won't go to their place, or visit only rarely. If we visit rarely, we will not develop feelings of affection [*prem bhaavnaa*]. [We might think about visiting but ask,] What will we do there? Today, if I need to do so, I'll go to [the carpenter's place] to get a wooden peg made [to tie cattle]. If we visit more often, we will also sit there for a while, listen to his concerns, share some of our own thoughts, meet four other brothers who are sitting there, and all of that encourages relations with others. That increases our affection for others instead of decreasing it. We use the same reckoning as you do when you visit us: you think that this is a place where I will receive some affection [*prem ki jagah hai*]. [You know that] when you come here, we will make arrangements for tea, we will make arrangements for food, and in this way our affection for each other will increase. But if you visit rarely, then we too will not give it much importance, then our affection for each other will remain low.

Ranbir thus traces the weakening of the once strong ties between people in the village community to changing means of production, as well as to the unprecedented ability of a younger generation of lower-caste people to distance themselves from low-status occupations. Both these changes could be directly traced to the developmental efforts of the postcolonial state. Although their specific origins lay in different development initia-

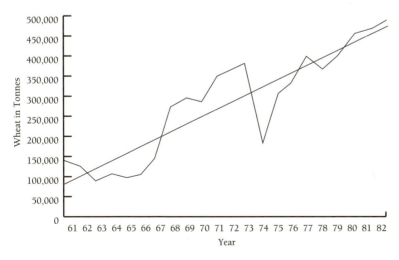

Figure 5. Annual Wheat Production, Bulandshahr District

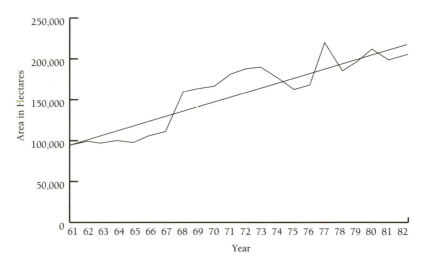

Figure 6. Wheat Cultivation Area, Bulandshahr District

tives, changes in the methods of production associated with the green revolution and a rapid expansion in job opportunities for lower-caste people both resulted from the state's efforts to bring about economic development.

Other people also commented on the decline of affection among villagers. Two older men took a frankly nostalgic view of the changes they had witnessed in their own lifetimes: "The degree of affection [*mohabbat*] that one saw before is no longer to be witnessed today. Now brothers are at one another's throats. Earlier, if there were four brothers, they would sit together in the evening and share their joys and sorrows. Children did not dare speak to their parents. A younger brother wouldn't even venture to smoke a hookah in the presence of his elder,[26] leave alone actually eat a meal. Now, even young boys tell their fathers, 'Let me take two or three puffs from the hookah, old man.'" In this view, the decline of affection for others is part of a larger transformation of an orderly social world in which age hierarchies were strictly respected.[27] Many people in the village suggested that one of the main reasons why "brothers [were] at one another's throats" was that increased consumerism and competition had led to the growth of envy. If someone prospered, others were jealous and wished him ill. If the growth of consumer desire can be charted to changing industrial policies in India's development plans, the change of abilities to fulfill that desire can be traced to the surpluses generated by the introduction of green revolution wheat to this region.

It was clear, however, that relations between lower and upper castes and classes were changing for reasons other than the fact that service castes had given up on "traditional" occupations. As my informants made clear, the majority of lower-caste people had always worked as agricultural laborers, rather than occupational specialists. Whether they were illiterate or semieducated, unskilled laborers or skilled craftsmen, lower-caste men preferred to seek employment outside the village rather than work for those upper-class, usually upper-caste households of Alipur that wished to hire wage laborers. When I asked why such was the case, I received sharply diverging answers, depending on the caste and class position of the person to whom I had posed the question.[28] Ranbir, largely a self-sufficient middle peasant, who hired laborers occasionally, complained that labor rates had risen faster than inflation. The reason, he claimed, was that laborers could find work more easily than before in the town. They went to town in the morning and found daily labor in factories. The farmer could afford to pay them only Rs 30, whereas they were paid Rs 50 in the factories; thus, they preferred not to work for farmers.[29] Ranbir's statements need to be contextualized by noting that the high cost of daily labor was the most frequently recurring theme in the discourse of farmers and landowners in Alipur.

Lower-caste and lower-class people had a completely different perspective on this question. I was speaking to a group of lower-caste men about why they preferred not to labor in the fields: "There is less work [the wages are low] in the village, and it is not available on time. Outside [the village], the wages are good and paid on time. We can work for a month or ten days outside, then come back to the village and stay for five days, then go out and work for another stretch." Not being paid on time for the day's labor was the workers' biggest frustration. Anil, a younger, jatav man, elaborated:

Laboring in the village means you have to go to work before the sun is out and can return only after the sun has set. Sometimes you get enough time to eat in the afternoon, and sometimes you don't. They make you work for fourteen hours, and after that, if the laborer goes to get his wages the next day, he is told, "Your aunt [*chaachi*] is not here, come in the evening." If you go in the evening, after the usual formalities, you are told, "Your grandma [*daadi*] has gone to such-and-such place, she has taken the key with her, come back tomorrow and take your money." In this way, one has to waste three days to get one day's wage. Where will you get the money to feed your family for the next two days? In the town, the wages are better, and you get paid in cash, so you can buy provisions for your family. For this reason, people don't like to work in the village.

Anil narrated this by exaggerating and mimicking the statements about "your aunt" and "your grandma" to the amusement of his listeners.[30] He deliberately used these terms to indicate how weak the excuses were for nonpayment. In most labor-hiring households, women were unlikely to have controlled the supply of cash or the access to it. The frustration of working hard and not being paid on time struck a familiar chord among the men present, all of whom, like Anil, were lower-caste laborers. Another group of lower-caste men told me that laborers especially disliked working for the thakurs because, they claimed, the thakurs had a habit of not paying workers promptly. This used to be a common practice and had declined to some degree so that the situation was better, but the worker always faced uncertainty. "Earlier, if they came to get us, we had to go because they were so powerful. Now at least we can refuse if we don't want to go [work for them]."[31]

At the time of this conversation in the last week of July 1989, there was frantic construction activity going on in Alipur as the village pond was being widened and deepened under a government program for village development. Tens of laborers had been hired for this job, but none of them was from Alipur. When I asked this group of lower-caste men, who made a living entirely from wage labor, why they were not working on this project, they said that they were all already committed to some other jobs which they did not want to leave. Most of the young men preferred to work in Delhi and had permanently left the village. Some worked in the nearby town of Mandi, where, depending on the kind of work, they earned Rs 20 or Rs 22 for a day's labor. Some jobs required more skill and thus commanded higher wages. I wanted to know why they would choose to go all the way to town when, after subtracting for transportation costs (Rs 4), they could get the same wage in the village. They agreed that wage rates were about the same but claimed that work was not always available in the village. Ram Singh, the unsuccessful candidate for headman, told me that the real reason that the younger generation preferred to work in the towns was because they could not tolerate working for the thakurs. Work on the village pond, for example, although financed by the government, was being allocated by Sher Singh in his capacity as headman. Getting a job in town may have meant freedom from local oppressions, but it also required living away from the village, thus removing these mostly young men from the village political scene.

The breakdown of forms of authority and deference that characterized a system of patronage in which laborers were dependent on landlords was due both to the changing means of production introduced by the green revolution and to the new opportunities for landless laborers to seek employment outside the village. Yet patronage did offer some security, however unequally it was institutionalized; therefore, the breakdown of patronage might have been expected to be accompanied by increased proletarianization. If by proletarianization we mean the growth of wage labor, then it was certainly true, as former tenants and farm servants become wage laborers.[32] But if by that we mean the growth of landless laborers, then this proposition is dubious and may even be false (K. Bardhan 1977). At first sight, the simultaneous growth of wage labor with landownership may appear counterintuitive. Understanding this phenomenon, however, gives us some vital insights into the nature of rural politics.

One can locate three broad causes of proletarianization (Byres 1982). Traditional village service castes had been displaced from their hereditary occupations, both because the changing methods of production no longer required certain tools and skills and because industrial goods had replaced their products (Berreman 1972; Appadurai 1989). "Development" in the form of the green revolution and consumer goods brought with it the displacement of certain kinds of labor. The dhimars (water carriers) of Alipur became tenants and petty shopkeepers because the introduction of tube wells and the abandonment of the village well made their occupation superfluous. Similarly, all but one person from the *teli* (oil presser) caste had abandoned their hereditary occupation because people preferred to take their mustard seed to town and have oil extracted by the cheaper, more efficient mechanical press. By 1984, none of Alipur's service caste households relied exclusively on their traditional occupation, and less than a handful practiced them as a secondary source of income. They had all become primarily wage laborers.

Another cause of proletarianization, directly connected to the decline of tenancy, stemmed from the increased profitability of agriculture (Byres 1982). Owners reclaimed land formerly leased to tenants for their own use. As green revolution technology had already been employed in Alipur for several years when I reached there in 1984, I did not witness this process. The low rates of tenancy I found may, in fact, have indicated that redemption had thoroughly run its course.

The final cause of proletarianization was the fragmentation and subdivision of landholdings as a result of the coparcenary system of inheritance. In this system, all the sons received an equal share of the property.[33] When a family's landholdings were split into several fragments, as they often were (on an average, there were 1.9 fragments per household), each son did not inherit one plot but a share of each of them. In this way, poor and middle peasants and sometimes rich peasants as well were reduced to marginal landholders in the course of one generation and were forced to enter the wage labor market.[34] This was one of the mechanisms by which landownership coexisted with proletarianization. Proletarianization was essentially Janus-faced: the other side to self-assertion and the growth of a class-based critique was increasing immiserization, marginalization, and victimization.[35]

The process by which landowners were driven to the status of marginal peasants, however, formed only half the picture. The other half concerned the rural landless who had gained some land and, thus, become marginal peasants. Some of these people were service castes who had lost their niche, others were tenants who had been evicted, and still others had always been landless laborers. I will discuss how the landless managed to obtain some land in the next section. To avoid terminological confusion, I will henceforth not refer to these people as "proletarians with land" (which appears oxymoronic) but as "the rural semiproletariat." To understand this phenomenon better, the following categories need to be kept distinct: rural semiproletariat, rural landless, agricultural laborers, and wage laborers. The relation between them, as I see it, can be illustrated by the tree in Figure 7. I have drawn only half of the whole tree—it can be followed identically for landholding semiproletarians. I think of these categories as jointly exhaustive but not mutually exclusive, except for the landholding/landless category, which is both.

The chief political implication of the proletarianization of the rural poor is to foster a new kind of dependence on village elites. The marginalization of semiproletarians is also true in a literal sense: their land is marginal both in terms of the size of the holding and in terms of its location—its distance from the settlement and from sources of irrigation. It is often also marginal in terms of soil quality. A pair of bullocks or a tractor is needed for plowing and sowing, a tube well for irrigation, and a thresher for cleaning the grain. Because the capital investment necessary for purchasing these machines is not justified by the size of the plot (and is, in any case, beyond their resources), the poor have to

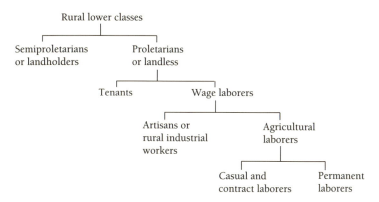

Figure 7. Categories of Rural Lower-Class People

rent these machines from upper-class peasants. The new high-yielding varieties are very sensitive to the timing of inputs: a two-week delay in irrigation when the winter wheat is ripening could mean a substantial loss of output. It is, therefore, not merely a question of access but of *timely* access, and in that sense, the poor are totally dependent on their upper-class suppliers.

One might wonder, then, why semiproletarians would cultivate their own plots at all. Given the uncertainty and seasonable variability of employment, every contribution to subsistence was necessary.[36] An important political consequence of retaining a toehold in cultivation was that the rural poor were co-opted into peasant movements which sought, for example, to increase subsidies for fertilizers and irrigation but which primarily benefited rich peasants.[37] Similarly, the *status* derived from being a landowner may have contributed to making a large proportion of proletarianization invisible in the compilation of official statistics. I found that even marginal peasants whose main source of income was wage labor invariably responded to queries about their primary occupation with *kheti* (farming) rather than *majdoori* (agricultural labor).

Development Programs and the Green Revolution

Instead of a straightforward story of capitalist expansion in which growing stratification resulted in a polarization between an increasingly more prosperous class of capitalist farmers and larger numbers of rural landless, the green revolution in Alipur saw the rise of a category of people who were primarily wage laborers but who gained possession of tiny plots of land. How did this come about? What was the relationship between this pattern of landownership and the development policies of the postcolonial state? How did agrarian populism affect the types of government programs that were implemented? What effects did this have on relationships in the village? In this section I explore some of the reasons for and consequences of land redistribution.

An understanding of this phenomenon has to begin with the wider context of Indira Gandhi's populism that I described in Chapter 1. Agrarian populism was partially a response to the increasing inequality accompanying the spread of the green revolution.[38] During the early seventies, the government introduced a series of subsidies and hand-outs oriented toward production but with essentially welfarist objectives. Targeted at small and marginal farmers, these consisted of small amounts of free seed, fertilizer, favorable credit for agricultural investment, and so forth and were administered by such new bureaucracies as the Small Farmers Development Agency (SFDA) and the agency for Marginal Farmers and Agricultural Laborers (MFAL).

In the decade before the introduction of the green revolution, some legal changes were put into effect to protect tenants and to break up large estates through stipulating the maximum amount of land that an individual could own, called a "land ceiling."[39] In the particular context of the simultaneous growth of capitalist agriculture and government programs, these laws were to have unintended consequences. On the one hand, the suddenly increased profitability of agriculture made cultivation by owners more attractive, and the new laws gave landowners a justification for not renewing tenant leases. The land ceiling, on the other hand, though seemingly at odds with the drive to accumulate, merely encouraged the legal (although seldom the operational) subdivision of property. Increased yields meant that profits could be raised without necessarily cultivating more land; and when land *was* purchased, it could be legally registered in the name of a family member of the cultivator.

At the village level, the effects of these changes were felt in two distinct ways. As mentioned above, the decline of tenancy and the increasing reliance on wage labor led to further class polarization. The joint impact of development programs targeted to small farmers and land ceiling laws can best be illustrated by an example. During my first round of fieldwork, the headman Prasad was the eldest brother of a joint family with a fairly substantial plot of fertile land. Legally, the land had been equally divided among the brothers;[40] as a consequence, each of them was technically a "small farmer." Prasad proudly told me what a good strategy that had been. As headman, he naturally had extensive social and official networks among the government bureaucrats responsible for programs for small farmers. He made full use of these contacts, seldom losing an opportunity to gather free inputs for himself and the rest of his family of small farmers. If there were allocations still left over, he would direct them to other close friends and kinsmen, almost all of whom were, like him, prosperous capitalist farmers.

Programs for small farmers were one part of the government strategy to bring development to the rural population. These programs could be placed alongside the establishment of other institutions, such as hospitals, credit cooperatives, fertilizer and seed stores, banks, crèches, ration shops, police stations, grain and sugarcane purchasing centers, and, perhaps most important, schools and colleges in rural areas. Another strategy of development consisted of building infrastructure in rural areas, for example, electric connections, roads, transportation and communication facilities, canals, housing, and so forth.[41] These efforts were critical for legitimation purposes because they provided jobs. Although the actual numbers of people thus employed were small, they acquired greater significance because of the number of people each government employee actually supported.[42] Further, perhaps more significant than the number of jobs created was the promise of job opportunities for an even larger number of people, particularly for the potentially troublesome group of educated, unemployed youth.

It is doubtful, however, that the direct and indirect accounting of heads in this way goes very far in explaining the legitimizing role of state institutions. Rather, their importance may lie in having usurped, reinvigorated, and enlarged the old patrimonial ethic of "looking after the little folk" through the provision of services. In the case of educational institutions, these services were accompanied by a conspicuously nationalist agenda.

Populism added a distinctive twist to the state's developmentalist agenda. Electoral pressures have always pushed dominant groups to seek support from the numerically populous lower classes. This has taken the form of a multitude of special programs aimed at the so-called Scheduled Castes (scs): reservations in government jobs, heavily subsidized credit for the purchase of productive inputs, distribution of small quantities of public land, subsidies for schooling,[43] food for work programs, free electric connections, and so on. Most of these programs operated within the institutional and infrastructural bureaucracies outlined above, but some of them were administered by special bureaucracies set up explicitly for that purpose. In her bid to obtain the support of lower castes and classes, Indira Gandhi bypassed the Congress Party machinery and attempted to tie those voters to her regime directly. Her ability to do so depended on the processes that had gradually weakened property-based ties of patronage described in this chapter, on the vigorous promotion of an ideology of "social justice" captured in her election slogan, and on a renewed emphasis on the implementation of laws against discrimination that had long been on the books. In Chapter 1, I presented some evidence for the "reception" of Indira Gandhi's populist messages in Alipur. But what was it about village social relations and discourses that had been altered to enable populism to succeed? So far, I have suggested that the two crucial elements of this story had been lower-caste assertiveness and the demise of patronage: I will now add a third element, which is the role played by state development programs.

This role can best be illustrated by the example of the manager of the state farm on which I stayed while doing fieldwork in Alipur. He was a lower-level, Class 3 employee of the UP state government. He had obtained the job by paying a small sum of money to a self-appointed "leader" [netaa], a broker who used his contacts with a lower-caste minister in the state government to obtain jobs for educated but unemployed lower-caste youth. Although he was a minor figure in a huge government bureaucracy, the Manager (as he was commonly called) effectively had complete control over the farm's substantial resources.

The state farm itself was splintered into three fragments. While the main segment, which contained the farmhouse where the Manager lived, lay on the periphery of the village, two of the smaller fragments were situated on the side where most of the fields were owned by thakurs.[44] The Manager, therefore, came into contact with the thakurs in the course of his work. For their part, they were eager to make friends with him so as to be able to utilize, on the basis of "friendship" (that is, without payment), some of the equipment owned by the state farm. For example, several of the bigger landowners often borrowed the farm's tractor and tractor trolley. The Manager, for his part, understood perfectly well why they wanted to make friends with him. He utilized the opportunity offered by the necessarily frequent social visits of the higher-caste thakurs to assert his symbolic and social equality. As a thakur told me (referring to the Manager): "As soon as he sees me at the gate (which was at some distance from the house), he orders his wife to make tea. Frankly, every time I drink tea at his place, I get blisters on my tongue." That this man nevertheless went regularly to the Manager's house and defiled his personhood in drinking polluting cups of tea (symptomized by the blisters) spoke to the immense transformations flowing from the intersection of development programs with relations of production.

This case was interesting because it demonstrated how the development programs launched by the state as part of its legitimizing efforts intertwined with the growing assertiveness of lower-caste and lower-class people. The Manager, like other low-level bureaucrats, acted as a patron, using his position as an officer of the state to "help" his own people. Most of the daily laborers that he hired (at state-stipulated wages, which were above the prevailing market rates) were people of his own caste. At the same time that he employed the resources of the farm for his own ends, however, he also served the purposes of the state. Although the lower-caste clients that he hired were grateful to him for providing them jobs, the significance of the fact that it was the long arm of the state that lay behind the Manager was not lost on them. They knew very well who he worked for, where their wages were coming from, and why he had attained such a "good" position. He was a lower-caste person like them, and both he and they had benefited from state development programs.

Pointing to the intersection of regime and lower-caste interests, however, does not completely explain why populist programs and policies have succeeded. We have to ask why rural upper classes supported such programs. At the very least, we have to account for why they did not oppose development programs aimed at lower-caste, lower-class people.

Any understanding of upper-class support for populist programs targeted at lower castes and classes has to focus on one crucial aspect of development programs. This is what is euphemistically referred to as the "leakage" of funds: corruption.[45] Institutional and infrastructural programs usually differ in this regard in that the former provide small and regular opportunities for "leakage," whereas the latter mostly provide large and singular opportunities. Together with the fact that "finance has been a major constraint" (Bardhan 1984:4) in funding these programs and that there is thus never a substantial enough sum of "leakage" to go around, I think we can locate here one of the most fundamental shifts in the political function of local-level leaders. That shift is the move from *patronage* to *brokerage,* a move that underlay the changing basis of the reproduction of relations of domination at the village level.[46] Village leaders no longer cultivated clients chiefly through the use of their own property—by leasing it to tenants, by employing an unchanging group of laborers, and so forth (that is, by acting as a patron) but rather by facilitating the delivery of state programs and services (that is, by acting as a broker). The centrality of brokerage was well illustrated by the politics of Alipur. Although Prasad was a rich farmer, he was not as wealthy and domineering as Sher Singh and certainly would not have been able to become headman in a scenario in which patronage was all important. He had used his position to disperse benefits from development programs to friends and supporters, higher-caste as well as lower-caste. In the bargain, he had accumulated a fair amount of capital that he invested in agricultural machinery and the education of his younger brothers.

Prasad looked back on his tenure as headman as a period in which the landless were the greatest beneficiaries. He took all the wasteland (*usar* land) in the control of the village panchayat and distributed it among lower-caste, landless people. According to Prasad, in the first round of land redistribution in 1983, he made thirty-six plots; he then created an additional forty-nine plots in 1987 (see also Wadley 1994:189–90).[47] This was the year before new elections were to be held for headman. The chief beneficiaries of the first round were the odhs, who had helped elect him and whose houses in the village were adjacent to his. In the second round, he claimed to have distributed plots chiefly to harijans who had, in fact, voted for Sher Singh. The land that he distributed in the second round had been "improved" by the Land Reclamation Department, which had spent over Rs 1 lakh (Rs 100,000) to level the land and construct irrigation and drainage channels. Prasad claimed that he chose not to divide up the land into plots that were too small to be useful. He made plots that were at least four bighas (about two-thirds of an acre), usually six or eight bighas, and sometimes as large as ten bighas. Some families received as much as twenty bighas in this way, because he allocated plots of four bighas adjacent to one another to several members of the family. Prasad maintained that it was largely due to his actions that there were no landless families left in Alipur. "The landless are now in good shape," concluded Prasad, when I spoke with him in 1992. A new round of elections were coming up. "People are asking me to run again," Prasad told me. "All the eighty-five people to whom I distributed plots have been requesting me to contest [the election]."

Apart from distributing farmland, Prasad claimed to have allocated house plots to lower-caste people as well. But his glowing assessment of his own actions was disputed by Ram Singh, Prasad's choice for headman in the elections after the last round of land redistribution. Ram Singh sarcastically noted:

> You don't make zamindars by giving people a small piece of waste [kallar] land. The thakurs opposed the land distribution, hoping that when they captured the headmanship, they would be able to distribute it to the very same people [that Prasad gave it to] and make money out of it. The fact is that from the poor the headman Prasad stole money, Sher Singh stole money, and if a third person becomes headman, he too will steal money [khaa raho ho]. Everybody steals from the poor.

From Ram Singh's perspective, there was little difference between Prasad and Sher Singh, because both were interested primarily in lining their own pockets rather than genuinely doing something for the landless. Ram Singh continued:

> That land does not yield any output even if you put water [and other inputs]. There is so much deception [gaddari] going on. They don't allow plots to be registered, just keep the paperwork unofficial. That is the difference between unofficial [kachcha] work and official [pacca] work. They have made it a business. Where one plot should have been allocated, they made six. That land has no value, it is just wasteland. The poor don't have the means to cultivate the land. To obtain water, they have to buy it from somewhere; to plow the land, they need to find a person with a tractor. There's no profit in those plots.

Having seen several pieces of wasteland that had been rehabilitated by the arduous labor of their owners, I was skeptical of Ram Singh's claim and challenged him. But he held firm in his conviction: "This is the kind of land where even grass doesn't grow; how can grain grow there?"

Although Ram Singh's general sentiments about the role of upper-caste leaders were soundly endorsed by another group of lower-caste men to whom I spoke, they directly contradicted his assertion that wasteland could not be rehabilitated. The plots that Prasad had distributed were not useless. Why, then, did people not choose to reelect Prasad or to elect someone that he had put up for the election? The explanation they offered was that lower-caste people voted for Sher Singh because "it is a herd mentality. Once one person decides to vote a certain way, they all decide to do the same. Once a person says, 'I'll vote for you,' he will vote for that candidate no matter what he stands for. It's an illiterate society [*unpadh samaaj*]. The candidates fool the people by promising them all kinds of things, then they forget it all afterward. These are just means to fool people." The "things" that were promised by Sher Singh were house plots, because everyone knew that there was no more farmland available for redistribution. They implied that the distribution of farmland was in any case no longer such an urgent priority: "With the exception of a few families, everyone now has a little bit of land. There is no family without *some* land. It is true that many of the new plots are on infertile land, but after working on them for two or three years, one can start planting them. They have to be leveled, lots of organic manure has to be applied, and only then are they fit for farming. The plots are small, just four to six bighas."[48] I wanted to know if those plots were adequate to live on. "No," came the reply. "One has to do wage work in addition [to farming]."

Sanwa was a relative of Ram Singh who had been elected to represent their hamlet in the village council. He claimed that Sher Singh approached him to endorse the drawing of several new plots. Sanwa knew that Sher Singh had already taken Rs 6,000 from several individuals to demarcate these plots and had accumulated the substantial sum of Rs 20,000 in bribes. In addition, a couple of wealthy jat peasants were eyeing some property that belonged to the village panchayat and had already paid off Sher Singh to get rights to those plots. So Sanwa refused to sign the register to indicate that the village council had met and approved the partitioning of new plots. He told me that as a matter of principle, he did not sign the register when he thought Sher Singh was doing the wrong thing, and only endorsed those proposals that he thought would benefit the whole village.

In July 1989, at the time this conversation with Sanwa took place, fresh national elections were imminent. The Rajiv Gandhi regime was desperately trying to woo voters in rural areas by seeking to reinvigorate rural development programs. Several new schemes for rural development had been launched, the most ambitious of which was the Jawahar Employment Guarantee Scheme (Jawahar Rojgaar Yojana, or JRY). In addition, there were programs to build houses for the indigent and lower-caste people in every village. In a bold departure from previous government programs, these new schemes handed over large sums directly to the elected village headmen rather than disburse them through development bureaucracies. The logic was that this would prevent corrupt bureaucrats from siphoning off most of the money intended for rural development programs.

On a hot and humid day in July, I was sitting and chatting with three men, two of them from middle castes and one from a lower caste. Sher Singh was passing by and, in response to a question from me about new government programs, mentioned that five new houses were to be constructed for harijans and ten for other "weaker sections."[49] In addition, two new houses were to be constructed under the JRY. Sher Singh told us that he had heard that the regime had an ambitious scheme to build as many as fifty new brick [pucca] houses in each village. He dismissed it as a gimmick to purchase votes in the upcoming elections.

We went on to discuss other topics, including the change in the manner in which government moneys were being disbursed. Sher Singh said, "This government has been very good for the health of headmen [sarkaar nay pradhano ki sehat banaa dee]." He was obviously referring to the newfound opportunities to divert some of the money from government schemes to his own pocket. The jat who was sitting there at once criticized Sher Singh for seeking his own profit at the expense of the villagers. Sher Singh defended himself: "This is a matter of one's intelligence. When there are fools around, the intelligent ones profit." "The only fools," came the retort, "are the people who elected a useless fellow like you." There followed a heated exchange of words in which accusations were freely traded. "I would be a fool," said Sher Singh, "if I paid everyone from the district to the block level and did not make some money for myself.[50] It is not I but the administration that forces people to be dishonest [mackaari]. When I have to pay off so much money to those above me, how can I get anything done [without diverting funds]?"

Sher Singh's open admission clearly indicated the shifting contours of village power. Populist programs for redistribution of land, creation of jobs for the unemployed, and construction of houses for the poor and lowest castes had resulted in new opportunities for the large-scale diversion of funds. It was easy to understand why the rural upper classes had readily shifted their activities from patronage to brokerage: the "fees" to be collected as brokers for development programs were a surer, quicker, and often more substantial source of surplus than the straightforward expansion of their agricultural operations. The two activities were, in any case, not exclusive, and funds derived from one were, quite literally, plowed into the other.

The shift from patronage to brokerage helps explain why the fact of thakur dominance of Alipur should not be interpreted too literally. The steady progression of control from the zamindar to Sukhi Singh to his nephew Sher Singh perhaps conceals more than it reveals. Not only had the bases on which dominance rested shifted, but there had also been profound changes in the legitimacy and "naturalness" of class and caste privilege. Relations of production that hinged on the social ties between landlords and tenants had given way to a class of capitalist farmers and wage laborers. However, wage laborers did not become pure proletarians, divorced from all means of production. Populist policies in a competitive electoral system resulted in the distribution of small plots of marginal land to poor, lower-caste, and landless groups. Politically, the redistribution of these small plots was significant. It bound lower-caste and poor people into quasi-clientist relations with the rural upper classes, as they were dependent on these upper classes for all the means that were necessary to make plots agriculturally viable, especially for irrigation water and tractors or bullocks for plowing.[51]

If poor and lower-caste people were bound to the wealthy for inputs crucial to farming, however, upper-class leaders were also dependent on lower-class, lower-caste people for their own positions. Sher Singh explicitly acknowledged what was common wisdom: that the profits to be made from the delivery of development services had become the chief source of surpluses for village leaders. But, apart from serving as a source of revenue, such a dependence also implied a commitment to the ideologies of caste and class equality, because that was the rhetoric with which these programs were justified.[52] This process was clearly visible in the state and central elections that were held in 1984, when several of the village elites went to work for their candidates. A thakur who was especially preoccupied with his caste status told me that the most distasteful thing about campaigning was that when he accompanied his candidate to lower-caste sections of villages, people would be standing in front of their houses with cups of tea. To demonstrate their sincerity, the canvassers would have to take a sip and thus publicly "humiliate" themselves for the sake of votes. That this man should have continued to court lower-caste voters, despite feeling quite intensely about food pollution, said a great deal about the importance of electoral politics and, by extension, of the competition for the "rewards" of public office.

Because funds for development programs were limited, it resulted in intense upper-class rivalry for the support of lower-class and lower-caste followers. This was clear in the struggle between Prasad and Sher Singh for the position of headman.

Programs aimed at lower-caste and poor people, integral to the project of developing a modern nation, were intended to achieve economic and social development. These programs accompanied the state-sponsored stimulus given to agrarian capitalism by the introduction of new agricultural technologies and subsidies that helped launch the green revolution in north India. Next, I will draw out some of the larger implications of the articulation of new agricultural technologies and state development programs in local politics.

Conclusion

In the previous chapter I demonstrated the importance of the green revolution and agrarian populism in the development strategies of the postcolonial state. In this chapter I have tried to show how the nationalist project of developing a modern agricultural sector intersected with populist policies to shape local politics and the everyday lives of people in one northern Indian village. The boost given to resource-intensive, capitalist agriculture by state policies resulted in a sharper cleavage between landowners and laborers. Landowners in Alipur who were net hirers of labor always complained that wage rates were rising much faster than the cost of other goods and commodities; laborers grumbled that wages were inadequate and that it was difficult to sustain, feed, and clothe their families at prevailing wage rates. On the other hand, state policies had also resulted in the redistribution of marginal land to the landless, so that "almost everyone" in Alipur had some small quantity of land (Wadley 1994:71, 213). This had the effect of weakening class antagonisms not only because it promoted relations of quasi-clientism, as stated above, but also because the owners of these small plots gained a stake in the subsidies that sustained the green revolution. Input subsidies for fertilizer, the electricity that powered tube wells, and seed benefited marginal farmers as well as big ones. Therefore, antistate farmers movements to preserve these subsidies, like that launched by the Kisan Union, had the potential to incorporate small and marginal farmers in addition to the surplus-producing peasant.

Lower-caste people also benefited from development programs that sought to bring "development" to them, such as those that aimed at providing housing, education, child care, production loans, and so on. These programs were important not only for the material benefits they delivered but perhaps even more for the changes they brought about in caste ideologies and opportunities for social mobility. Ram Singh, the lower-caste man who was defeated by Sher Singh in the election for headman, was reflecting on the changes that he had witnessed during his own lifetime. He felt that his grandchildren had much better prospects than he did as a child. There were schools in every village, whereas in his time, few people had their children educated. "In my days, there were barriers, people used to create difficulties for [lower-caste] children. Now, whatever they might feel inside, they don't say anything. When I was young, we [lower-caste children] could only study up to the first or second class. Those old things are now finished. They used to be extra strict with our children, so that discouraged them from studying. They didn't want our children to study. Now, whatever they may feel inside [*payt may jo bhi ho*], all children go to school."

But Ram Singh also maintained that children of his caste had not been able to take advantage of government schemes set up to encourage them to be educated because the money that was allocated for that purpose was "eaten up" by upper-caste groups who controlled the educational system. Thus, at the same time that Ram Singh attributed better opportunities to the government, he also criticized it for its inability to implement its programs effectively.

This criticism has to be seen in the light of the role that development has played in legitimizing postcolonial regimes. Discourses of development have been central to the postcolonial Indian state as part of larger strategies of decolonization and as a central strategy for building a modern nation. Colonialism was held responsible for the poverty of the country, that is, for its lack of development. Development programs, then, were mechanisms not only to bring economic and social progress but also to establish that national independence marked a complete break with colonialism and to launch the nation firmly on the path to modernity. Ram Singh delivered an eloquent critique of these premises:

> Whatever government schemes have been started to finish caste-ism [*choot-achoot*], it has been increasing rather than weakening. Casteism is increasing, not decreasing. People haven't been able to eliminate what is nested in their minds. Our [here Ram Singh was referring to the lower castes] people build these wonderful homes for the higher castes, but when the house is complete and the

hearth is laid, then we can't go into the house—isn't this casteism? This sort of casteism [*jaativaad*] is very difficult to remove. This country will be completely independent only when casteism is terminated.

Ram Singh's questioning of the country's independence clearly brought into doubt the claims to postcoloniality made by the state through its association with development.

Nationalist efforts to build a postcolonial nation-state tied economic development to social and cultural "progress" by holding colonialism responsible for poverty and "social evils" such as untouchability. Efforts to initiate "development," therefore, were seen as ushering in an epoch in which the national society would gradually be rid of invidious distinctions based on caste and creed. This phenomenon, which can be termed "developmentalism," became the hegemonic state ideology because it was successfully incorporated into programs and institutions, as demonstrated in the discussion of agrarian populism in the previous chapter. But efforts to promote economic development through productivity-enhancing technologies such as the green revolution often worked at cross-purposes with attempts to bring "development" to the poor and lower castes. In this chapter I have tried to show the complex interconnections between state sponsorship of the new technology of agricultural production, which worked to exacerbate class divisions, and populist programs that sought to reduce those divisions. A close analysis of their articulation in the context of one village helps explain why certain ideologies of development have proved so successful, as well as why challenges to this discourse of postcoloniality continue to be mounted. The next chapter holds up practices of agriculture to a more finely grained analysis, highlighting other contestations of development and differing characterizations of the postcolonial condition.

3

"Indigenous" Knowledges: Agronomy

uring my first spell of fieldwork in Alipur in 1984–85, a great
proportion of my time was spent conducting a socioeconomic
survey of agricultural production, covering the entire village in
two rounds of detailed interviews. During the course of administering
this intricate survey about farming practices, I noticed that there was a
yawning gulf between the technoscientific language of the survey form,
which had been adapted from similar surveys used by economists, and
the idiom in which the villagers of Alipur represented their own farming
practices (Appadurai n.d.). To gain a better appreciation of the epistemologies and practices of farming, I conducted a series of detailed
interviews with people from different castes and classes.

It was a sweltering June day in 1985, almost at the end of my fieldwork. The thermometer had consistently stayed above one hundred
degrees Fahrenheit, for the previous two months. Even at 7 A.M., when I
left the farmhouse and headed to the settlement to do my work, the sun
already felt hot on the skin. It was a good time, however, to seek out
farmers for interviews because agricultural work was pretty much at a
standstill. To make full use of the little time that I had left, I interviewed
people in the afternoon, when no one that I wanted to interview was
likely to be busy. It was at such a time that I spoke with Suresh in the
coolness of my room. Suresh was a small farmer (profiled in greater
detail below) who was explaining to me why he had plowed the field in
which he had planted maize only four times. This was quite unusual, for
farmers in Alipur tried to plow a field six times or more in preparation
for sowing. Suresh justified his decision, however, in the following
terms: "Say we plow six or eight times. Then the soil will drink more
water. If it drinks water, heat will come out of the ground, which will

appear to make the sapling yellowish. Thus the plant keeps sitting down there instead of shooting upward. It doesn't run upward. It just sinks into the earth and remains there as a twig. Underneath, its roots rot from the heat [bhabhkaa]. If the field is plowed less, then it is profitable. Plowing many times automatically results in lower production."

Because maize was sown just before the monsoons, the logic of the explanation is as follows: The ground had hardened over the hot summer months. When it was plowed, the soil was loosened up. The more it was plowed, the more water-retentive the soil became. Then when the rains came, the soil steamed because the water came into contact with earth that had been steadily heated over the dry summer months. This steam destroyed the roots of the plant and provided an environment far too hot and humid for the plant to grow. The plant's development was smothered by an environment that lacked the proper balance between moistness and heat. A smaller number of plowings, by contrast, dug up the weeds, brought them to the surface to dry, and also loosened the hard crust of the soil, which made it more porous and thus allowed rainwater to drain. Paradoxically, this enabled a better balance to be reached between moisture and heat because it did not trap the rainwater as effectively as did a well-plowed field.

Like other farmers in Alipur, Suresh brought an "indigenously" developed knowledge of agronomy to bear on an agricultural practice conducted largely with chemical fertilizers, electric tube wells, and "scientifically" bred hybrid seeds. When farmers in Alipur talked about wheat varieties, the names Number 2204, Number 2009, RR21, Sona, Kisan, Wonderful, and K68 rolled off their tongues. Although hybrid varieties of other crops also existed and were used in the area, it was the high-yielding varieties of wheat that were most widely adopted. Not only were the varietals themselves the product of bioscience, but so too was the entire technology of production. It thus surprised me to learn that bioscientific terminology played a relatively minor role in the discourses of Alipur's farmers. Their vocabularies of agriculture bore little resemblance to the "scientific" discourse that had given birth to the technologies which they employed in farming. This is not to say that bioscientific terms and explanations were entirely absent in Alipur. They were incorporated in a variety of creative ways in the agronomical discourse of farmers. But "scientific" explanations made up only one portion of agricultural "talk" and agricultural practices. Most of what farmers had to say about agriculture was expressed in a different discourse comprised of a "humoral" agronomy. This was true both in

Children bathing near tube well

their conversations with one another and in the interviews I conducted with them.

Such alternative epistemologies of agriculture and natural resources have usually been called "indigenous knowledge" in the scholarly literature. In this chapter I explore what it might mean to characterize the agronomical terminology, knowledges, and practices of Alipur's farmers as "indigenous." How does one theorize a condition in which disparate epistemologies and practices coexist and interpenetrate with such disarming ease? The farmers of Alipur, aggressively utilizing hybrid seeds, biochemical inputs, tube well technology, and state institutions, hardly correspond to depictions of "the traditional farmer." At the same time, they are not "essentially the same" as farmers in the United States or Europe. Where, then, does the difference lie? What makes these "modern" farmers distinctive? More broadly, is there something that these farmers can teach us about the different modalities of experiencing modernity in the postcolonial world? Some of the answers have already been hinted at in the first two chapters. Here, I extend the insights into social and political location offered earlier by considering the epistemology of agronomy and the practice of farming.

A detailed consideration of knowledges of agronomy and the practices of farming raises several difficult theoretical questions that run through this chapter. One of the chief problems is representing the inventive and contentious use of disparate and incommensurable discourses of agriculture without "cleaning them up," that is, eliminating their messiness. Farmers in Alipur often used discourses regarding the health of plants, which relied on a theory about a proper balance of humors—that is, elements that were hot, cold, dry, and moist. The balance of humors depended on the constitution of a plant, which depended on its intrinsic properties but also on the properties of the soil, fertilizers, water, and wind with which it came into contact. All these inputs conveyed their properties to the plant, which in turn conveyed its properties to humans when ingested as food. As I demonstrate very clearly, however, humoral explanations were not the only ones employed by farmers. "Scientific" theories of agronomy were freely interspersed with humoral ones in debates about agricultural issues, and when one examined *practices,* the situation became even more complicated. Farmers' explanations of agricultural practices interwove references to the politics of caste, class, and gender with theories of agronomy. What was one to make of a situation in which the discourses of development promulgated by a modern nation-state and a substantivist theory of plant life intermingled with seeming effortlessness? Was there something specifically "postcolonial" about these unexpected intersections?

In this chapter I employ an analysis of the epistemologies and practices of agriculture to delineate the hybridities that characterize the postcolonial condition. In particular, problematizing indigenous knowledges of agronomy enables me to demonstrate how the binaries of modernity—colonial and national—are destabilized by postcoloniality. Alipur's farmers neither fit the mold of indigenous people who have been uncontaminated by modernity nor that of progressive farmers on the brink of entering the takeoff stage of capitalist development. As such, they render ambivalent narratives of progress and modernity embedded in postcolonial discourses of development. They participated enthusiastically in green revolution agriculture, yet much of the time they employed a discourse of farming that was quite strikingly at odds with a bioscientific understanding of agriculture. At the same time, humoral understandings of agronomy constituted only one part of explanations and justifications given for particular agricultural decisions. Practices of farming were explained in terms of the relationship between humoral explanations of agronomy, local politics, development projects and programs, and the politics of household and caste. The destabilizing implications of postcoloniality for the identity of subjects of a modern nation-state become especially clear through such a lens, as farmers in Alipur failed to conform to the developmentalist vision of the citizens of a modern nation. The necessarily condensed argument in this paragraph will become clearer as it is illustrated through the detailed empirical material that follows. Before doing that, however, I wish to explain why I have chosen to use the notion of humoral agronomy rather than indigenous knowledge to characterize farmers' discourses of agriculture.

My discomfort in labeling hybrid understandings of agriculture as indigenous led me to the more specific and delimited concept of humoral agronomy. But while it does result in greater precision and clarity, the notion of humoral agronomy does not eliminate some of the questions that haunt "the indigenous." A brief consideration of these questions must begin with the relationship between humoral theories of agronomy and Ayurveda, a classical Indian system of medicine.[1] In an influential book, Zimmermann (1987) has argued that a structural distinction between *jangala,* the dry, grassy, savanna-type lands, and *anupa,* the moist, unctuous, marshy lands, lies at the basis of Ayurvedic classifications of land, fauna, flora, and human health. This "ecological" theme is then shown to run through Hindu medicine as a system of oppositions that motivates the classification of flora and fauna, of diseases, of body types, and of treatment. While such an exercise, built on the close reading of three ancient texts that date from the beginning of the common era to the seventh century, is undoubtedly valuable, it begs the question of the relationship of a classificatory system adumbrated in a few "great" books with the activities of practitioners across the centuries. As Obeyesekere (1991) has pointed out in a perceptive review article, a virtuoso structuralism cannot bridge the gap between the text and the world, and to posit Ayurveda as a transhistorical system is to reassert precisely those Orientalist reifications that so much of contemporary critical theory has helped take apart. The problem I have in reading the traces of a great textual tradition in present practices is that no evidence is ever offered of the mechanisms that translated those texts into practices and then preserved the entire system or elements of it intact over centuries. If the duality between jangala and anupa animated the agronomical theories that I encountered in Alipur, for example, peasants certainly presented no evidence of it in their discussions and practices.

Even if one were to consider not the Ayurveda of the ancient Hindu texts but the syncretic, hybrid version that is the legacy of the nineteenth century, which "took over Western ideas of physiology and anatomy and translated them in Ayurvedic terms" (Obeyesekere 1991:423), how would a theory of medicine concerning the human body be translated to plant life? Clearly, there were parallels between the notion that the good health of plants consisted of the proper balance of heat and wetness and the Ayurvedic analysis of the body as a balance of "humors."[2] But if the tripartite division between *dosas, dhaatus,* and *malas* (usually translated as humors, tissue or substance, and excreta, respectively) is central to the Ayurvedic understanding of the human body, I found farmers in Alipur employing no parallel explanation in referring to the health of plants. The closest that knowledges of agronomy got to this threefold division was in its parallels to the concept of the three *dosas* (called *vaayu, pitta,* and *kapha,* which are loosely translated as wind, bile, and phlegm, respectively); but even here, there was no literal correspondence between these terms and ideas of "hotness" and "wetness" used to describe the health of plants.[3] Thus, the notion that the understanding of the health of plants was analogical to "indigenous" explanations of human health should not be taken too literally.

If peasant understandings and explanations of farming were not merely a "corrupted" form of Ayurveda, where did they originate? Was there a "system" of "indigenous" agronomy that, while impervious to its users, could nevertheless be reconstructed by the analyst? I take it as axiomatic that originary systems of agronomy are not recuperable from an examination of current practices and discourses. After a quarter of a century of scientific, green revolution agriculture and at least a century of "modern" farming spanning independence and colonial rule, "indigenous" agricultural practices and agronomical theories form an ever receding trace on the horizon of the knowable.[4] It is this elusive quality that I wish to index in using the term "humoral," not some originary system of meaning. In contrasting humoral agronomy with "green revolution bioscience," I intend not as much to oppose "indigenous" knowledges to "scientific" ones but to pose existing, hybridized understandings of agriculture, themselves the outcome of multiple genealogies, against one, specific mode of agricultural practice, whose origin can be traced to the particular conditions of corporate agriculture in the United States in the twentieth century.

In this chapter, instead of searching for the Holy Grail of an indigenous system of agronomy, I have paid close attention to the practices and discourses of farmers in Alipur. In so doing, I have identified two features of farming that are often missed in structuralist analyses and in reconstructions of "indigenous knowledge." The first feature is the inescapable fact that agricultural understandings and practices are composed of disjunctive and incommensurably hybrid discourses, which I trace to the particular condition of postcolonial modernity. Second, discourses of agriculture are not a closed field of meaning and action but are profoundly shaped by the politics of caste, class, and gender differentiation. Using the analytic frame of postcolonial theory allows me to describe a very different practice of agriculture than has heretofore been the case.

The material in this chapter draws on the surveys, my observations of farming and village life, and detailed interviews conducted during three rounds of fieldwork. My objective was to explore systematically what I had heard regarding knowledges of agronomy. For the purposes of exposition, I will concentrate on the affairs of three farmers whom I got to know quite well.

I first met Suresh, the poorest of the three, a short, forty-two-year-old brahmin man with close-cropped hair and mischievous gray eyes, soon after I reached Alipur. He lived in a large cattle shed [*gher*] on the northern edge of the village. The oldest of his four children was a seventeen-year-old son, another son and a daughter were in their early teens, and there was a young girl of nine. Suresh was one of the few people in his generation to have obtained a formal education beyond high school. In one of the two little rooms in which his family lived, Suresh carefully preserved a picture that showed him among the graduating class at the technical institute, where he had trained to be a welder. He claimed to have moved back to the village, sacrificing a potentially financially rewarding career, because his presence was needed to manage the family farm. He had no regrets about his decision because he had heard that many welders eventually went blind at an early age; he felt that no amount of money could possibly compensate for the gift of sight given to us by God.

Due to conflicts with his uncles, Suresh and his family had moved from their ancestral home in the center of the brahmin part of the village to their family's cattle shed, a large yard with high brick walls. There, in three small huts built in different corners around a huge neem [*Azadirachta indica*] tree in the center, lived the six family members with their six animals. The two cows old enough to give milk were, however, too emaciated to supply much. The family relied for their livelihood on income from their two-acre farm and Suresh's activities as the village priest. In the kharif harvest, or monsoon harvest, in 1984, Suresh had planted maize on one-third of an acre; bajra, or pearl millet, on about an acre; and jowar (a variety of barley) for fodder on the rest. The total yield was 200 kg of maize and 600 kg of pearl millet or, if one assumes a four-month growing season, about 1.1 kg/day for each member of the family. But because 200 kg of millet was sold, the grain left for consumption was reduced to less than 1 kg/person/day.

In the rabi harvest, or winter harvest, they had grown three crops—a new variety of wheat, Number 2204, on just less than an acre; mustard on two-thirds of an acre; and barley on the remaining third. (This was considered the main harvest, and the yields were much higher.) The 1000 kg of wheat, 240 kg of mustard, and 280 kg of barley that were produced would have to feed the family up to at least late the next fall, when the monsoon crop would be harvested. Most of this harvest—all the mustard and barley and half the wheat—was sold to raise cash. The family's need for cash was more pressing than usual because loans incurred at the marriage of the older daughter needed to be paid back. Suresh even planted a mung crop on two-thirds of an acre that summer, but lack of water and a dearth of inputs resulted in a feeble yield.

The fact that Suresh managed to sustain a good reputation in a strife-torn little village such as Alipur was a testament to his tact and somewhat detached demeanor.[5] Of course, these qualities were also the result of economic necessity and political exigency. He had to stay above the hurly-burly of village politics and maintain good relations with all, especially the wealthy thakurs and jats, because the village was not large enough for him to earn a decent income from serving as priest for just one faction. At the same time, the marginality of his position as landowner and political actor was less likely to place him in structurally antagonistic relations with others. He had to speak carefully and (seem to) listen sympathetically to all groups. Appearing detached from worldly matters also conveniently played into Hindu notions of spiritual purity, an image that Suresh consciously aspired to cultivate. He did not farm, he claimed, because contact with the soil was contaminating and below the status of a true brahmin and because he wanted to keep himself away from worldly concerns.[6] Therefore, he left all the actual work to his sons and was content to supervise them. He spent most of his time reading the spiritual books that he ordered in the mail.

Suresh was one of the two people I was closest to during the time that I spent in Alipur. His religious training inclined him toward explanations framed in the "great tradition" of Hinduism, and his wish to impress me perhaps led him to frame things in "modern, scientific" terms.[7]

This led to some interesting contradictions that Suresh bridged rather creatively. At the same time, he tended to evaluate village practices negatively—that is, as "undeveloped" and therefore inferior.

The second example intensively employed in this chapter—that of Sompal Singh—converges in some regards with Suresh's situation but is different as well. As a thakur, Sompal was politically in the opposite camp and, for the most part, allied himself with the thakurs, "crossing over" mostly to go and talk to Suresh. Yet, he was friendly with at least one brahmin household and was on speaking terms with others (unlike, for example, the headman Sher Singh, who had no contact with most brahmin families). As in the case of Suresh, Sompal's ability to cross over was due to the combination of Sompal's tact and lack of political and economic muscle.[8] Although not poor by village standards, Sompal was one of the smaller landholders among the thakurs, owning just over four acres of relatively low-quality land near the village's western boundary. He did not own a tube well and was therefore dependent on Sher Singh (also a thakur) for irrigation water.

Sompal preferred to rent out his own property and earn his living doing odd jobs.[9] He was very skillful in working with his hands, especially with mechanical equipment. Toward the end of my fieldwork in Alipur, Sompal was steadily employed at a state farm, being paid to do maintenance and installation work on the farm's new tube well. But his continued employment was jeopardized by the impending transfer of the manager who had become his good friend. It seemed likely that, as in the past, his family, consisting of his wife and four young children, would have to subsist on rent from their land and income from occasional employment. Because Sompal's family lacked their own source of fodder, they could not even afford to sell milk by keeping buffalo and cows.[10]

The monsoon and winter harvests of 1984–85 saw Sompal take up farming for perhaps the first time after he had broken away from his father's household. But he did not farm his own land—that was rented out as usual. His father temporarily gave him ten bighas (approximately one and two-thirds acres) from his own plot on very favorable fixed terms. In the kharif harvest, Sompal planted four different crops on this land—maize on two-thirds of an acre, lentils on half an acre, oilseeds on a quarter of an acre, and fodder on another quarter of an acre. Lentils and fodder were grown for sale in the market, whereas maize and oilseeds [lahai] were meant for domestic consumption. Sompal's inexperience was evident from the poor returns. The maize crop yielded an abysmal eighty kilograms or one-half man per bigha, which Sompal claimed resulted from improper sowing techniques.[11] The same thing happened with the lentils, which were sown too close together; as a consequence, the lentil crop yielded a lot of wood but very little marketable output. The jowar, intended to be sold as a standing green fodder, found no purchasers because, according to Sompal, no one wanted to come daily into his father's property (which they would need to do to harvest it).

During the rabi harvest, Sompal planted barley after clearing the maize plot, wheat on about half an acre, and a fodder called *jai* (oats) on a quarter of an acre. He took a gamble by setting aside the rest—a quarter of an acre—for sugarcane. Because sugarcane takes approximately nine months to mature, he had hoped his father would allow him to keep the land for another year. But his father understood the ploy and refused to extend the lease. Since it was too late to plant anything else, Sompal then had no choice but to leave the area fallow. The yields from the rabi crop were also considerably short of spectacular. All of the barley and most of the wheat had to be paid as rent. Goats ate the fodder while it was still green. That left a net return of just 250 kilograms of wheat, which was not much for all the effort that had been required to farm.

During my first round of fieldwork, I did not get to know Sompal well until he started working regularly on the state farm on which I happened to live. On subsequent visits, I came to know his whole family much better. At thirty-three, he was just a few years older than I was in 1984, and we instinctively hit it off. What struck me about Sompal was his ability at—I might even say expertise in—negotiating his way through the maze of village politics. He had mastered the art of ambiguity, agreeing without commitment, if the situation so required, to convey his disagreement and, on the appropriate occasions, disagreeing without sincerity to indicate his actual agreement. On the surface, no one could fault him for saying the wrong things or acting improperly. And yet, paradoxical as it may seem, he was amazingly sincere. He let you know exactly how he felt without ever stating it explicitly. Sompal had mastered the fine art of representing intention. He showed very clearly that in the interpretation of experience, the equivocal qualities of interpretation could also be utilized, although perhaps not equally, by those peripherally placed in the loci of power.

Approximately twenty, Dhani Singh, the youngest of the three people whose voice informs this chapter, was the middle child of a jat family who had moved into the village within the last five years. They bought a substantial package of land, approximately seven acres split almost equally in two segments, just across the road on the eastern side of the village. In addition, in the year 1984–85, they had rented in two plots totaling three acres adjacent to their own. Although quite well off, Dhani Singh's family had been in a fair deal of trouble since they moved to Alipur.[12] Dhani Singh's elder brother was involved in at least two incidents that resulted in the village council subjecting him to the ultimate humiliation: being publicly beaten with a slipper by a woman. Toward the end of my stay, both the elder and the younger brother were, on separate occasions, hauled off to jail. The elder brother was a suspect in the theft of a tube well pump, and the younger brother had been caught redhanded trying to pick the pocket of a fellow villager.

After his brother broke away from the family to manage his own share of the property independently, Dhani Singh assumed the main responsibility for the household farm. His father was too old and feeble to be of much help, and his younger brother preferred to spend his time in town.[13] In the kharif harvest, they planted several crops in each of the four fragments, adding up to a total of nine separate plots. Half of all the land, owned as well as rented, was planted with maize. The rest was taken up by various kinds of fodder—pearl millet, jowar, and *gwal*. Like other farmers, Dhani Singh used almost no fertilizer or irrigation water during the kharif harvest.[14] The yields, although better than those of either Sompal or Suresh, were not very good (maize on all his plots yielded an average of 2.4 mans/bigha, approximately the villagewide average). Although the rented land required only a payment in kind at the end of the year, Dhani Singh agreed to a request from the owner to supply about 280 kilograms of maize and 80 kilograms of wheat immediately after the kharif harvest. This quantity would be deducted from the total owed, and the lower price of maize as compared with wheat made it profitable to supply as much maize as possible.

The rabi harvest saw Dhani Singh adopting a very unusual strategy in planting wheat on all the land, both rented and owned. What was even more surprising was that most of the wheat he planted was the traditional, or *desi*, variety. In 1984, practically no one else in the village sowed traditional wheat anymore.[15] When I asked him why he chose to plant desi wheat instead of one of the new high-yielding varieties, he told me that the seed was the only type they had at home at the time, adding, with some pride, "We have not bought seed to this day." The yields on each plot were predictably poor, ranging from a low of 2.5

mans/bigha to a high of about 4.0 mans/bigha. The "better" farmers, by comparison, achieved yields of 7 to 9 mans/bigha. Dhani Singh explained the poor yields by pointing out that he had been delayed in planting and harvesting the previous crop, that he lacked the resources to fertilize the land adequately, and that he could not supply enough water to the crop.

Dhani Singh was not considered particularly intelligent by other people in the village. In fact, when I was attempting to set up an interview with him, a man of his own caste who prided himself on his farming skills asked me why I wanted to waste my time talking to someone who knew so little about agriculture. Several people told me that he had taken on more land than he could possibly handle and might have been better off trying to give adequate inputs to the land that he did own. Dhani Singh agreed with them, claiming that his family would not even recover the amount of grain that they owed for the lease. When the landlord had come begging to him to lease the land, he had flatly refused, but his father consented behind his back. The result was that they could not afford the inputs that were necessary to get a good output and hence their entire crop would suffer.

Dhani Singh was not the best of respondents. Unlike other farmers that I interviewed, Dhani Singh seemed unsure of his own agricultural activities. It did not help that he was not terribly articulate and often could not explain what he meant. But he was always very friendly and often spent time gossiping with me, usually along with some other young men who did most of the talking. By the time I interviewed him, I had known him for a fairly long time; yet, I thought he appeared by turns uncertain and tentative and, as usual, reticent.

Before turning to a detailed examination of the agricultural practices of the three farmers whose profiles are sketched above, I wish to articulate explicitly some of the theoretical problems surrounding the notion of "indigeneity." In the next section I attempt to position "the indigenous" by considering the genealogy and politics of this term. What is the difference between the discussion of "indigenousness" in the last two decades and the role that indigenousness played in colonial and nationalist discourses? What are the continuities between colonial and developmentalist uses of "the indigenous"? In the section that follows, I show that the relationship between "the modern" and "the indigenous" is intimately connected to the modern/tradition dichotomy. The bulk of this chapter, however, is devoted to a close examination of "indigenous" knowledges of agronomy in Alipur. Although the theories of agronomy used by farmers in Alipur depend heavily on a humoral logic, a consideration of agricultural practices shows that they are not simply the outcome of "indigenous" theory. I then show how a discussion of agronomy becomes even more complicated by considering the political context of agricultural practices. Finally, I attempt to delineate how "the indigenous" has been conceptualized in postcolonial theory and what insights such theories have to offer when analyzing agriculture in Alipur.

Politics of "the Indigenous"

The past decade has witnessed an explosion of interest, scholarly as well as popular, in "the indigenous." Indigenous peoples, indigenous knowledges, indigenous medical practices, and indigenous flora and fauna are the subjects of flourishing discourses among academics, aid agencies, environmentalists, entrepreneurs, biologists, multinational corporations, new-age spiritualists, and the medical establishment (and this is, no doubt, a partial list). Discourses of indigenousness are everywhere these days, yet the term seems to be employed in an extraordinarily loose way to refer to a large variety of phenomena in different locations. Instead of clearing away the confusions that surround the term, so as to reveal its "true" meaning, I will ask what enables the indigenous to represent such a disparate range of referents. In other words, why does "indigenousness" prove to be such a productive signifier? What makes it possible for a diverse range of objects and phenomena to be brought together under the label "indigenous"? What does it mean to speak of the indigenous after centuries of colonial rule and a much longer history of global exchange? Why have discourses on the indigenous flourished in the last two decades, at the very moment that global capitalism has entered a renewed phase of expansion and legitimacy? At the same time that I recognize its utility and support its deployment in conjunctural political projects initiated by and on behalf of disempowered and marginal groups, I wish to evaluate critically the recruitment of the indigenous as a theoretical construct.

What could the notion of "indigenousness" possibly mean in the postcolonial, late-capitalist world, with the increased velocity of the circulation of commodities, services, finances, ideas, and images and its accompanying effect of time-space compression?[16] Although I do not explicitly pursue this question, it lies in the background in much of what follows as I pursue the task of relocating the indigenous through the thickets of nationalist and postcolonial theory. My intent is to chart the role played by the idea of "indigenousness" in colonial and national-ist discourses in India to understand why it continues to be so impor-tant in the postcolonial world. Perhaps more important for my purposes is to ask *how* ideas of indigenousness find their way into postcolonial theory and what the difference is between postcolonial representations of the indigenous and those found in colonialist and nationalist theories in India.

In this section I demonstrate the degree to which supposedly archaic attitudes to "the indigenous" suffuse present development practice. In so doing, I do not wish to imply that attitudes to the indigenous in development projects merely act to sustain colonialism by other means. There are several reasons for not equating dispositions to the indige-nous in "development" and colonialism, not least that nationalism itself shares much with colonial positions toward the indigenous. It is diffi-cult to explain why the indigenous has found such a receptive audience among national and transnational elites without tracing its connections to the role occupied by "native tradition" in colonial and nationalist imaginings.

Another way to frame this problem is to pose the question of the relation between indigenous knowledges and the contemporary, late-capitalist world. It seems paradoxical that the surge of interest in the indigenous in the last two decades has accompanied the geographic expansion and restructuring of capitalist processes so that marginal groups in "isolated" areas are increasingly drawn into the circuits of capitalist production and consumption. This has happened in a variety of ways: through tourism, particularly ecotourism and "ethnic" tourism; through the continued search for raw materials such as timber, pe-troleum, and minerals; through the efforts to locate new gene plasms for agriculture, pesticides, and insecticides as environmental pressures mount on chemical agriculture; through the search for new raw mate-rials for medicines by transnational drug companies; and through the encouragement given by Third World governments to various segments of the population to colonize the "low-density frontiers" of the nation. I do not for a moment wish to conflate what are in fact very different phenomena—a great deal separates "eco-marketing" from petroleum extraction, and it would be a mistake to suggest that the two phe-nomena have similar effects on the environment or on indigenous peo-ple. Although I do not pursue the relationship between capitalist expan-sion and the explosion of interest in the indigenous in what follows, I do wish to juxtapose those issues so as to stimulate some speculation about their relationship. Let me anticipate the argument of this chapter and suggest that for a wide variety of reasons, ranging from the struggles launched by indigenous people worldwide to imperialist nostalgia (Rosaldo 1989), there is a recognition in globally hegemonic discourses that capitalist expansion has indeed had a deleterious effect on indigenous people and indigenous culture. The growth of industries that reach more and more remote locations, therefore, is accompanied by renewed rounds of romanticizing and celebrating those who are found there— "indigenous" people and their cultures. Thus, at the very moment when the basis of their livelihood is being undermined and their way of life destroyed, "indigenous" people are being celebrated for their knowledge of the forest, their concern for the environment, and their "philosophy" of life. Such a recognition clearly enables certain kinds of resistance to be mounted, and this recognition has been used very effectively by some groups who have employed their "exotic" status to forge a measure of self-determination. But one needs to ask why resistance to processes of colonization and extraction are seen primarily in terms of "indigenousness." Of all the identities held by people who are subject to these processes, why is indigenous identity the one most privileged in analytic description and political recognition?

One would not have to be excessively paranoid or cynical to conceptualize this kind of recognition as yet another effort at domestication, as rich consumers in the West gulp down another container of Ben and Jerry's Rainforest Crunch ice cream or pay high prices for small (plastic) bottles of beauty products at The Body Shop, all in the name of the "indigenous people" who inhabit the rain forests.[17] Needless to say, paranoia or cynicism, even in moderate doses, hardly constitutes an adequate response. Ideas about incorporation or domestication do not acknowledge the destabilizing possibilities inherent in oppositional positions like that occupied by "the indigenous." It is precisely the ambivalence of the indigenous that I wish to explore more fully in this chapter.

In the next section, I sketch the role played by the notion of "the indigenous" in nationalist and colonial discourses in India. I will then show how these attitudes to the indigenous, far from being a distant memory, are redeployed in currently popular approaches to development.

Colonial and nationalist recuperations of "the indigenous"

To understand precisely what kind of oppositional space is occupied by "the indigenous" and how this space differs from colonial and nationalist discourses on "native traditions," I will outline an argument about the relationship between "the indigenous," colonialism, and nationalism in India. My purpose here is not to offer a historical trajectory but to bring into sharp relief *some* features of the relationship between colonial and nationalist views of "the indigenous," on the one hand, and postcolonial views, on the other. My concern is to highlight certain key elements of a larger narrative, at the risk of forsaking historical subtlety for what is no more than a schematic outline.

Let us begin with the observation that nationalism depends on the reversal, not the disavowal, of many binaries that are central to colonialism (Prakash 1992a:8). Thus, as demonstrated in Chapter 1, nationalist leaders shared colonial views of "progress," institutionalizing these ideas in the postindependence period through the notion of planned development (compare Ludden 1992; Chandra 1991). These ideas of progress and development had several features in common: a belief in historicity, a teleological narrative, and, combining the two, the notion that history charts the development of "man" in a unidirectional, if not necessarily linear, trajectory. Colonial and nationalist history differed in who was considered the Subject of history, the colonizer who was the agent of civilization or the native who was its forgotten heir. And the two versions differed as well in that the telos of nationalist history was the attainment of independence, whereas that could scarcely be the desired goal of colonial historiography.[18]

The reversal of colonial binaries was to be found in attitudes toward "the indigenous" as well. Here the situation is complicated by the fact that colonial attitudes toward the indigenous were themselves highly polarized. On one side were the Orientalists, who believed that indigenous traditions once possessed world-historical importance but that these great traditions had been lost, forgotten, or simply distorted by the passage of time. This was a way of viewing the world in which time and the "natives" were seen as sources of entropy, in which the greatness of Indian civilization lay in the dim recesses of the past.[19] In short, indigenous culture was worthwhile only to the extent that it was a museum artifact. The greatness of the Indian past had to be resurrected, but only in the manner that one reconstructs a civilization in a cultural museum. This attitude to history is by no means limited to colonialism and can still be found articulated in a number of academic and particularly in nonacademic contexts, in which an emphasis on ancient texts, high culture, great monuments, and the literary, religious, and artistic canon reinscribes a museum-like view of Indian civilization, whose shabby present state is implicitly compared with an enviable golden age. Such a treatment of "indigenous" society is closely linked to the spirit of "salvage ethnography" in that the emphasis lies in saving what survives of the past before it decays and disappears. Posey et al.'s (1984) call for saving what is left of aboriginal culture arises, at least in part, from the rapid decline of indigenous populations in Amazonia, but the same argument is also made because "cultures" and "societies" are threatened by "extinction" through assimilation (Rosaldo 1988).

However problematic the Orientalists' position, they actually constituted the liberal group, that segment of colonizers most sympathetic to the natives. On the other side stood colonial modernizers or Anglicists who regarded native civilization with disdain. This is the position made infamous by Macaulay's minute on education. Referring to the Orientalists, Macaulay wrote, "I have never found one among them who could deny that a single shelf of a good European library was worth the whole native literature of India and Arabia" (1952:722).[20] Colonial modernizers saw progress, civilization, industry, justice, and order as flowing from colonial rule, and they regarded the demand for independence with great apprehension. After the Great Revolt of 1857, they argued for the abandonment of liberal reform in favor of an unapologetic policy of rule by conquest (Metcalf 1964; Chatterjee 1993:14–34).

If Orientalists and modernizers shared anything, it was a disdain for that hybrid described by Homi Bhabha (1984:132) with the formula, "not quite/not white." This was the middle class, from which the leaders of the nationalist movement were drawn: too brown to be English, and too westernized to be "authentic" natives. And it was precisely this group that seized on Orientalist narratives about a golden past but altered its telling. The fact that India had been a great civilization was proof enough that there was nothing *inherently* second-rate or inadequate about Indians. If the India that they lived in had fallen on hard times and failed to live up to its ancient glory, it was not due to innate flaws in "the Indian character" but the historical fact of colonialism itself (Chakravarti 1989:32). It was colonial conquest that had drained India's wealth, rendered its people submissive, and robbed it of "its spirit." Accordingly, with the attainment of independence, the country would once again be able to ascend to its previous glory. It was colonialism, therefore, that was responsible for the decay in Indian civilization. Such a position, of course, fully participated in colonial discourses but inverted its judgments.

It was not only in references to a golden past that nationalist attitudes to the indigenous mirrored colonial discourse. The contrast between Orientalist and modernizing positions was incorporated as an agonistic splitting *within* nationalist discourses, so that diametrically opposed positions were found to cohabit uneasily within them. Thus, on the one hand, one finds the glorification of indigenous systems of knowledge, social organization, and aesthetic forms, often identified with the past but sorely in need of resurrection. Gandhi's construction of India as formed of "self-sufficient village communities" is a good example of nationalist appropriations of Orientalist conceptions of "village republics" (Dewey 1972; Brow 1992). On the other hand, these discourses display the reformist urge to change traditional practices, to eradicate superstition, "backwardness," "stagnation," and invidious distinctions based on caste, class, region, religion, and language (Chakravarti 1989:32–34).[21] Once again, we can see Gandhi's lifelong struggles for the "upliftment of untouchables" as part of an effort to alter tradition to render it "appropriate" for the contemporary world.

For middle-class nationalists, tribal peoples represented another basis of indigenousness. Tribal groups, after all, had an originary relationship to the land that anteceded even so-called Aryan arrival myths. The more nationalism employed temporal depth as a legitimating charter through its equation with a glorious past, the more problematic became the status of first peoples who preceded that "glorious past." Here I wish to borrow an argument from Trouillot (1991), who has demonstrated that the Renaissance built a triadic relationship between the savage, utopia, and conceptions of order.[22] "The West" was constructed as an ordered state by juxtaposing it to a Janus-faced Other, whose one side was the West itself in the form of a utopian projection and whose other face was a state of nature in the form of the savage. This "savage slot," far from being a creation of ethnography, was the precondition for its existence, the structural space which made possible the "discoveries" of anthropologists and which allowed a discourse on savages to be created and to be received.[23] Following Partha Chatterjee (1986), one could argue that the thematic of nationalism implied a similar positioning of a utopian past in contradistinction to a savage slot. Tribal peoples occupied the "savage slot" of nationalist thought, simultaneously as noble savages, simple and primitive, and as "scheduled tribes" most in need of "upliftment" because of their lack of agricultural, financial, and educational resources.[24]

As the "modern" industrializing state has developed, the tensions inherent in these polar attitudes have only increased. Thus, a utopian view of the savage is recovered by critiques of modernity articulated by environmentalists, nature religionists, spiritualists, and those interested in alternative medicine (see, for example, Sen 1992; Chaudhury 1991). At the same time, "modernizing" views of tribal peoples are espoused by bureaucrats and nongovernmental organizations interested in tribal "development," industrialists keen to exploit the raw materials on tribal land, and some "pro-development" politicians.

The discourse of indigeneity, therefore, is unstable in that it sometimes refers to the "high traditions" valued by Orientalists and nationalists but equally to the beliefs and practices of "first peoples." For example, discussions of indigenous systems of medicine in South Asia regularly include Ayurveda, whose origin in the Vedas locates it unambiguously in a nationalist construction of "high culture." On the other hand, indigenous systems of medicine can also include the use of wildflowers, roots, and berries among tribal groups, which may bear little or no relation to "high culture." While it could be maintained that these are merely two different *kinds* of indigenous traditions, one would then be placing side by side two bodies of practices that are in fact hierarchically ordered in contemporary South Asia. The only reason for placing them in the same category is that they are both non-Western "systems" of medicine. They both occupy a residual space defined by the absence of "modern," that is, "Western," medicine. So it is important to keep in mind that the term "indigenous" has many different referents, even within the "same" cultural context. To speak of "the indigenous" as a unitary category is to overlook its internally hierarchical and heterogeneous character.

The hetereogeneity of "the indigenous" is also visible in developmentalist discourse. In this discourse, however, some of the tension implicit in a "high tradition" versus "first peoples" view of indigeneity is sidestepped by the single-minded concentration on "indigenous peoples," who, by definition, occupy the margin of the nation-state system.

"The indigenous" in development discourse

The extent to which "indigenous knowledge" has become a key phrase in transnational ecological, agronomic, and development discourses can be gauged from the fact that it has been elevated to the status of an acronym (IK), which is also used as the logo of a publication, the *Indigenous Knowledge and Development Monitor*. For the most part, the indigenous knowledge movement has been led by a small group of international development advisers working in collaboration with national scientific experts and bureaucrats, consulting for agencies such as the United States Agency for International Development (USAID), the World Bank, and the Canadian International Development Agency (CIDA) and sometimes for nongovernmental organizations (NGOs). Information about "indigenous knowledges" occasionally comes from ethnographic immersion but, more often, from rapid-assessment surveys. "Natives" serve as informants and sometimes collaborate in eliciting data; significantly, they are rarely the "experts" who compile, systematize, and store the data in retrievable form.[25] This is not to suggest or imply that "indigenous peoples" or their leaders do not support this endeavor. All I wish to emphasize is that there is a division of labor that is rarely commented on in the literature on indigenous knowledge.

Reporting on the International Symposium on Indigenous Knowledge and Sustainable Development held in Silang, Philippines, in September 1992, the *Indigenous Knowledge and Development Monitor* recounted the difficulties of defining the two main concerns of the conference, "indigenous knowledge" and "sustainable development." The participants agreed to use the Brundtland Commission's definition of "sustainable development" but were less successful in forging a common understanding of "indigenous knowledge."

> Participants decided that it was easier to define what does *not* fall under this category and agreed on the following working definition formulated by Michael Warren: "The term 'indigenous knowledge' (IK) is used synonymously with 'traditional' and 'local knowledge' to differentiate the knowledge developed by a given community from the international knowledge system, sometimes also called the 'Western' system, generated through universities, governmentalist research centres and private industry. IK refers to the knowledge of indigenous peoples as well as any other defined community." (Mathias-Mundy 1993a:3–4; emphasis in original)

I propose to read the ease of defining "indigenous knowledge" by *negation* as symptomatic of its status as a residual category, where everything that is not part of the Western, international knowledge system is inserted. In fact, an effort to describe what "indigenous knowledges" are, rather than what they are *not*, throws together elements from different epistemological and ideological orientations into a haphazard mixture.

Negation is often a powerful political tool, one that has been quite effectively employed by marginalized groups and NGOs, for example, to resist the intrusions of the state and of international development agencies. The status of "indigenous knowledge" is much more ambivalent, however, because it has chiefly been used to create a space for alternative strategies of "development" within those international agencies. It is taken as a truism that knowledge is "indigenous" if it is possessed by, or resides in, a "community." But what is a community? That turns out to be a troubling and unproblematized concept, one built on implicit assumptions of small-scale, localized, face-to-face, bounded, homogeneous, and egalitarian societies.

Although indigenous knowledge is identified as "the knowledge of indigenous peoples as well as any other defined community," the relatively well-defined "community" of scientists is quite explicitly excluded. "Community" here means something quite specific (perhaps anthropologically self-evident?), as the various synonyms used for "indigenous knowledge" indicate. Sometimes indigenous knowledge is equated with "folk beliefs" (Brokensha and Riley 1980:115),[26] and at other points, with specificity and "the local." In an article arguing for the complementarity of "indigenous agriculture" to the research of international crop research institutes, Pablo Eyzaguirre states:

> Indigenous technical knowledge is a body of information applied to the management of natural resources and labor within very *specific* plots. Farmers' knowledge about the *specific* conditions in which they produce may be more exact than the knowledge of trained researchers who are producing new crop varieties or other technologies for these environments. This is not a failure of the research system or the idealization of the low-resource farmer, but a recognition of the division of labor between scientific agricultural research and the empirical knowledge that farmers acquire in order to produce with available resources. (1992:19; emphasis added)

Others, not as enthusiastic about the potential of cooperation with "Western" science, nevertheless emphasize the "localness" of indigenous knowledge. This is how the *Indigenous Knowledge and Development Monitor* put the matter: "Indigenous knowledge systems relate to the ways members of a given community define and classify phenomena in the physical/natural, social, and ideational environments. Examples are *local* classifications of soils, knowledge of which *local* crop varieties grow in difficult environments, and *traditional* ways of treating human and animal diseases" (Mathias-Mundy 1993a:4; emphasis added). Emphasis on "the local" is here clearly tied to an understanding of the "community" as a face-to-face, geographically circumscribed entity, one, moreover, that is "traditional." That this is not merely an accidental slippage is confirmed by the dualities that are brought into play between "indigenous" and "scientific" knowledge by contrasting "local" to "global" or "international" and "specific" to "general." These contrasts are brought out very clearly in this quote from the *Monitor:* "Parallel to and intertwined with the rapidly advancing body of *international,* scientific knowledge are bodies of *local* knowledge derived from the empirical trial-and-error of people struggling to survive over centuries. Little of this wisdom has been recorded or validated by the scientific method. Most is *localized,* is transmitted *orally,* and is typically not codified" (Mathias-Mundy 1993a:4; emphasis added). Indigenous knowledges thus are local, specific to particular people in particular geographic regions, and are found in spatially bounded communities; by contrast, scientific, "Western" knowledge is international, generalizable, and generated in unbounded settings. So far, we have a picture remarkably reminiscent of the "traditional" versus "modern" divide found in more confident versions of modernization theory.

The emphasis on local communities is sometimes given a nativist twist. Darrell Posey, for instance, argues that one of the reasons why indigenous agriculture is so well adapted to local climactic conditions in the Amazon is that it relies on "native" plants, which are more efficient in their use of tropical micronutrients (1983:246). This position is extended to its logical conclusion by those who reason that, because indigenous peoples form an integral part of the environment that they manage, "the best guarantee for the survival of nature is the survival of indigenous peoples" (Mathias-Mundy 1993b:7). In this manner, native plants and native peoples are brought together by their shared experience of "nature," which in turn is constituted by and through them. The loss of forests and species is seen as going hand in hand with the "disappearance and disruption of traditional societies," which is also destroying their "knowledge base." There is thus a need to preserve "knowledge, *in situ,* for its own sake" and to keep the indigenous system "isolated" and "unsullied" (Mathias-Mundy 1993a:4–5). Paradoxically, however, the justification for salvage ethnography is provided by "the onslaughts of industrialization, urbanization, and Western culture" (5), the very processes that advocates of indigenous knowledge would like to see ended. Thus, Posey et al. conclude their essay (1984:104) with the observation that "indigenous societies of Amazonia are in rapid decline. There are a few aboriginal cultures still relatively intact, but little time remains to salvage the valuable information resulting from millennia of accumulated ecological knowledge." Just as the argument about preserving nature through native people results in the spatial incarceration of the native (Appadurai 1988:37), so does salvage ethnography attempt to fix natives in time. I recognize that the agonistic relationship between "modern" and "indigenous," resulting from the structural inequalities of the world system, sometimes leaves no option but the strategic deployment of one pole of that binary. But when the struggle for survival of marginal groups comes to be equated to the often unabashedly nostalgic goal of "preserving" their "system of knowledge," is their agency acknowledged, let alone respected?

The need to preserve indigenous knowledge in situ follows from its property of being integrally connected to everyday life, religion, and ritual.[27] Unlike Western science, which separates religion and ritual from livelihood, indigenous knowledge is holistic and culturally bound. Religious practices and ritual performances can be central to managing and conserving the environment, a connection that is severed in "Western" science.[28] Holistic approaches contrast with the disciplinary specializations of science. This makes it difficult for centers in the IK network to "capture" indigenous knowledge systems. Whereas Western scientific approaches separate disciplines such as agriculture, forestry, natural resource management, aquaculture, human health, veterinary medicine, livestock management, communication systems, and organizational theory, indigenous knowledge systems make no such distinction (Mathias-Mundy 1993b:6). Of course, characterizing indigenous knowledges in this way raises fascinating questions about commensurability. How are different knowledges which are embodied and which are embedded in a particular cultural and moral milieu to be "translated" into the disembodied categories of a completely different knowledge system? How can people who are themselves practitioners and products of "the Western knowledge system" even begin to identify and describe, let alone analyze, systems of knowledge which are radically other and which have been constructed before, and lie beyond, "the West"? It is seldom appreciated in the "Indigenous Knowledge" literature that opposing indigenous knowledges to "Western" science in this way places its advocates in an impossible situation, for it undermines the epistemological foundations of their own knowledge claims. It could be argued, for instance, that the act of bringing a congerie of culturally specific knowledges into the singular category "indigenous knowledge" itself grows out of the homogenizing and universalizing tendencies of Western science. This is the very tendency that those transnational experts and national elites who are proponents of indigenous knowledge want to combat (Agrawal 1995).

Another questionable assumption made by proponents of indigenous knowledge is that all such knowledge is the cumulative result of generations or centuries of experimentation and wisdom. The evidence for this is simply the longevity of "the people" who possess the knowledge. Brokensha and Riley put the matter most clearly: "Mbeere and other folk-belief systems contain much that is based on extremely accurate, detailed and thoughtful observations, made over many generations. Without this basic 'scientific' knowledge (and disregarding any 'irrational' elements) the Mbeere would not have survived in their harsh and marginal environment. The point here is that accumulated familiarity and shared experience gives advantage to indigenous rather than to exotic evaluations" (1980: 115). "Survival" and "evolution" are the key indices that provide the evidence for a progressive theory of knowledge.[29] The view of knowledge as something that is accumulated over generations and tested and refined by experimentation is surprisingly like the hegemonic idealization of "Western science," which is purportedly most *unlike* indigenous knowledge. In a fascinating study of the role of trees in a Dogon village in Mali, van Beek and Banga (1992:69) note that the bush was considered the source of life, wisdom, and knowledge, which was used up and worn down in the process of being applied in the village. People in the past were considered to know inherently more than those in the present. Knowledge was viewed as something that dissipated and was consumed by use. Here is an "indigenous" view of knowledge that is anything but cumulative and progressive. If indigenous knowledge were not something that had accumulated over generations or millennia, would it be worth saving? Would it still be the object of "salvage ethnography?" These are complicated questions that one cannot even raise in the dualistic framework employed in discourses of indigeneity.

Because indigenous knowledge is identified as primarily local, culturally specific, and embedded in lifeways and worldviews, it would be easy to conclude that it is both widely shared and uniformly dispersed within an indigenous group. Although some versions of indigenous knowledge clearly take this position (Johnson 1980), others are keenly aware that knowledge is differentially available within an indigenous group. David Brokensha and Bernard Riley (1980:121) argue that "no informant has a total knowledge of his culture" and point out, for example, that among the Mbeere of central Kenya, older women are particularly well informed about herbs, boys who herd know a great deal about edible fruits, and honey collectors are sources of detailed knowledge about the flowering sequences of local plants. Not only is there internal differentiation, but it is sometimes argued that indigenous knowledge, taken as an entire system, may have "problems." Brokensha and Riley (1980:115) concede that "irrational elements" exist in indigenous knowledge systems, and Pablo Eyzaguirre (1992:26) evaluates farmers' knowledge systems in Honduras to be "incomplete and biased." Eyzaguirre's position follows from his desire to demonstrate the *complementarity* of indigenous knowledge to scientific knowledge, which he clearly regards as being superior.[30] The question arises as to which framework is being employed to make evaluations about rationality, and how one determines whether practices are safe or dangerous. Advocates of indigenous knowledge, therefore, unwittingly fall back on the seemingly "self-evident" norms of Western science in making assessments about indigenous systems of thought.[31]

Similar contradictions arise in the claim made by advocates of indigenous knowledge that it is neither a static nor a conservative system. Brokensha and Riley, for example, state that the Mbeere were not resistant to change but readily utilized new crops and technologies. Adoptions were especially likely to occur when they "could be absorbed into their social system" (1980:126). Eyzaguirre, too, reports that studies of farm households demonstrate that farmers change rapidly to exploit new economic opportunities as long as it does not affect crop diversity (1992:12). If this line of reasoning is followed to its logical conclusion, however, and indigenous knowledge systems are shown to have adopted, borrowed, and changed over centuries, inevitably including adoptions from "Western" science and technology, what essential core of authenticity is left untouched that makes it "indigenous"?

This is not an idle question, at least in the wake of colonial conquest. I can do no better than to echo Gayatri Chakravorty Spivak's skepticism about claims to purity and the apt strategy that she proposes for rethinking the question of the indigenous: "I cannot understand what indigenous theory there might be that can ignore the reality of nineteenth-century history. . . . To construct indigenous theories one must ignore the last few centuries of historical involvement. I would rather use what history has written for me" (1990:69). Not only must one contend with a few centuries of European colonial conquest in most cases, but one must also deal with a much longer history of connection in which people, goods, plants, animals, ideas, currencies, and so forth were exchanged between the far corners of the world (see, for example, Frank 1993; Frank and Gills 1993; Abu-Lughod 1989; Ghosh 1993; Wallerstein 1974).

Attention to the long history of connection is not a strategy to dismiss essentializing claims to authenticity. Rather, it enables a different kind of question to be posed whose goal is not primarily that of uncovering the "truth" about claims to indigenousness. Instead of asking whether particular practices, beliefs, or knowledges are truly "indigenous" or have been altered by "the West," we need to locate "the indigenous" within a discourse in which the question of origins becomes paramount.

Locating the Indigenous

Postcolonial critiques of nationalism have made the search for origins a problematic endeavor, enabling us to see that one way to understand the flourishing of discourses on "indigenousness" in the late-capitalist world is to relate "the indigenous" to the notion of "tradition." Comparing "the indigenous" with "the traditional" helps us realize that "tradition" and "indigenousness" are twinned concepts that occupy the role of the Other of modernity. Supporters of modernity find their Other in "tradition" that, not surprisingly, happens to be located primarily in the Third World. Critics of modernity, by contrast, find their Other in "the indigenous." As the project of modernity has come under increasing attack, the evaluative scale has shifted: "tradition," long-conceived as the chief stumbling block to the arduous pilgrimage into consumer heaven, has been increasingly replaced by "the indigenous," the alternative, eco-friendly, sustainable space outside, or resistant to, modernity.

To speak of "tradition" and "the indigenous" as twinned is to propose that the Other of modernity is Janus-faced. Supporters of the modernist project formed "the traditional" as a *residual* category, which contained everything that was devalued for not being modern. If there was one thing that "traditional" beliefs, practices, and institutions shared, it was a lack of modernity. They were defined by absence, and it is this absence that constituted a coherent, unitary "tradition" out of a disparate and inchoate mass of incommensurable beliefs and practices.

For the same reason, the "traditional" has always been a temporally unstable category. The telos of narratives of modernity would require the elimination of the residual. Such an emptying out was always immanent in the teleology of modernity; however, it could be reached only asymptotically. Although the "traditional," as a residual, fought a continuously losing battle to the forces of the modern, it could never be totally annihilated, because it provided the foil with which modernity defined itself.[32] The modern project thus became one of constant displacement of "the traditional" to ever more constricted domains.[33] This is what made "tradition" an unstable, shifting domain, and this is precisely what made the efforts to give it a pathetic privilege so futile. To fight for the preservation of "tradition" was to fight a battle whose outcome was already scripted.

What does this brief excursus into the relation between "modernity" and "tradition" tell us about indigenousness? If I am right in suggesting that "the indigenous" is a twin to "tradition," the other face of Janus, then we might reach the disturbing conclusion that some of the analysis presented above for "the traditional" holds for "the indigenous" as well. Indeed, I will argue that one of the reasons, perhaps the main reason, why "the indigenous" turns out to be such a productive signifier is that it too functions as a residual category. Critics of modernity have seized on "the indigenous" as a means to bring together an extraordinarily varied set of phenomena. It is not clear what could possibly unite all of them unless one understands that it is a grab bag for that which is *not* modern: unincorporated, resistant, incommensurable, originary, authentic, or, simply, an alternative. The discourse of modernity thus triangulates the relationship of "tradition" to "indigenousness" and finds postcolonial settings to be privileged locations for its operation in both cases. Keeping this relationship in mind may help us temper the celebratory tone that has accompanied the discovery of "the indigenous": there may be less that separates it from "the traditional" than meets the eye.

Although "tradition" and "indigenousness" are both located similarly as the Other of "the modern," there is an important difference between them: while "the traditional" is defined as the lack of modernity, "the indigenous" is defined by what modernity lacks. It is defined not by excess but by the failure of modernity. In this sense, the indigenous is not strictly the opposite of the traditional. Thus, "indigenous" knowledge about agronomy, forestry, and wildlife is premised on sustainability, equity, and harmony with nature, whereas "modern" science is destructive, exploitative, and patriarchal;[34] "indigenous" societies are based on community, sharing, and lack of hierarchy, whereas "modern" societies are based on individualism, acquisitiveness, and hierarchy (Guha 1989). Very often, the contrasting terms are left implicit, which only helps to underline the argument about "the indigenous" being defined as the Other of modernity.

The farmers I met in Alipur present an excellent case because they brought an "indigenous" understanding to an agriculture practiced with chemical fertilizers, electric tube wells, and hybrid seeds. The terms in which farmers in Alipur formulated, presented, and justified their agricultural decisions relied heavily, though not exclusively, on an "indigenous" understanding of agriculture. For this reason, perhaps, it might be tempting to refer to it as a shared system of knowledge. There are several reasons, however, why referring to indigenous agronomy as a "shared system of knowledge" is, in my opinion, misleading. First, as Appadurai has emphasized (1987), knowledge is not uniformly shared among different classes and castes or men and women in a village.[35] In Alipur, traditional agricultural castes such as the jats pride themselves on being good agriculturists and often express scorn for the farming abilities and work habits of other castes, both those above them in the ritual hierarchy and those below. Second, attributing a "systematicity" to indigenous knowledges of agronomy carries with it some questionable implications. To begin with, there is the implication that a coherent and systematic *theory* of agronomy is discursively available to peasants. It is further implied that indigenous knowledges of agronomy exist in some kind of stable (although not static) equilibrium and achieve a degree of closure as a complete system. This latter implication is buttressed by the fact that the new HYV inputs—seeds, fertilizers, irrigation sources, and pesticides—have, in what appears to be an effortless manner, been incorporated into a humoral agronomic system.

But such appearances are misleading. What gives "indigenous" knowledges of agronomy their power is that they represent culturally constituted recipes for dealing with the varying conditions and exigencies encountered in farming activities. They become important in this sense of informing and motivating the actions of peasants, and not because they are discursively retrievable as a complete system of thought.[36] Furthermore, agronomical explanations are necessarily entangled in the politics of agricultural operations and thus have an essentially disputed and unstable character. Finally, we have to recognize that differential access to the "legitimate" knowledge of agricultural officials (whose explanations are based on biochemistry) has resulted in an interpenetration of this incommensurable idiom of agronomy, therefore calling into question the degree of closure of the indigenous "system." In all these respects, then, indigenous knowledges of agronomy did not constitute a "system."

The best way to understand "indigenous" agronomical knowledges, I think, is to see them as acting in two essential ways: as logics that enable the classification of crops, soils, and other inputs (more on this follows), and as positing certain links or associations between the predispositions of soil, crop, fertilizer, and irrigation water. Of course, these two functions are closely related in that, on the one hand, classification entails both separation and connection and, on the other, notions of compatibility between the crop and the soil, for example, presuppose that both crops and soils are divided into several categories.

From discussions with farmers in Alipur in 1984–85, 1989, and 1991–92, I discerned two important dimensions to classification. The first of these is not limited to crops but is applied to all living organisms. In this view, all living matter must consist of appropriate proportions of humoral elements—hot, cold, dry, and wet.[37] As one of my respondents told me (employing the authority of the Vedas), good health for plants as well as for people consists of a balance of heat and cold, dryness and wetness. When any one of these elements is in excess, the living organism falls ill. According to Richard Kurin, who has presented an excellent, detailed analysis of humoral agronomy (1983:285):[38] "Hot and cold respectively refer to the expenditure and conservation of energy and wet and dry to the receptivity and resistance of matter. . . . Initially, life in plants . . . can only exist if sufficient levels of innate heat and wetness occur. As heat is expended, growth and development occur—matter is transformed from more amorphous and malleable wetter forms to more rigid drier forms." It was clear from what farmers had to say that at any point in time, the disposition of a particular crop depended not only on its innate disposition (which depends on its species as well as its stage in the developmental cycle) but also on the disposition of the inputs that had been applied to it and the disposition of the soil. Thus, a complex combination of factors works to determine the health of a crop at a particular moment.

A second dimension to the classification of crops was provided by one of my respondents, who broke down crops into three basic categories: those which grow under the soil (potatoes, onions, carrots, and so on); those which grow above the soil and have pods (lentils, peas, gram, mung, and the like); and those which grow above the soil but not in pods (wheat, rice, barley, maize, millet, and cane, for example). These can be further classified according to whether they strike deep roots and "pull" nutrients from below or whether they have shallow roots and gather their nutrients from surface soil. I was told that in the case of crops with pods, it is especially important to keep the ground clean and free of weeds. They should also be planted with enough space between rows so that the wind could pass "cleanly" through them: the seed inside ripens fully only if it receives the full impact of the wind.

The next section is devoted to a close analysis of how classifications of crops and soils actually operate in the discourses and practices of farmers in Alipur. For lack of a better term, when I first wrote about this topic, I labeled the agronomical practices of Alipur's farmers "indigenous" (Gupta 1988). Insofar as my concern was to demonstrate the distance of peasant agronomy from bioscientific conceptions of agriculture, that label was useful. But my choice of "the indigenous" erred on the side of emphasizing "difference" and failed to come to terms with the hybridities of agronomical knowledges and agricultural practices in Alipur, knowledges and practices that I would argue are constitutive of "postcoloniality" in contemporary India. The detailed examination that follows shows why ideas of postcolonial modernity are essential in theorizing what is meant by "indigenous" agricultural practices in Alipur.

"Indigenous" Knowledges of Agronomy in Alipur

There are two main agricultural seasons in the Gangetic plains of western Uttar Pradesh. The first is the monsoon or kharif harvest, which is usually sown around the time of the first rains in late June or early July and harvested in September and October. The winter or rabi crop is sown in November and December and harvested in April. Some farmers grow a third crop, called *zaid* (literally, "excess"), which is sown in April and harvested by the end of May.

Before the advent of tube well technology, farmers had to wait until the first rains to sow the monsoon crop. But the ability to pump out groundwater enabled them to start sowing before the rains came. Thus when I lived in Alipur in 1984–85, on early mornings in the month of May, before the first light spilled over the horizon, I could hear the oxen being goaded to plow in a straight line. Once the sun was up, it rapidly became too hot to do much work: people and oxen were drained of energy, and it was impossible to stay out beyond midmorning. Temperatures reached a scorching 110 degrees in the afternoon, and everyone took shelter beneath shady trees and thatched roofs. Late in the month, some farmers had already planted fodder [*jowar*], although most waited until the beginning of June. Maize was planted all through the month of June and especially intensively in the last week, around the time that the monsoons were expected. Pearl millet [*bajra*] was sown after the first monsoon rains, usually in the first half of July. July and August were spent weeding the standing crops and harvesting fodder for cattle. Green fodder was especially valuable at that time, for it coincided with the peak cattle-breeding season. Most of the kharif crops were harvested in September, including maize and the part of the millet (jowar) crop which had not already been employed as fodder. Some farmers used the time between the harvesting of the monsoon crop and the sowing of the winter crop to plant a fast-growing relative of mustard called lahai. This was also the time when chickpeas and peas were sown. The harvesting of pearl millet began in late September and extended into October.

After the fields were cleared of the monsoon crop, work began in earnest for the main winter crop, wheat. The fields were plowed as much as possible to prepare the soil for the winter wheat. All through October and November, this work, more than any other, preoccupied farmers. The work day began early, when the soil was still moist from the overnight dew and thus more malleable to being worked with the plow. Wheat was sown all through November and into December. Some varieties had to be sown early because they took longer to ripen than others. After the hard work to sow the wheat, there was a lull in farming activities. Most wheat plots are no longer weeded, so apart from supplying irrigation, there was not much to be done to the standing crop. Those who had sown sugarcane, however, were kept busy in January and February harvesting the cane and selling or processing it. Those who wanted to plant cane in a new plot did so in February and March. This procedure was very time consuming and frequently required the help of an extended circle of friends, who were then treated to a feast. From late March onward began, for a whole month, the harvesting of barley and wheat. Because harvesting was a slow and labor-intensive operation that required a significant amount of hired labor, wage rates and labor demand peaked at this time. Lest an unseasonal rain destroy the entire crop, harvesting was quickly followed by threshing. By this time, it was once again extremely hot, and much of the work of harvesting took place early in the morning and in the late afternoon. When there was electricity, threshing was done all night long, when it was cool enough for the laborers to work.

The few farmers who planted a zaid crop did so after the wheat had been harvested. But most farmers preferred to let the soil "rest" for a brief period over the summer. They plowed it to dig up weeds and to allow the heat of the sun to reach the soil, but this period was, for the most part, the slowest in the farming cycle.

Field being plowed with a pair of bullocks in foreground
and a pair of buffalo in background

Soils were classified into five categories: yellow [*peelee mitti* or *bhooda*], sandy [*raytiili* or *balui*], loam [*do-math*], clay [*chikni*], and white [*safayd mitti* or *usar*].[39] Loam, considered midway between sandy and clay, was thought to be the most fertile, and wasteland consisted of either yellow or white soil. Farmers believed sandy soil to be "lighter" than loam, and clay "heavier," the implication being that heavier soil retained moisture better, was more sustainably productive, and was less affected by the seasons.[40]

To understand the activities of farmers in Alipur systematically, I have subdivided agricultural operations into eight parts. (These topics correspond to the sequence of stages followed in farming operations.[41]) For each operation, I will closely examine the explanations offered for particular actions or sequences of actions.

Different agricultural operations were closely tied to a gendered division of labor in Alipur, as in most of northern India. Plowing and sowing were the only agricultural operations done exclusively by men.[42] In all other stages of the agricultural cycle, women were involved, and some stages of agriculture were largely the domain of women. Weeding was carried out by the whole family, including young children. Irrigation was done primarily by men. Fertilizer was applied by both men and women. Harvesting was not gender-specific, and harvest labor was paid as a proportion of the quantity harvested. Threshing and winnowing operations were conducted by both men and women, although other postharvest tasks such as the drying and processing of grains was done entirely by women. A great proportion of the work associated with cattle was done by women. Men mostly, although not exclusively, operated the fodder-cutting machine, but feeding cattle, cleaning them, and removing cow dung was largely the job of women.

Caste and gender interacted to specify which jobs were done by women. Thakur women did not do any work in the fields, almost never leaving the confines of the home for work-related purposes. Lower-caste women worked as wage laborers and thus had to be outside the home most of the time. Women belonging to castes such as brahmins and jats that owned substantial amounts of land almost never worked as laborers, although they did a fair amount of work on their own family farms. Women of all castes did almost all the household work, including child care, cooking, cleaning, washing the clothes, and pumping water from hand pumps for household needs. Almost all the purchasing of household goods was done by men, as they were the ones who went to the market. But women, or very often children, did go to the little shops in the village that sold household necessities.

My goal in the detailed descriptions of farming practices that follow is to demonstrate that an understanding of the lives of subaltern Third World people such as the farmers of Alipur is facilitated by an attention to questions of postcoloniality. Agriculture in Alipur does not conform to descriptions of "traditional" farming or to the idealized picture of subalterns earnestly guarding "indigenous knowledges" against the insurmountable odds of a homogenizing world system. At the same time, Alipur's peasants can be easily distinguished from industrial agriculturists in the "West." Neither occupying a position of pure opposition to the modern nor assimilable to a homogenizing "Western" episteme, farmers in Alipur constantly destabilized the oppositions that have framed explanations of subaltern, Third World peoples. It is this position of hybridity—practices of "mistranslation," alternative constructions of modernity—always structured in dominance and experienced through various modes of inequality, that I will try to emphasize in what follows.[43]

Crop choice

Contrary to my assumptions when I went to "the field" for the first time, understanding farmers' decisions about crop choice proved anything but straightforward. Three factors seemed to dominate the explanations that I was offered for why certain crops were grown as opposed to others. First, the disposition of the crop had to be carefully calibrated to that of the soil. If the soil in a particular plot was weak, sandy, or "cold," it could support only a crop that suited those properties. To plant any other crop was to create a mismatch that guaranteed low yields and perhaps even prevented regeneration of the soil. Because the ecological consequences of crop choice will be explored more fully in the next chapter, I will concentrate here on the match between the "character" of the crop and that of the soil (Vasavi 1994). The second explanation, proffered quite frequently, had to do with timing. Questions of timing were, on the whole, critical not just for crop selection but also for all agricultural operations. Third, there was the ever present difficulty of adequate resources. Farmers invariably explained the gap between what they *should* have done and what they actually did by referring to their inability to purchase necessary inputs. Sometimes, resource problems took the form of a shortage of adequate household labor and the inability to hire outside labor for agricultural tasks.

To begin with the first point, the notion that the disposition and "strength" of the soil should match the disposition of the crop was very widely shared. The soil in certain places was said to be able to "catch" or "get hold of" [*pakadnaa*] certain crops. The ability of the soil to get hold of a particular crop stemmed from its inherent qualities—its disposition in terms of heaviness, strength, and texture.[44] The success or failure of new varieties was often judged in terms of how well the soil reacted to them, whether it "caught" the new species or not [*pakadti hai ya nahi*]. As Suresh put it: "There are places where the soil gets hold of jowar, somewhere else it catches bajra, and in some areas it helps maize more. In some areas, rice is mostly grown. So where there is a tradition, wherever the soil holds onto a particular crop, people there start growing that crop. Our land is sandy, so bajra caught on well. It started growing well, thus everyone started growing it." The agency attributed to the soil was critical in the conceptualization of the relation between the land and crops. The land was not merely the object of labor or the medium through which the agency of the farmer could be exercised. It had its own volition, its own character, its own disposition, its own ability to act on the plant.

The dispersion of several crops on the same field was explained in terms of a careful evaluation of the strength of the soil in various parts, as well as the ability of the soil to get hold of the crop. Dhani Singh had rented a plot adjacent to the one he owned and in each plot had planted some parts with maize and some with jowar. Puzzled by this, I asked whether it would not have saved him time and labor to have planted all the maize in one place and the jowar in another. His explanation for what seemed, at first glance, a classic "risk-aversion strategy" was the following: "Suppose a field has less strength, then we do fodder [*nyaar*] or jowar in it. And maize is grown only in a strong field so that output is good. There were small portions in both fields that were strong, so we could grow just a little maize. If there are some barren spots [*kalri* or *usri*] in the field—usri means places where the field has less strength— we plant gwal in that. And where it is slightly better, where the soil helps the crop grow well, jowar is planted there. And the land which is even stronger, that's where we sow maize." Therefore, significant local variation in the quality of the soil determined the choice of crop, with both the quality of the soil and the properties of the crop suggesting the best course of action.

One of the most important properties of crops, of course, was the time that they took to ripen and harvest. A delay in planting or a long-standing crop could affect the output of the subsequent crop. This was particularly true of the kharif crops, because the chief source of income was the sale of wheat planted in the rabi growing season. Concerns about timing were ubiquitous in discussions about crop choice. An example was provided by Dhani Singh, who was telling me why he chose to plant legumes in a field:

> We didn't sow *arhar* or *urad* [different kinds of lentils] in that field because the next crop—wheat—is delayed. It gets late. If, for example, arhar is sown in a plot, then if you get late for wheat, what will you do? You will fling [*maarangey*] twenty to twenty-five kilos of fertilizer for every bigha, by broadcasting it. Only then will you plant it. For the small farmer, that turns out to be a heavy burden. It's not at all a heavy burden for the big farmer. The small farmer [*chotey kisan*] will want to get by with fewer inputs. Arhar should not be sown because it is harmful to the next crop.

The implication of the long cropping cycle for lentils is that it leaves very little time to prepare the fields for wheat, which is, after all, the main food and cash crop. Dhani Singh implies that one way to compensate for the shorter preparation time left after harvesting lentils is to apply large doses of chemical fertilizer. Twenty kilograms of fertilizer per bigha was approximately double of what was considered standard or "good" practice in Alipur in 1984–85. Dhani Singh made it clear that such high doses of inputs were beyond the means of small farmers, presumably including himself in such a category. As the owner of 20.5 bighas, however, he did not really fit such a description.

One possible answer to the dilemma of growing lentils would be to sow them early, so that they were harvested in time to prepare the fields for the winter wheat. Dhani Singh ruled out such a strategy for other reasons:

> Suppose you sow lentils [arhar] early [aghaii]. Then, it will grow excessively and the output will be low. Its stem grows too much and so it has fewer beans. Now, if you plant late or in the middle of the planting season, then the production will be greater. More beans will appear, its stem will grow less, it'll spread out a lot. Then production will be greater. For example, the person whose field is over on this side, Hamir Singh, he has planted lentils within his maize. After sowing the maize and harvesting it, he dropped fertilizer in the lentils. Only then has his output of lentils been all right. There has been no significant shortage. In a farm of six bighas, the owner [maalik] has put ten sacks of fertilizer.

"Ten sacks?" I could not contain my amazement. "Yes, ten sacks. Ten of a *dhadi* [ten kilograms] each." Normally, one sack of fertilizer has approximately fifty kilograms, and if ten normal-size sacks had been applied, it would have been the equivalent of putting five hundred kilograms in an area a little less than an acre. One hundred kilograms of fertilizer was still very high, especially for the monsoon harvest, but well within the range of possibility. In Dhani Singh's view, intercropping lentils with maize was preferable to any other strategy. If lentils were planted early, output was poor; if they were planted in the middle of the season or late, there was not enough time for the next crop. Thus little advantage existed to planting arhar. However, many farmers believed that planting lentils had beneficial effects on the soil, a theme that is explored in greater depth in the following chapter.

Finally, resource constraints were frequently mentioned as a reason for planting a particular crop. Suresh explained why he chose to grow bajra (pearl millet) rather than maize in the monsoon harvest:

> It's like this. What we do depends on our circumstances at that time. The first thing is how much we have by way of resources, for example, whether we have water or not. I grew bajra because I

thought it would grow with less inputs and we would be able to get higher yields—that is possible with bajra. Maize would have required more inputs. If I could have managed the production of maize, with regard to weeding, irrigation [which has to be administered in quick succession], as well as fertilizer, then I would have planted maize. But since we didn't have that capability, we just caught hold of one crop, we just planted bajra. . . . We sow only the crop that we are capable of managing.

Suresh's explanation of the choice of bajra as flowing out of resource constraints was perfectly compatible with the other factors mentioned above—namely, sowing bajra would not lead to problems with timing, and there was a match between the properties of bajra and his land. Yet even when resource constraints were mentioned as an important reason for planting something, they were combined with explanations that would defy a straightforwardly instrumentalist logic.

For once, Dhani Singh was not accompanied by anyone when I interviewed him in the room where I lived on the state farm. We had set up a time earlier at which he had failed to show up. We made yet another appointment, and just when I was beginning to wonder if Dhani Singh had hidden reservations about being interviewed, he appeared at the door. I began, as I did with all others, with questions about the kharif harvest and then went on to the winter crop. Dhani Singh had made the highly unusual decision of planting his entire plot with "traditional" (desi) wheat, the only farmer in Alipur to do so in 1984–85. Everyone else had switched to the new high-yielding varieties, which could be coaxed to yield higher returns with appropriate doses of fertilizer and water. Dhani Singh explained that the decision to plant desi wheat was partially made because it required less resources than the new varieties. But on further questioning, he revealed two other reasons. One reason was that the rotis made from the new varieties were not as tasty as those made from desi wheat, an opinion that was almost universally shared in Alipur. Yet, that fact alone did not prevent others from switching to the new high-yielding varieties. When I pointed that out to Dhani Singh, he told me that they had planted whatever seed was in the house. Although his family might consider exchanging seed with other farmers, they would never purchase it on the market. In fact, the preferred strategy was to keep some of their own output as seed for next year's harvest.[45] The importance of non-purchased inputs and the taste of the new varieties thus entered as important qualifications to a straightforwardly resource-constrained, decision-making model of crop choice.

The qualities of the crop and its compatibility with the qualities of the soil, factors of timing, availability of household labor, and resource constraints thus combined in complex ways to determine the choice of crops. Arguments about compensating for the lack of time for preparing the field with additional doses of chemical fertilizer and discussions of how the choice of crop is determined by the availability of water and fertilizer went hand in hand with matching the disposition of the crop to that of the soil and positing that the land had its own agency.[46] "Modern" explanations were thus inextricably woven into "indigenous" ones, and any effort to reinstate this dichotomy would have the inevitable consequence of reading the evidence tendentiously.

If compatibility between the crop and soil was important, what affected the qualities of the soil? The labor expended in preparing the land for sowing and in looking after the crop clearly affected soil quality, and it is to this topic that I turn to in the next section.

Field preparation and plowing

Preparing the land for sowing was perhaps the most labor-intensive and time-consuming activity for men in Alipur. Women did not plow or sow but carried out most of the weeding, took an active role in harvesting, and often did much of the threshing.[47] The plow used was produced of either iron or wood [desi] and made a single furrow behind a pair of oxen, although buffalo were sometimes used. In 1984–85, only two households in Alipur owned a tractor. Rather than bear the expense of keeping oxen, those with very small landholdings sometimes preferred to pay a tractor owner to plow their land rapidly. But, tractor owners were loath to work someone else's fields before their own. Thus those who could afford to keep oxen did so because it enabled them to control better the timing of plowing.

Although most farmers in Alipur generally believed that the more times the ground was plowed in preparation for sowing, the better it was for the crop, not everyone was convinced of this connection. At the beginning of this chapter I quoted Suresh, who claimed that plowing less often was better for his maize crop. On the other hand, there was almost universal agreement that the winter crop of wheat gave higher yields if the field was plowed many times. Suresh had plowed his wheat fields only four times and was speculating about the effect of a greater number of plowings:

Field being leveled with wooden block

More plowings have a positive effect on wheat. The more times wheat is plowed, the better. There was enough time according to my calculations to have plowed eight times. Yes, I would have done eight plowings. If my health had been okay, I would have continued to use the plow in this field. It would certainly have made some difference. Another thing was that since there was no grass in this field, we didn't even think that the right time would pass. That's why I thought, "Why waste time?" And so I went ahead with sowing. There was no time left. Even so, we got quite late. On the one hand, the bajra was harvested late, then we plowed so we got even more late. To plow at the right time requires preplanning. If we had planted maize in this, it would have given us the time to plow. Planting bajra did not enable us to find the time—it is cut later than maize, a whole month later. For this reason, the wheat sowing had to be a whole month late too.

Suresh was unable to plow as many times as he wished to for two reasons. First, both he and his two teenage sons fell ill at the time most critical for sowing. Second, he harvested the previous crop of bajra late, which did not leave enough time to plow the field properly for wheat. One factor working in his favor was that the bajra field had very few weeds in it. He therefore felt that he could go ahead and sow wheat in it, despite the low number of plowings that the field had received.

Why was plowing many times helpful for the wheat crop? The usual answer was that the more times the soil was turned, the more productive it became. If the soil was well turned [goond], it retained water better and imparted its nutrients to the crop relatively easily. The wooden plow turned over the earth almost a foot deep, which helped to hold water. It went into the earth at a slight angle, operating like a spade in alternatively going up and down as it pulled up and dug in by turn. By contrast, the iron plow had a wider cutting edge and a shorter bit. It dug almost vertically into the ground, displacing weeds but not turning the soil over. I was told that iron plows became popular only after the introduction of chemical fertilizers, as these plows made the use of fertilizers mandatory to maintain the productivity of the soil.

How many times a particular field was plowed also depended on the number of weeds present during the previous crop and after it had been harvested. Suresh was pointing to the difference between three areas on his field. In the monsoon harvest, he had planted maize, bajra, and jowar. He had plowed the area with maize four times, that with bajra three times, and the fodder field just once. What accounted for the differential treatment of the three areas? Suresh explained that it was due to the presence of weeds:

It's like this: the field in which I saw black grass [kaali ghaas] . . . a kind of grass grows. To kill the grass, the average number of plowings [required] was excessive. [Normally] I keep plowing until the time the field is ready for sowing, until the day when there is no grass or no weeds [kharpatvaar], no matter how many plowings are needed. On the other hand, one has to be aware of the time too. If the time to sow is at hand, then I may leave the plowing half-done too. So this was the reason. The maize field had black grass so it needed one extra plowing. The bajra field was clear, and for this reason we could get by with plowing it less. The jowar field was plowed just once because there was no grass or leaves underneath. It was clean from before. We have to see how much grass there is to decide how much to plow.

The desire to plow the field as many times as possible before planting wheat is tempered by the necessity of not delaying sowing operations.

Certain parts of the field are then plowed more than others, depending on the quantity of weeds and on the previous "cleanliness" of the field.

Once again, as in the case of crop choice, we find that field preparation depended on a complex mix of factors. Decisions about how many times to plow were based on a number of different elements: humoral understandings of the relationship between the land and the crop, as seen in Suresh's decision to plow the field only four times to prevent the land from becoming excessively hot and moist; issues of timing, evident from Suresh's conflict between plowing more or sowing before it got too late; the effectiveness of certain tools and techniques, as revealed by the comparison between the effects of the wooden and iron plows on the soil; and, finally, the presence of weeds that needed to be uprooted.

Selection of seeds

Once the land was plowed, it was ready to be seeded. For most crops, there were only one or two varieties of seed available, but several generations of commercially marketed wheat hybrids were in use in Alipur. How did farmers determine which variety of wheat to sow? How were new varieties of seed introduced into the village?

The most obvious means, of course, was through the recommendations of other farmers. Suresh had planted varietal Number 2204 for the first time in the winter of 1985. I asked him where he had obtained information about this variety. It turned out that relatives of his had praised it very highly the previous year. So he obtained some seed from them and planted it on his land. And where had his relatives obtained the seed? They had procured it from a neighboring village. By the time Suresh acquired the seed, it was already at least two generations old. This fact did not seem to bother him, for he claimed that a simple test told him when the seed had become too old:

> Wheat seed lasts quite a few years. As long as it keeps giving good production, we understand the seed to be all right. If there is any shortage in production, if we irrigate and fertilize it, and it still doesn't grow, and if everyone around starts saying that your seed is now old, then we change it. The old desi wheat seed used to last a fairly long time, it lasted ten to fifteen years. And these new varieties, these last at least seven years, and sometimes ten. Now take Number 2009: it has been used for a fair amount of time, and if we see some weakness in it, then we'll change it. Like the Number 312 cane we had, it worked for a fair while, then it became weak, it

started drying, it started uprooting, so we stopped cultivating it because it dries, uproots . . . the cane dries. . . . It's the same way with wheat.

Suresh had switched from Number 2009 to Number 2204 because the former was not as profitable as the latter. He told me that Number 2009 fetched a lower price in the market. Even if he were to sell it at the government scales set up to purchase wheat surpluses at a preannounced price, he would have to be content with "number two" rates. So he decided to cultivate a variety that would fetch a higher price on the market. He did not know if Number 2204 would work on his land, because it was recommended by people who belonged to a different area. But he decided to take a chance and plant it. If his land "got hold of" the new variety and the output was good, then he would cultivate it the following year. Otherwise, he would just have to swallow the loss.

Another farmer who had planted RR21 told me that he preferred RR21 to another variety, Sona, because it needed fewer inputs—fertilizer and water—and still gave good yields. If for some reason one was unable to irrigate the crop on time, the yields from Sona would drop sharply, but that was not the case with RR21. Because he obtained good results with RR21, he had planted it for three years in a row and had not ventured to try any of the newer varieties that had been released. His neighbor planted a newer seed called Kisan and achieved very good yields. But this farmer attributed that yield to the fact that his neighbor owned a small amount of land and was therefore able to pay more attention to his crops and provide higher doses of inputs for them.

There was widespread agreement that the traditional varieties of wheat were much tastier, although only one farmer had planted desi wheat in 1984–85. When the wheat crop was being harvested, Raj Singh, an older thakur and owner of just over six acres of land, was praising an "improved" version of desi wheat called K68. According to Raj Singh, it was a sight to behold, with the grain round and fat, a beautiful white color, and it had an excellent taste; if you saw it heaped along with other piles of grain in the market, it would immediately catch your attention. For this reason, it sold for a higher price than other varieties. Its flour was "nice and white," as were its rotis, and it was genuinely tasty. The problem with K68, he added, was that the stalks were far too tall and thus tended to lodge, or fall down, on windy and rainy days. It was also more responsive to organic manure than chemical fertilizer, a fact that became important in light of the constant complaints in the village

Dividers being made in field for irrigation

about the "shortage" of organic manure (this theme is explored at greater length in the following chapter). Another problem was that it needed to be planted relatively early. Because people were growing several crops a year, the fields were not free at an earlier time. The implication was that, apart from difficulties caused by lodging, K68 disturbed the timing of other crops and hence had repercussions that extended beyond the wheat-growing season.

To purchase new wheat seeds on the market, one could obtain loans in kind from government agencies to be repaid at the end of the harvest. Loans of this kind were usually made by farmers cooperatives, which were monitored closely by local officials. Suresh told me that he chose not to go through the banks to purchase new seeds because the officials created trouble [*gadbad*]. The purchase orders approved by bank officials were valid only with particular dealers, with whom the officials had made arrangements in advance. The dealers palmed off old seed and fertilizer to the farmer, which, predictably, failed to perform up to expectations. This, in turn, started a cycle of debt, because the farmer could not afford to pay back all that was required under the terms of the loan. If there was a bad harvest and most of a farmer's crop was lost, he was in deep trouble because, unlike local moneylenders who were flexible in demanding repayment, government officials blindly followed the rules in following repayment schedules.[48]

It was not only the fear of debt that prevented farmers from approaching government agencies for seed loans but also the insensitive response of bureaucrats to the importance of getting inputs to the farmer in a timely manner. For example, Suresh complained that the approvals for seed loans were invariably delayed. By the time the bank officials got the orders for the distribution of seed, the best time for sowing was past. He felt that monetary loans would be better than loans in kind. Most people sitting in those offices, he said, have no experience of farming. They would not recognize a head of wheat if they saw it. All they knew was how to shuffle paper. Bureaucrats would not dream of releasing funds before they obtained orders to do so, and by the time the orders came, it was invariably too late for the farmer's crop. They just did not understand the importance of timing in agricultural activities.

A consideration of the seed selection process of even a few farmers reveals a complex mix of determinants. The recommendations of trustworthy neighbors and relatives clearly played a central role. On the other hand, one had to test whether the new seeds would "take hold" on one's own land. Many farmers in Alipur tested new seeds on a small portion of their land; if the output was satisfactory, they adopted it wholesale the following year. A new variety was sown as long as results from it were satisfactory and no clearly superior variety was available. Again, the demonstration effect of neighbors was critical, but it was balanced by a careful consideration of the manifold factors that went into high yields. Thus the farmer who saw his neighbor obtaining good yields with the varietal Kisan attributed it not to the variety itself but to the application of large doses of inputs. Although farmers preferred desi wheat for consumption and often rhapsodized about its properties, as well as about the high prices it fetched in the market, they rarely grew it because of its tendency to lodge and because its long growing season disrupted the crops in the previous harvest. The nonavailability of credit was suggested as a factor that played a part in sowing decisions, especially the fact that the timing of credit did not always match that of agricultural production. "Indigenous" knowledges of agronomy, therefore, combined with "satisficing" forms of behavior, a whole host of market factors, and the operation of state offices to determine the selection of seeds.[49]

Sowing

Crops either were sown in straight rows behind a plow or were "broadcast" by taking fistfuls of seed and throwing it across the land. All the major crops in Alipur were sown in straight rows. In sowing operations, two men usually worked together. One operated the plow while the other trailed behind dropping the seed. Working in this way, it was possible to sow approximately one acre in a day. I saw only a couple of farmers broadcasting grain, and they did so because they were desperately late or short of labor. Creating the furrows for sowing is a delicate operation, requiring the plow to be operated at an angle so that it does not dig in as deep as it does when plowing. Planting the seed too deep might cause it to rot; conversely, planting it too high left the plant vulnerable to lodging. The depth at which seeds were planted was an important factor in accounts of low yields.

I asked Suresh why most farmers preferred to do the sowing themselves when they could rent a tractor to sow in a fraction of the time. He replied:

> I have heard one other thing about tractors, namely that the seed drill [kudi] drops the grain somewhat high. So when too much water is applied to it and the wind blows, its roots give way, and the wheat falls over. Often one sees wheat sown by a tractor lodging. With the plow one sows slightly lower than that, the seed reaches a bit low, then it cannot fall. This is one hypothesis held by people, that the tractor places the seed high. So its root slants in this manner, water is applied, the soil gets wet, and it falls over. This is one reason for not using tractors. The second reason is that the tractor owner has to be given cash. To save money, it's good to get by using just the plow. The small farmer works with just his plow.

Dhani Singh used almost identical reasoning. He too traced greater lodging to the fact that the seed drill on a tractor deposited the seed higher up in the soil as compared with a bullock plow (three to four inches instead of six inches): "Output will be greater in the bullock-plowed one. Why? The reason is that the bullock-plowed seed reaches somewhat deeper. Therefore its roots are firmer. The seeds sown by tractor have higher roots. If the fertilizer is of good quality, and water is applied, later if the wind blows, then the plant will fall, and the result will be lower production." It might appear that this is an argument for planting seeds somewhat deep. But there are also good reasons to ensure that seeds are not placed excessively deep. Dhani Singh accounted for

Sowing

the poor production he obtained from his mustard crop by saying that the seed had been planted too deep. He had plowed the field once, then broadcast the seed, and plowed the field again. The result was that the seed was embedded far too deep into the soil and rotted. Some plants haphazardly pushed through the earth, but even these grew only to a short height and failed to yield any mustard. Several farmers told me that the reason why seeds planted too deep failed to yield anything was that, at a greater depth, they could not obtain the heat that they needed to sprout. Consequently, they rotted from the wetness. On the other hand, planted at the correct height, they received just the right combination of moisture and heat to enable them to grow rapidly. Because different crops varied in their constitution, as did the soil in different plots, the "correct" height at which seeds had to be planted varied. Thus, a skillful farmer used his understanding of humoral agronomy to plant seeds at varying heights and times, depending on the properties of the crop and the soil.

Even for a particular crop, there was considerable debate as to what was the correct depth for planting. Contrary to what has been quoted above, the practice of planting the seed relatively high was supported by some farmers by referring to changing practices of irrigation. The depth at which seed was planted depended on a combination of factors related to the properties of the soil and the increased availability of water. Sompal explained it this way: "It depends on the moistness of the soil. Earlier, there were no sources of water, and people depended on the rains. So the moisture remained lower down, and the seed had to be planted at a greater depth. And now that people irrigate before sowing, the seed should naturally be higher." By 1984–85, tube wells were enabling farmers to irrigate their crops plentifully and relatively inexpensively. Under those circumstances, the argument for planting seed deep was less persuasive. When farmers depended on the rain, it made sense to plant the seed lower down because the soil was more moist the deeper one went. Irrigation made it possible to plant the seed relatively high because the land could be kept wet even in the absence of winter rain. A humoral theory of "adequate" moisture was thus employed to assess the significance of tube wells on the depth of planting.

Apart from the failure to plant seed at the right height, the chief impediment to high yields mentioned most often in my interviews was the failure to sow on time. Despite irrigating his wheat crop six times, Suresh's output was poor. When I questioned him about it, he told me that the main reason for low yields was that he had been late in planting. Even though water and fertilizer had been put in a timely manner, planting late had prevented the crop from being a good one. Suresh told me that to assure a good output, one needed to plant on time *and* provide adequate amounts of fertilizer and water. All three things were necessary for a good harvest. An additional factor that affected the timing of sowing was the availability of labor. Suresh was delayed because he and his sons fell ill at the critical period when the field had to be plowed and sowed. Sowing time was one period when finding hired labor became more difficult than normal, although these shortages were minimal compared with those at harvesting and threshing, when labor was short despite the fact that wage rates were at their annual peak.

From my interviews, the reasons cited most often for the success of sowing were the timing as well as the depth at which the seed had been planted. The depth at which seed was planted depended on the technology of plowing—that is, whether tractors or bullocks were used—and the technology of irrigation—that is, whether the land had access to tube well water. Evaluations about the interrelation of techniques of planting, depth of planting, and irrigation depended on humoral agronomical knowledges. The most interesting aspect of the new technologies of irrigation and plowing was how they entered into sharply conflictual assessments of sowing. Thus, different farmers could not agree as to the "proper" depth of planting seed because they accounted for tractors and tube wells in very different ways.

As with crop choice, field preparation, and the selection of seeds, the new technologies of agriculture had crucially altered Alipur farmers' decisions about sowing. The depth at which seed should have been planted, the technology (tractors or bullock-driven plows) that should have been used, and the timing of planting were all determined by a mixed set of explanations drawn from humoral agronomy, the exigencies of household cash and labor supplies, the properties of these machines, and the access that individuals had to them. Tractors, tube wells, and hybrid seeds were the emblems of the green revolution, the revolution that would make agriculture and the nation modern, self-sufficient, productive, developed. A close examination of the microtechniques of agriculture shows the extent to which epistemologies and practices of farming had been shaped by the hybridities that characterize postcolonial conditions.

Weeding

"Weeding once is worth two coats of fertilizer," a farmer in Alipur told me, emphasizing the importance of this activity. Once the crops were sown, they had to be periodically weeded and irrigated. This was time consuming but could be done over a period of days by the entire family. For most crops, a small hand hoe was used. The person weeding would squat in the field, grab the offending plant with one hand, use the hoe in the other to dig up its roots, and then put it in an improvised bag slung around the waist. It was an extremely labor-intensive procedure but, compared with the use of herbicide, ecologically benign. It was not unusual to see entire families—men, women, and children—weeding together. Hired labor was almost never used for weeding purposes. Because "weeds" were used as green fodder for cattle, the speed of weeding was regulated by the need for fodder. People usually started from one corner of their plot and stopped when they had collected enough green fodder for that day's feed. The following day, they began weeding from where they had left off.

Suresh had weeded both his maize and bajra crop twice, whereas the normal practice would have been to weed maize more than bajra. Asked about the importance of weeding, he clarified that the weeds [kharpatvaar] would have competed for nutrients [tatv] with the maize, resulting in a weak crop. He speculated that not weeding might have reduced output to as little as half of normal. No fixed number of weedings was

A family weeding their plot

considered "necessary"; the number of times one weeded depended on the plot. Full production could be obtained only if the fields were cleaned every time weeds appeared. After sowing, it took fifteen or twenty days for the plant to grow enough for four or five leaves to appear. That signaled the right time to begin the first weeding. One of the advantages of using the hand hoe was that it turned the soil and made it more fertile. Thus, if it rained immediately after one had weeded or if the field was irrigated soon after, the soil retained moisture better and did not dry out rapidly. The next step, according to Suresh, came after the maize plant was a little bigger.

> And then after this when the knot explodes [*gaanth phutthi*], when the ear [*kukdi*] emerges, when the maize leaf comes out, then it is very important to weed. It is extremely necessary because we people have estimated [*andaz*] that it is only because of the heat that the leaf emerges from the green plant. From below, we will weed it, make it dry [*khushki*]. The sun's light will fall on it from the top, then maize will come out from the entire plant. When the maize is ready to come out, at that very time we weed it, and at that very time apply potent [*urvarak*] fertilizer—urea, or whatever fertilizer one wants to apply.

Clearly, the most forceful notion operating behind this explanation is the humoral reasoning that a burst of "heat" will push the growth of the plant in the crucial stage of cob production. Weeding both cleared the ground of other plants that were competing with the maize plant for nutrients and turned the soil over, thus further drying it. At the same time, a potent fertilizer like urea, which was considered extremely hot and dry, would accelerate the process. Once again, the timing of the application of chemical fertilizers was based on a humoral logic about the life stage of the plant as well as an understanding of the properties of that fertilizer. Suresh told me regretfully that in his own fields only half the plants bore cobs because he did not have the money to apply fertilizer and the late rains did not allow sufficient time for the entire plot to be weeded.

Suresh told me that if he had had the money to apply fertilizer, he would have applied one coat at the time of sowing, another one after the first time the corn was weeded, and a second dose when the cob first emerged. Those who did not apply fertilizer at the time of sowing applied it after the crop was weeded the second time. Bajra did not need to be weeded as often as maize, because after weeding it twice, it became so tall and grew so dense that one was unable to squat in the field without damaging the crop. So the right time to weed was when the first leaves emerged and then after two or three weeks. And if the field had been plowed a larger number of times to prepare it for sowing, then it could be weeded just once, and that too would be sufficient for bajra.

The term sometimes used for weeding was "dressing" the field [*khayt sajaana*].[50] "Sajaana" suggests "to make beautiful" or "to adorn." Thus apart from its instrumental effects of being "worth two coats of fertilizer," weeding also had an important function in the aesthetics of farming. Was the use of this phrase related in any way to the visual differences between agriculture before and after the introduction of green revolution wheat? Even in 1984–85, farmers in Alipur typically intercropped several minor crops into a major one: thus mustard was normally grown in the raised mounds that separated plots of wheat; a number of smaller crops were typically raised in corn; and sugarcane too had minor crops grown between the rows. Some farmers suggested that raising crops in rows, a practice deemed necessary in "scientific" agriculture to maximize the efficiency of inputs, was a relatively recent practice in Alipur and may have become "normal" only after the introduction of high-yielding varieties. "Modern" farming, with crops growing in straight lines, had its own aesthetic in which heavily intercropped plots appeared hopelessly haphazard and unkempt. Was this judgment incorporated in describing the uprooting of weeds as "adorning" the field?[51]

Explanations of the need for weeding and of the speed at which it was done were therefore composed of a balance between considerations that emerged from a humoral understanding of the effects of weeding and those from the household's requirements for fodder and from the substitution effects of plowing. Suresh's account, for example, drew on humoral agronomy and from a particle theory of matter.

Irrigation

Tube wells had enabled the farmers of Alipur to grow multiple crops in a year. Most farmers grew at least two, and those with good sources of water and ample supplies of household labor sometimes grew as many as four crops in an annual cycle. Of the two main growing seasons, tube wells were used mostly for supplementary purposes during the kharif growing season; by contrast, the rabi crop relied heavily on this relatively new technology.[52]

Tube wells are so named because they consist of a thin pipe that is sunk into the ground and attached to a pump on the surface. In Alipur, the water level in 1984–85 stood at a mere thirty-six to forty-two feet. The pipe on the surface pumped water into a small holding area, from where it was distributed by gravity flow to small irrigation canals. Fields were partitioned into rectangular plots by building embankments a few inches high to separate them from one another. Then, the irrigation canal was "cut" to allow water into one plot until it was saturated and so forth until the entire field had been irrigated. Getting the job done was a challenge under conditions of uncertain electric supply. Most tube wells in Alipur were electrically powered; hence irrigation could be accomplished only when there was electricity. In 1984–85, the supply of electricity alternated between days in one week and nights in the next. But there were often times when there was no electricity at all, either because there was no supply in the grid or because a local transformer had burned out. If, for instance, the electric supply suddenly stopped after water had been pumped for an hour and only two-thirds of the first rectangular plot had received water, then when the supply resumed the patch that had been previously irrigated would have to be saturated again before the water reached the unirrigated portion of the plot. Thus, stop-and-start electric supply extracted a high price in terms of the inefficient utilization of water.

One of the advantages of tube wells was that people had started to

Tube well powered by diesel pump set

plant crops before the first monsoon downpour, whereas previously they had to wait for the rains. However, although widespread, this practice was not considered desirable by everyone. In the first week of July, after a long, excruciatingly hot, and seemingly unending summer, I talked to different individuals about the effect of monsoon rains on the crops. The monsoons had teased us the previous week, providing a sprinkling instead of the sheets of rain that announced the beginning of the rainy season. We could feel the moisture in the hot air, the wind would even pick up on occasion, but the rain stayed frustratingly out of reach, testing our patience.

Walking back on the main road from the village to the farm where I lived, I had to pass by the small, thatched hut of an impoverished brahmin family. They were so poor that the eldest son, Hukum, had to work on a long-term wage contract with a politically powerful thakur family as, in effect, an indentured laborer. The younger son managed the family's own land while the elder tried to raise some cash for inputs. In the evening, on my way back to my room, I saw Hukum on the side of the road, and we started talking about the lack of rainfall and the state of the crops. Hukum announced that he believed that one good monsoon rain was equivalent to irrigating four times with a tube well. The plants started growing only after the monsoons and would shoot up rapidly once the rains arrived. He pointed to some fodder growing on the side of his plot and said that if the rains had come, they would have grown up to his chest, but because the monsoon had been delayed, they had not been doing so well.

As we were talking, another young man, Devendra, came by and joined our conversation. Devendra was an enterprising jat whose family was widely considered to be the richest in Alipur. Devendra expressed the wish that the rains be delayed by a few more days. He had already had to replant his maize once because of the light sprinkling of rain the previous week. Instead of soaking the soil, the rain had wet the soil enough to form a hard crust that the new seedlings had been unable to pierce. Thus, he had sown maize for a second time. If it did not rain the following week, the seedlings would break through the ground, and then the timing and amount of rainfall would matter less. If it rained heavily, the whole ground would be soft, and the seedlings would easily come up through the moist soil. But if it rained lightly once again, the same problem would arise and most of the plants would stay inside the ground, thus yielding a poor output. Most of all, it was the uncertainty of rainfall that was harmful. Many farmers had lost even the second round of maize because the heat that year had proved to be too intense for the young shoots. Only very heavy rain would have cooled the land enough and provided the moisture necessary for a good harvest.

One difference between a crop such as maize and a millet like bajra was that the former required regular irrigation. Suresh emphasized the importance of water to me: "For all crops, it's necessary to get water on time—for maize as well as for bajra. Whenever the crop needs water, then it should be given. Maize too demands water. If there is no rain, and the clouds go away sometimes in the middle of the monsoons [*sawan*], it gets dry. Then we apply water to the maize from our electric tube wells. Bajra stays put for many days, although it reduces the output, but maize dries completely. [Without water] a little bit of bajra is still produced." The ability of bajra to withstand irregular irrigation made it a favorite among people with poor access to irrigation water. This included farmers who had no tube well, who did not have the resources to purchase irrigation water from neighbors, or who did not have neighbors who were willing to sell water to them.

In the winter harvest, those with inconsistent access to water resources chose to grow barley rather than wheat for much the same reason. Suresh stressed that barley should not be irrigated more than four times, as compared with a desired six or seven irrigations for wheat.

I received one irrigation late anyway and more than four irrigations should not be applied for the reason that barley does not grow with much water. In barley, more water is not needed because when its head is quite big, when its shape is fully determined, then if water is given, it is good. This water carries over, the plant doesn't dry out. If there is a shortage of water, barley doesn't dry but keeps growing like bajra. Whereas wheat will wilt. It affects wheat a great deal if water is not given. Barley is not so sensitive. It ripens in less time, whereas wheat takes more time to ripen because it is irrigated more.

Timing was of crucial importance. It was not only that wheat had to be irrigated a greater number of times but also that it was "less forgiving" if water was not applied at the right time. Barley "allowed" greater leeway as long as it was irrigated once soon after the head of grain first emerged. The length of the growing season was of great consequence here. Frequent irrigation was required in the last three weeks to a month before wheat was harvested. This was when the heat began to get more intense, the days lengthened, and the crop risked drying out if its need for water was not closely monitored. By harvest time, in the first half of April, the sun was blazing. Harvesting was done early in the morning and in the late afternoon. Not even people used to the heat dared to be out in the fields between ten and three in the middle of the day. The fact that barley was harvested earlier quite significantly correlated to its lower "demand" for irrigation water. In speaking thus of the crop as possessing the "ability" to withstand irregular irrigation, of being "less forgiving" or "needing" or "demanding" water, I employ the same vocabulary as that used by farmers in Alipur. In this view, crops are not conceptualized as inert objects that are acted on by external "forces" such as human beings and the weather but as possessing a constitution, needs, and desires.

Despite the lower demands for water made by barley and its relatively forgiving nature if irrigation was inadequate, timing was critical not only to stave off disastrous outcomes but also to obtain good yields. Suresh explained the sequence in which the four irrigations should be applied to barley.

One in the beginning for when the field is sown. The second irrigation when the plant begins to progress, when it pushes out of the soil. And the third irrigation is applied when it starts growing upward, when the plant becomes approximately one foot or one-half foot. Then the field itself tells you, the leaves shrivel—water is applied then. Three irrigations are done! The fourth irrigation is applied when hair emerges from the head. It should be irrigated then because fairly long hair emerges by applying water. But water should not be applied on ripening; otherwise, the barley will lodge and turn yellow. It will no longer stay white. Why? Because of steam from the ground. Or the plant is uprooted because the soil becomes soft from the water. That's how barley becomes yellow and weak. So for this reason, it does not need water on ripening. If it rains, the barley will get spoiled too.

The chance of rain late in the harvest season, when the barley was almost ripe, was rather small. The danger, therefore, was not as much from a freak rainstorm as from an inexperienced farmer, who might irrigate the barley when it was ripe. That could be disastrous because the hot and wet atmosphere provided by the water would cause the grain to turn yellow. By upsetting the humoral balance, excessively moist heat damaged the quality and shine of the grain and gave it a sickly, yellow appearance. If not that, then the soil became so soft that the plant lodged in the stiff breeze prevalent at harvest time.

The most interesting feature of Suresh's exposition was that the correct times for different irrigations were all indicated with reference to the stages of the plant's growth, rather than by dates on the calendar, the days from sowing, or the interval between stages. In fact, a crucial irrigation, the third, depended entirely on the land announcing a need: "The field itself tells you."[53] The notion of wetness was consistently used to estimate the appropriate time to irrigate a crop, the goal being to maintain the appropriate balance of moistness at all stages of the plant's growth. Suresh, for example, attempted to steer between the extremes of the leaves shriveling and the grain becoming yellow.

With reference to his mustard crop, Suresh told me that the third and final irrigation was applied after the mustard was ready to ripen. The water entered the mustard seed and made it plump. "After flowering, when it starts becoming a pod, then apply water once. It's not applied during flowering because if water is applied to the flower, the flower at once sheds and then the pod cannot form." But why did irrigating the plant in its flowering phase cause it to shed? Again, the explanation was offered in humoral terms: "When water is applied below, then rot is produced in the flower because of the wetness of the water. From above, it receives heat. The flower is extremely delicate so it sheds its petals and falls. So it affects the crop, the output, because pods cannot form. If water is administered only when it is ready to form seed, then the seed will form completely." The flower possessed a finely tuned and easily disturbed "constitution." In its flowering phase, the plant was at an exceedingly delicate stage of its life cycle, and extra precautions had to be taken to maintain the proper balance of elements required for good health. Excessive wetness, combined with the sun's heat, would have disturbed the fine balance required for the flower to survive. The logic of explanation of indigenous knowledges, therefore, imposed on their practitioners a pattern of timing with regard to their agricultural activities. The growth and health of the plant, understood in relation to humoral categories and explanations, thus determined the timing and frequency of the application of water.

At the same time, farmers in Alipur also discussed irrigation in relation to the properties of electric pumps and the design of tube wells. Because the method of irrigation employed was gravity flow, an intimate knowledge of the topography of the land was essential to understand differences in the output of crops. Talking to one another, villagers in Alipur did not use directional indicators to refer to places within a field. For example, instead of saying "at the southwest corner of the plot," they were more likely to say "the lower part of the field." One had to know not only where a particular peasant's fields were but also its microtopography. I frequently found myself clueless on encountering statements about location that were obviously very meaningful to everyone else. For instance, I once asked Dhani Singh why he obtained a yield of only 3¼ mans/bigha in his wheat crop, whereas others in the village had obtained yields of twice as much, despite the fact that he had irrigated it no less than six times. He replied patiently: "So how does it matter? That field comes down like this—it's a sloping field. For example, if this [gesturing] is a flat [eksaar] field, then the water will fill it equally. So the production will be okay. And those fields that are like this [indicates slope], the field can drink only as long as the water is flowing [chaltaa rahegaa]. All the water goes down the slope. The production on the higher side is killed." And was there a technique to overcome this problem? The only method that he could suggest was to take a leveling board and attempt to level the field as much as possible. Obviously, all fields had some slope, otherwise gravity irrigation would not work. However, Dhani Singh was pointing to the negative effects of a field tilted at too steep an angle. The higher ends of such a field could not retain enough moisture to support a good wheat crop. An intimate

Plots are irrigated by gravity flow in small segments

knowledge of the quality of the soil and the topography of the field was thus essential for decisions about what kinds of crops to grow, how much fertilizer and water to give them, and when to supply inputs.

Humoral theories relating to "wetness" were thus woven into explanations about the timing of irrigation, the number of irrigations provided, the resistance of particular crops to shortages of water, and the topography of fields. An understanding of the relationship between irrigation, crops, and land was not limited to that which could be provided by humoral agronomy but combined with other factors. The fate of the crop did not depend merely on what was done to it; it too had an active role to play. The crops and fields had dispositions and needs and made demands: a crop could be "forgiving" for being supplied irrigation unevenly; the field itself told the farmer when it needed water; and a sharply sloping field could "kill" the crop by "drinking" water unevenly. In the last section of this chapter, I demonstrate the political contexts for irrigation decisions in order to complicate the "readings" presented here even further.

Fertilizer use

In 1984–85, chemical fertilizers were used by practically all farmers in Alipur, except those few who were too poor to afford them. Fertilizer was not applied uniformly to all crops, being used much more heavily for the main cash crops—wheat, sugarcane, and mustard—and less for other crops. Three types of fertilizer were most frequently employed: diammonium phosphate, popularly called "Di" or DAP; NPK (a mixture of sodium, phosphate, and potassium); and urea, a nitrogenous fertilizer that was by far the most popular. Fertilizer could be applied either at the time of sowing or later on, when the crop was growing. For those who could afford it, DAP was the preferred fertilizer to sow with (called the basal dressing), although NPK was also used. Urea was almost always employed as top dressing. Most farmers in Alipur applied at least one top dressing in wheat and sometimes two, but very rarely did they apply urea three times. I was questioning Suresh about the amount of urea he had applied in his wheat crop. Why had he used 8 kg/bigha and not more? (The modal amount was 10 kg/bigha; those well off used even more.) He replied: "The VLW [village-level worker] has told us that the diet [khuraak] for one acre is one sack DAP and two sacks urea.[54] This is what we have been told for wheat. He has also told us the calculations for nitrogen in terms of sacks, that so much percentage nitrogen should be present. All I know is a rough [mota-mota] approximation: sow one sack DAP on one acre and apply two sacks of urea as a top dressing at two different times. I just keep the broad principles [mota-mota sidhaant] in mind."[55] I reminded Suresh that he had not actually stuck to these broad principles, for he had used only one sack of urea instead of the two recommended. He replied that they had not been able to afford more fertilizer at that time. He continued: "I also believed that there is some manure lying here that will have a positive effect, so why waste money? For this reason, we didn't put more fertilizer." The superiority of organic manure to chemical fertilizer was a common theme in the discourse of farmers in Alipur. In fact, chemical fertilizers were considered a poor replacement for manure, resorted to only because of the lack of adequate supplies of the latter. Thus, Suresh's justification for not using additional fertilizer was not at all unusual, although he clearly did not have the resources to purchase more chemical fertilizer even if he had wanted to do so. One of the reasons manure was considered so effective was that farmers believed that it released its heat slowly, thus imparting strength to the soil over a period of three years.[56] In a humoral agronomy, the effectiveness of fertilizer was a consequence of the "heat" it imparted to the plant. Heat pushed the plants upward, providing the energy necessary for growth. The difference between chemical fertilizer and organic manure was that the former released its heat all at once and with great intensity, whereas the latter released its heat slowly over several years. Suresh's account thus freely combined recommendations based on the need to supply a certain amount of nitrogen, translated by means of a rough approximation into so many sacks per acre, with a humoral theory that encouraged the substitution of manure for chemical fertilizer.

Such vigorous eclecticism is not terribly unusual in South Asia, as numerous studies of the use of healing practices have demonstrated (Leslie 1992; Obeyesekere 1992; Trawick 1992). However, it is not merely the fact that farmers in Alipur relied on radically different, or perhaps incommensurable, prescriptions for agricultural practice that makes this such an interesting case. Rather, as I will presently demonstrate, it is that biochemical inputs were simultaneously incorporated into a humoral agronomy and retained within a "scientific" discourse whose autonomy was recognized and maintained. Contrary to some of the functionalist assumptions of theories of "indigenous knowledge," it was not only knowledges compatible with the "indigenous system" that found widespread acceptance. In fact, as noted above, very few of the connotations of "systemness"—coherence, order, some stable relation between parts, functionality, and clear boundaries—could be found in this case. For example, Suresh explained the difference between diammonium phosphate and NPK in this way:

> DAP turns out to be good. Why? At the time of sowing, DAP gives the seed enough heat for the plant to maintain itself till the very end. NPK cannot manage to give as much heat as DAP. This is what's special about Di, DAP. So DAP is better compared with NPK while sowing. On top, we put nothing else, only urea. Ammonium sulphate is applied only in maize. But now everyone applies urea. The vw [village-level worker] tells us that increasing the growth of the plant requires nitrogen. Thus, when the plant begins to grow, then just give urea as the top dressing, that's what they say. We have sown phosphate below. For growth, give it urea. The phosphate gives it heat. As the hen gives heat to its egg by sitting on it, so DAP gives heat to the seed, then the production is good. And to make that plant grow on top, as a top dressing urea works. Urea makes it grow, DAP makes it sprout. For this reason, the crop is good with both things.

Suresh here effortlessly switched back and forth from the "scientifically" based recommendations of the VLW to "indigenous" knowledges based in a humoral agronomy. The analogy with the hen "naturalized" chemical fertilizer so that it appeared integral to the production process rather than a fairly recent innovation. Basal and top dressings of fertilizer played very different roles in the life of the plant: the fertilizer planted with the seed gave it the heat required to make it sprout, whereas top dressings made the plant gain height—that is, "shoot up."

However important top dressing may have been to the growth of the plant, one had to be careful about using too much of it. Sompal Singh, the thakur introduced at the beginning of this chapter, explained why: "If you put more fertilizer, barley will grow taller. When it grows tall and you irrigate it, there is the danger of it falling. If the standing barley lodges, the production will be lower. So thinking this, one can't put too much fertilizer." Urea, the intensely hot and dry fertilizer used as top dressing, caused the stalk of the plant to grow too much. Irrigation, which was then necessary, increased its wetness and pliability, thus making it more vulnerable to lodging on a windy day.

From these explanations of agricultural practice in Alipur, it should be clear that biochemical agriculture is not merely "translated" into an indigenous system, which has merely incorporated new elements into an old structure of oppositions and correspondences. Rather, what one finds is that farmers draw on diverse modes of explanation simultaneously, combining in sometimes startling and ingenious ways modes of thought that cannot be recuperated into an analytically neat "whole."

Wind

One factor that made an important difference to the growth of plants was the wind. Explanations of good output (or, conversely, of poor output) frequently depended on the direction and timing of the wind. If there were periods of gusty wind immediately after the final irrigation, for example, the crop would lodge, and output would be low. On the other hand, some crops needed to be exposed to the wind to give adequate yields. The wind did not merely serve to dry the moisture in the stalks (that function was largely attributed to the sun) but also was a factor that, like heat and moisture, was inherently necessary for crop growth. As Kurin (1983) has pointed out, air is considered one of the primary constituents of matter and is accordingly considered an input in a sense that is absent in "Western" agronomy.

For example, one of the really important factors in getting good yields from lentils was to plant them far enough apart that the wind could pass through the rows. Sompal explained why he had obtained such a poor yield in these terms: "When the wind doesn't pass through

Winnowing mustard

it, how can the pods emerge? They only come out on top, on a little bit of the stalk. If the lentil (arhar) is sparsely planted, then it gets pods all around because it's exposed on all four sides." Sompal had broadcast arhar instead of planting it in rows. Lacking experience in farming, he had used too much seed per unit of land. As a result, the arhar plants grew very close to one another. Urea helped them grow, but they yielded very few lentils. So Sompal harvested mainly firewood from the lentil crop, getting pods only from the very tops of the plant, which were exposed to the wind.

It may seem that I have overlooked the obvious explanation that the injunction to allow the "wind to pass" between the rows is simply a means to ensure that the lentils are planted in rows and spaced far enough apart. But this example really points to a class of explanations in which the direction and timing of the wind is held to be responsible for certain consequences. Thus, the reason a crop did badly might be explained by the untimely presence of "gusts from the south" or "unusually hot winds" and so on.

Unlike Sompal, Narain was an experienced farmer, considered one of the best in the village. He attributed his superior farming skills to the fact that he had grown up on a farm and, additionally, had learned quite a few things from the various government farms on which he had served. Narain was technically a civil servant and was employed full-time on the government seed farm in Alipur. But he also did his own farming by renting in land from someone in the village. Narain managed what was the equivalent of two full-time jobs with a great degree of skill, doing just enough work on the government farm to get by and devoting his prodigious energy to getting good outputs on the farm that he had rented. He proudly told me that every piece of land that he had rented had yielded superior output because he never skimped on inputs. By the time his wheat would be harvested, he would have irrigated it nine times. "Can you find another farmer in the village who has put as much water in their wheat as me?" he inquired. Not even those who owned their own tube wells could match that figure. In the previous year (1984), however, Narain's crop had not been as good as he expected. Interestingly enough, the explanation he offered for that fact was that an ill wind had affected it [*buri havaa lag gayee*].

A similar incident involving the effects of malevolent winds was recollected by a group of farmers on another occasion. This was the year of India's first atomic explosion in the neighboring state of Rajasthan, which they variously dated as 1974–75 and 1978.[57] They said that the crop that year was destroyed because of the effects of the radiation. The farmers claimed that, as a consequence of the explosion, "ill winds blew

Threshing wheat with an electrically powered machine; women play an important role in postharvest operations

our way and destroyed our crops." They found very little grain inside the pods. In each bundle of cut grain for the bullocks to stamp (for threshing), there were hardly one or two mans of grain, whereas there should have been at least fifteen. Some of the farmers with whom I talked claimed that the government had deliberately suppressed the news of the bad effects of the explosion, and they were hence unable to estimate the extent to which the explosion had damaged the crops.

Once again, we find an almost stereotypical instance of indigenous knowledge—the importance of the wind in humoral agronomy—rendered unstable by its imbrication in modernist discourses about the nation-state. The effects of an ill wind are almost uniformly recognized, but the sources of the ill wind are in dispute. Is it the weather or the desperate efforts of the postcolonial nation-state to assert itself as a world power? Rather than ironically juxtaposing the scientific achievement of modernity symbolized by the atomic bomb explosion with the traditionalism of hapless farmers talking about malevolent winds, I suggest that the two phenomena are intimately linked in the consciousness of farmers themselves. The residents of Alipur knew that the atomic bomb was connected to the "development" of their nation. Even without an awareness of exactly what the atomic bomb was, they recognized it as a symbol of "progress" toward that exalted state of "development" that they, as citizens of a poor nation, were aspiring toward. At the same time, in connecting the ill winds to the power of the atomic bomb, Alipur's farmers displayed an understanding of the destructive potential of modernity, as well as a disturbingly clear assessment that it was people like them who would have to pay the price of "progress."

From "Indigenous Knowledge" to the Politics of Practice

What alternative descriptions might one provide for the agricultural practices portrayed above? It has already been hinted that "indigenous knowledge" is an inadequate basis for understanding agriculture in Alipur. What other forms of explanation—hybridized, incommensurable, mistranslated—might be necessary for a better understanding of farming in a postcolonial setting? In this section I argue that a move away from explanations that rely on the *alterity* of "indigenous knowledge" to those that embrace contradictory and perhaps unremarkable combinations (ranging from the imperatives of market prices, responsibility to the family, caste solidarity, and humoral agronomy) is a necessary step in order to understand the epistemologies and practices of farmers in postcolonial settings. To go from knowledges to practices is also to shift from cognitive conceptions of culture toward those which emphasize the embodied and enacted realities of the postcolonial *condition*. My goal in this section is to take a few instances to clarify this point and to deepen the explanations offered already.

Dhani Singh and his brother jointly owned one of the few tube wells on the far side of the Mandi road. In one detailed interview with Dhani Singh about his farming practices, he explained why he had not planted a high-yielding variety. A new variety, he said, would suffer if it was insufficiently irrigated. I expressed astonishment that a person who owned a tube well could conceivably have a problem with water. This is what he said: "We both have a problem with water, and to some extent, we don't. What is the reason for this? The reason is that a two-hundred-bigha area nearby has come under the command of our tube well. So we have to fulfill their needs too."[58] But why couldn't he fulfill his needs first *before* selling water to other neighbors? Because a system for sharing water allocated particular days to particular fields [*vaar pad jaaten hain*]. Agreements to purchase water were typically made at the beginning of the cropping season. It was decided in advance who would get water on a particular day of the week.[59] Given the erratic and highly uncertain supply of electricity, it was possible that a particular field that was to be irrigated every Wednesday, for example, might not receive any water for two successive weeks. Even the owner of the well, as in the case of Dhani Singh, might have found himself in that situation.

Although Dhani Singh, as the owner of his own tube well, was "free" not to share water with his neighbors, there were other models of water sharing in Alipur. Three farmers had split the expenses for a tube well, two of them having put in a quarter share and the third having put in a half. Water from the tube well was allocated by turns: three days to each of the two minor partners, followed by six days for the major partner. All three owned farms of roughly the same size, so the quarter partners were at a distinct disadvantage as compared with the one who owned half. But all of them were assured water at least once every nine days, again depending on the supply of electricity.

There was, of course, a solution to the unpredictability of the supply of electricity: to purchase a diesel pump set as a substitute for the electric motor. The diesel pump was more expensive to operate but it could be used at any time. Dhani Singh had considered purchasing a diesel engine, but at that time, there were conflicts in his family. Although I never did find out the source of this conflict, I gathered that it had to do with his elder brother's dissatisfaction with the sharing of the proceeds of farming. Dhani Singh's father was elderly and frail; rather than waiting until his father's death, as often was the case, to split the property among the three brothers, Dhani Singh's elder brother wanted his share of the property to be partitioned. That way he could move out of the joint household and save the income from farming his share of the property for his own nuclear family. The existing tube well fell in the elder brother's part of the property. If his elder brother paid them half the price of the tube well, Dhani Singh told me, they would use that money to install their own diesel pump set. But the elder brother gave no sign of buying out his share of the old tube well. So things stood as they were, with no prospects for change on the horizon.

One response to the unpredictability of the water supply was to change the crop mix. Sompal Singh, the thakur who was an inexperienced farmer, explained that he decided to grow barley instead of wheat because it required less irrigation. The specific actions taken by farmers in Alipur to combat the erratic supply of water relied on an understanding of the health of crops derived from humoral agronomy—for example, which crops were inherently hotter and wetter and would therefore do well with less irrigation or which crops were able to maintain their moisture for a long time and could sustain long periods of dryness with minimal loss of output. Humoral theories blended into explanations about social obligations and family politics to suggest why, for example, Dhani Singh did not irrigate his wheat more often or install a new tube well. An explanation based entirely on "indigenous knowledge" would be unlikely to account for this case. The pattern of irrigation employed by Dhani Singh was informed by both an understanding of the health of his crops derived from a humoral agronomy and, to the extent that they affected his ability to obtain water, negotiations with neighbors and conflicts within his family.

Such a conclusion emerges particularly forcefully in the case of Sompal Singh, who owned a not insubstantial piece of property—about twenty-eight bighas—on the western side of the village. But instead of farming his own land, which he had rented to someone else, he chose to cultivate a small plot rented from his father. Once, walking toward a distant grove in search of mangoes, I asked him about this unusual arrangement. I was unprepared for Sompal's intensely emotional response, which revealed his troubled relationship with his parents. Although Sompal lived *in* the same home as his parents, he did not live *with* them. The family home had been partitioned into two spaces, each with a separate hearth, an act that had crucial symbolic significance. As the middle of three brothers, Sompal felt that his parents treated him unfairly, giving him neither the privileges afforded the elder, who lived in his wife's village, nor the attention given the younger. These problems were evident in the handling of the family land. His parents owned sixty bighas (approximately nine and a half acres) in Alipur and an equal amount of land in his mother's village. The land in his mother's village had already been given to the eldest brother; now, the elder brother was insisting that what remained in Alipur be split equally among the three brothers, which Sompal thought would be unfair. His father had held on to most of the land, postponing the inevitable decision, but had already given Sompal a little less than half the total. Although his father had leased Sompal some land in 1984–85, he had refused to do so earlier, instead preferring to lease it to other people. He knew that Sompal did not have any other source of employment, yet he continually turned down Sompal's requests to lease additional land. When Sompal tried to cultivate sugarcane on the part of the land that he had leased, his father flatly told him that he could not expect to rent the land the following year and therefore should not plant an annual crop such as sugarcane.

Sompal's disillusionment with his parents stemmed from the periods shortly after the birth of his first child and his youngest daughter. Each of the two children had fallen seriously ill, and Sompal had no source of income on both occasions. He requested some monetary help from his parents but was rebuffed. "My parents could very well afford to spend some money on my sick children and my wife, but they just refused to do so. Now, even when I feel sorry when I see my old father toiling in the fields and sometimes think I should go and help him, my feelings refuse to assist me. My heart doesn't go out to him at all." Sompal's voice cracked as he spoke, reliving the bitterness and disappointments of the past. We walked silently for a while, the space between us heavy with this revelation, listening to the steady clatter of the bicycle that he was pushing with one hand. Sompal proceeded to tell me that his parents had spent a lot of money paying for the treatment of his elder brother, who had been seriously ill for the previous two years. He did not grudge the fact that his parents were looking after his elder brother; what really hurt him was the fact that they had discriminated against him.[60]

Sompal explained his rather unusual situation (of renting in property from his father while renting out his own land) by telling me that the main reason why he rented out his own property was that he had no ready access to irrigation. The tube well that supplied irrigation water to his field was owned by Sher Singh, with whom he was on polite, but distinctly cool, terms.[61] Operating his own fields would have placed him in a position requiring frequent contact and exchanges with Sher Singh, exchanges, moreover, in which he would be in a weaker, dependent position. For this reason, he preferred to rent out his property, earning a combination of up-front cash and, at the end of the year, a fixed quantity of the wheat harvest.[62] His tenant had to be a person who could get along well with Sher Singh. More often than not, Sher Singh himself chose the tenant and brought him to Sompal for approval. Sompal felt comfortable with this procedure because if later there were conflicts between his tenant and Sher Singh, he did not need to get involved on behalf of his tenant, as might reasonably have been expected of a landlord. On their part, prospective tenants knew that Sher Singh was the person who could get them land to lease. In turn, Sher Singh carefully looked for a man who had young, unwed daughters with whom he could enjoy sexual liaisons. A complex triangular relation was thus set up between Sompal, the tenant, and Sher Singh.

Sher Singh's ability to use his tube well as a source of power forms an interesting contrast with the case of Dhani Singh mentioned earlier. Dhani Singh was unable to use his tube well to irrigate his own fields in a timely manner because he was "bound" by the arrangement made with his neighbors to share water with them. Therefore his ownership of the means of production—that is, the tube well—did not, by itself, enable him to exert control over others either directly or through their recruitment as clients. Sher Singh's importance in village politics flowed, as I have argued in the previous chapter, from the intersection of his class position and his status as a broker by virtue of the "contacts" he had in the state bureaucracy. The importance of his class position, in fact, is what enabled him to convert ownership of the means of production into political power through his ability to recruit clients and establish his position as village strongman. By contrast, Dhani Singh was unable to push people around. His family had arrived in the village only a few years ago and occupied a peripheral position in every sense of the term—politically, socially, and in terms of prestige.[63] He had to establish a bank of goodwill that could be drawn on for the sort of everyday conflicts that frequently afflicted families in the village. Thus, even though it sometimes had adverse effects on his own farming, he had "no choice" but to distribute the sale of irrigation water in a regular and socially acceptable manner.

The politics of agricultural decisions illustrated through this contrast between Sher Singh and Dhani Singh adds a further twist to the consideration of "indigenousness" pursued through the detailed discussion of specific agricultural practices. It reminds us of the importance of not overlooking structural inequalities in discussions of hybridity. Although neither Sher Singh's nor Dhani Singh's agricultural practices could be explained solely with reference to indigenous knowledge and even though both farmers were interpellated by the discourses of a developmentalist nation-state, the significantly different structural positions they occupied had enormous consequences for their everyday lives. In Alipur, caste-specific practices provided an important, articulated marker for underlining social distinctions. One of the most important mechanisms by which caste was naturalized was with reference to the activities of women in different caste groups. For instance, whereas women from the thakur households rarely ventured outside the home and were not allowed to do any work in the fields, jat women worked alongside their husbands and fathers at almost all agricultural tasks.[64] This does not imply that thakur women did not make an important contribution to agricultural activities—a lot of the postharvest work was done inside the house. Nevertheless, the restriction that they could not work in the fields did constrain the household labor supply in crucial ways. Interestingly, the mechanization of postharvest operations further reduced their importance and pulled more severely on the cash reserves of these households.[65]

An interesting case of the manner in which class status and caste ranking combined to influence agricultural action is provided by Sompal. Forced to rent out his own land, Sompal preferred to remain unemployed and do odd jobs rather than become a tenant himself. When I asked him to explain why he was reluctant to rent land for farming, he replied: "I'm also a farm owner, and so I feel ashamed to work for another person. If I didn't own any land, then I could go and rent land from someone else. But to go and take in land from someone else while possessing your own—one hesitates a little, that's all." He then told me that none of the thakurs would think of being tenants because "all have fields so there's no reason to rent in anybody else's land." At the same time, he acknowledged that the practice of tenancy was common among even those jats who were substantial landowners ("Oh, yes, those people do rent land"). Obviously, owning land had different implications for tenancy in the case of thakurs than in the case of jats. These implications were so obvious to Sompal that it did not even strike him as a contradiction that the fact of landownership satisfactorily explained why thakurs did not rent in land and, simultaneously, failed to explain why jats did so. The ideological transparency of Sompal's beliefs lay in the hegemonic position historically enjoyed by the thakurs as "owners" of the village. To be a tenant in the old order of things was to be a client of the thakurs. The previous chapter has demonstrated that patrons no longer use tenancy as an important means to recruit clients. The jats who, in any case, were tenants in the old order incurred no symbolic losses in capitalizing on the new opportunities. But old associations persisted, so how could a thakur, lord of the village, become a tenant and "work for someone else"? Although no longer inconceivable, becoming a tenant could not have been an appealing prospect to someone like Sompal.

The hegemony of the landed castes played a very important role in the justifications given for assessing "proper" or "appropriate" rates for goods and services. For example, wages were fixed at ten rupees per day[66] for all agricultural tasks performed by men except for a brief period during the harvesting of the rabi crop.[67] Although wholesale shifts in the wage rate could be masked by changes in labor contracts, one might still have expected a dispersion of wage rates reflecting the difficulty of the task and the quality of work. In fact, such market-clearing adjustments were noticeably absent. "Good relations," not the promise of higher wages, is what attracted a laborer to a particular employer, providing a sharp contrast to the individualistic and merito-cratic ideology of what a "just wage" should "naturally" have been. However, a laborer who made a reputation for himself as a "good worker" could choose where he wanted to work but could not demand a higher wage.

A number of farmers in the village claimed that the need to obtain fodder for their animals was an important reason for planting particular crops such as barley. I asked Suresh why he did not plant the most profitable crop and buy the fodder he needed from someone else. At first he said that fodder was not available in the village. When I pointed out that the lower-caste households who were in the buggy (buffalo cart) rental business had more work on their hands than they could handle transporting surplus fodder from the village to the market in town, he said that they would not sell him a small enough quantity of fodder. Finally, it emerged that the main reason for his reluctance to purchase fodder was that he did not think they sold it at the "proper" or "appro-priate" rate. This sentiment was widely shared, as evidenced by the fact

Harvesting with a sickle

that farmers frequently cited a desire for homegrown fodder as the most important reason for planting a particular crop.

The manner in which production decisions were entangled in the politics of family, community, and state is best illustrated by the example of Suresh. Suresh owned a plot of fairly rich land to the northern side of the village that was considered small even by village standards (approximately two acres). With three of his four children in their teens, there were many mouths to feed, but the ratio of "productive" to "nonproductive" members in the family was high.[68] His two sons had dropped out of school and worked full-time on the family farm. Suresh himself preferred not to do any farmwork.[69] Instead, he devoted himself fully to his role as the village priest, which brought in a steady but meager stream of cash income. In the summer, not too long before I was to leave Alipur, Suresh disappeared from the village for an extended period of time. His children and wife claimed not to know where he had gone. Soon I started hearing rumors that he had left the village for fear of being imprisoned. The source of his troubles, I learned, was some transactions with the "Society," the local production cooperative housed in a nearby village.

I reconstructed the sequence of events by talking to many different people, including Satvati Devi, his wife, who everybody called "pandi-taini";[70] some of his friends and neighbors; and his uncle. Despite

After the crop is harvested, it is tied into small bundles;
every twentieth bundle is given to the laborers as wages

spending innumerable hours with me, Suresh never directly talked to
me about his problems. While interviewing him about his farming activities, I discreetly raised the issue by asking him why he did not obtain
fertilizer on credit from the Society. I had hoped he would launch into
the details of his own case to explain why he did not use the Society, but
he kept his pride and gave me a "straight" answer instead. The "straight"
answer was that the cooperative failed to deliver fertilizer to the farmer
in time for sowing and if for some reason the crop was ruined, the
interest continued to accumulate, proving too burdensome to pay back.

After the death of his father, Suresh was still living with his two
uncles in a joint household. The family lands were also farmed jointly.
At that time, they decided to take a seed loan from the Society, with
Suresh as the official borrower. The panditaini told me that instead of
sowing the seed so obtained, Suresh's uncles decided literally "to eat it
all up." On their part, Suresh's uncles alleged that he had sold the seed in
the market and spent the money in gambling and on liquor. The pandi-
taini agreed that her husband had never fancied farming and may even
have been considered lazy, but she vehemently denied that he would
ever have squandered money gambling or drinking. "A person just
doesn't change overnight," she said, appealing to the "good" reputation
that Suresh enjoyed as a priest.[71] In any case, the net result was that the

loan was not paid back and the interest started to mount. To add to the complications, the secretary of the cooperative society was alleged to have manipulated the books to increase the amount of the outstanding loan. At first, Suresh refused to pay on principle. Later, because he had split to establish his own household and was no longer in possession of enough land to make a go of it, paying back the loan was beyond his means. But since he was still legally responsible, he had been jailed for a few days in 1984. When I was in Alipur in 1985, at that time of the year when the Society's books were balanced, he was afraid that the police would be informed again and he would find himself in jail once more. He thus left the village temporarily, and rather than risk the humiliation and perhaps the financial burden of imprisonment, he spent a month and a half with relatives in a nearby city.

This case is interesting because it demonstrates very clearly why paying attention to the politics of production is so important. As a highly regarded priest, Suresh's father occupied a position of great moral authority in the village. Even when I was in Alipur, people talked of him with an affection bordering on reverence. Although he had not farmed, Suresh's father clearly controlled the family's agricultural activities. After his death, the ideology of mutual responsibility underlying the joint family forced Suresh, as the only educated person, into the position of official borrower. But Suresh had been unaware of the impending dissolution of the joint family. When the family split, Suresh's resource base dwindled to his small share of the property, a position from which he would have had to struggle very hard to pay back the loan. Lacking both his father's authority to force his uncles to pay their share and the ability to muster the support of other villagers, Suresh was unable to pin the responsibility for the loss on his uncles.[72] Further, the conflict in his family and his peripheral position in the village enabled the cooperative officials to take advantage of his situation. Brahmins did not have much of a say in the management and functioning of the cooperative. One of the ways of balancing the books was to pass on the unpaid loans of locally powerful men to the accounts of those who were either illiterate or weak, preferably both. Suresh's "contacts" in the bureaucracy, which were mediated entirely by the brahmin headman, were ineffective in this case. Furthermore, his class position was marginal: he had neither the resources nor the connections to revise the doctored accounts.

Deeply in debt, Suresh might easily fit the classic modernization theory profile of a "backward-looking," tradition-bound nonadopter. Yet, if anything, the opposite was true. It is clear that Suresh's agricultural decisions could be understood only by placing him in the context of a wider political sphere—that is, by situating his actions at the intersection of the politics of family, village, and state. The intergenerational tensions implicit in the joint family precipitated, typically, in a rupture shortly after the death of the patriarch. The politics of family life, in turn, played into what was now an even more peripheral class position. Separation from his uncles left him without the well-established contacts needed with the state bureaucracy and quasi-state institutions such as the agricultural cooperative.

The detailed examination of agricultural practices in this section has been necessary to illustrate the complex interrelationship between "indigenous" knowledges and "modern" farming practices. What is apparent from the description of farming practices in Alipur is not so much the continued existence of a separate sphere of "indigenous knowledge" but the divergent ways in which "modern" farming is constructed in different parts of the world. In this section I have emphasized that the experience of modernity for the residents of Alipur is crucially mediated by the structural positions of subjects situated along specific axes of power. I have focused on inequalities flowing from the politics of family, caste, class, and gender and the imbrication of the farmers of Alipur in the postcolonial project of "development."

The earlier chapters have shown that the relation of postcolonial subjects to modernity is mediated by the development discourses of the nation-state. This chapter has demonstrated how scientific agriculture promulgated by the development efforts of a modern nation-state, in the form of hybrid seeds, tube well technology, chemical fertilizers, and "scientific" agronomy, *articulates* with price support programs, markets, village politics, and humoral agronomy to shape "indigenous" understandings of agriculture. Focusing on *practices* of agriculture, rather than on "indigenous" *knowledges,* gives substance to the interrelationship between humoral theories of agronomy, local politics, and the development-oriented institutions and policies of the nation-state.

If, from what has been described above, it is clear that "indigenousness" is a much more troubled notion than is admitted in the literature on "indigenous knowledges," how can we theorize such a location? What does "indigenousness" mean in the postcolonial world? Next, I explore these themes by surveying the role played by "the indigenous" in postcolonial theory.

Postcolonial Versions of "the Indigenous"

There are many contrasts—and no doubt some points of similarity—between the recuperation of "the indigenous" in nationalism and in postcolonial theory. Instead of rehearsing the debates about the term "postcolonial" that I mentioned in the introduction to this book, I will for my limited purposes here group what may appear to be very different approaches under this rubric. I will interpret the "post" in "postcolonial" broadly, not merely to indicate the end of colonial rule or administrative colonialism but also to signify the endless deferment of teleological narratives of progress, the abdication of what may be called the "temporalizing imperative." I interpret the "colonial" in "postcolonial" to be interrogating the limits of the Western episteme, as questioning the applicability of Enlightenment categories and epistemological grids to the "Third World." This is obviously a minimalist strategy that throws together positions which may be characterized as antimodernist, subalternist, and a stance defined both by anticolonialism and antinationalism. At the very least, what makes these positions different from colonial, nationalist, and developmentalist discourse is that "the indigenous" occupies a much more complex location within postcolonial theory.

For the purpose of this chapter, I will make one rather rough cut within postcolonial theory: between those versions which seek to create a space for indigenity and those which call its entire rhetoric and politics into question. In the first group, I will distinguish between four different approaches.

To begin with, certain approaches are premised on the negation of modernity. Here, "the West," colonialism, or nationalism can stand for modernity (Nandy 1980, 1983; Chatterjee 1986). In "Smallpox in Two Systems of Knowledge," a complex and richly detailed study that illustrates this viewpoint clearly, Frédérique Apffel Marglin (1990) argues that smallpox vaccination replaced an indigenous system of inoculation that was inseparably connected with the worship of the goddess Sitala. The British government's Western, statist, and logocentric approach to the eradication of smallpox is contrasted with the indigenous, popular, and nonlogocentric approaches to controlling the disease that existed prior to colonial rule. Although the new vaccination was technically superior to the indigenous method of inoculation it replaced, Marglin emphasizes that its widespread employment was accompanied by a great deal of symbolic violence and state repression. Marglin's conclusion forcefully brings out her critique: "Today's post-colonial governments have made the colonial governments' mode of thought their own. Decolonization has taken place on the land but not in the mind" (1990:140). This theme is echoed in the influential works of both Partha Chatterjee (1986) and Ashis Nandy (1980, 1983). Whereas the West first assails the indigenous in the context of colonial conquest, the end of colonialism witnesses the displacement of Western, Enlightenment, logocentric, modernist attitudes onto the postcolonial state. In this way of thinking, "the indigenous" that previously represented resistance to colonial power now represents resistance to the postcolonial state.

In critiques of modernity built on negation, the recuperation of Gandhi as an antimodern figure has been critical. Claude Alvares, for example, has this to say: "Gandhi remained an indigene *par excellence,* seldom apologetic for the positions he held" (1992:133). He approvingly quotes Gandhi's call for a return to "our own distinctive eastern traditions" in contradistinction to "an anglicized, denationalized being" (1992:134). Similarly, both Chatterjee (1986) and Nandy (1983) argue that Gandhi's opposition to modernity derives from his place "outside" the "West." But one could make a compelling case that Gandhi, far from being a paradigmatic figure of "indigenousness," is emblematic of both its *ambivalence* and its *multivalence.*[73] His criticisms of modernity derive both from his conversation with "Western" antimodernists and from his creative reinterpretations of "Indian tradition," as well as an intimate knowledge of rural life gleaned from living for several years in the countryside.[74]

There is a subtle but important difference between those who embrace the "indigenous" for its antimodernism and those who posit that it is implicated in a *necessary* relation of alterity within hegemonic constructions of difference. (This is the second approach to "the indigenous" that I wish to highlight.) I have already referred to Trouillot's argument that the "savage slot" arose in a triadic opposition to Renaissance conceptions of utopia and order. The indigenous, therefore, was "discovered," described, and mapped within a discursive field whose origins preceded that of the discipline of anthropology itself and perhaps even created the conditions for its emergence.[75] V. Y. Mudimbe (1988: 16–23) makes the further point that the reification of "the primitive" occurs in a period in which both imperialism and anthropology take shape. Far from being a vantage point that is opposed to modernity because it is "outside" it, "the indigenous," these analysts suggest, is a position that is not merely anticipated by modernity but demanded by it as well. Michael Taussig makes this point most forcefully when he says that "the phantom figure of the pure Indian becomes the object of desire by the First World" (1993:142). It is the desire for the indigenous that enables "the West" to construct its own identity through alterity. Taussig underlines that "alterity is every inch a relationship, not a thing" (1993:130), and one of the most powerful ways in which sameness can be maintained through alterity is by desiring a pure space of otherness, inhabited not by those who destabilize constructions of Self and Other but by phantom figures who occupy a space of pure oppositionality. In this view, the indigenous represents the desire for difference encoded in Western constructions of the Self.

Recognizing this does not by itself rule out the possibility that the indigenous can form the basis for resistance to hegemonic projects. The third position that I wish to elucidate here—namely, that of "the indigenous" as an invented space of authenticity—is precisely such a project. While the literature on the invention of tradition (Hobsbawm 1983) has most often been interpreted as providing the intellectual armory to undermine the claims of indigenous peoples to property rights and native practices, I want to suggest that the "invention of tradition" argument is far more open-ended, politically and practically, in its applications. One of the consequences of stressing that traditions are invented is that it fractures the chain which links authenticity to temporal depth, because the question of origins becomes paramount with a teleological view of history. Thus, the possibility of immobilizing movements of resistance or the construction of oppositional identities on the grounds that they are "invented" is undercut if one maintains that this is a feature of *all* traditions.[76] What matters is not the temporal depth of these identities but their existence. Therefore, claims to recompensation made by people dispersed by genocide, forced resettlement, and slavery need be justified not by reference to an originary or continuing cohesion but because of the wrongs committed against them (see Clifford 1988 for a brilliant case study of the Mashpee Indians).

A more directly effective political strategy than the antifoundationalism of the literature on the "invention of tradition" is the use of "the indigenous" as a strategic essentialism (this is the fourth, and last, position). Spivak (1988b:13) uses the term "strategic use of positive essentialism" to suggest that even when taking a critical position toward essentialism, one has to recognize not only that the essentializing moment is irreducible but also that it can be deployed in the pursuit of "a strictly visible political interest." This view of things is compatible with the position that "the indigenous" is located in a necessary relation of alterity within hegemonic constructions of difference. A strategic essentialism would acknowledge the imbrication in hegemony but would reclaim that identity strategically within the logic of an unfolding war of position. Examples of such strategic uses of positive essentialism might be the claims made by aboriginal groups against colonizing immigrants in settings such as Australia, Canada, and the United States.

I now turn to those approaches which are not as much concerned with creating and defining a space for indigenousness as they are in bringing the notion of "the indigenous" into question. Here I will distinguish three closely related positions. The first of these follows from Spivak's call to employ "what history has written for me" and embrace the hybridities engendered by the multiplex histories of colonialism in the Third World. This would mean exploring the "strategies of mimicry, hybridity, incommensurability or translation" that are "the unspoken, unexplored moments of the history of modernity" (Bhabha 1989:67). It is important to move beyond the view of hybridity as a singular location that is an in-between, temporarily suspended space, between two (or more) rather securely positioned and stable locations. Only by paying attention to the specificities of the historical construction of place, forged out of the violent history of colonialism and, most crucial, the continuing role of power differentials that shape new forms of global discipline, can one account for hybridities that allow for the play of difference. Thus, explanations of hybridity as an identity of difference themselves need to account for the multiple (often hierarchical) positions that are encapsulated within that term, so as not to universalize a particular relation to colonial discourse, namely, that occupied by colonized elites. It is for this reason that I prefer to use the plural form, "hybridities," rather than the singular, "hybridity."

Concepts of hybridity have been most persuasive in upsetting the spatialized security of notions of "culture," "society," and "nation." Postcolonial settings are themselves borderlands, spaces of marginality and impurity, that render unstable the secure identities of "the West" built on spatial exclusion. This instability has resulted from processes of exile and displacement, from what Edward Said (1979:18) has termed "the generalized condition of homelessness," from travel and tourism, and from "body shopping" and new forms of indentured labor in the high-tech transnational circuits of late capitalism, among other processes (Anzaldúa 1987; Clifford 1992; Ghosh 1989a, 1989b; Gupta and Ferguson 1992; Ong 1987; Prashad 1994; Rushdie 1989; Said 1983; Wolf 1992).

Another way to theorize why the postcolonial continues to unsettle the self-construction of "the West" is suggested by Homi Bhabha's insight that one has always to keep in mind a temporal disjunction that lies at the heart of modernity (1993:1–6). At the time that civil society, the state, the nation, civilization, and citizenship were being consolidated in the centers of colonial power, racist disciplinary forms, discrimination, prejudicial governmental policies, economic exploitation, and subjection were being practiced in the colonies. Bhabha argues that "the very creation of the national, Western metropolitan nation is always in a differential relation to the colonies upon which it projects its own internal, contradictory, cultural trace; or, in an alternative gesture, it often constitutes its metropolitan society by disavowing the colonial space" (1–2). What is the effect of the colony's creation as the disjunctive double of the modern, "Western" nation? To put it simply, it is to destabilize the relation of alterity through which the identity of "the West" is stabilized.[77] The "indigenous" peasants of Alipur who enthusiastically use chemical fertilizers; the native who wears a "traditional" necklace carefully crafted from lightbulbs (Clifford 1988); the shaman who uses Coke bottles in a healing ritual (Taussig 1987): all are "inappropriate subjects" who spurn the desire for a pure difference (the indigenous) that would stabilize the identity construction of "the West." Clearly, these inappropriate subjects who render ambivalent Western narratives of the self, of progress, and of modernity are not doing so out of the desire to make choices or demonstrate resistance. I want to steer clear of *any* suggestion of the celebration of cultural plurality and point instead to the overdetermined nature of mimicry, at once produced within and unsettling of the representational efficacy of global relations of inequality.

The differential relationship with an inappropriate Other prevents "the indigenous" from functioning to coalesce redemptive narratives of liberation or return. For example, narratives of progress in the West employ "the indigenous" as a point of contrast in order to redeem a utopian vision of capitalist cornucopia, a liberation from want. This is the teleology, or theology, that lies behind development discourse, and this is why nationalist projects of development in the Third World continue to produce "the indigenous" as their Other. Opposed to redemptive uses of "the indigenous" in narratives of liberation are those of *return*, an example of which is provided by some of the eco-friendly discourses of environmentalists and experts on ik referred to earlier. Here, the notion is that sustainable and sustaining practices of agronomy, forestry, and so on can be recuperated from those who came *before* or who stayed *outside* the West. Although these narratives represent very different ethical and political positions, whose differences I do not wish to diminish, both pivot on their alterity with "the indigenous."

To what extent do these positions on "the indigenous" within postcolonial theory help us understand the conditions of peasants in Alipur? Or perhaps the question needs to be asked in the reverse manner: Do the detailed descriptions of farming in this chapter substantiate or interrogate the insights of postcolonial theory? Unlike its employment as a strategic essentialism in other contexts, the notion of "indigenousness" is not similarly deployed in Alipur. People in Alipur were not interested in defending their knowledges, practices, or institutions in the name of "indigenousness." Nor were they considered to exemplify "indigenousness" by outside observers and analysts (although I did initially characterize agronomical theories in that way). Rather, if they are considered prototypical of anything, it is as *failed* subjects of the project of modernity, a position whose burden they feel acutely. In the first chapter, I showed how this feeling of being "left behind" forms the basis for peasant mobilization against the dominant vision of national development.

Agronomical knowledges that blend humoral and "scientific" explanations offer a good example of the strategies of hybridity and "mistranslation" that lie at the heart of that alternative form of modernity that goes under the name of "postcoloniality." Thus, we have the example of Suresh, who explained the properties of the fertilizer DAP by drawing an analogy with the hen incubating its egg, switching back and forth between the recommendations of development officials and theories based on a humoral agronomy. It is this unobtrusive commingling and coexistence of incommensurable beliefs that makes it impossible to position peasants in Alipur as occupying a space of pure difference. They spurn the desire for alterity that would stabilize the identity construction of "the West." Possessing neither the wisdom of noble savages nor the technology of industrial agriculturists, they can be looked at neither as shining examples of development nor as exemplars of ecological correctness. As hybridized, syncretic, inappropriate, postcolonial subjects, they enter as a disturbing presence that continuously interrupts the redemptive narratives of the West (Bhabha 1994). They serve to remind us that the continuist temporalities implicit in discourses of progress and development, born of the confidence of privilege, depend on a disavowal or sanctioned ignorance of the heterogeneous and discontinuous temporalities of subaltern groups (Bhabha 1993). Thus, the

IMF and the World Bank continue to report the news of "development" with a happy face, while more people face starvation around the world, more children die from malnutrition and war, and more ecological refugees, displaced by "development," abandon the countryside and migrate to overburdened cities and First World countries. Through mimicry and mockery, parody and protest, riots and rebellion, the "not-quite-indigenous" and "not-quite-modern" disrupt the complacent march of continuous progress implicit in discourses of growth and development.

4

"Indigenous" Knowledges: Ecology

The previous chapter charted the relationship between "indigenous" knowledges of agronomy and "modern," scientific discourses of agriculture to delineate the specificities of postcolonial modernity. In this chapter I extend the concern with indigenous
knowledges of agronomy to examine the ecological understandings embodied in them. Concern over the quality of the land and the availability
of water loomed large in discussions about farming in Alipur. I therefore
concentrate on these features of the agrarian ecology. It is not surprising
that farmers should be so concerned with what are, after all, their principal means of production. What is interesting, however, is the manner
in which connections are made between land and water, on the one
hand, and the body and social life, on the other. The main feature of
these relationships between the "environment" and the body is their
lack of exteriority with respect to one another. This lack of exteriority is
exhibited most clearly in the intimate relationship between the production of food and its consumption.

Two features stand out in farmers' discourses about the production of
crops and their use as food. The first is the similarity between the terms
employed to understand the health of plants and the soil and the health
of humans. I was initially tempted to consider this an example of analogical thinking, in which understandings of the body had been extended onto other realms of life. But the second aspect of these discourses made it clear that such a perspective was questionable. The
health of the soil and plants is not analogous in the sense that they
constitute living systems that parallel and mimic the body. Rather, they
are connected to each other and to the body in an intricate web in which
actions that influence the quality of the soil, for example, have direct

effects on the quality of the food produced; the food, in turn, has implications for the health of the people who consume it. In this manner, qualities or properties flow through the chain of processes involved in the production of food.[1]

To subsume peasant understandings of the relationships between the soil, plants, air, water, and humans under the rubric of "ecology" would merge different conceptual histories and genealogies that might better be used to interrogate each other. Do the connotations of "ecology" thus have to be stretched beyond recognition to take account of interpretations of their "environment" by Alipur's farmers? Substantivist explanations of the relationship between plants and the wind, for example, were clearly quite different from those discourses of "ecology" that are imbricated in mechanistic and systems-theoretical premises about "nature." I recognize that there are many different positions on "ecology," and many ecologists question the view of nature as an ecosystem in homeostatic balance (for some alternatives, see Botkin 1990; Colwell 1985; Joseph 1990; Petulla 1980:30–34, 60–74, 103–5; Sneddon 1996; and Zimmerer 1994). But what differences, if any, exist between revised and reformulated theories of "western" ecology and substantivist theories about bodies, plants, and the earth that begin from radically different positions (Kurin 1983; Zimmermann 1987)? In the previous chapter I demonstrated how the qualities of the soil, water, and other inputs are passed on to crops. When these crops are ingested by humans as food, their qualities [*gunas*] infuse the body of the eater (Daniel 1984; Marriott 1989; Trawick 1974).

The concern with the properties of crops and their possible relationship to ecological processes and the body is all the more acute given that Alipur has seen drastic changes since the late sixties, both in terms of the crops that are being grown and the methods employed to grow them. There have been two "green revolutions" in the last third of the twentieth century: the first referring to increased food production in the Third World—the promise of green fields overflowing with cereals—aided by high doses of biochemical inputs and water; and the second referring to environmental awareness, the promise of sustainable development. It is ironic that the second "greening" should have followed so closely on the first, whose premises and results were, if anything, diametrically opposed to it.

My own perspective on the "ecological" consequences of high-yielding variety agriculture has been shaped by a concern with sustainability and "green" politics. Yet, an engagement in this chapter with the "ecological" practices and discourses of peasants in Alipur, who have their own versions of both green revolutions, has enabled me to reach a different perspective in my own environmentalism. Implementing a complex triangulation between an ecologically green perspective, a high-yielding green revolution viewpoint, and the stance of farmers on both not only enables me to decenter "Western" theories of agronomy and ecology but also to destabilize the telos of modernity. Could the farmers of Alipur seem simultaneously *more* "modern" because they were ecologically green before they became high-input farmers and *less* so because they lacked the purposive directionality of scientific "progress" (which would find their present practices to be "unsustainable")? In this chapter, rather than pronounce judgment on their practices, I have chosen to present the interpretations and understandings articulated by farmers in Alipur about the relationship between their "environment" and farming.

In their discussions about the differences in soil quality and the effects of contemporary agricultural practices on the land, farmers commonly employed comparisons between the present and the past. However, my efforts to pin down the exact year that was being referred to in historical recollections about farming practices were continually frustrated. The farmers I spoke to seemed completely uninterested in specifically *when* that past happened to be and would often wave their hands impatiently when I attempted to obtain greater precision by asking them to relate the time they were referring to by connecting it to their own life cycle, to the ages or presence of their children, or the like. "Was your eldest son born at that time?" "Yes, he must have been, it was sometime then." "Had your second child been born yet?" "Yes, it was somewhere in those days." And so it went. My attempt to use ethnographic tricks of triangulation were met with the disdain that such nit-picking deserved. Gradually, I stopped trying to use the scale of temporalizing prevalent in my scholarly discourses to identify points on theirs. Perhaps the narratives of temporality implicit in our respective views of "the past" were incommensurable. It was not a question of what *happened* in the past, not the narratives of events and identities, but of "the past" itself. What made a period "the past" in their discourse was not its distance on a linear time line. "The past," instead, was a *time of difference*. That is what made it "the past," and that is what was significant about it. "The past" was defined by specific practices of leaving land fallow, cultivating rain-fed agriculture, or displaying an exaggerated deference to the upper castes, all of which were no longer valid. In the material that follows, "the past" is continually invoked in this manner to speak of ecologically meaningful changes.

What do these attitudes to time and "the environment" imply? Are we to read the ecologically sustainable agriculture practiced by farmers before the advent of the high-yielding varieties as the stance of subjects resisting modernity? Or does the practice of *unsustainable*, green revolution agriculture indicate that Alipur's farmers are resisting the call for sustainable agriculture flowing out of modernist premises about scientific evolution? Do the farmers of Alipur critique ecological destruction caused by "modern" farming? Or, conversely, are they enthusiastic supporters of industrial agriculture and unconcerned about its ecological consequences? Far too often, the ecological practices of indigenous peoples have provided a means to construct romantic critiques of the industrial world. Alternatively, the transfer of technology from the First World is seen as a crucial step in halting environmental destruction in the Third World. Where do the ecological practices of Alipur's peasants fit within these dichotomies? Have the farmers of Alipur been carefully preserving the environment for centuries before the onslaught of "modern" technology, or do they need modern technology to avert environmental disaster?

This chapter is divided into three main sections, corresponding to what I have identified as the three most important themes in the "ecological" discourses of farmers in Alipur. The first section deals with land quality and presents an inquiry into how different crops, changes in crop rotation and the crop mix, fertilizer, and weeds affect the quality of the soil. Many farmers in Alipur expressed anxieties about the fall in the level of the water table and suggested diverse explanations for it. In the second section, therefore, I proceed to analyze farmers' discourses on water resources. In the final section I attempt to link "ecological" degradation with perceptions about the decline in the well-being of the population, especially that of the poor.

Land Quality

Concerns about land quality were pervasive in the discourse of farmers in Alipur. This is not entirely surprising, because their livelihood depended on a knowledge of the soil. I have already explained the system of classification by which soils were graded. Farmers often used the terms for land [*zameen*], soil [*mitti*], plot, and field [*khayt*] interchangeably.[2] Here, I will concentrate on explanations about the "strength" of the soil. The decline of the quality of the land was expressed primarily in concerns about the "weakness" of the soil.[3] As indicated in the previous chapter, one of the most fascinating aspects of this discourse on land quality was the sense that the land had its own agency and was not merely inert raw material to be employed as an input toward human ends.[4] The active *participation* of the land was apparent in many ways. It had an "appetite" similar to that of humans and needed a "diet." Chemical fertilizers were used to fulfill that need by providing what was in effect a high-energy, but poorly balanced, meal. Similarly, the land needed time to "relax" [*sastaana*], to regain its strength after a prolonged period of intensive work. Farmers also talked about how a certain field "had taken hold" of a particular crop [*pakad liya*] and had helped that crop to grow especially well.[5] Talking about the importance of timing in irrigating barley, Suresh told me that the field itself "tells you" when it needs more irrigation, and then you know the time is right. Were these statements merely metonymic?

The agency of the land combined with humoral theories of agronomy and green revolution agricultural practices to shape a unique form of modernity, neither "the same" nor the Other of "the West." It is precisely for reasons such as this that postcolonial settings provide the rationale for the idea of *alternative* modernities. By this I mean the multivalent genealogies of modernity at the limits of "the West," where incommensurable conceptions and ways of life implode onto one another, scattering, rather than fusing, into strangely contradictory yet eminently "sensible" hybridities.

I begin by describing how farmers' conceptions of land quality may be understood in terms of the effects of different kinds of crops on the strength of the soil. Next, I examine how changes in the cropping cycle and the mix of crops may affect land quality. A third factor dealt with here is the difference between organic manure and chemical fertilizer: this was a favorite topic of discussion among Alipur's residents. Finally, I move to the role of weeds and the consequences of weeds and weeding patterns on the soil.

Effects of particular crops on soil quality

According to the farmers of Alipur, crop selection affects the quality of the soil in many respects, chiefly in its consequences for how strong or weak it is likely to leave the field. Whether one plants millet (bajra), cane, or wheat has different long-term implications for the strength of the soil and productivity of the field. In this section I present three very different perspectives on whether such crops as sugarcane and bajra weaken the soil. The objective is to give a sense of the divergent assessments of this phenomenon in order to emphasize that indigenous perspectives are neither unitary nor do they constitute a closed and consistent "system" of thought and practice. I have deliberately chosen people whose opinions differ so that they can be read against one another.

Ram Singh was an older, lower-caste man who lived with his family and the families of his three brothers in an independent little cluster of houses situated at one edge of the village land. There were three such hamlets around Alipur, two situated between the village and adjoining villages and one between the village and the paved road that ran a short distance from it. Ram Singh was a well-to-do farmer by local standards, for he shared approximately fifty acres with his three brothers. In 1992, each brother farmed independently of the others. Unlike his father, who, despite being the sole heir to a fairly substantial piece of property, took little interest in farming, Ram Singh had been involved in farming activities for almost all his life. At the time (1992) of the conversation reported below, he continued to participate regularly in farming activities, although most of the work was now done by one of his adult sons, Inder Singh, who was also present during the interview.

Ram Singh distinguished between crops which weakened the soil greatly and those which did so only slightly, or even strengthened it, by discussing the paradoxical properties of millet: "Bajra is the one crop that weakens the land; otherwise, there aren't any that weaken the land excessively. In reality, bajra weakens the farm, but it also grows in a weak field [*kamjor khayt main bhi ho jaaye*]—this is one of its distinctive marks." Inder Singh intervened, "It can grow with just rainfall, but it also weakens the land, and one cannot grow wheat after it." Bajra had the advantage of growing in a weak field without any means of irrigation, but it had the disadvantage of weakening the land to such an extent that it retarded the production of the major crop, wheat. This was partially due to the lateness of its harvesting, which did not leave enough time to prepare the field adequately for the wheat crop. Bajra's effect on the land, however, was also connected to its other properties, which underlined the complexity of evaluations about soil quality. Ram Singh and Inder Singh contrasted bajra with maize in the following manner:

Ram Singh: Growing maize requires the use of fertilizer. We have to apply both manure [*bhooday ka khaad*] and market fertilizer [*ba-*

zaar ka khaad], and we have to weed it with a hand hoe. The land is well turned with the hand hoe, and that helps raise the production of wheat to its fullest. In the bajra field, we can weed only once. We can't even put much fertilizer in it because it needs fewer inputs. But bajra does not produce much wheat.

Inder Singh: Bajra extracts nutrients from the top. That is what enables it to grow so well, but that also weakens the earth. If we sow crops that pull nutrients from below, if we had sown gwal [a green legume] or sown arhar [lentils], they would have pulled nutrients from the bottom. This way, both crops, bajra and wheat, become top crops. For this reason, the wheat is weak.

Farmers had a choice between planting maize and bajra in the monsoon harvest, and their choice of crop had a great impact on the subsequent crop, wheat. Bajra contrasts with maize in terms of two features that had a bearing on the residual quality of the soil: the effect of the inputs required to grow the current crop, and the depth to which the roots of the crop had to go to draw nutrition. The cultivation of maize required that the field be weeded on several occasions and that both organic manure and chemical fertilizers be used. By contrast, it was not possible to weed bajra more than once; the plants grew so close to one another that, once the crop had grown more than a few inches, it became impossible for anyone to sit in the field and weed with a hand hoe. In a similar vein, although there were no prohibitions on doing so, using fertilizer was considered a waste because bajra did not need higher levels of inputs. Growing maize, therefore, had favorable consequences for the production of wheat, the chief food crop *and* the main cash crop in Alipur. As we will see, turning the soil over and using organic manure were considered two of the most important mechanisms for preserving and improving soil quality.

The second aspect of this explanation centered on the sources of nutrition for various crops (see Chapter 3), a feature that had important consequences for the crop cycle.[6] Growing wheat on a bajra field turned out to be an unsuccessful strategy because both grains drew their nutrients from the top layers of soil. Thus, it was a question not only of whether a certain crop weakened the soil but also of the stratum at which the weakening occurred.

Ram Singh and his son argued that *jowar* (another millet) and bajra should not be grown on "good land," that is, in fields that retained moisture: "[Jowar and bajra] are mostly grown in fields that lack access to irrigation. They grow better in sandy soil. We don't plant them in other fields because, if the water accumulates, they won't grow. They need less water and sandy soil, that is, fields where the water keeps drying. The water shouldn't be standing in the field." Going one step further, Ram Singh and his son pointed out that a good, "strong" field was actually wasted on bajra and jowar because such a field was likely to retain rainwater longer than did sandy soil. Thus, not only did these crops grow better in weak fields but they should also not have been cultivated on fertile fields because they weakened the soil and they may actually have failed to grow adequately in good soil.

By contrast, wheat and cane could grow well only in soil that "had strength": "Wheat and cane require strong land [*tagdi zameen chahein*]. They don't really weaken the land. They are potent things [*taakatvar cheej*] and so grow only in potent fields." The repeated references to the soil "having strength" and "giving strength to the crop" once again underlined the fact that the land was conceptualized not as an inert substance but as something that *acted* to impart its qualities or properties to the crop. Of course, the crop had to be predisposed to receive those qualities; not every crop, for example, would benefit from land that had strength. Both the land and the crop acted on each other in a complementary manner.

Ram Singh and his son gave the example of sugarcane, whose beneficial effects on the soil were questionable, and addressed their absent interlocutors (the majority of farmers who held a contrary opinion): "When you uproot cane, it isn't as if the field doesn't have any strength left. If, after cutting the cane, you have it plowed with a tractor, the wheat that follows immediately afterward is really abundant [*bahut tagday gayhoon*]. The tractor just shreds the roots. Then we plow in the remainder, and it produces very good fertilizer. It's like putting manure, it makes the soil black. Maize, wheat—all these crops grow very well on a cane field." Although cane was deemed a "potent" crop that was widely perceived to weaken the soil, Ram Singh and his son argued that growing cane was beneficial for the soil if tractor technology was employed as a crucial intermediate step. But only a couple of the richer farmers in Alipur owned tractors. Others, too poor to afford even a team of bullocks, would sometimes get their fields plowed with a rented tractor. If the field was plowed with a bullock team, as was normally the case among farmers in Alipur, the cane stumps that remained in the soil were uprooted but were unlikely to be shredded. By contrast, plowing with a tractor tore them into little strips, and these turned the soil black, just like manure, reinvigorating the soil so that a good harvest of wheat or maize could be obtained after harvesting the sugarcane.

This explanation of the beneficial impact of sugarcane on the soil was disputed by Prasad, the prosperous brahmin who was the previous headman of Alipur (see Chapter 2). Prasad advanced an alternative understanding that owed a great deal more to "scientific" explanations, perhaps as a result of his higher level of formal education and his closer ties to the government bureaucrats who administered agricultural programs.[7] In Prasad's explanations, the contrast between crops which benefited the soil and those which taxed it was clearly marked:

> The *do-dal* crops [legumes], like *masur* and all the other lentils [*daals*], never weaken the farm. Chickpeas, peas, those that have *do-dal,* those that are called lentil crops—they never weaken the field. Rather, they make the field good and strong. Other crops like wheat and barley—these weaken the field a little. Cane, too, weakens the field because it needs more nutrients [khuraak]. Cane requires more fertilizer, more water, it needs more of everything. If we plant another crop immediately after harvesting cane,[8] it doesn't do well because cane weakens the field. There are some crops that do well in a cane field, for example, peas. If you plant peas after harvesting cane, it will grow well.

Prasad thus articulated an important viewpoint about the effects of growing sugarcane on soil quality. In this perspective, the sugarcane crop's enormous "appetite" for inputs demonstrated that cane actually consumed many nutrients from the land and left it weaker, more so than did wheat and other grains. But even Prasad left open the possibility that sugarcane's effects on the soil did not have uniformly negative consequences for productivity. He acknowledged that some crops, for example, peas, could still do well in a cane field. He added that if the harvest of peas was followed by maize, the maize crop would do exceedingly well.

Asked to compare the effects of new varieties of cereals with "traditional" ones, Prasad categorically denied that there was any difference: "There is no effect on land, but there is more effect on water." Despite the implications of Prasad's statement, most farmers denied any relationship between new varieties and the falling water table level (this is explored further in the second part of this chapter).

Pitting Prasad and Ram Singh's interpretations against those of a small farmer, Suresh, helps us gain a perspective from another class position. When I first interviewed him in 1984, Suresh's household was suffering from a severe resource crunch. He had almost no money to pay for inputs like fertilizer and seed. He was making a transition from farming, an occupation at which he was not particularly successful, to becoming a full-time priest. When I returned to Alipur in 1991, Suresh's priestly "business" was booming, as was his household's farming, which his two grown sons were handling with consummate skill.

Suresh's justification for planting bajra in 1984 was that he did not have the resources to grow maize:[9] "I grew bajra because I thought we would be able to get higher yields and it would grow with less inputs. Maize would have required more inputs. . . . Because we didn't have that capability, we just caught hold of one crop, we just planted bajra. . . . We sow only the crop that we are capable of managing. Now people see that bajra takes away the nutrients from the field so that wheat doesn't grow. For that reason, they have left it. In this way, things are being done according to their usefulness [priyog], seeing which land is good for what."

The knowledge that bajra would adversely affect his land did not prevent Suresh from planting it, because that was the only crop for which he could afford the necessary inputs. Although maize would have been better, its good properties resulted partly from its need for expensive inputs. Suresh attempted to balance his crop mix by assessing the impact of different crops on the soil:

The way this is thought out, first, that our field's growing power not be diminished. For example, if I continue growing wheat and bajra, then the strength of our fields is reduced. They take too much nutrition from our fields. By contrast, if we keep growing maize, then it [the land] gets some respite, the farm gets some time. Less nutrition is lost from the field. Maize is cut early, the field is plowed, it may rain, the soil is turned over, and it is weeded continuously. The soil is continuously turned and is less depleted. [The problem] with growing wheat and bajra is that bajra takes too much nutrition. The bajra is weeded, but it takes more nutrition from the soil than maize—that's the only thing, it takes the nutrition away.

Whereas there was a fair degree of consensus about bajra, Suresh's views on sugarcane were closer to Prasad's than to those of Ram Singh. One reason for this may have been the correlation that Suresh drew between class position and the production of sugarcane:

No, one should never plant cane in a cane field. Usually, first the sugarcane field is turned over, then the field is prepared. People grow a lot of maize, for example, after cutting the cane. [A gap of several months separates these two crops.] They leave the plot empty and keep preparing it. Then they grow maize. Other crops are not sown because there are too many weeds lying in the sugarcane. Then it becomes necessary to prepare ["make"] the field in the summer to kill the grass. When the field is clean, then maize is sown. [The entire cycle] takes one and a half years. Cane takes more time. For this reason, those who have more land grow sugarcane. Cane weakens the soil quite a lot, just as bajra does. With sugarcane, the crop that is planted afterward does not get a good yield. Only by giving a high dose of inputs can anything be grown [afterward].

Growing sugarcane meant devoting almost a year and a half to one crop. Suresh made it clear that small farmers could not afford to set aside a part of their land for such a long time. Only those who had more land could afford to grow sugarcane. Therefore, Suresh's understanding that cane weakened the soil was reinforced by the observation that the opportunity to grow cane varied differentially according to one's class position—in particular, according to how much land a farmer owned.

Unlike the others, Suresh was also more explicit about the deleterious effect of wheat, which was by far the main crop of the area, on soil quality. When I asked him why he used a large quantity of manure in a field where he had just planted bajra, he explained that he had sown wheat in it earlier and the land had therefore become weaker. The manure was meant to reduce the weakness of the field.

Suresh pointed to the positive results of planting lentils in contrast to crops such as sugarcane and wheat: "Lentils [dalhan] impart nutrition to the field. For this reason, the field is strengthened, and the second crop is stronger. For example, we might want a big wheat harvest. The seed which has two pods [dufaada], which can be split into two—what we call lentils—gives additional strength to the field. With lentils, the winter crop—wheat, barley, peas—grows well even if we apply less nutrition [by way of fertilizer]." Lentils, like other crops, are here clearly seen as possessing agency—imparting nutrition and giving additional strength to the soil. Despite a widely shared perception that lentils were good for the soil, they were a relatively minor crop in Alipur owing to the excessive length of time that they took to ripen.

One of the most interesting things about these statements was the extent to which the use of the technology associated with high-yielding varieties had been completely "naturalized" as if it represented the properties of the crops themselves. Thus, Suresh explained that less nutrition was lost from a maize field than from one in which millet was grown, as if the chemical fertilizers that were necessary for maize production were a feature of the maize plant. Rather than being seen as a supplementary input, the additional nutrition supplied to the field by using chemical fertilizer was completely naturalized as a feature of maize. Similarly, Ram Singh's defense of cane was predicated on the use of tractors which shred the cane into little pieces that formed a valuable fertilizer for the next crop. Rather than seen as an innovation that became possible only with the help of tractor technology, the operation of shredding was assimilated to the properties of cane itself. Assessments of soil quality, therefore, were not just traceable to indigenous agronomy but also reflected the complex interweaving of different theories and practices, of which the new technologies of production were an essential ingredient. Suresh's incorporation of chemical fertilizers as a feature of maize was widely shared by other farmers in Alipur; however, as was evident from the comments of Prasad and Suresh, Ram Singh's use of tractor technology as intrinsic to cane production was less common. Hence differences existed in the degree to which the technology of production had been assimilated to the properties of the crop.

The farmers quoted here help clarify several aspects of the relationship between crops and soil quality. First, different crops such as lentils, beans, maize, wheat, cane, and bajra could be arrayed in a rough order, ranging from beneficial to detrimental effects on the land. However, such a statement has to be qualified at a number of different levels. Not all these crops could or would grow equally well on the same kind of land. Therefore, whereas wheat and cane were potent crops that required strong land, bajra was a potent crop that could grow on weak soil. Those whose roots were shallow, such as bajra or wheat, did not have a strong effect on other crops, such as lentils or beans, whose roots went deeper. Then there was a crop like maize. The detrimental effects of maize were countered to some extent because one needed to apply manure to it and weed it several times, which turned the soil over and prepared it for the planting of wheat. To consider the *effects* of individual crops on the land was thus to miss the intertwined nature of cropping cycles, in which the mix of crops at any one time was determined by the effect of previous decisions on soil quality and which in turn helped determine what could be grown in the future. It is to this topic of crop rotation that I now turn.

Crop rotation and crop mix

The cropping cycle [*fasal chakra*] was a recurring topic in discussions about the soil. In referring to the effects that individual crops had on the soil, farmers in Alipur inevitably linked soil quality to crops that had been grown previously. They also claimed that the current crop was restricting or influencing their decisions on what could be planted subsequently on any particular plot. In considering the entire mix of crops that had been grown on any plot of land, farmers relied on evaluations about the "strength" [*taakat*] or "weakness" [*kamzor*] of the soil. They contrasted the present system of multiple or serial cropping with their practices in the past, repeatedly pointing out that the earth did not get the time to relax any more. The belief that the strength of the soil depended on its ability to relax and recover from the previous crop was widely held. At the same time, however, this belief was regarded with some ambivalence. Some farmers thought that the new technology made it unnecessary for the land to relax between crops and that not allowing land to lie fallow had made them better off financially in the short run.

Comparisons with a past that was at odds with the present were often invoked by the Subedar, a veteran of the British army's African campaign in the Second World War.[10] He was shipped to Egypt in 1939, where he was part of a unit that prepared defensive positions for British forces. The Subedar was very critical of the British: "They took us there to protect themselves," he said. "They thought that if fighting starts, these Indian soldiers will die first. They were very cunning." But his anger at the British paled in comparison with his bitterness toward the government of independent India, which refused to pay him a pension on the grounds that he had fought for the colonizers.

When he came back to the village after a long stay at the hospital where his leg was amputated, his family denied him land to cultivate or a home to live in, arguing that his pension should be sufficient for him to support himself. Eventually, he managed to obtain a part of his ancestral land to cultivate on his own. In contrast to the specificity with which the Subedar recounted the dates of his term in the colonial army, he was surprisingly vague about the time when farmers stopped leaving land fallow—that is, when tube wells were first installed in the village. Except for asserting that he was the first to do so and that he got the idea in the army when he heard that water could be pumped from under the ground, he considered the year in which that happened to be quite irrelevant.

The Subedar contrasted present cropping patterns with those of "the days before tube wells."

> People used some plots for kharif and other plots for rabi. The land didn't retain enough moisture. If there wasn't enough moisture, how would the crops grow? That's why they used to keep plowing it, then would level it, and keep the ground covered [leveled] so that it retained its moisture until the time of sowing. Only then did the ground retain its moisture. Then they would put the seed this deep [the Subedar indicated several inches with his hands], in the moisture, right at the tip of the plowing blade. If it was left any higher, the air would go through it earlier, the seed would dry. It didn't get any irrigation; the crop had to depend on the rain.

Plots were used either for the monsoon crop or the winter growing season but not for both. Those left fallow in the monsoon season were plowed intensively to turn the soil and then leveled to retain the moisture of the rainy season into the winter. It was for this reason that the seed in the winter crop had to be planted deep. If it were planted closer to the surface, there was a risk that it would dry out, because the deeper one went, the more moisture was likely to be retained. The Subedar indicated that the field in which the kharif crop had been grown "was left dry, just left as it was. Now, no one leaves fields fallow. People now want to take two or three crops." "Does that contribute to making fields weaker?" I asked. "Yes," said the Subedar. "The field does not receive any warmth. Earlier, when you cut the wheat harvest, you plowed the land and left it. It continually received the sun's warmth. Now there is no time for the heat [to warm the soil]." At this point, Sompal Singh, who had been sitting there and patiently listening to our conversation, chipped in, "It used to invigorate the field." The Subedar continued: "The field would become stronger [*taakat aa jatee thi*]. People changed the crop, sowed something else the next year. If they used the field for kharif one year, they used it for rabi the next. They kept interchanging fields and didn't grow the same crop. If they kept one field fallow this time, they kept the other one next time."

Therefore, it was not just the lack of irrigation that led farmers to leave fields fallow but also the belief that the heat the field received while "resting" helped to reinvigorate it. This heat rebuilt the strength of the soil. Fallowing was thus crucial because it allowed the field to "relax." In addition, the fields that were left fallow were not used to grow the same crop every year, nor were they even used in the same growing season. Thus, if a plot was used to grow the kharif crop one year and the rabi crop in the following year, it was allowed to remain uncropped for just over a year. As the Subedar pointed out, no farmer in Alipur would allow that to happen today. The demise of the practice of fallowing could probably be traced to the increased availability of groundwater for irrigation.

The same features—fallowing and crop rotation—were emphasized by a group of mostly lower-caste jatav men who were describing agriculture in "those days" to me. One day we sat on a cot in front of the cattle shed owned by the brothers Chotu and Lakhman. The cattle shed was wedged between the tube wells of two large, landholding thakur households and the homes of a group of well-to-do jats. It was late in July 1992, toward the end of the monsoon season. As we talked, we were joined by their sons who had been cutting fresh green fodder in the machine in the cattle shed. One of the jat men who lived nearby came and participated in the conversation. The discussion meandered, making its way through many topics—land ownership, the conditions of agricultural labor, the dietary regimen of the poor, and the pressure to expend money on consumer goods. Surprisingly, Chotu and Lakhman criticized the thakurs quite openly and explicitly. Although I knew from my previous experience that the resentment toward thakurs among the lower castes ran deep, I had expected more dissimulation and evasion. Chotu and Lakhman began by telling me how they had come to own the substantial property that they farmed. Both brothers were now well on in years; their adult sons managed the day-to-day activities of farming. The brothers recounted what had changed from the time when there were no wells and hence no form of irrigation on their land:

> In those days, for the kharif crop, we grew moong, bajra, urad, jowar, maize, cotton—a lot of cotton used to grow. Then there was arhar, there was a kind of arhar planted in the rainy season [baisaakh]. For example, if we were to plant maize, urad, arhar, bajra, jowar in one year, then that field would have to rest for six months. We would have to grow crops on it just once. After it had rested for one year, then, in the second year, wheat would be sown in it and peas and barley [jon]. The following year those fields would have jowar, bajra, maize, and such things. Different crops.

Referring to the dominant practice, I asked if one wheat crop would ever be followed, in the next year, with another wheat crop. Chotu replied:

> No, no, no. [In the past] the field had to rest for one season because there were no facilities for water and fertilizer then. Now people grow [as many as] three crops! There were no facilities for irrigation then. So these were the things that grew. But the yields were good. Without inputs, the output used to be quite good. If you calculate yields now, given the inputs, it comes out to the same. Now, inputs are higher. Then, we didn't need as many inputs, one did it all with one's labor [*haath-pair*]. Now one needs to buy water, one needs to buy fertilizer. The earnings are higher, but so are the inputs, and more money is needed. But there is more profit now than before. The output is greater than before. Because earlier we had to be content with just one crop, and now we take three crops.

It should be evident that "the past" was not being employed just as an ecologically sustainable vantage point to criticize the present. Indeed, there was a fair degree of ambivalence about older farming practices. On the one hand, the jatav men claimed that high outputs in the present were offset to a large extent by the increased demand for inputs, implying that expensive inputs may have merely substituted for hard labor. Interestingly, when Chotu talked about inputs, he included purchased goods but not labor; in fact, he explicitly contrasted "inputs" to "labor." On the other hand, Chotu and Lakhman acknowledged that "there is more profit now" and spoke with pride of the fact that farmers now grew three crops a year. What was clear, despite their ambivalence, was that even when they were being critical of high-input practices, subaltern groups in Alipur never voiced a romantic longing for a lost, ecologically desirable past. Unlike some advocates of indigenous knowledge, subaltern views of "the past" were remarkably unencumbered by a nostalgia for origins.

Crop rotation and fallowing did not, however, necessarily go hand in hand. Prasad, the "progressive" farmer quoted earlier, spoke with some pride of the greater intensity of cultivation, while defending the practice of crop rotation: "Now, the system is that people usually grow three crops: first maize, after maize, mustard [*laahi*], and after mustard, wheat.[11] They take three crops in this way. And in the next year the same crops are grown again. They change the fields, not the crops. They grow these crops in one plot this year and in another plot next year. What is there to change in the crops? They change the plots instead. Because if the same crop is grown in a plot, the field imparts a little less strength [to the crop.]" Prasad's description of crop rotation was premised on the perception that a plot was unable to impart the same degree of nutrients in the second round as in the first. At the same time, Prasad steadfastly maintained that the new varieties, with their higher demands for inputs, did not have a negative impact on the quality of the land. If plots were changed regularly and if particular sequences of crops were planted on any given plot, then the increased intensity of cultivation accompanying the new varieties would not adversely affect the land.

There were other farmers who did not share Prasad's even relatively minor doubts about the new methods of farming. Suresh was one such person. He stressed both the importance of fallowing for agriculture as it had been practiced in "the past" and its irrelevance for the present: "After growing wheat and bajra, one sows lentils and so forth. And after that, wheat, maize, things like that. Bajra isn't planted again because it makes the field so weak. . . . Earlier, people used to leave the field in which they planted bajra alone for a year. They didn't plant anything in it. They left it free so that the soil could relax and regain some strength. Then, during the second year, they would sow it again. Some even left it free for two years—so that its strength returned, so that the farm, the soil could regain its strength. Growing bajra is very weakening for the soil." Suresh contrasted this picture of "the past" with the present, when it was possible to grow even four crops a year if one owned a tube well. But, he warned, it was essential now to provide a "very good diet" to the land by using large quantities of chemical fertilizer and water. As long as adequate nutrition was supplied to the soil, he maintained, it made no difference how often one sowed or how quickly one crop followed another. "If, for several years together, wheat/maize or bajra/wheat are grown in one field, then the soil will become so weak from both those things that the output will keep decreasing. It is only because of the crop cycle that the soil is affected. Otherwise there is no weakness in the soil, it has the same particles, the same everything else, it's just a matter of nutrition. The crop cycle is spoiled. One [crop] should be with high roots, and one should be with deep roots." Suresh's statements betray an interesting tension between divergent modes of explanation. He started out by asserting that in the past—"earlier"—people allowed a field where bajra had been planted to rest for at least a year and perhaps for several years. He then went on to say that, as long as adequate inputs were applied to the soil, it made no difference how many crops one grew in a year. But he also seemed to believe that specific crop cycles did affect the soil adversely and that crops with shallow roots should be alternated with crops with deep roots. At the same time, he maintained that *apart* from a failure to rotate crops adequately, there were no reasons for the soil to be getting weaker. He seemed to draw on a particle theory of matter to show that soil was no different from other substances. There was, therefore, a disjunction between his "scientific" insistence that adequate nutrition was all that was required to replenish the soil and his acknowledgment that the soil was getting weaker as a result of high-yielding wheat becoming a virtual monocrop in Alipur's winter growing season.

A view similar to that of Suresh was advanced by Satish, a small-boned man belonging to the odh caste (according to Government of India categories, the odhs are a "backward" caste). He and his brothers owned a small piece of land that was inadequate to support their families. So Satish worked as a tenant farmer, renting land from others on a sharecropping arrangement. When I talked to Satish in 1992, he had rented land immediately adjacent to the macadamized road that runs past Alipur. Satish, the thakur Sompal, a man from a neighboring village, and I sat on a piece of cloth in the middle of a partially weeded maize field. The shoots, just a few inches out of the ground, had the glossy sheen of young plants in the monsoon. It was late July; the monsoon was still in full swing. Although it was a bright and hazy day, the breeze, when it wasn't drowned out by the horns of buses passing each other on the narrow road, blew noisily into my tape recorder lying in our midst. Satish agreed with the other farmers quoted here that one should not grow a single combination of crops for any length of time. But he also felt that what mattered more was the quantity of inputs employed: "Bajra weakens the land the most, pulls all its strength; therefore, we will just have to put a little more fertilizer. However much effort you put into the crop, however much you apply by way of inputs, it will produce that much more. If you don't put anything in it, next time the crop won't be plentiful unless you put fertilizer. Even if I were to leave this field fallow and didn't apply fertilizer with the next crop, the crop won't be that good." Satish felt that regenerating the soil by leaving it fallow was an inadequate method to make it productive. It would still need fertilizer, and the more fertilizer one could put, the more plentiful the crop would turn out to be. More clearly than the others, Satish felt that fallowing, while beneficial, was not terribly important to maintaining the quality of the soil.

What emerges from these long quotations from various farmers in

Alipur are discrepant and contested views on the importance of the cropping cycle and crop mix to the quality of the land. On the one hand, there seemed to be a broad consensus that growing the same crops over and over again weakened the land and that the best strategy was to switch plots for any given combination of crops or to switch crops for any given plot every year. No one seemed to think that leaving land fallow was a good option for the present. On the other hand, there was some disagreement over whether fallowing had been a sound alternative in "the past." Some thought that multiple cropping, at least two and perhaps even four crops a year, was financially beneficial even if it resulted in the deterioration of the soil in the long run. Others categorically denied that multiple cropping was responsible for declining soil quality, blaming instead the inability of farmers to provide adequate nutrition by way of inputs.

Although I have been using the phrase "soil quality" in describing farmers' evaluations about the growing power of the land, their own descriptions relied on notions of "strength" and "weakness." For this reason, they recommended that a plot which had been unduly weakened by a crop such as bajra be allowed to "rest" for a while. The term used for the soil was the same one used for humans: sastaana, or sometimes *saytaana*. As I trudged around the village in the hot summer and monsoon days, I was often greeted with the words, "Guptaji, where are you going? Come, relax for a while [*thodi dair saytaa lo*]." This could denote a range of things—resting, relaxing, taking it easy, gossiping, enjoying a siesta, or just sitting quietly in the shade.

I now turn to another aspect of land quality, namely, the effects that fertilizer had on the soil. Fertilizer use complemented the effects of crops, cropping cycles, and weeds, and all these phenomena together had detrimental or beneficial consequences for the soil.

Effects of fertilizer

So far, I have described the effects of particular crops and cropping patterns on the quality of the soil. Decisions about which crops to grow and the order in which they are grown were directly tied to the availability and timing of inputs. Of the inputs used in Alipur, the one considered to have the most significant effect on the soil was fertilizer. In the discourse of farmers, comparisons between manure [*gobar ki khaad*] and chemical fertilizers [*angrezi, sarkaari,* or *rasaayanik khaad*] loomed large.[12] While speaking of the strength of the soil, farmers inevitably pointed out the differences between manure and chemical fertilizer and between different kinds of chemical fertilizers. They had differing explanations for why there was a shortage of manure and how this shortage was connected to the cropping pattern and to cropping intensity. Similarly, the farmers I spoke with attempted to make sense of why the ground now needed larger amounts of chemical fertilizer than in the past. Finally, as I will explain shortly, the terms in which farmers spoke of manure and chemical fertilizer revealed a great deal about how they located themselves within a larger political realm.

All the farmers that I got to know in Alipur thought that (organic) manure was better for the land than chemical fertilizers: manure released its heat slowly over several years, whereas chemical fertilizers released their energy all at once. Prasad explained it to me in the following manner:

> There is an enormous quantity of nitrogen in *gobar* [cow dung] fertilizer. No other fertilizer has as much nitrogen as gobar fertilizer, not even NPK. The second thing is that gobar fertilizer increases the growing strength of the land. Gobar fertilizer makes even hard land soft and fertile [*kadi zameen ko bhee mulayam banaa daytee hai, zameen ko bhurbhurri banaa daytee hai*]. When the land becomes fertile, the output will increase. If you put gobar fertilizer once, its effects last for three years. It doesn't dissolve all at once [*ghudansheel nahi hai*]. . . . It exhausts itself in an even pace in three years. . . . [I]t slowly becomes like the soil, becomes mud. Then we apply it again.

The same point, about manure being a kind of time-release fertilizer, was made to me by another farmer. Prasad "translated" this knowledge about the effectiveness of manure into terms equivalent to those employed to explain the potency of nitrogenous chemical fertilizers. He claimed that it was the nitrogen in manure that made it effective: how else could one explain its strengthening impact on the soil? But Prasad did not think that the property of slowly releasing its heat was the only thing that made cow dung manure so effective. It did something else: it made the land soft and fertile, which chemical fertilizers, for all their potency, were unable to do. It was for this reason that, although chemical fertilizers failed to be useful in such circumstances, manure could be used to make even wasteland [*banjar zameen*] fertile.

The difference between the sudden release of heat displayed by chemical fertilizers and the effects of manure was given a different emphasis by Ram Singh and Inder Singh, who contrasted the real strength imparted to the soil by manure with the sudden release of energy provided by chemical fertilizer (their comments are presented in greater detail in the Introduction). Despite the perception that manure benefited land quality in the long term, it was not applied in the needed proportions. Why was that the case?

According to Ram Singh, one reason was that there was less manure available "these days" (1992) because people kept fewer cattle: "People still use manure but very little. Many of them have tractors. If they kept animals, they could make more [manure], but they don't even keep oxen. So they can use less of this [desi] fertilizer. Unless they put green fertilizer like hemp [sani]—that's another matter. But otherwise they cannot put much [desi] fertilizer." A very similar explanation was advanced by the Subedar: "There isn't enough manure for all the land. People don't keep enough animals to make manure. People use tractors and have fewer oxen. If you take the estimate of two oxen [per household], they will eat and produce cow dung which would go back into the farm. Now one can't get enough manure." Between my first extended field trip in 1984 and the time of our conversation in 1992, the number of cattle had grown dramatically, thanks to a concerted effort by the state to increase milk and cheese production for the major metropolises around Alipur. The government's label for this development program, intended to emulate the "success" of the green revolution, was "the white revolution." For some reason, the visible increase in the total population of cattle was not acknowledged by many farmers. When they spoke of how people now kept fewer animals, farmers invariably referred to oxen [bail, bhainsaa], not milch cattle [bhains, gaay]. Pressed on the matter, they were likely to acknowledge that the number of cattle had gone up. But they quickly added that the additional cattle could not meet the increased demand for manure that followed more intensive cultivation. The following conversation with Ram Singh and his son demonstrates this point particularly clearly.

AG: You mean, are there less cattle now than before?
Inder Singh: There are more than before. But the production [of food grains] has gone up more. Earlier, what was the level of production?
Ram Singh: We can't make enough [manure] for all our farming, only one plot can be provided for.

Inder Singh: One or two plots are filled. But it is not that all fields get manure.

That farmers should gauge the quantity of organic manure relative to the needs of production, as opposed to some absolute scale, was not entirely surprising (Appadurai n.d.). But the vastly increased scale of production was not the only reason why manure was in short supply.

Some farmers offered other reasons. Prasad, for example, mentioned the competing uses to which cow dung was put: "People are paying more attention to manure. But in our village it is used more for cooking. People are using cow dung more for burning: that is resulting in a loss [of fertilizer]. There is a shortage of fuel. If it were not used for fuel, there would be a lot of cow dung fertilizer, there would be adequate quantities of it. Now look how many cow dung stores are standing in the village. If it were all made into fertilizer, how much fertilizer would there be? But people prefer to use it for fuel." Prasad drew on his knowledge that there were successful gobar gas plants operating in nearby districts (although there were none in Alipur or its adjoining villages) to underline that Alipur was an exception: "In our village it is used more for cooking." These plants, apart from generating valuable methane gas for cooking, had the additional advantage of leaving a highly concentrated residue that served as an excellent fertilizer, thus averting the choice between cooking and fertilizer production.

The Subedar proposed a different explanation for the decline of organic manure. In the middle of a conversation about the use of chemical fertilizers, I suggested that there was a trend among farmers in the United States to switch to organic inputs. Catching the implication, he laughed heartily but expressed pessimism at the prospect of substituting manure for chemical fertilizer completely. When gobar gas plants were first built in the area, a number of people had them installed, partly because they were heavily subsidized by the government. But after a while, the plants were abandoned because they were considered a bother to operate. The Subedar noted that the plants left behind a residue that was a very potent organic fertilizer. But, he said, "people have become lazy because of machines." I was curious and pressed him by noting that it worked well in other districts. He replied that many such plants had been set up in the neighboring villages, but none worked successfully. The few that did operate stopped after a brief period. The almost complete failure of gobar gas plants meant that there was no way around the trade-off between the use of cow dung for manure and its use for cooking. The Subedar attributed the lack of interest in gobar gas plants shown by people in the area to the fact that they had become lazy and did not want to do the work that was required to operate and maintain these plants.

Another reason advanced for the lack of manure was that farmers no longer knew how to make it. This was Ram Singh's view: "There is this difference between manure and [chemical fertilizer]. If one makes manure in a pit, then it takes [properties] from different elements and becomes very good. Now no one does this. One should have the knowledge to do it: if the farmer puts salt in it, then collects good waste material, it makes a real powerful fertilizer. This fertilizer displays many good properties for the land." Ram Singh implied that farmers no longer used as much manure as they effectively could because the knowledge of how to make good manure had been lost. Thus, one had to go beyond mere laziness, the presence of machines, and the easy availability of chemical fertilizer to understand why manure was no longer used, although these factors may indeed have been responsible.

In fact, Ram Singh and his son went further and claimed that the *only* reason why anyone even cared to purchase chemical fertilizer was that there was not enough manure available:

Ram Singh: If there was enough organic fertilizer for all our fields, we wouldn't touch market fertilizer [*nishaan ko naa lay*].
Inder Singh: Then no one would get market [fertilizer] because organic manure makes good gas [*achee gas banaavay*] [in the soil].

It was unclear to me whether Ram Singh and his son used the English term "gas" because they somehow connected the fecundity of manure to gobar gas (methane) plants or whether they had some more specific and direct explanation for why "gas" made land more fertile. They evidently felt strongly that using market fertilizer was a necessary evil rather than a desirable thing to do.

The explanations for not using more manure depended on whether farmers owned the plot they were cultivating or had leased it for the season. Because the beneficial impact of manure lasted three years, tenants with year-to-year leases had no incentive to use manure on a rented plot. Sompal emphasized this in talking about the farm he had leased from his father in 1984–85: "This is the first year the plot has been self-cultivated. An outsider will never put organic manure; he will only use chemical fertilizer. Once a certain amount of chemical fertilizer is put, if a smaller amount is put subsequently, the production will keep decreasing. If you put the same amount of fertilizer or more, its output will remain constant. Now, it's not possible for me to put so much chemical fertilizer. . . . I've got the field for one year; why should I put any organic manure?" The owner of a farm who leased it for a stretch of three years risked losing it entirely because the existing laws allowed a tenant to lay claim to any land that he had regularly cultivated for three years or more. But even if it were possible to lease a farm to the same tenant for three years, Sompal claimed that the tenant would never use manure. I was puzzled: wouldn't it be to the tenant's advantage to apply manure since its effect lasted only three years? But Sompal replied that the tenant would first use the manure on his own land: "When it is insufficient for his own land, who will put manure on another's property?" The theme of a shortage of manure was thus repeated, but Sompal also articulated a clear preference in the way in which he used manure, namely, that it was always applied first to one's own land as opposed to land that had been rented. That may have been due to the belief that a broad range of long-term benefits flowed from manure and that using it did not merely increase output in the short run.

Whatever the reasons given by farmers in Alipur for the "lack" of manure, the fact was that they had become increasingly dependent on the use of chemical fertilizers. As compared with five kilograms per bigha of diammonium phosphate, or DAP, and ten kilograms per bigha of urea used earlier, farmers in 1991–92 used ten kilograms per bigha of each. Prasad pointed out that one measure of the increased use of fertilizer was that farmers had started fertilizing maize, traditionally a low-input crop, twice. However, applying fertilizer in the rainy season was a tricky business: "When there is excess water, urea dissolves in it and goes underneath and doesn't give its benefits to the crop. If I put urea, and then it rains really hard, it will have gone to waste. Suppose we put it now, then if it doesn't rain for four to six hours, then it is all right. A minimum of six hours is needed for the plant to absorb the nutrients. If it rains immediately after the application, it will go to waste." Prasad contrasted the low wheat output of not more than five to six mans per bigha obtained ten or fifteen years ago with the present, when it was possible to obtain ten mans per bigha with "adequate" quantities of fertilizer and water.[13] He pointed to the doubling of outputs possible with high doses of inputs, as well as to the uncertainty involved in applying expensive fertilizer. If it rained immediately after the fertilizer was applied, there was a chance that its benefits would be squandered. The chance of rain occurring unpredictably was particularly high during the monsoons, when maize was harvested. Prasad did not repeat two points made earlier by Ram Singh and Sompal. First, the new varieties did not grow without chemical fertilizers. Second, a pervasive belief had become part of the discursive consciousness of Alipur's farmers, despite their short historical experience with this technology: articulated earlier by Sompal, the belief was that once a certain amount of chemical fertilizer was used in a plot, subsequent harvests required more fertilizer to match the output from that first harvest.

The explanation most frequently proposed for the soil's increasing "demand" for fertilizer was predicated on the notion that chemical fertilizers did not give sustaining strength to the *soil* but merely gave a short-term boost to the *crop*. For example, Satish said: "The effect [of chemical fertilizers] is that if I put more fertilizer next year, the output will be good, but if I put less, then I won't get much. The reason is that the strength of the land declines. It can't get what it needs." This was corroborated by a man from the neighboring village of Sulemanpur, who gave the example of some land that used to give very high yields of grain (millet and barley) in the days when only one crop was cultivated on it. Those high-yielding fields had been ruined to such an extent that they did not produce as much as wasteland [*banjar bhoomi*]. The man felt that the decline in productivity was caused by the use of the new fertilizers and seeds. There was a solution to soil degradation though, which was to plant ramās (a bean, *Dolichos Sinensis*), a green fertilizer, allow it to grow to a height of two feet, and then plow it into the ground. After that, one could use the new chemical fertilizers without fear; otherwise, they were capable of completely destroying the soil.

There were, however, alternative explanations for why larger quantities of chemical fertilizer were necessary, one of which focused on the quality of fertilizer available in the market. This was the Subedar's view:

We now have to put more fertilizer to get the same output as before. The reason? Fertilizer is not so good anymore. At first, aluminum sulfate was used, now you don't even hear its name. I had maize in my field, about two feet high, and it got waterlogged once. I said, "Put aluminum sulfate," and we put it right in the water. Instead of turning yellow, that crop turned black, and it produced really fat cobs. That fertilizer is no longer available. Now that chemical fertilizer has to be put in larger quantities, the factories have started cheating. They have increased the price and reduced the quality of the product. At first you had DAP[14] which was excellent; now even that is less effective.

As we shall presently see, the Subedar's suspicion of "factories" was founded on a fundamental opposition inscribed in the names given to chemical fertilizers. Thus his view of the matter was not idiosyncratic but deeply enmeshed within the categories in which farmers made sense of their use of chemical fertilizers.

A completely different explanation for the decreasing efficacy of chemical fertilizers was offered by Prasad. On the one hand, Prasad claimed that new high-yielding varieties had no effect on the land. But almost immediately he added: "This is for sure, that the land isn't working without chemicals. It used to work without chemicals earlier; now, it doesn't." When asked why that was the case, Prasad advanced the following as one reason: "Earlier a fair amount of land used to lie empty; now nothing remains unused. Now, wasteland, ditches, highland, lowland, whatever land is available, is all being cultivated." The implication was that the extension of cultivation to low-quality land led to an increased use of biochemical inputs because farming such land would not be possible without the aid of large quantities of irrigation and chemical fertilizers. But this explanation appears to displace the problem of whether chemical fertilizers were less effective, for other farmers consistently maintained (as, indeed, did Prasad at other moments) that even plots with fertile land needed more biochemical inputs than before. Prasad, however, may have been quite right in suggesting why aggregate quantities, as well as the average intensity, of fertilizer use had gone up: marginal land that had previously been left barren was now being brought under cultivation with the help of chemical fertilizers.

It is clear from the statements quoted in this section that the increasing use of chemical fertilizers, their decreasing effectiveness, and lack of manure, which was considered superior in imparting strength to the soil, all had negative consequences for land quality. These effects combined with other concerns in the very terms that farmers used in referring to manure and chemical fertilizer. Manure was called "country fertilizer" [desi khaad], "cow dung fertilizer" [gobar ki khaad], "waste fertilizer" [kooday ki khaad], or sometimes "animal fertilizer" [pashuon ki khaad]. By contrast, biochemical fertilizers were referred to as "government fertilizer" [sarkaari khaad], "English fertilizer" [angrezi khaad], "market fertilizer" [bazaar ki khaad], or, more infrequently, "chemical fertilizer" [raasayanik khaad]. It is significant that the terms "English," "government," and "market" are used interchangeably. The substitution of these terms reveals how, in peasant discourse, nationalist critiques of colonial rule came together with suspicion of government policies and urban merchants. This convergence of discourses lay behind the Subedar's anxiety about fertilizer factories cheating farmers by pushing lower-quality material onto them. Once the land cannot do without chemical fertilizer, he claimed, it becomes possible for the producers of fertilizers to "increase the price and reduce the quality." Similarly, Ram Singh's insistence that he would not even have touched market fertilizers if they had had large quantities of manure underlined how much these farmers resented the dependence that accompanied the necessity of purchasing inputs.

When farmers in Alipur expressed frustration at their dependence on purchased inputs or their involvement with the market, however, they were not simply harking back to some golden age of putative village self-sufficiency. Farmers in Alipur did not, after all, begin their engagement with markets only when high-yielding varieties were first introduced. Rather, this resentment has to be explained in the context of the antigovernmental populism of farmers movements described in Chapter 1. The populist positions of farmers movements charged the pro-industrial development policies of the Indian state of acting against the interests of farmers; of setting terms of trade against farm products (hence the opposition to markets); of neglecting rural areas in terms of infrastructure; and of adopting a model of development that was urban and Western—that is, "foreign"—in its orientation. It was for this reason that "English," "government," and "market" could be used synonymously to describe chemical fertilizer. Thus, a critique of the particular model of development being pursued by the state was inscribed in the various terms for chemical fertilizer. In so doing, however, and in contrasting chemical fertilizer unfavorably with organic manure, peasants were proposing that other paths to development were possible and desirable. Rather than some retreat into "tradition," these development options constituted alternative forms of modernity.

The effect of weeds

So far, I have dealt with the impact of crop rotation, the cultivation of particular crops, and fertilizer use on the quality of the soil. I now turn to the effect of weeds or, more accurate, the effects of weeding on the soil. When I did my first round of fieldwork in Alipur in 1984–85, almost no one in the village used herbicides or insecticides. Since then, thanks to aggressive governmental promotion, there has been a decided increase in the amount of herbicides employed, although the level and quantities used, as well as the number of people using them, is still very low.

Had weeds increased in the last few years? Were they due to almost continuous cropping and increased use of inputs? What was the best way to deal with them? When I posed these questions in 1991–92, the answers I received were quite divergent. Prasad, for example, maintained that there were no more weeds now than in the past and denied that the amount of weeds had any connection with the high doses of fertilizer being given to the crops: "No, weeds have not increased, they are about the same. Now there are medicines [*davaa*] to destroy weeds. If we sprinkle it, the weeds are destroyed. Earlier, no one used medicine. Now they do." At the same time, Prasad also conceded that the weeds plaguing the wheat crop were not found in the area earlier: "There is this grass *baluri* which grows in the wheat. It wasn't present earlier. Now we have that and there is a *jungli jai,* a black jai. These two grow in the wheat and destroy it. In some plots, they destroy it completely. I don't know where it has come from [but] it has come here in the last four or five years." I inquired if the heat released from biochemical inputs might have caused the weeds to flourish. Prasad categorically denied that that might be the case: "No, no, there is no such thing. The weed has its seed, and the seed sprouts in the right season. Now take jai. Jai is harvested in March or April. Its seed will fall in the field and lie there the whole year. And then, in October or November, it will come out. It will grow again in October or November—so this is it. The medicine destroys both the jai and the baluri." Prasad was so completely convinced of the effectiveness of the "medicine" (that is, weedicide) that he compared it favorably with the older, labor-intensive technique of hand hoeing:[15]

> Hoeing doesn't remove [weeds] completely. It does reduce them a great deal. Even if you do nothing but put excess seed in the plot, [the weeds] will be less. [The weed's] seed won't get space to grow and so will become weak. There are many solutions. [Weeds] are reduced by plowing, and they are reduced by hoeing, but they don't go away completely. Only medicine destroys them completely. Some [of the weed] is always left in the wheat. It then spreads again. Earlier, sowing was done with wide furrows, and now they are very close. The hand hoe [*khurpi*] won't pass through it. Earlier, nine or ten inches used to separate the lines for sowing. Now, it is three or four inches at most.

Prasad expressed a preference for herbicide because, unlike weeding, it was a more radical solution, removing weeds completely, whereas hoeing or preparing the field by repeated plowings always left some weeds in the plot. One of the solutions to the rampant growth of weeds was to plant excess wheat seed in the plot and space the rows closer together. Unlike the traditional wheat, which needed more space between rows to grow, this was a strategy that the new, high-yielding varieties had made possible. But one of the consequences of spacing rows three or four inches apart was that it made it much more difficult to use the hand hoe, thus forcing farmers to use herbicides. Prasad's enthusiasm for herbicides was hence directly connected to the widespread use of high-yielding varieties. It is significant that Prasad did not react favorably to my suggestion that the presence of weeds might be explained by the "heat" provided by chemical fertilizer. He rejected an explanation based in humoral agronomy and instead used the "English" calendar to make his case. This is a good example of how farmers in Alipur sometimes explicitly turned away from indigenous knowledges to justify their agricultural decisions.

Other farmers I spoke to were no less impressed by the wonderful new "solution"; however, some were much more circumspect about its economic viability and hence somewhat reluctant to try it. Ram Singh, for example, could report on herbicides only through hearsay:

> If there are weeds, they are mostly taken out with hoeing. We can't use that many medicines. We don't even know enough [about medicines]. Some farmers know [how to use medicine], and some don't. We do weeding, as much as is possible, and the output is good. We haven't put the medicine, the one that they say burns the grass, destroys it [*jalaa day, nasht kar day*], but doesn't affect the crop. . . . They tell us that the grain in the wheat will remain safe and the weeds will be destroyed. When villagers were talking, they said there is this medicine. . . . I don't know what medicine they said, I can't even remember the name now. If it is released in the grain, all the weeds will be destroyed. I asked, "Does it kill the mustard and the stem of the wheat too?" "No, that is saved." [Tone expresses wonder.] What kind of thing is this . . . ? It saves the mustard, it saves the ripening wheat, it just destroys the weeds. We haven't tried it out and seen it for ourselves, but we sure have heard about it, that there are such medicines. These weeds are due to water, [due to] the humidity. If you clean the ground, then there won't be any weeds. We haven't used the medicine until now.

Ram Singh's diffidence in trying the "medicine" followed from a belief that keeping the ground "clean" was sufficient to keep weeds away. But at the same time, his voice conveyed his wonder, laced with skepticism, at this new substance that could selectively kill weeds without "harming" the crop. He stressed that he "didn't know enough" about these new medicines and that he could not even remember the name of the herbicide discussed by other farmers. He therefore continued to assert the effectiveness of traditional forms of weeding while expressing his wonder at the new technology.

Not everyone, however, was convinced of the utility of herbicides. The Subedar thought that they were not worth the money one paid for them.

> There are weeds, but now there are medicines to destroy them too. The farmer has a country tool that we call the khurpi. Those who have [enough] people in the family take the thorns out with [the hand hoe], but there are many others who can't [weed with the hand hoe]. The medicine is too expensive; some use it and others don't. Even now, very few use [medicine]. It turns out to be expensive, that's why. The country [desi] remedy for weeds is hoeing. There is no other remedy. If you take it out at the very beginning, when the crop is young, then you can do it. It is not possible to do it later.

Once again, the Subedar set up a contrast between the effectiveness of village methods and that of expensive medicines. He emphasized that apart from hoeing there was "no other remedy" for weeds. But he also acknowledged that this technique worked best for those who had enough family members to do the labor-intensive work of sitting in the field and taking out each weed with a hand hoe (I did not come across a single example of the use of hired labor for weeding). Despite the fact that he had to do the farming on his own and had a difficult time weeding his plot, he did not endorse the use of herbicides.

Weeding by hand had other benefits. Satish, whose plot lacked easy access to irrigation, had a fascinating insight into the relationship between weeding and irrigation. Pointing to his plot, Satish commented that there were less weeds on it because the soil was "poor." By definition, poor soil is less conducive to all plants, including weeds. He said that weeding made a big difference in allowing him to extend the time between irrigations. If he weeded the plot regularly, he could afford to postpone irrigation by ten days or so. The reason for that was simple: weeding reduced the number of plants that were competing to absorb irrigation water. Because the supply of water was a major source of uncertainty for him, this was no small benefit. Apart from allowing the crop to be grown with lower inputs, it made him a little less dependent on the person from whom he had to purchase water for his crop.

The insight offered by Satish about the relation between weeding and irrigation could be reversed for farmers who owned their own tube well. Because farmers were weeding less, there arose the distinct possibility that irrigation was being used as a substitute for labor-intensive weeding operations. Perhaps this was one reason why, despite Prasad's denials, weeds had become a bigger problem for farmers in Alipur in the years since my first trip in 1984–85. Some of them thought that the increase in weeds could be attributed to irrigation, but others did not link it to the use of more water or fertilizer. Most, but not all, farmers felt that the new "medicines" were a potentially useful remedy. None of the people I spoke with, and this included the agricultural "experts" in the local office of the extension service, had any idea that herbicides were potentially dangerous to humans as well. In contrast to my earlier trip, I found government officials responsible for extension and rural development enthusiastically promoting the use of herbicides. Farmers, however, expressed some skepticism about the necessity of herbicides and especially about their cost, which may have hindered their more widespread use. Although no one interviewed mentioned the turning of the soil as one of the beneficial effects of weeding in the context of the use of "medicine," it was raised in other contexts. In 1991–92 I frequently heard the comment that people no longer bothered to weed wheat plots, partially because growing the hybrid varieties in rows so close together left no room to wield the hand hoe. The consequences of not turning the soil over for the productivity and strength of the soil, however, were rarely mentioned, although they remained implicit in the disapproving tone used in making such statements.

In bringing the first section of this chapter to a conclusion, let me recapitulate the main points. I have explored the effects of crops, cropping patterns, fertilizer, and weeding practices on the strength of the soil. I have endeavored to present both a range of positions on every issue and to note significant convergences. Indeed, my effort has been to underline, rather than explain away, the contradictory evaluations and logics employed by Alipur's farmers in understanding how each of these factors influences the quality of the land. My point is that it is precisely this mix of hybridity, mistranslation, and incommensurability that lies at the heart of postcolonial modernities. Those eager to discover systems of indigenous knowledge have, too often, downplayed the theoretical importance of these contradictions. The reason is that any effort to reconstruct a "system" can accommodate contradiction only within an overarching unity, whereas what is distinctive about the situation I have described is the lack of any such higher-order unity. It is exactly this situation of the uneasy coexistence of a multiplicity of logically contradictory discourses that characterizes the postcolonial condition of Alipur's peasants. Such a situation resists the holistic logic of "culture" as an integrated totality, a system of meaning to be deciphered semiotically or to be read as a text.[16] What one finds instead are overlapping discourses that are interknit not in a seamless unity but in a manner in which the dislocations and seams are, analytically, all too readily apparent. It is for this reason that the hybridity of postcolonial "culture" frustrates those searching for "patterns of culture" or an understanding of "whole" cultural "systems." The ecological discourses of peasants in Alipur display neither the systematicness of indigenous knowledge, the "green" consciousness of environmentalism, nor, paradoxically, the colonizing attitude toward "nature" exhibited until recently by discourses of "development." What emerges, rather, is a contested domain where divergent explanations are advanced to account for the failing "strength" of the soil.

Water Resources

The first part of this chapter dealt with the effects of different factors on land quality. The other primary "ecological" concern of Alipur's farmers was water resources. In this section I explore the perceptions and practices surrounding the use of irrigation water for farming. In the eight years since I had first gone to Alipur in 1984–85, the water level had dropped to twice its former depth. I begin by presenting farmers' perceptions and understandings of the drop in the water table level: predictably, one of the chief explanations they offered was that of a lack of rainfall. I next attempt to show how an understanding of the use of water is tied to types of irrigation technology, the cropping pattern, and the intensity of cultivation.

The falling water table level

At the time of my most recent visit in 1991–92, there was near unanimity among residents of Alipur that the water level had fallen dramatically in the last decade or so. I wanted to obtain the perspectives of the farmers I met on these questions: How much had the water level fallen? What were the chief reasons for this fall? What would happen in the future? In this section, I explore the first and last of these questions. The other subsections of this part of the chapter explore the *competing* explanations given by farmers in Alipur for why they thought the level of the water table had dropped.

Comparing the effects of the new varieties on land and water, Prasad, the former headman, said about the dropping water levels: "There is no effect on the land, but there is more effect on water. There is very little water now. One of the reasons is the lack of rainfall. There are very few trees and greenery; for this reason, rainfall is less."[17] Although Prasad linked the falling water level to the new varieties of cultivars, he did not explain it in terms of setting forth a causal connection. Instead, he pointed to the "lack of rainfall," which he attributed to the decrease in greenery (Gold forthcoming:11). Subsequently, his emphasis shifted completely to the low levels of rainfall in the preceding years.

> I mean, because of a lack of rainfall, the water has gone down very low in the ground. It has gone down really low. In the summer, in the month of June, the crop does not get any water. On the other side, the supply of electricity is also low. When [water] goes down too low, the pump can't pull it up. The pump too has a limit, it can pull from a certain depth and throw it up to a certain height. [When you came earlier], then the water supply was good. Now even the tube wells can't pump it out. Last year, the rains were good, so we managed to get water. This summer, we got water, but it was not much. Now it is raining. If it continues to rain like this, then it will increase, the level of water will come up. Presently everyone is irrigating with pumped water.

May and June were the driest and hottest months in the agricultural year. Before tube wells became common in Alipur, almost no one could grow a crop during May and June except those who had plots adjacent to one of the village wells. I must confess that when I heard Prasad blame the lowering of the water table entirely on a lack of rainfall, I was somewhat incredulous. But Prasad was by no means an exception. Almost everyone with whom I spoke had a similar explanation. It is true that the previous three years had seen a period of exceptionally poor rainfall. But could that be all there was to it? Ram Singh's explanation echoed that given to me by Prasad: "If there is a good strong rainfall, then the water level will be all right, otherwise it will keep going down. If it kept raining, then the level would be high. Now that there are many tube wells all over the place, there can be no shortage of water." Far from blaming tube wells for lowering the groundwater level, Ram Singh reversed the chain of causality. Had there been enough rainwater, the tube wells could have done the job of distributing it spatially and temporally. But without rainfall, the water level would keep dropping. The only person who admitted a link between the operation of tube wells and the falling water table level was the Subedar. But even his explanation was qualified: "[The falling water level] is due to the lack of rainfall and, of course, due to the operation of tube wells. The water is pulled out rapidly. Now the level [of groundwater] can rise only if there is rain. That's why it hasn't risen and it keeps going down."

But how far had the water table dropped? By seeing the operation of various tube wells and talking to people about hand pumps, I had an idea that water levels had declined at rates that I would regard as precipitous. But I was interested more in the *perceptions* of the decline among farmers in Alipur. Clearly, given their impression that it was linked to the cyclicities of rainfall patterns, they were not alarmed at the drop: they attributed it to the fact that the region had passed through a few dry years. Prasad explained just how much of a change there had been: "Those hand pumps that are big and extra deep—more than one hundred feet deep—they give water even in the summer. Those that are less than one hundred feet, they will yield less water, they won't be able to give water. Most hand pumps used to be twenty-four hands [deep] previously, all our tube wells were twenty-four hands [approximately thirty-six to forty-two feet]. Now, they still work but they give less water. Previously the machines on top [in hand pumps] were small, one or two meters [deep]. Now the machine is twenty feet deep. So that [machine which is deep] is successful. Smaller machines don't work now." The water table had plunged precipitously in the eight years that separated my initial and most recent trips to Alipur. Hand pumps that were traditionally about thirty-five feet deep had been replaced by others that went much deeper.[18] Apart from changes in the design of traditional machines, entirely new ones had been installed by the government that used a vastly more complicated technology to pull water from a depth of one hundred feet or more. Whereas the old design was one that could be repaired by people in the village, the new one depended on the intervention of expert mechanics from the block office nearby. Consequently, when one of the three fancy new hand pumps broke down, it remained in that state for extended periods until a mechanic was finally sent to repair it.

I wondered where the trend in the falling water level would lead. The answers I received took me completely by surprise because of the matter-of-fact attitude adopted by farmers to the possible demise of agriculture in the area. As early as my first trip, in 1985, a man from a neighboring village had told me that the high yields being obtained by the new varieties would not last. The entire area would soon be converted to a desert as the water in the ground was drying up.

In 1992 I asked Prasad, referring to the experience of the last decade, "If the water level continues to drop in this fashion, what will happen to farming in five or ten years?" His response was that "farming will finish then. No one knows about the future, who knows the future? One doesn't know anything about the future, maybe it will rain, who knows." Prasad's answer was far from exceptional. Everyone else I spoke to was more unequivocal about the unsustainability of current trends. At the same time, there seemed to be a displacement of responsibility to the government. Ram Singh's response was similar to Prasad's: "This won't last terribly long, just a few years more. It will start looking like Rajasthan. Unless there is a canal that goes through here. It will cost a lot of money to dig deeper tube wells." The reference to Rajasthan is to the adjacent state with India's largest desert. Ram Singh went on to say that the government would build a canal and make some arrangements for water if the groundwater ran dry. Yet he had no idea where the canal water would come from. I asked the Subedar a similar question: What would they do if the groundwater level kept dropping as quickly as it had in the past few years? He responded in this manner: "What will happen, farming is going to collapse [*thap honay waali hain*]; where will the water come from? If there isn't enough to drink, where will the water for farming come from? We will have to leave the area—what else is there to do? [He laughs.] Unless the government comes up with some scheme to get drinking water." I didn't know if the Subedar's laughter indicated helplessness or resignation or was the laugh of someone who suddenly realizes the onset of a calamity. If future rainfall proved inadequate and the water level dropped to a point at which farming could no longer be sustained, the government was expected to intervene and rectify the situation. But poor rainfall was not the only cause for the dropping water table level. As I talked to these farmers in greater detail, other explanations emerged.

Effects of irrigation on the water table
Predictably, all the farmers I interviewed saw the advent of tube wells as a highly significant episode in changing the patterns of groundwater use.

The first tube well was sunk and run by the government and depended on the installation of rural electric lines. The Subedar recollected how it all began when I asked him about the first tube well in the area:

> When the "rural line" [here the Subedar used the English words] started, they gave us the government tube well. Once the line was installed, then private tube wells began [operating]. The people from the state sanctioned the private ones almost under them, near them, so the state tube well started being less [successful]. Farmers nearby started taking less water from the state tube well because, at the rate they had to pay, their own water proved cheaper. So they made their own [borings]. In this area of ours, I was the first person to make a boring from the [rural electric] line. But I had to go through a lot of trouble in the boring [he laughs].

As we sat and talked, many years after the fact, the Subedar could afford to laugh as he recalled the struggles he had had to endure to start his own tube well. He expressed surprise that the irrigation department that managed the state tube well would undermine its effectiveness by allowing people to get electric connections to start their own tube wells in its immediate vicinity. Those who bought water from the state tube well soon discovered that it was cheaper and more reliable to sink one for themselves. The Subedar attributed his own pioneering role to family pressures and his overseas experience:

> That's it, I was also the first to put a tube well. I came back from the military. My family wasn't giving me land, they weren't giving me a house either. [They told me,] "Get out of here, go anywhere you like." I said [to myself]: I have been sanctioned a pension of eleven rupees, my in-laws aren't rich enough to support my family, and I have three children. Where will I take them? It was difficult. I too was not able to do things on my own because my legs were useless. Then I agreed to take what little land my family gave me. Now there was no provision for water on it. Then I thought hard and said, "*Bhai,* in Assyria the earth throws water from below in pipes, from a [well] boring."[19]

I wasn't sure I had heard correctly. "Where? In Australia?" Without missing a beat, he continued, "In Australia. The water comes from below." I was genuinely puzzled. "How do you know about Australia?" He laughed at my presumption: "Why wouldn't I know? So I thought hard. I told myself, whether it works or not, I should make arrangements for water. So I first showed it was possible with a boring for a hand pump. At twenty-four, water came out. At twenty-four hands—that means at thirty-six feet." The story of the Subedar's struggle to sink the boring and operate the first private tube well is a fascinating one. There were numerous false starts, and he had to endure the jealousy of other villagers. The efforts to sabotage the project reveal that a privately owned tube well was perceived to be a threat, although it was unclear who was sabotaging it and what kind of threat it constituted. It signaled the rearrangement of relations of production and prophesied the beginning of a process of social differentiation based not as much on land ownership as on capital investment. When the Subedar started his boring, none of the equipment for it could be obtained in the nearby market town. To obtain a reflex valve, he had to go all the way to Delhi. The boring, a simple hole in the ground that was open to the elements, was left exposed in his absence. When he came back, he found that the boring had been filled with little pebbles and sand. When he tried to remove the pebbles, they did not come out. Then he discovered that there were two small sticks at the bottom, crossed together and tied with a fuse wire. The pebbles had been heaped on top of this contraption. It was clear that this was not an accident. Someone had deliberately tried to jam the boring so that it could not be used. Despite clearing it as much as possible, that boring did not yield any water.

The mechanic who was responsible for the boring decided it would be best to abandon that one and begin anew. So they started digging at another place. This time, they hit water at twenty-two hands instead of twenty-four. The Subedar thought to himself, "Fate is on my side." The mechanic had one long pipe of approximately twenty feet and another piece that was much smaller. He inserted the small piece underneath and then threaded the longer pipe to it. The result was that it was too long. Instead of cutting the full-length piece, he decided that it might be better to put the longer pipe underneath; he could then cut the smaller pipe such that the joint, always a potential source of trouble, would be higher up and thus easier to repair. But in taking the pipe in and out, the side of the boring was cut by mistake, so they had to start the process once again in a third place.

The third time, they hit water at a depth of just twenty-one hands. Although the mechanic was skeptical about the quantity of water at that site, he insisted they try it. When they hooked up the engine, water just flooded out [*paani diyaa khoob rayj ka*]. But just as he was soaking in that delightful scene, the Subedar received an urgent message to come home: one of his calves was in serious trouble. He asked Lakhanpal, who had been training to be a mechanic, to guard the tube well. Lakhanpal assured him that nothing would happen to it. When the Subedar got home, he discovered that a calf had broken its leg. No sooner had he tended the calf than he returned to his farm to discover a horrible noise coming from the tube well. In his absence, Lakhanpal had cranked the tube well's motor to full speed. Because the well was still very new, there wasn't enough water in it. The Subedar screamed when he reached the well, "What are you doing? What are you doing?" "Nothing," came the nonchalant reply. "I was just checking its speed." So much sand had been pumped out in an hour that the entire plot was white. At first, the Subedar felt that misfortune was assailing him from all sides, but when he discovered that no damage had been done to the motor, he concluded that fortune was truly with him.

The Subedar's narrative, with its plotline of eventual triumph over adversity, stopped with the installation of the tube well. This is important to note: he did not talk about the *benefits,* agricultural or financial, that flowed from the successful operation of his tube well. The narrative stopped not with an image of the bumper harvest that ensued but with the success of the installation itself. The arrival of the era of the tube well was thus a marked moment. From that time on, agricultural practices in the village were permanently altered, from cropping patterns to labor requirements. Of course, the state tube well initiated some of those changes. But because ownership of the state tube well was not in the hands of any one person and because a large number of people shared its water, it did not have the kind of effects on farming that individual wells were soon to have.

The Subedar's description of Lakhanpal cranking up the engine to its maximum speed carried a veiled suggestion of foul play within its overall depiction of Lakhanpal as an irresponsible buffoon. The efforts to sabotage the tube well could undoubtedly be understood as arising out of envy, but could it have been something else as well? Tube wells were to usher in dramatic changes in agriculture, leading to a more labor-intensive, capital-intensive, natural resource–intensive regime. Some people, no doubt, gained more from the introduction of tube wells than did others, but as a result, everyone worked harder.

The Subedar's tube well continued to function on its old site. But it no longer yielded water at a depth of twenty-one hands. "The pump had to be lowered because the 'water level' [said in English] has decreased. The pump had to be lowered, but it is supplying water."

Implicit in the Subedar's story is the premise that the tube well was a beneficial technology. Not everyone, however, shared this assessment. Neerpal Singh, a jat farmer with a substantial piece of fertile land near the main road, pointed to the loss of control experienced by farmers in the use of tube wells. The reason, of course, was that to operate tube wells, farmers were dependent on the supply of electricity. Almost all the tube wells in Alipur were electric-powered, although there were a couple of farmers who owned diesel-powered pump sets. There was a big difference in their respective operating costs, however, which served to inhibit the use of diesel pump sets. On the other hand, the capital costs entailed in buying diesel pump sets prevented their employment solely as a backup. It was this dependence on electricity that Neerpal Singh decried:

> Talking of the "current," when they don't give it, that field doesn't get water. They never give it, the government gives electricity whenever it wishes. The government owns it and decides what it wants. Now, whom does one go and ask? Nobody feels for anyone else. It is all in the hands of the government. Sometimes it sends electricity. Whenever it wishes, it sends electricity. Everything is in its hands, water, et cetera, for the farmer, is all in its hands. Earlier it wasn't like this. Earlier, it was individually owned. . . . We sank a well and used bullocks to draw water. You could irrigate two bighas or four bighas. . . . The wheat produced was so much, that with four bullocks, you could produce one hundred mans or fifty mans. Now the wheat is much weaker.

Neerpal Singh suggested that despite being able to irrigate only a few bighas of land with the older technology, farmers were compensated by much higher yields than they obtained in the present. With the onset of the new technology, he implied, they had lost much autonomy. Everything that the farmer needed was now in the hands of an unresponsive government which did things according to its own whims and was not accountable to farmers. It was for this reason that Neerpal Singh complained that "nobody feels for anyone else." The "nobody" to whom he was referring were state officials in charge of the various services needed by farmers.

In addition to serving as the chief source of complaints among agriculturists, the lack of reliability in the supply of electricity helped determine the use of water resources in a number of ways. The infrequent supply of electricity limited the amount of water that could be pumped out of the ground. This was partly a consequence of the system of billing. Based on the size of the motor installed in their tube well, farmers had to pay a fixed amount per month for electricity. Therefore, if electric supply was plentiful, farmers merely pumped out more water because the additional cost of pumping out groundwater was essentially zero. For the electricity department, entirely owned and operated by the Uttar Pradesh state government, this also meant that they were obtaining less revenue per unit than they would if they limited the supply of electricity. So the only way of regulating the price of electricity was to control its supply! This had several unintended consequences for the use of groundwater and for capital investment, some of which are brought out very clearly in a comment made by Ram Singh in response to a question about his tube well.

> This must have been twenty years ago. At first we—all four brothers—put a tube well together. We used that for some time, and when irrigating, if one field was left [unirrigated], it didn't matter because we had so much land. So all our work was done with one tube well. At that time, the electric supply was also very good. Then we started getting less electricity. When we first installed the tube well, we used to get electricity all twenty-four hours, lots of electricity. And with one tube well, we could irrigate all the land we have.
>
> At first they had put a meter, then irregularities [*gadbad*] were found. Farmers must have been cheating [*gaddari*]. So then they removed the meters, and there was no guarantee any more. At that time, the electricity supply was [still] very good. Then we started getting six hours of electricity in twenty-four hours, and we couldn't get by. All four brothers couldn't get by with one tube well. So then each had to sink his own well. We have four wells now.

The inability to monitor individual use through meters had resulted in a fixed-rate system. As a result, the only way to regulate prices was by limiting supply. But reducing the number of hours that electricity was supplied made it more difficult for a single tube well to irrigate several different fields. The need to irrigate several plots simultaneously thus required the sinking of more tube wells. This meant that although water was being pumped out of the ground for fewer hours each day, much more of it was being drawn in those hours. Furthermore, since a tube well represented a very substantial capital investment, the capital investment per unit of irrigated area multiplied manyfold without a corresponding increase in productivity. The aggregate statistics on private investment in irrigation, therefore, might misleadingly suggest that there was a spurt of fresh "improvements" in the form of new private capital formation; the situation on the ground, however, revealed a different picture altogether.

The multiplication of the number of tube wells was not solely the result of the uncertainty in electric supply. It also had to do with the system of property rights in land. Like some other parts of northern India, Alipur had a coparcenary system of inheritance.[20] On the death of the parents, male heirs received an equal share of the property. The first few years after such a division were usually accompanied by bitter fights among the brothers, with each suspecting unfairness in the apportionment. Poor relations among the brothers often translated into a lack of cooperation in basic agricultural necessities such as irrigation. This meant that brothers tilling adjacent plots often sank their own tube wells in order to have an independent source of water. Because irrigation was done by gravity flow, tube wells were usually located at the highest spot on the field, so that water could flow from there to other parts of the plot. Very often, the highest spot on adjacent fields was on the border that divided them. Prasad identified this phenomenon as being the main reason why too much water was being drawn out of the ground, seemingly contradicting his earlier statement that the lack of groundwater resulted chiefly from a shortage of rainfall:

> Excess water is being pumped in some places and there is a reason for it. Earlier, there were only a few tube wells, just one or two. Now, the [traditional] wells are lying empty. Why are they empty? Because tube wells are pulling the water away. Too many tube wells have been sunk. Each place has two tube wells. It's like this, that if there are two brothers, one of them puts it here and the other there [indicating adjacent spots on the ground]. They pull each other's water so that if one of them works, the other one shuts down, and if the other one works, then this one shuts down. It's useless. Inside the village, there are three working [tube wells]. [When] one of them works, the other two cannot be operated.

The three tube wells inside the village refer to those on the boundaries of the settlement and not to the number of tube wells on village farmland. All three were located at one end of the settlement, separated from one another by a distance of approximately fifty yards. When I first went to Alipur in 1984, they could be operated simultaneously without any problem. But, by 1992, the water table had fallen to such an extent that this was no longer the case.

Explanations about the drop in the water table thus derived from a multiplicity of sources, in which the introduction of a new technology—tube wells—was refracted by changing class relations, new ties between peasants and the state, and inheritance patterns. The advent of tube well irrigation itself owed to the sinking of the state tube well, which had its intended effect in demonstrating the feasibility of a new technology. The state tube well, in turn, was part of an effort to "modernize" agriculture and became possible only with the installation of electric lines. The "electrification" of rural areas (I am here using official government terminology) was, and continues to be, the benchmark of a "modern" nation-state. Advertisements by state governments proclaiming their success in "development" rarely failed to mention the number of new villages that had been "electrified." Tube wells, therefore, were not just about pumping groundwater; they lay at the end of a chain of signifiers indicating the modernity of the nation-state.

Tube wells were a means of pumping groundwater, but they were machines which also changed class relations and which reshaped the relations between peasants and the state. Dependence on tube wells thus initiated a complicated relationship between peasants and the state. The supply of electricity, the repair of electric lines, and the payment of electric bills became central to farming. This dependence on the state led to an antagonistic relationship between officials of the Electricity Board and peasant activists, as the latter contended that runaway corruption, irregular supply, and high bills were part of the government's strategy to keep rural areas poor. It was this structural antagonism between urban-based officials of the state and rural producers that was successfully exploited in peasant mobilizations that pitted rural "Bharat" against urban "India" (see Chapter 1 for details). The use of groundwater resources, therefore, was the outcome of a complicated intersection of factors beyond the technology of tube wells themselves.

The advent of tube wells and the increased use of groundwater were also related to cropping patterns, the intensity of cropping, and the qualities of the soil. These themes are explored further in the following section.

Effects of cropping pattern and intensity of cropping
How did changes in what was grown and the manner in which it was grown affect the use of groundwater? Clearly, drastic changes had oc-

curred in cropping patterns and cropping intensity in the last two decades. For example, since tube wells were first introduced into Alipur, new varieties of wheat had completely replaced traditional desi wheat. With the encouragement provided by support prices, farmers had started cultivating sugarcane as never before. Not surprisingly, new types of crops were accompanied by altered patterns of land use. Double cropping had become the norm. Some farmers attempted to obtain three or even four crops in an agricultural year, a pattern of cultivation that would certainly not have been possible without a regular and dependable source of irrigation. As compared with the elaborate discourse surrounding land quality, what farmers had to tell me about the use of groundwater was decidedly sketchy. What little they had to say about the relationship between the decline of groundwater, the kinds of crops grown, and the intensity of cultivation displayed far sharper disagreement than did the statements about land quality presented in the first section of this chapter.

Farmers noted that tube wells enabled them to extend dramatically the area under cultivation as often as they remarked on the importance of tube wells in extending the growing season. I was told that irrigating with the leather *chars* allowed only four to five bighas to be irrigated in an entire day.[21] In response to a question about the difference in *farming* methods between the past and the present, Ram Singh chose to focus entirely on changes in *irrigation*:

> Before, there was no source of water. There were many difficulties earlier. People used to work hard, but due to [the shortage] of water they could not profit from farming. There was a well here with *chars*. And then after that we put *rahat* [persian wheels]. We were very young when rahats first began. The rahats [supplied enough water] to enable the fields to be plowed. Only a little bit of farming was possible with it. All the fields could not be filled. They remained unirrigated [*padwa, padua*]. So the fields on the other side kept getting spoiled. The government tube well irrigated some [of our] land. Some was done here, some there, just enough to get by. It wasn't like one could profit from so much land. We didn't profit in the least. Then these tube wells started. Tube wells have been beneficial. Nothing else was profitable.

Ram Singh and his brothers could irrigate only small patches of their substantial property with older technologies of irrigation. The fields immediately surrounding their well received water, and those close enough to the government tube well also managed to get some irrigation. But that was just enough to eke out a living. Despite possessing a lot of land, they did not produce a surplus from it until they started irrigating by tube wells.[22]

Tube wells were probably even more important for having extended the growing season. Earlier, most of the land could be used to grow only one crop. Now, tube wells enabled almost all the land to be double cropped. Ram Singh explained:

> The monsoon crop, that which could be grown from the rains, was the only crop which grew. The rest was left uncropped [*ashadi*]. Now, each farm is taking two crops. The moisture of the rains did not last. If it rained a little bit the crop would sprout somehow, and it would progress a bit, but otherwise it would dry. Some land that we would bring under control by plowing [*kaabu main kar day jyot kay*] would retain moisture. Grain was sown there. But we couldn't cultivate all the land. Due to the arrangement of water from the well . . . only a little land could be used. All the land couldn't be farmed. It allowed production only for one season [*chamai*]. All this changed with tube wells. It then became more convenient. Now, water reaches every field.

I wondered about the degree to which the fall in groundwater level could be attributed to the extension of cultivation and how much of it was due to the kinds of crops being grown. Was the falling water level to be explained by the fact that more land was being irrigated now? And that this land was being cultivated for at least two seasons rather than one? Or was it due to the growth in acreage devoted to sugarcane and to high-yielding varieties of wheat, both "thirsty" crops? When I asked Ram Singh, his response was unequivocal. The water level was not falling because of the new, high-yielding varieties. Rather, it had to do with the amount of land under irrigation. The combination of tube wells and hand pumps left very little water under the ground: "The only reason for the shortage of water, *babuji*, is because of too many tube wells. There is not enough water left down below. The water here is finishing." In Ram Singh's reckoning, the shortage of water was caused not by crops that require more irrigation but by the increase in the cultivated area. This view was seconded by Prasad, who also felt that the decreasing water level had little to do with the crop mix. Prasad's view was that all crops required approximately equal quantities of water, with the possible exception of two or three crops that could be grown with somewhat less irrigation. I pointed out to him that barley [*jon*], for example, required a lot less water than wheat. But he was not convinced: "A lot of jon is being sown even now. But when there is no water, there won't be enough even for jon. [If the amount of water decreases], then even less can be used for jon." Prasad acknowledged that some crops required less water than others. But their potential to save water was limited by the fact that they were already cultivated quite extensively. All remaining crops required roughly equal amounts of irrigation; hence, changing the crop mix would do little to save water. Prasad emphasized that to conserve water, one could always irrigate such crops as sugarcane less. But, he pointed out, the more times it was irrigated, the better the yields were. It was the same for crops like wheat. Water use, therefore, depended less on the crop than on the decisions made by the farmer about irrigation (irrigation decisions, in turn, accompanied choices about the quantity of fertilizer, the number of weedings, and so forth). Correlating water use to the crop, therefore, was a kind of shorthand that bypassed the complex calculations that actually went into the use of water. Prasad suggested that, in practice, these other factors were more likely to be important to water consumption than was the kind of cultivar.

Another result of extending the irrigated area was that poorer-quality land was being brought into cultivation. (The consequences of this fact for soil quality have already been explored in the first part of this chapter.) I wished to find out if poor-quality land needed more water in addition to larger quantities of fertilizer. Satish told me that his field was "cold" and that he had to irrigate it more frequently than normal.[23] I asked him why, if the field was "cold," it needed more, rather than less, irrigation. He replied:

> Fertile [*do-math*] land starts drying from the bottom. It appears to be wet on top, but if you dig it, it is absolutely dry. This [pointing to his plot] land is dry on top, but if you dig it, you will find it absolutely wet [*tar*]. There is nothing wrong with the land. All it lacks is water. The only difference is that better land has an advantage of ten days as compared with this land. If this plot can go for fifteen days without water, good land can go for twenty-five days. But the output will be the same if you put water in this plot every ten days and, in the other land, every twenty or twenty-five days. Only irrigation expenses will be higher, that's all.

Crops, such as wheat, that have shallow roots are obviously better suited to land which retains moisture on top. By Satish's calculation, the "cold" plot that he was cultivating would need twice as much water to obtain as good a yield as fertile land.

Satish's observation that poor-quality land required higher inputs of irrigation becomes more significant in light of statements quoted earlier about the extension of cultivation. One of the important points made about the increase in a cultivated area was that it enabled poorer-quality lands to be farmed. If Satish was right, lands with poorer soil required more irrigation than did high-quality land to yield a given level of output. Thus, increasing the cultivated area resulted in a more than proportional increase in the use of groundwater resources.

My attempt to understand peasant perceptions of the decline in groundwater and their explanations for this decline have thus brought a number of considerations into focus. These explanations have combined in various ways the extension of cultivation to new areas, the increase in the intensity of cultivation to two or three crops a year, and the cultivation of poor-quality land. Farmers were much less convinced that the crop mix or the cultivation of high-yielding varieties was responsible for the sharp drop in groundwater.

Tube wells were welcomed because they made it possible, even convenient, to grow several crops on a larger cultivated area that included fields with poor soil. At the same time, the excessive pumping of water made necessary by multiple crops, large cultivated areas, and poor soil was held to be an important reason for the decline of the water table level.

The same processes that affected land quality and water resources, or, more generally, the health of the environment, also had an impact on the health of humans. The next section explores some of these relations.

Health and the Cultivated Environment

The ecological understandings advanced by farmers in Alipur depended on substantivist interpretations of phenomena in which properties, and not merely elements, were passed on through the food chain. Properties were imparted to the food by the soil, fertilizers, water, wind, and sun. These properties were then imparted to the people who ate this food, thereby changing their constitutions, bodies, minds, and temperaments.[24] Inputs that had ill effects on the health of the soil, for example, also adversely influenced the health of humans through their effects on the crop.[25]

Soon after I arrived in Alipur for my first round of fieldwork in 1984, Suresh was explaining how technologies of irrigation had changed over the years. He concluded his narrative by emphasizing the role of water in the constitution of the body. At that time, I was unaware of Suresh's inclination to attribute scriptural origins for his pronouncements. He attributed this insight to Lord Krishna: "Water creates food, and food creates the body" [*jal say ann banta hai, ann say shareer banta hai*]. This was a straightforward, commonsensical notion that needed no explanation in Alipur. The idea is not merely that water is necessary for the production of grain but that it is constitutive of it. *Banta* implied "to make" or "to create." Thus, what is implicit in this statement is that the *properties* of water find their way into the grain, and the properties of the grain, in turn, find their way into and constitute the body. One of the most common questions which people in Alipur ask about any region and which they constantly asked me about America was, "How are the water and air [*havaa-paani*] over there?" The question was based on the premise that in some places these elements were conducive to good health, and in others they were not (Zimmermann 1987). For example, the water of a region could be "sweet" [*meetha*] and "tasty" [*swaadisht*] and thus promote good health.

Because foods passed on their properties to the body, one had to regulate carefully the kinds of food one ate in different seasons and at different times of the day. Also, because each body was different, the intake of food had to be regulated to the constitution of the body (Gold forthcoming:16). For instance, two varieties of hemp were grown in the village. Oil was extracted from the fruit on top of the plant and used for medicinal purposes. This oil was thought to be especially useful in treating breathing problems and coughs and was sometimes ingested in the form of sweets [*ladoos*]. The fruit could also be eaten like a vegetable by peeling and cooking it. It has a taste similar to that of okra and was considered a delicious vegetable. One variety of hemp, called *pat-sann*, was considered to be a very "hot" food and cooked only during the winter. The other was known as *phool-sann*, so named after its bright yellow flowers, and was thought to be so "hot" that it was deemed unfit for human consumption. If it was fed to oxen, it was believed that they broke out into knotlike sores from which they started bleeding. This was because of the excess heat released by the food in their bodies.

Many people in Alipur expressed the opinion that wheat grown with chemical fertilizers did not possess the qualities of traditional varieties. These qualities or properties were expressed in terms of its purity, sweetness, taste, strength-giving nature, and softness. (An extended example of these beliefs is given in the Introduction.) A conversation in

1992 with a group of mostly low-caste jatav men who were commenting on the change in dietary patterns brought out these beliefs quite clearly.

> Earlier, when people sowed wheat, they didn't apply fertilizer, they didn't apply chemical fertilizer. They used to apply manure. That grain was pure, and chickpeas, peas, wheat, and jon were eaten, there was nothing heat-producing in those grains. Chickpeas-wheat rotis help purify the blood and cleanse the stomach [achchaa khoon banaavay aur payt ki safaii raakhay]—chickpeas, wheat, barley [chanaa, gayhoon, jon] mixed together. Even if you eat them dry [rookhi—that is, without ghee, condiments, or vegetables] and go to sleep, they can be digested. And these [chemically grown] wheat rotis, if you eat them once and go to sleep, they will stay like stones in your stomach. They will cause only trouble.
>
> Earlier, we had desi wheat, which was very strengthening and good to eat. If you made a roti of that in the morning and kept it, it would stay soft like a cotton ball till the evening; it was so soft. These rotis, you take them out of the fire and put them on the plate, and they are like leather. It is a matter of taste and also of strength—there is a lot of difference between this grain and that.[26] Earlier, we used to eat a lot of chickpeas, now even the gods can't get it [ab chanaa na milay devtaon ko; laughs].

The tastiness of rotis made from desi wheat was partly due to its softness. The softness also indicated that it was easy to digest, that it wouldn't lodge in the stomach like a stone, and that it was not excessively heat producing. Unlike the new varieties, which excited the body by their excess heat, rotis made from desi wheat imparted "real" strength that sustained hard, physical labor for long periods. Its effectiveness owed much to the strength of the organic manure used to grow desi wheat. By contrast, new varieties, nourished by chemical fertilizers, were less pure and thus less sustaining and strength giving. In fact, rotis made from a combination of chickpeas, wheat, and barley were considered more nutritious and sustaining than those made from plain wheat. But the price of chickpeas had risen so much that even ritual offerings had been curtailed, thus provoking the ironic reference to the deprivation suffered by the gods. The knowing laughter that ensued from that clever turn of phrase indicated that humor was the only weapon in the face of deprivation.

Farmers in Alipur had stopped planting chickpeas because the output had been declining to the point where they could no longer recover even the cost of the seeds. They attributed this decline to the fact that the soil had become weak from the widespread use of chemical fertilizers and thus could not support a crop such as chickpeas, which required a "strong" field. Even if they put nitrogen and calcium in the soil, the chickpeas failed to grow. The plants grew tall, but there would be very few pods on them. Thus, one could neither purchase them on the market nor successfully grow small quantities for domestic production. The soil had become too weak to support a crop like chickpeas; this, in turn, contributed to the poor health of humans because they could no longer afford to eat such nutritious food.

Chemical fertilizers were also directly blamed for the poor health of the population. It was believed that eating grain grown with chemical fertilizers failed to provide the nourishment necessary to ward off disease. During the same conversation with the jatav men described earlier, Anil, a young man, articulated a common perception about the spread of illness. "There weren't as many diseases earlier [chorus of agreement from others]. Earlier, illnesses spread in 10 percent of the people. In approximately August, September, or November, illness spread in 10 percent of the people. And in today's era, 10 percent remain healthy, whereas 90 percent are sick."

The use of chemical fertilizers that had accompanied the introduction of high-yielding varieties of wheat also had the consequence of changing the mix of crops grown. Wheat became, by far, the dominant crop in the winter harvest. This change in the crop mix had implications for the health of the local population as well. Although the connection with chemical fertilizers and greater access to groundwater was less direct, it was evident to everyone. Anil articulated his misgivings, with some help from the other men present, with particular reference to the poor: "Earlier, there was ghee and milk for food; and in grain, we mostly [ate] chickpeas, peas, and barley. With wheat, it was like this: if a relative came, rotis were made for him. Otherwise our own food was ghee and milk. And among grains, chickpeas, barley, and peas were eaten most often. So people's strength was maintained at a high level. Now those things are not available to eat and nor can you get them." In the discourse of villagers, ghee and milk are synonyms for a time of plenty. Anil first presents a picture of "the past" in which the most highly valued dairy products are plentiful. At the same time, however, he points out that wheat was a "prestige" good eaten only at times when an honored guest came along. When people in Alipur talked of "relatives," they usually meant a very specific relation, the father-in-law or brother-in-law of one of the daughters of the house. Apart from these rare occasions when wheat rotis were made in the house, the everyday food used to consist of a "strength-giving" combination of grains like chick-peas, barley, and peas. My upper-caste informants told me that these "coarse" grains were eaten mainly by the lower castes such as jatavs and that they never ate anything but wheat, which seemed very unlikely except for the richest households in the village. In Anil's commentary, the health-giving food eaten by them in "the past" was intimately connected to his earlier statement about the spread of illness. One of the reasons nutritious foods were no longer available was that chemical fertilizers had weakened the soil so much that it was unable to support such crops as chickpeas. Once this nutritious food was no longer available to farmers, their strength could not "be maintained at a high level," and they became prey to different kinds of diseases.

Anil went on to explain why people had started eating less nutritious food in the present:

> The food [eaten in the past] still has greater strength. If someone wants to eat it, then that food still has great strength. One of the reasons why people are not able to eat it now is that their families have become too big. Few in the household earn and many eat [kamaanay waale ghar may kam, khaanay waale adhik]. Another reason is that the price of chickpeas used to be very low. In today's world, it is very high. It is much more than [the price of] wheat, approximately four times [the price of] wheat. That is why people cannot eat those things that are good for their health, that are beneficial for them. They sell it instead of eating it. They can't eat it because they are constrained. They eat wheat instead.

Anil identified two primary causes for the inability of people to eat the food that they used to in "the past." One was that the population had increased, and families "had become too big," with the result that the ratio of dependents to earning members in a family had gone up. The other reason was that the logic of the market forced people to sell products such as chickpeas because they fetched a much higher price than staples such as wheat. The "constraints" that he identified as responsible for poor nutrition were precisely that farm families needed cash to purchase inputs such as chemical fertilizer. So they felt that they could not afford to consume chickpeas when cheaper food was available. In a similar manner, despite the large increase in the amount of milk produced in the village, almost all of it was sold. The reason was that urban consumers in the large towns around Alipur could afford to pay a lot for the milk, and farmers needed the cash to purchase fertilizer, machinery, and consumer goods. As a result, very few children in the village drank milk. Most households kept just enough milk to make tea and a little bit of yogurt. The rest was sold (see also Sen 1981 and Alvares 1992 for discussions of the negative effects of markets).

Those who owned enough land to grow their own wheat could at least eat that for the entire year. But the situation in poorer households was much worse:

> [People] eat a lot of potatoes, whereas potatoes are not good for one's health. In winter [their growing season], potatoes are used much more than anything else. If a poor man does not have grain to eat in his house, he will get one kilo of wheat flour and two kilos of potatoes for his family, boil the potatoes and stuff them into the rotis, and feed it to them. In this way, they get by. If they [the family] want to eat wheat or chickpeas/peas [*chanaa-matar*], then he won't be able to afford it. [Their deprivation] reaches such an extent that children come to the brink of dying from hunger. They [poor families] take inexpensive ration rice, boil it, eat it at night, and go to sleep, thinking that this way no one will get up at night from hunger. [The food that the poor eat nowadays] is less beneficial [chorus of agreement]. Their situation is worse. When their position is down [situation is bad], they are unable to earn [a wage]. If they are not able to earn, the possibility arises that their children will die of hunger. This period is quite harmful for the poor.

In Anil's view, the pressure to eat less nutritious but cheaper food resulted in the consumption of potatoes. Potatoes, while quite filling, did not supply much by way of strength. The potato output had shot up in recent years because of a rise in the number of cold-storage facilities where they could be stored all year. For several years, immediately after the harvest, the price of potatoes had been extremely low. Because the potato crop was harvested well before the wheat harvest was in, wheat prices were high at that time, which made potatoes an especially attractive food for the poor. Similarly, Anil suggested that the poor obtained rice at subsidized rates from the public distribution system and ate it at night. Rice filled people up and prevented them from waking up due to hunger. But it did not give the poor the energy that they needed to work well the following day. Anil's statement that the food eaten by the poor nowadays was worse than before was met with widespread agreement by all the men participating in the conversation. They concurred when he suggested that eating unhealthy food inserted the poor in a vicious cycle because the inability to work affected their earning capacity, which in turn had repercussions for the health of their families. Anil indicated that the poor had been brought to the brink of starvation not merely because of the quantity of food that they could afford to consume but because of its *quality* as well.

At first glance, the explanation offered by Anil and the other men for the declining state of the health of the poor may seem only tangentially connected to the use of the new agricultural technology, with its attendant use of chemical fertilizer, groundwater, and so on. What one has to keep in mind, however, is that the shift in cropping patterns to a more input-intensive regime has occurred almost entirely as a result of the introduction of hybrid wheat varieties. Thus, the fact that wheat displaced more nutritious crops such as chickpeas, peas, and barley was directly related to the availability of fertilizer and groundwater and to the stable prices of wheat guaranteed by the government. In comparison with wheat, new, high-yielding varieties of chickpeas, peas, barley, and maize were almost unknown. Farmers in Alipur, like other farmers in northern India, had almost completely stopped growing chickpeas; this is why the price of chickpeas had risen so sharply that "even the gods couldn't consume them." By contrast, the potato harvest had boomed because the number of cold-storage warehouses had increased, which enabled the consumption of potatoes to be spread throughout the year.[27] Again, it is important to note that the stored potatoes went to cities, not to village homes. At the same time, the spurt in demand for potatoes had led to bumper harvests, which had made it the cheapest food product in the winter season. The compulsions of the market also led most village homes to sell their milk rather than keep it for domestic consumption. Alipur and other villages in the area participated in a government program that bought milk at fixed rates from a significant radius around large metropolises such as Delhi. The pulls of the market thus worked in multiple ways to draw out nutritious food from the village and to force the poor to depend on food that was filling but not sustaining.

Conclusion

In unfavorably comparing their present state to "the past," a time when they had nutritious food to eat, poor peasants in Alipur were drawing attention to ecological changes that had a direct impact on their dietary intake. What I found especially significant in villagers' narratives of "the past" was not that such stories helped to determine whether the poor "actually" ate better in "the past" than in the present but that they detailed how villagers experienced the changes that they were living through. The perception that their current diet was less nutritious than in "the past" and that the condition of the poor was worse now than before was an eloquent critique of the claims made by the modernizing state about the "development" of the countryside and the lifting of record numbers of people above the "poverty line." The very programs that were supposedly "improving" the lot of the rural areas through high support prices, cold-storage facilities, and the organization of milk producers cooperatives were also sucking out all the nutritious food from the villages to supply consumers in urban areas who had the resources to pay for it.

This chapter has demonstrated that the degradation of the quality of food and thus of human health was not merely the result of market pressures but also of changes in the production process. Hybrid wheat, chemical fertilizers, and tube wells represent a new technology and, more important, a new relation between the land, crops, and human health. The use of chemical fertilizers and groundwater does not merely affect the output but also has implications for the health of the land and the qualities of the grain. The food produced by these methods is both less tasty and less nutritious. When this food is ingested, it fails to impart strength to the eater, who is, as a result, left vulnerable to illnesses. The health of the soil, the health of plants, and the health of humans are thus intrinsically and intimately linked. Qualities imparted to the soil by chemical fertilizers find their way into the crop, which then transmits these qualities to the person who eats them. It is for this reason that "ecological" degradation is not something that happens to a "nature" that surrounds and is thus external to the self: it is a set of processes that degrades the qualities of human life as well. Hence, rather than think in terms of the "impact" of environmental degradation on human health, perhaps it is more appropriate to conceive of "the environment" and "the body" not as two "systems" that interact with each other but as linked by a highly conjunctural flow of qualities or properties.[28]

Substantivist theories of the relationship of the soil, fertilizer, air, water, plants, and bodies to one another are very similar to theories of the interconnectedness of all things in nature in certain strains of West-

Threshing with a tractor; the wheat is lying in the foreground

ern environmentalism. Taking the example of England, Keith Thomas shows how the relation between "man" and the natural world changed from the seventeenth century, when the dominion of man over nature was an unquestioned objective of human endeavor, to the nineteenth century, when doubts about human dominion of nature and the uniqueness of humans began to arise (1983:17–91). Seventeenth-century travelers were "baffled" by the Jain, Buddhist, and Hindu respect for the lives of all animals, even insects (21). The elevation of nature to a subject worthy of study in its own right and not merely for its utility to humans allowed naturalists to reconceptualize the relationship between plants, animals, and their environment. It was in this context that the German zoologist Ernst Haeckel coined the term "ecology": "By ecology we mean the body of knowledge concerning the economy of nature—the investigation of the total relations of the animal both to its inorganic and to its organic environment" (Bate 1991:36). Thus, from the very beginning, ecology was conceived of as a holistic science concerned with the relationship between living things and their environment. From its basis as a means to understand plants and animals, notions of ecology were extended to denote the symbiotic relationship posited between the economy of nature and the activities of humans by nineteenth-century writers such as Thoreau and Wordsworth (36–61). Indeed, Wordsworth's notion of "dwelling" in nature appears to strain against the original separation between humans and nature that makes their reconciliation a possible goal.[29] And it is precisely the nineteenth-century notion of holism that Carolyn Merchant underlines in her influential text *The Death of Nature,* in which she makes a distinction between ecology and its philosophy of nature, holism: "The idea of cyclical processes, of the interconnectedness of all things, and the assumption that nature is active and alive are fundamental to the history of human thought" (1980:293).[30] Mechanistic and cybernetic models were grafted onto these formulations and resulted in a notion of ecology as a self-regulating ecosystem. These ecological theories continue to exert a tremendous influence on popular understandings. By contrast, holistic theories of the interconnectedness of all living beings resemble the substantivist theories of peasants in Alipur in that they too posit that changes in one sphere will make their way through the ecosystem to affect humans. For example, changing the microbes and nutrients in the soil would eventually affect humans through the food chain. Yet something fundamentally disrupts too strong an identification between holistic approaches to ecology in the West and the substantivist ideas of Indian peasants, and that has to do with ontological assumptions that underlie those understandings. Peasants in Alipur thought that all living matter was connected because it was interchangeable. Such a view of connectedness rested on a belief in the transmigration of souls. It was not merely the case, as Merchant (1980:293) argues of ecology, that it levels the value hierarchies between humans and other living things because any part of the ecosystem is as valuable as any other part; rather, a human life could *become* any other form of life in the next birth. It was a question not of the *equality* of all forms of life but of their *transmutability.* It was for this reason that cutting down trees was considered a polluting act to be performed only by specific lower-caste people (see also Gold n.d.:14). Substantivist theories of the interconnectedness of all living beings thus rest on somewhat different premises from those supporting holistic ecology.

Substantivist theories of "ecology" were also a key ingredient in a critical conversation about indigenous practices that emerged among Alipur's farmers, to which chemical fertilizers and the new agricultural technology were integral. What I saw was not the loss of indigenous knowledge, with its attendant implications of the lack of agency of indigenous peoples to resist the forces of historical change, but the careful evaluation of indigenous practices. Arguments for the preservation of indigenous knowledge, when not based on nostalgia, are built on the utilitarian premise of saving knowledge potentially "useful" for "humankind." But for whom is such knowledge useful? By positing a unitary subject (humankind) that is experiencing this loss, the discourse of indigenousness ignores that inequalities of power might result in divergent needs, effects, perceptions, and experiences. It glosses over the real possibility that there may be very different assessments between, for example, First World conservationists and subaltern, Third World people as to what constitutes a "loss" of indigenous knowledge and which losses are significant. Discussions or efforts to "preserve" indigenous knowledge end up privileging certain kinds of knowledges over others. In some instances, the interests of "first" peoples and First World conservationists have coincided in preserving indigenous knowledges; however, when that is not the case and subaltern groups find themselves in opposition to those who want to preserve "indigenous knowledge," whose needs and experiences will be invoked to judge whether to save a particular instance of indigenous knowledge?[31]

The larger question that I wish to raise here is about the exclusions implicit in the project of conserving indigenous knowledges. Proponents of "indigenous knowledge" have clearly played an important role in empowering marginalized peoples, who have been able to establish that they have a culture and an identity that is distinctive, original, and shared by an identifiable group with a continuous history. This has enabled important political gains to be made by extremely impoverished, culturally marginalized, and politically disenfranchised groups all around the world. No one would dispute that such efforts need to be recognized and encouraged, nor can the political efficacy of such claims be underestimated. Yet, at the same time, one needs to distinguish between the strategic political projects based on an essentialist invocation of indigeneity given the pressures of hegemonic discourses nationally and internationally and the cultural theory that is used to support such claims. I fear that there is a heavy price to be paid for the emphasis placed by proponents of indigenous knowledge on cultural purity, continuity, and alterity. Such efforts at cultural conservation make no room for the vast majority of the world's poor, who live on the margins of subsistence and the most degraded ecological conditions[32] but who cannot claim to be "indigenous people" in the limited definition accorded that term. Like the residents of Alipur, the large proportion of the most indigent people in the Third World find their lives shaped by impure, hybrid, and modern forms of culture and identity. Instead of taking an analytic and political position that ignores such people or, worse, regards them with contempt for having lost "their culture," I would like to argue for a concept of culture that is robust enough to enable the empowerment of disparate groups of subalterns. Instead of using ideas of cultural alterity embedded in Enlightenment projects of modernity (see Chapter 3 for details), might it be possible to rethink notions of alterity so that alternative formulations of culture and different models of political affiliation and political practice emerge?

It would, for example, have been easy to conclude that the substantivist connection made by peasants in Alipur between the health of the soil, of plants, and of humans represents a form of resistance to their imbrication in "modern," "scientific" farming. But one would then have to ignore their enthusiasm for tube wells or the sentiment, expressed by many, that high-yielding varieties and chemical fertilizers had been beneficial to farmers because they had increased farm surpluses and farm incomes. This goes to underline that indigenous perspectives on ecology are neither consistent nor unitary. Indigenous ecology is itself a hybrid, constituted of incommensurable discourses, practices, and evaluations that cannot be neatly encapsulated in the master narratives of modernity and development. The postcolonial subjects of Alipur frustrate their positioning within relations of alterity that would make of them examples of backwardness or tradition, on the one hand, and lost exemplars of ecological sustainability, on the other. They mimic industrial agriculture, yet criticize its effects. They are both resistant subjects who critique the ecological destructiveness of "modern" farming and "industrial" farmers who employ resources unsustainably.

Simultaneously positioned within the discourses of modernity promulgated by an international system of development and as marginal subjects at the limits of "the West," their critique of "ecological" destruction has itself to be read in alternate terms. I have attempted to demonstrate that their understandings of ill health, based in substantivist theories, are themselves incommensurable with explanations of "ecological" destruction, because the latter presumes a certain kind of relationship between subjects and "nature" that is not shared by the peasants of Alipur. It is precisely these strategies of mimicry and hybridity that characterize the postcolonial condition—technologies of farming that are the same and yet very different, and understandings of the "environment" that make their critiques at once familiar and very strange.

5

Peasants and Global Environmentalism: A New
Form of Governmentality?

T he previous chapter charted the ecological effects of a global
discourse of development incorporated in the green revolution. The ecological crisis precipitated by globally dominant
models of development led to the world convention on the environment, which, in conjunction with other international treaties, promises
to alter drastically rural peoples' relationships with agriculture. Negotiations for these global treaties, conducted half a world away, nevertheless drew strong protests from farmers groups in India.

On March 3, 1993, between 18,000 and 200,000 farmers from different
parts of India converged on New Delhi.[1] Led by Mahendra Singh Tikait, president of the Bharatiya Kisan Union (literally, Indian Farmers
Union), who came leading seven thousand tractors and trolleys overflowing with people, the Karnataka Rajya Ryotu Sangha (KRRS; Karnataka Farmers Association), and the Gene Campaign, the meeting was
called to demand that the Indian government reject outright the Dunkel
Draft on the Trade-Related Intellectual Property rights (TRIPS) section
of the General Agreement on Tariffs and Trade (more popularly known
as GATT). The farmers called for an amendment to the constitution to
make mandatory the ratification of all international agreements by a
majority in both houses of parliament as well as by at least half the state
legislatures. The Dunkel Draft, they insisted, must be discussed in all
state legislatures before the Government of India signed the Uruguay
Round of GATT.[2] Another demand voiced at the meeting was that the
Dunkel Draft be translated into all Indian languages.[3] Dr. Nanjundaswamy, leader of the Karnataka Farmers Association, explained and
criticized the Dunkel Draft, to loud cheers and the waving of green
shawls.[4] Farmers, he said, had every right to produce, improve on, and

sell seeds, a right that they would now lose to multinationals: "We are going to launch a one-point programme—to drive out the multinationals. *Our genetic resources are our national property*" (*Hindu*, March 4, 1993, 9; emphasis added).[5]

From a North American perspective, a discussion of the finer points of TRIPS appears hopelessly specialized, if not esoteric. This response is perhaps itself a reflection of a particular intertwining of structural and geographical location. For many poor people living in different parts of the globe, however, the effects of international governance are visceral and often calamitous. Biogenetic resources have become a highly charged issue not only in the context of GATT but against the backdrop of the entire debate on biodiversity (Khoshoo 1993; Vyasulu 1993). Trade and environmental issues come together because the new trade regime adopted in the Uruguay Round proposes for the first time a standard for the patenting of life forms, a process made easier by the Earth Summit, which pronounced the genetic material found in "nature" to be a global commons (more on this below).[6] Environmental agreements such as the Rio Accords are an essential part of a set of instruments being forged for global governance that have grave implications for the current world order of nation-states. Peasant groups in India are aware that global accords signal important shifts in the territorial basis of nationalism and are struggling to articulate what this postcolonial space represents for peasant organization and resistance. In this chapter I attempt to analyze some of the extraordinary links articulated by farmers' leaders between environmentalism, multinational capitalism, and the nation-state.

I use as my primary example, as well as my point of entry into a thicket of hairy questions, global environmentalism, as exemplified by the 1992 Earth Summit in Rio de Janeiro. Debates about the global environment have created a novel intersection of discourses of development, the world food economy, and agricultural technology. The concern with a deteriorating environment has led multilateral development agencies to stress "sustainable development" as the next stage in the "evolution" of development discourse. At the same time, the concern for "intellectual property rights" embodied in GATT and the application of techniques of genetic engineering to plants has meant that transnational corporations stand to play an even more important role in the world food economy than has been the case so far. Because the rhetoric of "sustainable development" has been accompanied by the demands of multilateral agencies for neoliberal policies in highly indebted Third

World countries, there is a convergence between the actions of the development apparatus and the interests of transnational capital. What implications does this have for the sovereignty of nation-states? Is it likely to lead to a global order marked by forms of neocolonialism? Or are the relations of inequality established by this articulation genuinely postcolonial, in the sense of going beyond a mode of domination that rests on the centrality of the nation-state? If so, what effects is this new global order likely to have on the everyday lives of subaltern people in the Third World?

I argue that in the same way that the notion of "postcoloniality" marks a temporal break where many living elements of colonialism are reconfigured into a new series, it also marks a break with the *spatial* order of nation-states such that elements of the spatial regulation and control exercised by nation-states are reconfigured into novel modes of governance. Perhaps no other issue so clearly and dramatically illustrates this proposition than global environmental regulation.

Environmental concerns, however, are important not just for the attention that recent spectacles like the Earth Summit have focused on them. Vandana Shiva (1986:272) puts it dramatically when she says: "Killing people by murdering nature is no longer an invisible form of violence. Claude Alvares has called it the Third World War—'a war waged in peace time, without comparison, but involving the largest number of deaths and the largest number of soldiers without uniform.'" The premises of this argument lead one to the inescapable conclusion that environmental problems, like world wars, can best be understood in terms of conflict between coalitions of nation-states. I wish to argue that extant understandings of the relationship between the local and the global, the micro and the macro, the West and the rest, need to be drastically rethought in order to comprehend some of the most important changes happening in the world today. My contention is that global environmentalism is part of a qualitative transformation of the world economy whose ramifications go far beyond mere *intensification* of existing trends. It foreshadows the creation of a set of institutions and practices that make up, in Foucauldian terms, a new technology of government. To talk about these changes entirely in terms of the geographical expansion of capitalism is thus to *under*specify what is distinctive about the new world order (or, as some prefer to call it, the "new world *dis*order").

Global environmental problems, specifically atmospheric warming, biodiversity, and the ozone layer, prove to be a particularly good subject to interrogate a series of concepts that have so far provided the means to map the relation of "local" peoples such as peasants to "larger" institutions and structures such as the world economy.[7] The ones that I will concentrate on in this chapter are those of territoriality, sovereignty, and the nation-state. Together, this triad has been completely naturalized to constitute the social sciences as a form of knowledge that inhabits the discursive space of *nationalism*. The confrontation between nationalism and colonialism (or neocolonialism) is made possible by shared conceptions of territoriality and sovereignty. The optic of nationalism, I will argue, proves especially limiting in its ability to see the peculiar dangers posed by environmental problems. Yet, its hegemonic status has the function of foreshortening the discursive horizon, such that certain ways of conceptualizing the question of environmental degradation are metaphorically "out of sight," while others are squeezed uncomfortably into a Manichaean logic.

I begin by analyzing the discourses surrounding environmental problems, especially those circulating at the Earth Summit. I describe the agreements reached at the Earth Summit and put them into the context of other treaties and accords that have been signed and implemented in the more recent past. The next section provides a critical analysis of two of the main interpretations that have been offered of the Rio Accords. Although the proponents of each have emphasized the differences between the two interpretations, I will demonstrate that they have a great deal in common as well. These points of convergence enable me to reach my second objective, which is to tease out some of their larger theoretical implications: I suggest how one might begin to rethink the question of environmentalism as a new disciplinary technology. This leads me to the final objective of this chapter, which is to analyze farmers' collective reactions to new institutions that affect ecological practices in terms of their likely implications for the future. I end by relating forms of governmentality with the organizational structures emerging to contest these new disciplinary technologies. It is these novel forms of discipline and resistance that characterize postcolonial conditions. I use the term "postcoloniality" to indicate that the terrain on which the new forms of governmentality are operating has (perhaps irrevocably) altered from the order of nation-states that enabled colonialism and nationalism to thrive. Just as in Chapter 3 (on "indigenous" agronomy) I demonstrated the link between global discourses on the green revolution and agricultural practices, so here I attempt to show why changing forms and modes of global regulation are being resisted by peasant groups that are afraid of the consequences of global environmental and trade treaties.

The Earth Summit and Other Global Accords

Agreements reached at the earth summit

The Earth Summit held in Rio de Janeiro from June 3 to June 14, 1992, was organized by the United Nations Conference on Environment and Development (UNCED). It had as its objective the signing of two major treaties, the Framework Convention on Climate Change and the Convention on Biological Diversity. In addition, there was Agenda 21, a program and set of green guidelines for the twenty-first century, and a statement of Forest Principles, which was also intended to be an advisory document to preserve forests and monitor the impact of development on timberlands. The summit was attended by 117 heads of state and government, the largest such gathering until then at an international conference, and by 35,000 accredited participants from 178 countries (*Facts on File,* June 18, 1992, 440).

The global warming convention aimed to reduce the emissions of carbon dioxide and other greenhouse gases (nitrous oxides, methane, and CFCs [chlorofluorocarbons]) believed to be responsible for heating up the atmosphere. Because the industrialized countries are responsible for 90 percent of the carbon dioxide that has so far been accumulated in the atmosphere, they were required to implement policies that freeze their emissions of these gases to 1990 levels (Bidwai 1992; *Facts on File,* June 18, 1992, 440–43). Although the twelve nations of the European Community (EC) unilaterally pledged to stabilize their emissions at 1990 levels by the year 2000, U.S. opposition to any targets scuttled efforts to set binding deadlines for emissions reductions. Similarly, the tax on fossil fuels proposed by the EC ran into rough weather with oil-producing countries and had to be dropped (*Facts on File,* June 18, 1992, 442). By the end of the summit, 153 countries had signed the global warming treaty, led by the host nation, Brazil.

The other major treaty signed at the Earth Summit was the Convention on Biological Diversity, which was intended to protect endangered plant and animal species. This treaty aimed to reduce the alarming depletion of genetic diversity on the planet. Signatories committed themselves to drawing up inventories of native plants and wildlife and to preservation of threatened species. Most of the biological diversity in the world exists in the poor countries of "the South," whereas the primary industrial and commercial demand for it exists in the rich countries of "the North."[8] The most contested aspect of this treaty called on industrialized countries to share the results and profits from biotechnological inventions with the countries that supplied them the genetic raw materials. The United Kingdom and Japan, countries that were initially hesitant, signed the treaty at the last moment. This isolated the United States, which became the sole major power to refuse to endorse the pact.[9] By the end of the summit, 155 nations had signed the Convention on Biological Diversity (*Facts on File*, June 18, 1992, 441; Grubb et al. 1993:82).

In addition to these major treaties, an agreement was also reached on a nonbinding statement of Forest Principles. This was perhaps the most controversial subject, with rich and poor countries taking strongly opposed positions. The eventual compromise recognized the right of all countries to "develop" their forest resources as they saw fit but in a way that minimized damage to ecosystems. Efforts to push a binding treaty that would mandate conservation failed owing to strenuous opposition from Brazil, India, and Malaysia. The argument advanced by delegates from these countries was that forests were sovereign resources, not a global resource to be commonly held by all. On the other hand, the United States wanted to make a forest conservation treaty the cornerstone of its own efforts. Two days before the Earth Summit began, President Bush announced a doubling of U.S. contributions to international forest programs to $270 million. But the last-minute nature of the effort alienated even its allies and resulted only in greater suspicion among those already wary of the United States' tactics and role.

A major new institution was also set up—the Global Environment Fund (GEF). The GEF would be administered by the World Bank in conjunction with the United Nations Environment Programme (UNEP) and the United Nations Development Programme (UNDP). In its pilot phase (1990–93), the GEF would be funded at an annual rate of $300 million (Grubb et al. 1993:175).

All three treaties signed at the Earth Summit have significant implications for farmers in rural India. Although the nonbinding nature of the statement of Forest Principles makes it the least effective of the agreements, it could result in international pressure on the Indian government to limit access to firewood, which would raise the price for cooking fuel all over the country, particularly for the poorest (see Agarwal

1986 for a detailed study of the wood fuel crisis). Similarly, the global warming convention could indirectly raise prices for oil-based chemical fertilizers. It is the biodiversity convention, however, that most directly threatens the interests of Indian farmers. It declares the genetic diversity carefully nurtured by farmers practicing "traditional" agriculture over millennia to be "the common heritage of mankind [sic]" but abrogates to (mostly First World) capitalist institutions the "intellectual property rights" that flow from tinkering with and genetically altering this painstakingly preserved resource (Agarwal and Narain 1992).[10]

Precursors of the earth summit

Although it was the largest and grandest international environmental conference to be convened until then, it would be incorrect to view the Earth Summit as initiating a new era in transnational environmental regulation. By 1992, there were more than 170 environmental treaties already in effect on issues ranging from ozone depletion to pollution of oceans, acid rain, protection of endangered species, and the preservation of the Antarctic (Frank 1994).[11] Nearly half these treaties have come into effect since the 1972 UN Conference on the Human Environment held in Stockholm, which was a watershed event in the growth of environmental consciousness at the level of nation-states (A. Agarwal 1985:4; French 1992:6–7). At the time of the Stockholm conference, the project of "developmentalism" reigned supreme. This was an ideology of nonsustainable growth vigorously promoted by Western countries since Bretton Woods and successfully disseminated to most Third World states by the early seventies. As the Brazilian delegate to the Stockholm conference put it, "Smoke is a sign of progress" (A. Agarwal 1985:4). Now, those very nations in the First World were expressing concerns about the exhaustion of resources, population growth, and the degradation of such global commons as the atmosphere, oceans, and biodiversity. One of the chief results of the Stockholm conference was the setting up of UNEP and the signing of conventions on marine pollution, conservation of world cultural heritage sites, and the protection of seals in the Antarctic (Hecht and Cockburn 1992:848–50).

Of the many treaties concluded after Stockholm, the one most widely regarded as being a model of international environmental regulation is the Montreal Protocol on Substances That Deplete the Ozone Layer, which was signed in September 1987. The treaty arose out of the urgent recognition that there was a big hole in the ozone layer over Antarctica and that rapid depletion over the Northern Hemisphere was imminent.[12] Since the chief culprit was identified as chlorofluorocarbons, the protocol initially set a target of emissions in industrial countries to be cut in half by 1998.[13] Several innovative features help explain the treaty's rapid acceptance and implementation. Developing countries were given a ten-year period to stabilize CEC emissions. Punitive measures in the form of trade embargoes against noncompliant nation-states were built into the agreement. When new evidence emerged that the ozone layer was being depleted faster than initially estimated, ninety-three nations signed a new treaty in June 1990, agreeing to stop using CFCs completely by the year 2000. Pressure from India and China, which argued that the expense of switching to CFC substitutes would constitute an unfair burden on their growing economies, led Western countries to set up a fund of $240 million to help developing countries make the transition and purchase the necessary technology under "fair" and "favorable" conditions (Cairncross 1992:17–18; French 1992:12–14; *India Today,* June 15, 1992, 78–79).[14]

These precursors to the Earth Summit remind us that global environmentalism does not arrive like a bolt from the blue but is the culmination of a series of efforts to build institutions, rules, and processes of regulation in the world system.[15] What implications do these new institutions and regulations have for the spatial order of nation-states that underlay colonialism and nationalism? Is global environmentalism part of a truly "postcolonial" and postnational mode of global governance? How does it affect subaltern groups in countries such as India? I will begin to answer these larger questions by putting global environmental treaties in the context of other kinds of global treaties.

Other global accords

Environmental treaties constitute but one component of a wider pattern of global accords and institutions that seem to have swept across the world of nation-states, particularly since the early seventies. Environmental agreements have to be seen alongside mechanisms that seek to regulate and promote international trade, finance, technological transfers, communications, travel, weapons, development efforts, and human rights. In the case of agriculture, there have been sustained attempts to boost output in developing countries through a network of international institutions of which the Consultative Group on International Agricultural Research (CGIAR) is perhaps the best known. These institutions have been funded by agencies such as the Ford and

Rockefeller Foundations, USAID, Canadian International Development Agency (CIDA), and other First World "development" agencies, with infrastructural support provided by the World Bank and bilateral agencies.

A primary mechanism in the economic arena is the GATT, which dates from 1948 and whose eighth round (called the Uruguay Round) was signed on April 15, 1994. During the last two decades, the growing internationalization of the world economy has been accompanied as well by greater control of Third World economies by the World Bank and the IMF. Also reached during the same two decades were such agreements as the Convention on the Rights of the Child, the Convention on Wetlands of International Importance of 1971; the World Heritage Convention of 1972; the Convention on Trade in Endangered Species (CITES) of 1973; the International Convention for the Prevention of Pollution from Ships (MARPOL) of 1973; the Law of the Sea Treaty of 1982; the International Whaling Commission ban on commercial whaling (since 1986); the Basel Convention on the Export of Hazardous Wastes of 1989; the International Labor Organization's Convention 169 on Indigenous and Tribal Peoples of 1989 (Bijoy 1993); and the Convention on the Prohibition of Chemical Weapons of 1992.

The scope, width, and breadth of global accords, of which environmental agreements form an essential part, have grave consequences for the territorial bases of nation-states. How do social-scientific concepts, that are themselves caught within the frame of nationalism, enable or limit our understanding of global accords? Does the proliferation of global agreements initiate a spatial order that represents an important shift from the territorial claims of colonialism and nationalism—a "postcolonial" space? How are peasants in India positioned by these transnational fields of power and knowledge? In this book I have attempted to chart the relationship between one set of rural, subaltern people in India and the global phenomena of development, capitalism, green revolution technology, and, in this chapter, environmentalism, in the process delineating the conditions of postcoloniality. Before I can address the questions about global environmentalism posed above, I will present the dominant interpretations of global agreements such as the Earth Summit, which will enable me to examine the role of existing frameworks in understanding and critiquing such agreements. At the same time, an analysis of dominant positions on the environment will also demonstrate how prevailing paradigms place certain kinds of interpretations beyond the discursive horizon.

Interpreting Global Environmentalism

Two positions on global environmental issues emerge most clearly from debates surrounding the Earth Summit. The first position emphasizes the environment as a global commons, suggests that it is a problem for all inhabitants of the planet, and urges that "we" work for "common" solutions. The second major position sees the environment as a staging ground for conflict between the rich countries of the North and the poor countries of the South. This is a view widely shared among governments, policymakers, industrialists, and environmental activists in poor countries (for example, *India Today,* the leading mainstream, pro-business, English-language magazine in India headlined the Rio extravaganza "Earth Wars"). Although it will be evident that I endorse many of the criticisms articulated by activists and leaders of the South, my analysis leads me to a position that goes beyond merely validating that view.

A position that follows from a "North" versus "South" view of the environment provides an explanatory foundation with a more specific and concrete genealogy. This is the view that global environmentalism constitutes a new form of imperialism—that is, ecological imperialism. The idea of "imperialism" is used in a rather loose way in much of this discussion, often as a synonym for "neocolonialism." It substitutes northern nation-states as agents where the more rigorous classical definition placed blocs of monopolistic finance capital organized along national lines. In the classical sense of "imperialism," blocs of nationally consolidated finance capital provided the driving force for conquest, colonialism, resource extraction, and the superexploitation of labor in the periphery (Lenin 1939). What is the status of these claims? Is "ecological imperialism" or "environmental neocolonialism" a helpful conceptualization of the problems raised by global environmentalism?

Before proceeding to elaborate on the two positions on global environmentalism mentioned above, let me stave off possible misreadings by stating what I am *not* arguing in the rest of this chapter. First, although my sympathy with southern critiques of "the North" will be readily apparent, I do not end up wholeheartedly endorsing a view from "the South." In fact, I argue for the need to move beyond *both* positions to understand why global environmental governance is such an important phenomenon. I suspect that the obviousness of the differences between North and South leads to an underappreciation of their commonalities. My strategy in counterposing "One World" to "North versus

South" positions on global environmentalism is aimed at accentuating dominant positions that are emphatically unlike each other. Obviously, in both the North and the South there exists a multiplicity of beliefs on global environmental issues held by diverse groups of people. My aim, therefore, is not to portray homogeneity and commonality where neither exist; at the same time, a great deal is gained in analytic clarity, and often in political efficacy, by focusing on *dominant* positions. Thus I do not deny or erase the multiplicity of positions and organizations within either the North or the South. On the contrary, I wish to point to the necessity of existing efforts to build coalitions across geographic divides. A superb example of such coalition building has been provided by the various grassroots groups who fought the World Bank's sponsorship of the Narmada Dam in central India (see particularly Udall 1995; also Baviskar 1995; Esteva and Prakash 1992; Fisher 1995; Kalpavriksh 1985; Morse 1992).[16] At the very least, the discussion of coalitions demonstrates that government representatives, environmental organizations, and grassroots groups have very different views of global environmental problems and sometimes pursue quite diverse avenues of action (although what is equally interesting is the extent to which their discourses converge). I do not pursue this question in great depth here because to do so would have taken me in a somewhat tangential direction from my main argument. The recognition of different institutions and actors is, however, implicit in my analysis and is discussed explicitly in the section "Peasant Protests" with reference to farmers groups.

In the analysis of global environmental discourse that follows, my concern is not to uncover the "interests" of various parties in taking the positions that they did but to see why they chose to forward their interests in one specific idiom and not another. Why, for instance, did northern leaders talk about environmental problems in terms of the "common problems facing the human family"? It seems to me that if other, unspoken interests were being forwarded in global environmentalist discourse, it is worth understanding what kinds of positions were implicitly supported or inhibited by that discourse.[17] Furthermore, my critical evaluation of global environmentalist discourse should not be taken as a criticism of all kinds of internationalism or a pessimism about the possibility of constructing empowering forms of transnational coalitions. My argument, in fact, leads to the conclusion that it is very important to build transnational organizations that can resist the kind of governmentality that is being instituted through global accords like the Earth Summit. Any such effort will necessarily draw on previous models of internationalism but also modify those models to meet the changing configuration of the nation-state system.

It is well beyond the scope of this chapter to spell out a theory of the new world order. My objective, for now, is to draw attention to some important processes, and I rely on other scholars to fill in aspects of what is a very large picture indeed (see Aglietta 1979; Brenner and Glick 1991; Davis 1978, 1984; Lipietz 1985, 1986, 1989; and Mandel 1975). Finally, I have not here attempted to explain how global environmental treaties have been forged; that is a related, but entirely separate, question. Instead, I am interested in the assumptions that are implicit in dominant global discourses surrounding environmental problems and their implications for poor rural people in the Third World, such as the farmers I worked with in Alipur. While I do not believe that this is the only or should be the exclusive way to study these questions, my contention is that a close examination of global environmentalism reveals a great deal about some central questions regarding the nation-state and the condition of postcoloniality. With this long list of caveats in mind, then, I turn to the analysis of "one world" positions on global environmentalism.

"Our common future?"[18]

In his opening speech at the Earth Summit, UNCED secretary general Maurice Strong said: "The most important ground we must arrive at in Rio is the understanding that *we are all in this together*. . . . If the agreements reached here do not serve the *common interests of the entire human family*, if they are devoid of the means and commitments required to implement them, if the world lapses back to 'business as usual,' we will have missed a historic opportunity, one which may not recur in our times, if ever" (Hertsgaard 1992:14; emphasis added). The idea that "we are all in this together" forms a cornerstone of global environmentalist discourse. During the late eighties, when leaders of some of the most important industrial countries such as Mikhail Gorbachev, Margaret Thatcher, George Bush, and Gro Harlem Brundtland started proclaiming themselves to be environmentalists and "competing to be the greenest actors on the world stage" (French 1992:7), this was a common slogan (*New York Times*, May 10, 1989; May 15, 1989). This is also the sentiment that lay behind the efforts of nongovernmental organizations, think tanks, and celebrity citizens to foster global environmental consciousness. The notion of "one earth," a fragile ecosystem suspended in the vast space of the solar system, is captured in the recurring motif of "Spaceship Earth" and the view of the earth from outer space. The

Brundtland Commission report, in fact, begins by noting the potential historical significance of this moment: "In the middle of the 20th century, we saw our planet from space for the first time. Historians may eventually find that this vision had a greater impact on thought than did the Copernican revolution of the 16th century. . . . From space, we see a small and fragile ball dominated not by human activity and edifice but by a pattern of clouds, oceans, greenery, and soils (Brundtland 1987:ES-1).[19] Apart from the obvious questions of who is represented by terms such as "we" and "our" (Who had the privilege of seeing "our planet"?), the Eurocentrism of this statement is striking. Far from representing an enormous historical break, what is striking about this picture is its *continuity* with a long tradition of Western representation in which *vision* and *objectivity* come together. *Looking* from a fixed point in the distance (the objective position) was what enabled the construction of the modern map, which represents the land as seen from a bird's-eye view (Raman 1994), and what gave rise to the notion of perspective in painting (Ruggie 1993:159). The urge, as well as the ability, to "step back" to "gain perspective" dates to the Renaissance and initiates a new relationship to the world in the "physical sciences, literature, landscape painting, architecture, and the principles of garden design" (Garb 1990:265).[20] The National Aeronautics and Space Administration (NASA) control crew brought out the premises implicit in the Whole Earth image by calling it the "God's eye view" of Earth (266). This notion of infinite vision, where nothing is hidden, where the disenchanting reach of modern science brings clarity and light, ties objectivity to the control of nature (Haraway 1988). It is a view from nowhere in particular, a disembodied vision, that insists not only on the transparency of its representation but on its univocality: this is the one true picture, the "real" representation of the world in its authentic fragility (Garb 1990; Haraway 1988).

The idea that behind the petty regional and national squabbles that beset the earth and the pursuit of narrow economic and geostrategic interests lies the true vision, the real truth that we all share one earth, "a small and fragile ball" as seen from space, is thus a call for a "larger vision" (once again the optical metaphor) that is itself firmly ensconced in a parochial conception of what *constitutes* a larger vision. In other words, if, in the unmemorable words of Maurice Strong quoted earlier, "we are all in this together," who defines what "this" is?[21] Is globalism, as envisioned by the Brundtland Commission and other First World environmentalists, itself deeply implicated in Western modes of knowledge, classification, and representation, a kind of moral position that makes it unable to comprehend other perspectives, let alone address them in any way that enhances dialogue?[22]

To be fair, the Brundtland Commission puts the question of international inequalities at the center of its explanation for the lack of sustainability observed in the world. Driven by the realization that economic and ecological changes have dramatically enhanced the interdependence of nations and peoples on one another, it issues a call for the recognition that we all inhabit one world (Gill 1991; Lipschutz and Conca 1993). Whereas previously concern was always with the ecological effects of economic activities, the interest has now shifted to the impact of "ecological stress" on economic endeavors. "Ecology and economy are becoming ever more interwoven—locally, regionally, nationally, and globally—into a seamless net of causes and effects" (Brundtland 1987:ES-4).There is thus a structural explanation for "one world" which goes beyond a feel-good liberalism that, in the face of all available evidence, declares "oneness" with the rest of humanity. Using this explanation as a backdrop, the Brundtland Commission report promotes the notion of "sustainable development" as a solution to the world's interwoven ecological and economic dilemmas. *Sustainable development* has become the new mantra of the large transnational institutions that dominate development theory and practice (the World Bank, USAID, the various regional development banks, and so forth), as well as of the Western environmental establishment, such as the large, wealthy environmental groups that have successful track records lobbying in Washington (Buttel 1992:18; Stephens 1992a:7). After all, what reasons could there possibly be to oppose an environmental strategy that promises growth with greenery?[23]

The explanation of interdependence contained in the Brundtland report, however, is firmly anchored in a developmentalist and technocratic vision in which the "problem-solving" approach is employed to deal with complex questions in a systems-theory framework (see Visvanathan 1991). Unsurprisingly, among the six major problems considered by the commission, the first three—population, food security, and the loss of genetic resources—are primarily "Third World" problems. The fear of overpopulation, for some time now out of center stage in development discourse, has been rediscovered in the guise of global environmentalism (*Economist,* May 30, 1992, 11–12; Tokar 1988).[24]

As Agrawal and Sawyer (n.d.) demonstrate quite convincingly, the overpopulation thesis is the latest incarnation of an old colonial theme in which a feminized tropical nature is sought to be protected by white scientists as the patrimony of mankind.[25] It is significant that despite its rhetorical acknowledgments of inequalities in trade and income and of overconsumption and waste in affluent countries, the Brundtland Commission report falls back on population as the chief threat to sustainability. This was clearly a reflection of the predilections of its leader. In her address to the Earth Summit, Gro Harlem Brundtland admonished the gathering for failing to address issues of overpopulation (*Facts on File*, June 18, 1992, 443).

A significant point made by the Brundtland Commission report, one echoed by others working on environmental questions, is that there is a lag between the nature of the problems and the institutions that are in place to deal with them:[26] "These institutions tend to be independent, fragmented, and working to relatively narrow mandates with closed decision processes. Those responsible for managing natural resources and protecting the environment are institutionally separated from those responsible for managing the economy. The real world of interlocked economic and ecological systems will not change; the policies and institutions concerned must" (Brundtland 1987:12–3). But to the extent that such a critique results in a call for greater *inter*national cooperation in the creation of new institutions that cut across traditional issue areas and sectors, it remains firmly anchored within the nationalist project.[27] As Liisa Malkki (1994) has shown in an insightful essay, nationalism and internationalism presuppose each other in that the presence of the nation is "premised on the existence of analogous national units in a global community of nations." It is the existence of other similar entities called nations that enables another major premise of global environmentalism, namely, that of "the human family."

Of the universalizing strategies employed by global environmentalists, the notion of humanity as a family is absolutely central. It finds its way, with minor modifications, in almost all the justifications given for what it is that is "common to us all" in dealing with the environment. Maurice Strong, in his previously cited speech, urges that the Earth Summit reach agreements that serve "the common interests of the entire human family." The notion of the human family is integrally connected to the idea of "the family of nations" because relations between members of the human family are mediated by their national affiliation. At the same time that it suggests an intimate and enduring bond between peoples, the image conjured by the idea of a family is one in which gender and age inequalities are deeply institutionalized and naturalized.[28] That it is a heterosexist, patriarchal family is left in no doubt; metaphors of the rational control and management of a feminized nature are freely employed (Agrawal and Sawyer n.d.).[29] As I demonstrated in Chapter 1, the role of "the human family" in development discourse is to naturalize the control exercised by the rich industrialized countries over the rest of the world. In global environmental discourses, this is done quite overtly. The ruling classes in the Third World often occupy the role of children who need to be disciplined by a (usually) kind and paternalistic father.[30] The discussion of population, environmental safeguards, and deforestation is similarly densely infested with patriarchal, filial, and heterosexist imagery. What I am suggesting, therefore, is that the universalizing humanistic impulses of global environmentalism ("the human family") embody a fundamentally inegalitarian conception of a global order and that such inequalities are not incidental but are central to the "management" of the environment by paternalistic Western experts.[31]

It is significant that so much of the concern for sustainable development has, in practice, focused on rain forests. The alarming figures of tropical deforestation dispersed widely in the media might lead one to believe that rain forest destruction was the leading cause of the buildup of greenhouse gases in the atmosphere. In fact, tropical deforestation contributes no more than 15 to 20 percent of global warming (Buttel 1992:19), and the much maligned Amazonian rain forests contribute a paltry 4.5 percent (Sawyer 1992).[32] One of the consequences of what Buttel (1992:19) has called "rainforest fundamentalism" is that advocates of sustainable development have paid little attention to those agroecosystems and semiarid zones where the majority of the world's populations live and work. Once again, concerns about "our common future" turn out in practice to be rather more parochially focused on the future of the wealthy industrial countries.[33] The "growing mental shorthand that sustainable development pertains mainly to rainforest zones" (Buttel 1992:19) also underlines the fact that, despite the fervent hopes of many of its proponents, sustainability does not necessarily entail outcomes that would be seen as positive by those committed to social justice.

"South" versus "North"

In contrast to the humanistic pronouncements of "sharing one world," made mostly by leaders and activists from the North, is the view of representatives of poor countries that the environment is a crucial arena where conflict between the haves and have-nots manifests itself. This is a perspective that is likely to increase in importance in the future. As Gus Speth, president of the World Resources Institute, put it after Rio, the United States "has totally missed the point that the axis of world affairs has shifted from East-West to North-South" (*Newsweek*, June 22, 1992, 46). Maurice Strong, the UNCED secretary general, emphasized the same point when he said, "If we fail at Rio, it will be one of the greatest breakdowns ever in international relations, especially concerning North and South" (*India Today*, June 15, 1992, 71).

The general outlines of the argument made by the South are the following: Most of the pollution in the world (CFC emissions, carbon dioxide emissions, toxic wastes, pollution of oceans) and the overwhelming proportion of resource depletion have been caused by rich countries in the North in the process of industrialization. For this use of common resources, the North did not pay anything. Now that poor countries in the South are industrializing, the North wants to put up barriers on the grounds that the commons cannot be allowed to deteriorate any further. As *Newsweek* pithily put it, "This is the global application of the well-known phenomenon that one's willingness to make 'sacrifices' for the environment goes up in proportion to the number of Volvos one already owns" (June 1, 1992, 22). The South wants to get equal access to the commons. Or, put another way, it wants compensation from the North for having used up common resources so that it can industrialize without using the same polluting, wasteful technologies employed by the North in its industrialization. However, the countries of the North are not willing to make such transfers, and because they control the few instruments of international governance that exist, they usually have their way.[34] I will illustrate this viewpoint by analyzing in greater detail some specific issues that came up at the Earth Summit.

The first point of contention at the Earth Summit had to do with its agenda.[35] Thus, greenhouse gases, biodiversity, and the preservation of forests were discussed on the grounds that they constituted global issues requiring global negotiations and treaties, whereas issues such as desertification, soil erosion, drinking water availability, and sanitation were ignored on the grounds that they were "local" issues best left for sovereign nations to deal with (Centre for Science and Environment [CSE] 1992:2; *India Today*, June 15, 1992, 90).[36] Environmental concerns were discussed in isolation from the economic processes in which they were embedded. So, for example, matters relating to protectionism practiced by northern countries or an end to tariff discrimination against goods manufactured in the South were avoided. Dawood Ghaznavi, head of the

Worldwide Fund for Nature in Pakistan, said "GATT is crucial to saving the environment. The fact that trade was largely left out of the financing discussions is the most regrettable thing that happened at UNCED" (in Schwarz 1992:61). A major trade-related issue that has very significant implications for the environment is Third World debt. Indeed, it has been argued that the North could achieve more by debt forgiveness than any explicit policy aimed at ecological degradation and resource conservation. Although they have been much admired as creative solutions to tropical deforestation, debt-for-nature swaps end up supporting the current global debt regime rather than seeking to dismantle it. "Only desperately-indebted countries have their debt sufficiently discounted on the world's secondary debt market so that it can be purchased in debt-for-nature swaps. Debt stress, and the implicit threat of terminating the flow of loans and bridging funds, is typically in the background as environmental organizations and development agencies have worked to prompt developing countries to strengthen their environmental conservation policies" (Buttel 1992:20). Environmental organizations and development agencies thus rely on the presence of debt stress to provide leverage for their own interventions.[37]

Perhaps one way of understanding the divergence between North and South at the Earth Summit is to see that of the two themes that the conference was trying to bring together, environment and development, the North focused on the former while ignoring the latter, whereas the South focused on the interrelationship between the two.[38] Third World environmentalists point out that environmental problems in the North arise from different sources than do those in the South (Shanmugaratnam 1989). In rich countries, the chief problems have to do with the control of pollution and the disposal of wastes. In poor countries, by contrast, the chief problems arise from the overexploitation of the natural resource base (CSE 1992:1).[39] This overexploitation is not due to "population pressures" or "poor management," as northern experts would have it, but to economic linkages in which the raw materials from the South serve as essential inputs into goods manufactured, and largely consumed, in the North. Anil Agarwal, for example, points out that "despite the worldwide process of decolonisation, there is today many times more land being used in the developing world to meet the food needs of the Western countries than in the 1940s" (1985:5). In a World Bank paper, Piritta Sorsa acknowledges that "as a transmitter of many externalities, trade may contribute indirectly to environmental damage" (1992:3). He goes on to argue that only 1 percent of yearly destruction of tropical timber can be attributed to international trade, the rest being the result of "land clearance for agriculture, and the poor's use of wood for fuel" (3). He neglects to ask if the clearing of forestlands or cutting of wood may be related to the use of the best agricultural land to grow crops for export or the use of wood in industrial products also employed for the same purpose. The counterfactual question should be, If the First World's consumption per capita were the same as that of the twenty most densely populated Third World countries, how much destruction of forests would there be?

The potentially more "open" agricultural trade regime that will result from GATT certainly does not bode well for the future of sustainable agriculture in the Third World. Those regions that use mechanisms to force prices of agricultural goods to reflect externalities such as nonrenewability or pollution would find their markets flooded with cheaper commodities from regions that do not adopt such measures (Harold and Runge 1993). The speed with which sustainability is exported to the rich countries of the North is likely to be accelerated, as highly indebted Third World countries set up efforts to increase agricultural exports to the West to meet their interest payments. Because increases in output with methods of industrial agriculture also involve increased outlays for petroleum-dependent inputs such as chemical fertilizers, the balance of payments consequences of agriculture-led export growth are unlikely to be highly favorable for poor countries and may even turn out to be only one bad harvest away from being negative (see also Buttel 1993). On the other hand, sustainable agriculture, presumably conducted with organic inputs, would have the effect of reducing expensive petrochemical inputs and hence reducing foreign debts for poor nation-states, but they would, as a result, make debt-for-nature swaps less attractive for banks, donors, and environmental organizations. It would thus undercut one of the key programs mounted by First World environmental organizations to promote sustainable growth.[40]

Transnational trade is one of the most effective ways to transmit the ecological costs of overconsumption on to others. One way to theorize the transfer of materials processed at enormous environmental costs in the South to the North through "free" trade is to see that such transfers represent a subsidy to northern consumers. A report by the Centre for Science and Environment (1992:2–3) makes this point very clearly: "Developing countries export sustainability while industrialized countries import it at the cost of the former. This discounts the future of the South and passes on the immediate costs of environmental degradation onto the world's poor living on the margins of their environment."[41] This transfer is exacerbated when the terms of trade turn against the raw materials that poor countries export to the North. And this is precisely what happened throughout the 1980s.[42] If the current effort to institute Trade-Related Intellectual Property rights is successful, it will further disadvantage many poor peasants in the Third World vis-à-vis powerful transnational corporations. Farmers, who now save, modify, and sell seeds of high-yielding varieties to one another will be prevented from doing so by the new arrangements. A sense of the importance of farmer-to-farmer transfer of seeds can be gauged from the fact that only approximately 38 percent of the seed requirement of Indian agriculture is sold by formal agencies.[43] Henceforth, this will be the exclusive right of the companies that hold the Plant-Breeders Rights to the seed in question (*New York Times,* May 16, 1989). Patent rights (Intellectual Property Rights) thus become a code to protect the "rights" of multinationals to corner the surplus from the sale of seed varieties. Anyone who has the resources to alter seeds genetically and then, very important, has the ability to patent such an "invention" obtains the monopoly to market such seeds (Khoshoo 1993; *Economist,* May 30, 1992, 64; June 13, 1992, 93–94).[44] It is for this reason that the leader of the Karnataka farmers announced that their "one-point program" was to "drive out the multinationals" (Sahai 1993a, b; Shiva 1993a).

The argument about the South's export of sustainability finds support in the fact that northern countries are willing to promote global environmentalism as long as it doesn't affect their consumption practices. The data here is compelling: "The haves form just 23 per cent of the population, occupy 50 per cent of the land area, account for 60 per cent of the energy consumed and earn 85 per cent of the world's income. . . . an average American consumes over two tonnes of steel every five years in the form of cars and eats 112 kg of meat, whether beef, lamb or pork, every year. And consumes 7,822 kg of oil equivalent annually. In contrast, an average Indian consumes 50 kg of steel in the form of a cycle and eats only 2 kg of meat annually. And consumes barely 231 kg of oil in the form of energy" (*India Today,* June 15, 1992, 96).[45] If, as a thought experiment, one were to multiply India's per capita consumption figures by four to compensate for its larger population, consumers in the United States would still end up using ten times as much steel and oil as Indians. This is entirely consistent with other studies of consumption (Bidwai 1992:853). That Western styles of consumption were not sustainable was evident a long time ago. In 1908, Gandhi asked, "If it took Britain the exploitation of half the globe to be what it is today, how many globes would India need?" (cited in CSE 1992:4). Southern leaders at Rio insisted that the real issue was overconsumption by the North; predictably, there was almost no acknowledgment of this fact except in Gro Harlem Brundtland's opening statement, in which she said, "We can't tell the Third World, 'The waste-basket is full because we filled it, now you have to help us empty it'" (*Facts on File*, June 18, 1992, 442).[46]

These positions were prominently displayed in the debates over the global warming treaty, which called on all industrial nations to return to their 1990 levels of emissions of hothouse gases. Developing countries would be permitted a ten-year grace period before restrictions were imposed on them. The twelve nations of the EC had made an earlier pledge to reduce their emissions to 1990 levels by the year 2000, and they repeated that pledge at the summit. Germany, which is responsible for 3.2 percent of global carbon emissions, unilaterally agreed to cut them by 25 percent by the year 2005. In the face of stiff U.S. opposition, however, the treaty was signed without specific deadlines. Together, the United States and the former Soviet Union account for over half the carbon dioxide emissions in the world, and as a group, the North is responsible for 90 percent of the carbon dioxide that has accumulated in the earth's atmosphere so far (*New York Times*, May 2, 1989; Tokar 1989; Bidwai 1992:854). Yet a plan to impose a carbon tax in industrialized nations was foiled owing to heavy lobbying by oil-producing countries.

Given the inbuilt inequalities in the treaty that favored industrial countries, the U.S. reluctance to sign was surprising.[47] Praful Bidwai offers the following example: "If U.S. per capita annual emissions (5.2 tons) were to be frozen and India's (0.22 tons) were to grow at recent rates, India would not reach one ton a year until 2024—a level surpassed by the United States well before 1900" (1992:854). Although industrial countries are required under the treaty to assist developing nations financially and technologically to control their emissions of greenhouse gases, the financial commitments do not approach the true cost of atmospheric exhaustion. "If Northern emissions could be traded with the South at $15 per ton of carbon equivalent and damages were to be paid at $25 per ton, the top fifteen polluters would have to pay $110 billion to the South; the United States alone would have to pay $45 billion a year" (Bidwai 1992:854). When the UNCED secretariat pressed the industrialized countries to contribute $125 billion toward resolving *all* major environmental problems faced by the South (an effort that they estimate will cost $625 billion annually), they met with little success. Members of the EC and other industrial countries agreed to increase their aid levels to 0.7 percent of their GNP "as soon as possible" (but with no date specified). The United States refused to agree to the aid target that it, along with other industrial nations, had pledged to meet during the Stockholm Conference in 1972!

Many people in the First World, policymakers and environmentalists alike, held up the Montreal Protocol on Substances That Deplete the Ozone Layer (1987) as an example to be emulated in the design of international environmental treaties (Babbitt 1992:36; French 1992:12–14; *Economist*, June 13, 1992, 39). The Montreal Protocol had delayed deadlines for developing countries, a provision to transfer resources, and punitive trade measures for nonimplementation. The view from the South, however, saw the ozone layer treaty as a disastrous pact that would permanently institutionalize global inequalities. Bidwai offers this opinion: "Since no responsibility is attached to different countries for their varying contributions to the CFC burden, no rights and obligations follow. So the South, with its current emission of 12 percent of CFCS, is asked to make the same commitment, albeit over a longer period of time, as the North, which produces 88 percent of the total. The underlying assumption is that it would be a disaster if every Chinese or Indian (not American or Japanese) had a refrigerator, but that it is not necessary for the rest of the world to find substitutes for CFCS" (1992:854). What has gone unnoticed about the ozone layer agreement is that it was enthusiastically supported by the handful of multinational corporations who produce CFCS. The reason is that they are also the only companies that manufacture CFC substitutes, and "a world ban on CFCS was obviously an ideal way to lock up the largest possible market for substitutes" (Cairncross 1992:18). Countries in the North were also far more concerned about the consequences of the depletion of the ozone layer, as it had immediate effects on the health of their populations.

The struggles between North and South were sharpest, however, over the proposed forest convention, which was scaled back to a nonbinding statement of forest conservation principles in the teeth of stiff opposition from such countries as Malaysia, India, and Indonesia (*Far Eastern Economic Review,* June 25, 1992, 62; *Facts on File,* June 18, 1992, 442; Lakshman 1992). Northern countries, led by the United States, were very keen to push through a forest convention. Tropical forests in particular are excellent "sinks" that absorb carbon dioxide and thereby minimize or reverse global warming. They are also the sites where most of the world's genetic diversity is preserved.[48] The northern countries thus felt that they would benefit on two different fronts with one policy. Countries such as Malaysia and India argued that forests were a sovereign resource.[49] Malaysian prime minister Mahathir bin Mohamed said that a forest convention made sense only after a worthwhile agreement on industrial emissions was reached. Like other developing countries, Malaysia felt that the United States had no justification for pushing for a forest convention while failing to agree to a timetable for halting global warming.[50] Mahathir bin Mohamed (1992:57) argued that timber sales were crucial to the economic development of his country: "The extraction of timber can easily be reduced without making us pay for it: if the rich will pay twice the price, logging can be reduced by half. It is that simple." Once again, the deteriorating terms of trade of primary goods entered the picture in a central way. The Malaysian prime minister suggested that instead of poor countries having to shoulder the responsibility to provide carbon sinks for the entire world, an aggressive worldwide program of *re*forestation be conducted in which northern countries would be responsible for shutting down their inefficient farms and their polluting industries and foresting the land on which they stood (1992:58).[51]

So far, I have attempted to draw a contrast between "one world" versions of global environmentalism and "North-South conflict" views of the same phenomenon. Both these perspectives underplay the significant differences between states, environmental groups, and subaltern groups within the North and the South, suggesting a degree of homogeneity that does not in fact exist. In the next section, I argue that despite their sharply opposed viewpoints, "one world" and "North versus South" positions share a modernist discursive space shaped by common ideas about territoriality, sovereignty, and the nation-state.[52] It is this modernist space that enabled Dr. Nanjundaswamy of the Karnataka Farmers Association to say, "Our genetic resources are our national property" (cited at the beginning of the chapter). What are the commitments entailed by such a view? Does this perspective obscure emergent processes of global regulation and control? Specifically, are there *postcolonial* forms of global discipline and global regulation that are elided by Dr. Nanjundaswamy's emphasis on national sovereignty? It is to these questions that I now turn.

Rethinking Environmentalism: Governmentality on a World Scale

Global environmental problems have brought about an interesting convergence between otherwise radically distinct political and theoretical positions. People who hold different perspectives on environmental issues all agree that they somehow bring into question the premise of national sovereignty on which the existing order of nation-states is based (Wallerstein 1991b: 140; Young 1982, 1989).[53] What continues to differentiate people along lines of "one world" or "north-south conflict" is their understanding of exactly how national sovereignty has become problematic, what is to be done to deal with this new situation, and how one goes about theorizing the emerging world context (Walker and Mendlovitz 1990b:1). In this section I argue that one way to understand global environmental accords is to see them as part of a larger process that is weakening the intimate links between "nation" and "state." I see this as a fundamentally "postcolonial" moment in that it initiates a break with a spatial order of sovereign nation-states that was forged in the anvil of colonialism and fired in the furnace of national liberation.

Typical of nongovernmental North views is the one expressed by French.

> National sovereignty—the power of a country to control events within its territory—has lost much of its meaning in today's world, where borders are routinely breached by pollution, international trade, financial flows, and refugees. Increasingly, they may be eroded by such forces as climatic warming, migrations, and the depletion of the earth's ozone shield. Because all of these forces can effect environmental trends, international treaties and institutions are proving ever more critical to addressing ecological threats. Nations are in effect ceding portions of their sovereignty to the international community, and beginning to create a new system of international environmental governance as a means of solving otherwise-unmanageable problems. (1992:6)

Similarly, in the wake of the pessimism expressed by many at the failure of the Earth Summit to approve binding treaties, there were those who pointed out that the real gains of Rio should not be overlooked. One of the benefits of the Earth Summit was that "for the first time in history, nations vowed to take into account global environmental concerns when making *internal* economic decisions" (*Newsweek*, June 22, 1992,

46). Jessica Tuchman Mathews, vice president of the World Resources Institute, is quoted as saying, "[The global warming treaty] has the potential of forcing governments to change domestic policies to a greater degree than any international agreement I can think of" (*Newsweek*, June 15, 1992, 33). Maurice Strong brought together the ideology of markets with concerns about security in speaking of a "new global compact in which the industrialized nations understand that they cannot secure their future without a partnership with developing nations" (*Far Eastern Economic Review*, June 25, 1992, 61).

The view from the South also recognizes that discourses of environmental degradation pose a distinctive new kind of threat to national sovereignty because of their stress on northern control of remedial measures.[54] In southern interpretations, the emphasis has so far been either on northern dominance, sometimes glossed as "ecological imperialism," or on the necessity of seeking broader coalitions. In the former case, national sovereignty is at peril because control over national resources (forests, and flora and fauna embodying biological diversity) is threatened by powerful northern countries in the name of preserving the "world's heritage" (Chengappa 1992). This is clearly the view expressed by Malaysia's Mahathir bin Mohamed: "The North should begin to clean up its own back yard and stop scapegoating the South for the ecological sins it committed on the road to prosperity. . . . Eco-imperialism should be brought to an end once and for all. . . . [T]he developed North, having destroyed its natural heritage, wants to declare that whatever is left intact in the developing countries *also* belongs to them" (1992:56, 57).[55] In the latter case, national sovereignty is rendered ambivalent because the only way to defend it is to merge one's own national interests with some other nation's. Traditional enemies, China and India, banded together, and the Group of 77 united in the face of strenuous northern attempts to split them up (*India Today*, June 15, 1992, 70).

Another way to see the growing recognition of the crisis of sovereignty is to look at opinions about the role of *international* organizations in dealing with environmental issues (Keohane and Ostrom 1995). The present system of international governance, organized largely in the immediate aftermath of the Second World War, is considered to be ill-equipped to deal with global environmental questions. Whereas the Brundtland Commission identifies the narrow mandates of existing institutions as the source of their inability to deal with global environmental problems, however, others believe that a more radical overhaul of the *system* of international institutions is necessary.[56] There is thus a recognition that environmental issues are raising questions about national sovereignty and inter*national* governance, about national order and the order of nations. But to understand precisely what this challenge means theoretically, I will first briefly trace the historical relations between sovereignty, territoriality, and the nation-state.

However odd it may appear from the perspective of the present, the notion that systems of rule should be, or need be, territorial is not at all self-evident.[57] It is a peculiarity of the particular history of modern Europe that a system of rule came to be institutionalized that had at its basis states that were *territorial;* that were, moreover, territorially *fixed;* and that entailed the *mutual exclusion* of others from the territory (Agnew and Corbridge 1995:79). In medieval Europe or precolonial India, for example, territorial exclusion was not an operative principle of political power.[58] "The distinctive feature of the modern—homonomous—variant of structuring territorial space is the familiar world of *territorially disjoint, mutually exclusive, functionally similar,* sovereign states" (Ruggie 1993:151; emphasis added).[59] A strong centralized administrative state is not found in Europe until the end of the fifteenth century (Foucault 1991:103), and it is another two centuries before a *system* of states comes into effect (Young 1988: 29). Charles Tilly called the sixteenth century "a time of significantly rising stateness" and characterized the later seventeenth century as constituting "a frenzy of state-making" (1975a:34).[60] In other words, a long period of conflict over the *nature* of political units was followed by conflict over the *boundaries* of those units (Ruggie 1993; Tilly 1975a:28). Yet by the beginning of the eighteenth century, the practice of the mutual acknowledgment of sovereignty that it termed the "state system" was already in place.[61] That this was a highly contingent outcome was underlined by Tilly when he wrote: "The Europe of 1500 included some five hundred more or less independent political units, the Europe of 1900 about twenty-five. The German state did not exist in 1500, or even 1800. Comparing the histories of France, Germany, Spain, Belgium, and England (or, for that matter, any other set of West European countries) for illumination on the processes of state-making weights the whole inquiry toward a certain kind of outcome which was, in fact, quite rare" (1975a:15).[62] State sovereignty, which is today often elided with national sovereignty, actually emerges in a period historically prior to the consolidation of the nation (Wallerstein 1991b:143). That this curiously hyphenated entity, the nation-state, does not evoke constant surprise is a testimony to its complete ideological hegemony. Scholarly work has tended to underestimate seriously the importance of that hyphen, which simultaneously erases and naturalizes what is surely an incidental coupling (Kaviraj 1994; Nandy 1992). Tilly emphasized this when he said, "In Europe . . . [nation building] generally occurred after the formation of strong states, and by no means as a direct or automatic consequence of state-building alone." He summarized the contributions to a volume on state building in Europe by emphasizing that the authors "insist on the analytic separation of state-building from nation-building, and consider *the nation-state only one of several possible outcomes of state-building*" (1975a:70–71; emphasis added).

Scholars of nationalism ask what holds such an imagined community together; what the mechanisms are that produce and reproduce the structure of feeling that is termed "nationalism"; what its exclusions and silences are; how it emerges; and where it is likely to lead. Scholars of states inquire into the circumstances that led to the centralized system of administrative rule that is called the state system; what conditions ensure its reproduction; the situations in which states are transformed, come into existence, die, or fall; what enables them to get things done, to defend their borders, and to secure their existence. When the concept of *national sovereignty* came to be conjoined to the territorial basis of statehood, then the ideology of the modern order of nation-states, as it exists today, was firmly established (Ruggie 1993:163; Walker and Mendlovitz 1990:6).[63] Just as states need the interstate system to establish territorially based authority, so do nations need the international system to engender, regulate, and normalize the feelings that are dubbed "nationalism." In fact, neither statehood nor nationalism is possible or intelligible without the interstate and international systems.[64] What has to be understood about the nation-state is that it fuses these powerful forces in one entity. Not enough attention has been paid in the scholarly literature so far to the implications of this fusion, both for the study of nationalism and "the state" and, equally important, for the study of internationalism and the interstate system.[65]

Once the problem is laid out in this manner, it becomes clearer why the idea of sovereignty is so paradoxical. The claim of sovereignty is one that attempts to stabilize and fix territorial boundaries, specify identities, and establish unambiguous control over goods and people (Onuf 1991; Shapiro 1991:448, 473; Walker 1993:161).[66] But insofar as the sovereignty of nation-states depends on the recognition of *other* nation-states, of other units that are different in their culture, history, and even "temperament" but alike in their constitutive modality, then the pretense to self-sufficiency is revealed for what it is (Malkki 1994). In other words, sovereignty is a *relation* that, to be exercised, must "misrecognize" itself as a self-sufficient identity. Starting from the premise of state sovereignty, therefore, already structures the analysis of "interdependence" or "world politics" in such a manner that alternative forms of alliance, community, spatialization, or identity are suppressed or erased (Agnew and Corbridge 1995; Shapiro 1994; Walker 1993; Walker and Mendlovitz eds. 1990).

The paradoxical nature of sovereignty as absolute individuation first became visible with problems of diplomacy. The question was how to recognize the sovereignty of some other state *within* your own territory through the person of the ambassador and the ambassador's staff and their offices and residences. The solution was to carve out a particular space (the embassy) that was recognized as "extraterritorial" in that the laws of some other nation-state operated on that particular territory.[67] Not just diplomats and common property resources challenge the ideology of sovereignty: flows of all kinds across the borders of territorial nation-states, most notably trade but also images, finances, and people, call the construction of stable identities into question.[68] Ruggie suggests the notion of the "unbundling" of territory as a way to come to grips with the means employed by nation-states to "attenuate the paradox of absolute individuation" (1993:165).[69]

Another way to theorize this growing phenomenon of the "unbundling" of territory is to think about its consequences for the hyphen between nation and state (Appadurai 1993c). What I would like to suggest is that there is a growing tension between nation and state so that the particular enclosure that was conjured by their historically fortuitous conjunction may slowly be falling apart. The clearing does not hold in the hyperspace of late capitalism. The kinds of activities and meanings that were ideally brought together by nation-states—the regulation of industries, goods, and people; the control and surveillance of populations; the exercise of the monopoly on violence within the territory; the provision of "security" with respect to other nation-states (Dalby 1992); the employment of laws; the feeling of belonging to "a people"; the belief in particular historical narratives of identity and difference—may be untangling (Comaroff forthcoming).[70] It is very likely that they will reconstitute themselves into different bundles. But it is highly *unlikely* that the reconstituted entities will simply be reproductions of nation-states, writ large or small. As Étienne Balibar has said of the European Community, "The state today in Europe is *neither national nor supranational,* and this ambiguity does not slacken but only grows deeper over time" (1991:16).[71]

This focus on the "unbundling" of territorially based sovereign nation-states may help us see that much of the discussion on whether nation-states are declining or increasing in importance may be missing the point. For one can often point to persuasive evidence that leads to *both* conclusions for the *same* cases. Rather than be cursed like the equivocator "that could swear in both the scales against either scale,"[72] I wish to argue that the "postcolonial" be employed to signify that the hyphen between nation and state be written "under erasure." Arjun Appadurai uses the term "postnational," arguing that it has three possible implications: that other forms of allegiance and identity are replacing the nation-state; that alternative forms of organizing the flow of resources, images, and ideas are contesting the nation-state or constituting peaceful alternatives to it; and that national identities are taking hold that have no foothold or basis in territorial states (1993c:421).[73] To suggest that the particular historical conjuncture that brought "nation" and "state" together into a stable form of spatial organization may be coming to an end is not to argue that forms of "nation-ness" or forms of "state-ness" are in danger of disappearing altogether.[74] New, more menacing, racially exclusionary forms of national identity are emerging in Europe and the United States, for example, and statelike functions are being performed by organizations such as the European Union and transnational corporations. One way to understand the enthusiasm with which "big" government has been attacked in the North is to see that the Fordist project of regulating the national market through government intervention is no longer viable. Fordist mass production proved to be an unusually efficient engine of growth, particularly in the United States since the Second World War (Aglietta 1979; Brenner and Glick 1991; Davis 1984). However, late-capitalist forms of capital accumulation have been straining against the fetters of a national market, and so the national state now appears to be an overbearing presence.[75] National states are by no means obsolete, but their statelike functions are being increasingly "privatized" except insofar as they represent direct subsidies to transnational corporations. What is one to make of this retreat of "state-ness" in the very heart of the capitalist West? And how is the selective rollback of the functions of the state to be related to the virulence of an exclusionary, racially charged nationalism? Are these twin movements connected in any way to postcoloniality? What I wish to suggest is that if postcoloniality is the condition that registers the exhaustion of the promise of the modern nation in the former colonies, its other face is the superannuation of the Fordist nation in "the West." The two movements, one toward poststate forms of capitalist organization in "the West" and the other toward postcoloniality in the Third World, come to be linked at this historical juncture by new modalities of global discipline and regulation.[76]

Instead of the decline of the nation-state, I prefer to talk about the tension between "nation" and "state," arguing that a particular relationship that coalesced in the formation of nation-states may be unraveling. Of course, in many parts of the world, particularly those whose borders were arbitrarily drawn by departing colonial rulers, that relationship between nation and state was never a convincing fiction.[77] Another way to theorize the growing crisis of the hyphen is to shift our attention to a process that Foucault (1991) has termed "governmentality." By government rationality or governmentality, Foucault refers to that ensemble of institutions, procedures, and tactics that allow the exercise of a certain kind of power whose object is population in the sense that it seeks to regulate the relations between people and things (Gordon 1991). In Europe, the problem of government expanded in the sixteenth century in the face of opposing tendencies to state centralization and religious dissidence. Thus, the government of the self, the government of souls and lives, the government of children, the government of the family, and the government of the state by the prince all become important questions in that period: "how to govern oneself, how to be governed, how to govern others, by whom the people will accept being governed, how to become the best possible governor" (Foucault 1991:87). The model of government was provided by economy, the art of managing a household wisely for the common welfare of its members. The problem was to extend this model of the household to the government of the state, to exercise over people and things within a particular territory the kind of surveillance and control that the head of the family exercised over his patrimony—his family and his goods. This became possible only with the rise of statistics (with its etymological root as "the science of the state"), which provided the technology to envision the "economy" and "the population" as concrete and palpable realities through tabular representation. By the middle of the eighteenth century, the craft of governing well thus became the art of managing the economy and the population for the common welfare of all.[78] The sole purpose of rule was no longer just the defense and expansion of the sovereign's wealth and territory; rather, it became the provision of security more generally.[79] This technique of governmentality was instituted both inside and outside the state. It was a "very specific albeit complex form of power, which has as its target population, as its principal form of knowledge political economy, and as its essential means apparatuses of security" (Foucault 1991:102), a form of rule that Foucault suggests continues to operate in the present.

What I am suggesting in this chapter is that we may be witnessing the birth of a new regime of discipline in which governmentality is un-hitched from the nation-state to be instituted anew on a global scale.[80] In this project, global environmentalism comes together with other global accords and treaties, and the institutions through which these "compacts" are monitored and enforced, to regulate the relationship between people and things on a global (not simply international) scale. The Earth Summit, GATT, and other international treaties are attempting to institutionalize a new form of governance, this time not within the territorially defined boundaries of the nation-state but across an "un-bundled" space for which there is not as yet a name, a brave new world order (Gill 1991).[81] These shifts in forms of governance are integrally related to the reorganization of capitalism in the last quarter of this century (Mandel 1975; Harvey 1989). Just as the nation-state was integral to Fordist manufacture by *multinational* corporations, which had the backing of powerful imperialist states, so is the tension between nation and state related to the industrial dominance of *transnational* corporations in post-Fordist capitalism, which are themselves ambivalently positioned in regards to their nationality. But these new modes of governmentality are not going unchallenged by groups that are likely to be adversely affected by them. I turn now to an analysis of the actions of peasant groups in India that have organized a series of successful protests against global treaties.

Peasant Protests

No one can predict how emerging modes of governmentality will affect the everyday lives and practices of peasants in different parts of the world. Vigorous reactions to the GATT were recorded during the year preceding its formal signing on April 15, 1994, however. In this section I analyze peasant protests in India, reflecting on the interpretations implicit in their actions.

The farmers' rally with which this chapter began had its origin in another act, the daring "raid" of December 29, 1992, in which members of the Karnataka Farmers Association ransacked the Bangalore corporate offices of Cargill Seeds India Private Limited, an Indian subsidiary of the giant U.S. grain-trading multinational. Seventy-five farmers climbed the four flights of stairs to the Cargill office, burst through the door, announced that they did not intend to harm the dozen or so employees but were there as a protest. The farmers then proceeded to smash windows, break open filing cabinets, and throw papers and financial records through the window to the crowd of four hundred waiting below. Once the stack of papers grew tall, Nanjundaswamy handed over a box of matches to a farmer who lit the flame, bringing all traffic on the road to a halt. "Bon fire," Nanjundaswamy proclaimed, adding, by way of explanation: "From the French origin. Good fire." The farmers gathered in a ring around the fire and shouted "Quit India" in Kannada (Tolan 1994:18).

This action drew a formal protest from the U.S. government and is credited with "opening the Dunkel debate to the public" (*Frontline*, January 14, 1994, 42). Professor Nanjundaswamy, the leader of the Karnataka Farmers, was unrepentant. Using the same logic displayed by Union Carbide in rejecting responsibility for the actions of its Indian subsidiary in the Bhopal disaster but inverting its ends, Nanjundaswamy claimed that because Cargill India is registered under the Indian Companies Act, "what happened at Bangalore was between Indian farmers and an Indian company. There is no room for diplomatic interfering. America's interference exposes their ulterior motives. The Indian government should not [have] tolerated this, let alone apologized." He went on to add that he had received congratulatory telegrams from all over the country after the attack (*Times of India*, January 11, 1993). This raid was followed by another attack on the Cargill factory in Bellary. In protest against the patents taken out on the biopesticide qualities of the neem seed, the Karnataka Farmers threatened to destroy the factory owned by the Indian partners of the American multinational W. R. Grace Company (*Deccan Herald*, November 23, 1993). Eventually, they did not go ahead with their plan because of the presence of a hydrogen plant next to the targeted factory.

In Nanjundaswamy's discourse, the Farmers Association was carrying on a struggle against colonialism that had first been launched by the nationalist movement. He proclaimed the farmers' intentions as being "to banish all multinational seed companies which are here to ransack our country." He explicitly referred to the farmers' actions as initiating the "second Quit India Movement against imperialists" and reiterated their commitment to Gandhian socialism, "which has been forgotten by all political parties" (*Times of India,* January 11, 1993). Very similar themes were voiced by other leaders at a giant rally of half a million farmers that took place in Bangalore on October 3, 1993. Mahendra Singh Tikait, the leader of the primarily north Indian farmers organization, the BKU, warned those present to be prepared for a second round in the freedom struggle. He compared the multinational seed and pesticide firms with the East India Company, which had looted the country of its wealth. "We should not permit the recurrence of such an act. The country is still to attain prosperity" (*Hindu,* October 4, 1993, 11). Similarly, Sesha Reddy, one of the most prominent of the Karnataka activists, said: "We call Cargill the West India Company. We don't want a West India Company to once again dominate our economy, our freedom, our politics. We are prepared to die for this." Graffiti on city walls declared, "Reject Dunkel, Reject Imperialism" (Tolan 1994). Tikait, even more than Nanjundaswamy, reproduced a nationalist discourse in which prosperity and modernity constitute the telos of national liberation. Both leaders used development discourses, premised on teleologies of the nation, that had been hegemonic internationally until the eighties to organize against the contemporary paradigm of "open" economies touted by the international aid system.

The nationalist rhetoric of such peasant leaders as Tikait and Nanjundaswamy might appear to be anachronistic in 1993, especially given the disappointments faced by the large majority of rural Indians in almost half a century of independence. But the peasant leaders' rhetoric is mixed with a shrewd recognition of the current global historical conjuncture and of the importance of forging coalitions with similar groups in other parts of the world. Like those movements of indigenous peoples that have formed, on the basis of an indigenous identity, transnational coalitions that are simultaneously above and below the nation-state, peasant leaders worked actively to make connections with other groups across the world. Thus, of the resolutions adopted at the meeting, one proclaimed that "plant wealth, seed wealth, and intellectual property were the property of the *farmers of the world* and called upon all countries to launch a direct struggle to protect the collective rights [of farmers] and prevent them from being robbed by multinational companies" (*Hindu,* October 4, 1993, 11; emphasis added). An international research center to develop intellectual property rights on behalf of farmers was initiated and a pledge made to continue the free exchange of seeds among farmers of the Third World. The international institute for sustainable agriculture was formally inaugurated on May 30, 1995, as a joint project of the KRRS and the Third World Network, a development and environmental organization based in Malaysia.[82] Apart from the promotion of organic farming techniques, the aims of the institute include helping farmers store traditional varieties of cultivars in community seed banks and revitalization of those cultivars to preserve genetic diversity. Farmers brought two hundred varieties of various crops with them to start the institute's seeds banks. Explaining the need for the institute, Nanjundaswamy said that farmers had been incurring mounting debts because of input-intensive modes of cultivation, that they had become dependent on a few varieties of cultivars promoted by large seed companies, and that the soil had been made infertile by large doses of chemical fertilizers. Therefore, it was necessary to turn to productive, sustainable, organic farming (Khor 1995).[83]

Nanjundaswamy featured prominently in an anti-Dunkel protest meeting of farmers, ecologists, and consumer groups from around the world in Geneva on December 4, 1993, while the final GATT negotiations were taking place. Contrary to positions attributed to him earlier, he maintained, "Our stand is that India should remain a member of GATT, but should have demanded drastic amendments in the agreement" (*Frontline*, January 14, 1994, 42). In what follows, I will briefly pursue the interesting contradictions between the explicit emphasis on national sovereignty and self-determination and the populist appeal to "farmers of the world" and to other transnational, intermestic (*international/ domestic*) coalitions that put sovereignty into question.[84]

These tensions were harder to find in the statements of various peasants at the March rally, which, in conscious reference to the Independence Movement, was called the "seed protest" (*beej satyagraha*).[85] As one farmer put it, "We are aware that these foreign proposals are an attempt to deny the best seeds to us and put us at a disadvantage when compared to farmers of richer nations. If they are accepted, the multinational companies will start determining *our domestic* agriculture policies. We are also protesting against other anti-farmer steps taken by the government in the past" (*Times of India*, March 4, 1993; emphasis added). In virtually the same sentence, this farmer articulated both the kind of nationalist position historically espoused by the government in India and a critique of the same government for emphasizing the industrial, as opposed to the agricultural, sector in its pursuit of modernity and self-reliance. Deewan Chand, a small farmer from Muzaffarnagar,

UP, voiced a more unambiguous nationalist position: "Our leaders have said that the foreign paper [Dunkel Draft] is an evil design to sell Mother India to foreigners. For a *kisan* [farmer] the life support are his land, seed and plough. If the Rao Government sells these to foreigners what will happen to the national pride?" (*Hindustan Times,* March 4, 1993, 5). Another farmer, from the prime minister's electoral constituency, expressed incomprehension at the changing objectives of the government. Assuming that the long-held nationalist goal of self-reliance was a worthwhile one, Sesha Reddy pointed to the crisis of food production that had plagued the country in the second half of the sixties: "But not today. We are now self-sufficient in crop production. So why this sell-out to MNCs [multinational corporations]?" (*Hindustan Times,* March 4, 1993, 5).

It would be misleading to portray the massive protests *against* the Dunkel proposals as if all peasants were unanimously behind them. A newspaper editorialized that "those opposed to the Dunkel proposals are the nation's traditional farmers, predominantly small and medium peasants, whereas those who support Dunkel are from those areas where farming is advanced and has assumed the characteristics of a profit-making business" (*Navbharat Times,* March 4, 1993; my translation). Despite its indubitable political appeal, such a dichotomy is not defensible. The great majority of the supporters of the vociferously anti-Dunkel BKU were relatively well-to-do landowning farmers, with large marketed surpluses, who belong to the prosperous agricultural castes that have been the chief beneficiaries of the government's green revolution policies. Their demands and agitations largely reflect this orientation, calling for loan write-offs, increasing the subsidy for fertilizer, the nonpayment of electric dues, increasing support prices, and so forth.

An analogous class of farmers forms the backbone of the Maharashtra-based Shetkari Sangathana (Farmers Union), which supported the Dunkel Draft. Sharad Joshi, the leader and chief ideologist of the Shetkari Sangathana, declared: "What's wrong with Dunkel? I prefer to pay royalty for good quality seeds than pick up bad subsidised ones" (*India Today,* North American edition, January 15, 1994, 19). The pro-Dunkel group also held a farmers rally in New Delhi on March 31, 1993. Explaining the significance of the demonstration, Joshi stated: "We fully support the Dunkel proposals and a totally free economy. We shall seek an alliance with other forces which stand for a free economy. This will be a producers versus parasites demonstration" (*Hindustan Times,* February 17, 1993). Joshi pronounced the end of the first republic in which the state controlled the economy, and he issued a call for the second republic, with no government control on exports, imports, or the rest of the economy (*Hindustan Times*, February 17, 1993).[86] This was in keeping with his belief that if government restrictions on them were lifted, farmers in India could profitably sell on the world market without subsidies. The organizations present at the meeting presented a five-point charter of demands to the government that included calls for stopping the dumping of agricultural produce from abroad on the Indian market (*Times of India*, April 1, 1993).

The Shetkari Sangathana's position underlines the fact that the class implications of the new modes of governmentality are far from transparent. There are splits even within the politically powerful class of relatively well-to-do farmers with marketable surpluses, and the forces allied against international treaties regulating biodiversity yield no simple mapping in terms of class positions, geographical contiguities, or crop regimes.[87] If the argument advanced in this chapter is correct, the "unbundled" space in which these forms of governance are exercised creates its own possibilities for opposition to coalesce. Just as international and interstate regimes of control and discipline were instituted through the nation-state, the new forms of governmentality operate through this postcolonial space created out of the chasm where the hyphen once stood between "nation" and "state." And just as older modes of resistance coalesced around the politics of the nation-state, employing the rhetoric of nationalism and development, so too will new modes of resistance find their tactics in this "unbundled" space of global discipline (see Walker and Mendlovitz 1990:10).

Conclusion

I began this chapter by juxtaposing two events that, for all practical purposes, may have occurred in different worlds: one, a rustic event filled with the sounds of country bugles, fiery speeches, and the colorful waving of green turbans and shawls; and the other, an urbane gathering of official representatives from 178 countries and a large number of heads of state. I suggested that the farmers rally in India and the Earth Summit in Rio were both addressing similar questions. But my efforts to make sense of that connection had to overcome the enormous distance—geographic, political, social, rhetorical, and disciplinary—that seemed to separate them. This chapter represents, as does indeed the entire book, an attempt to draw together disparate events, contexts, and

levels of analysis to think precisely of the overlaps between the discourses and actions surrounding biodiversity of some Indian farmers
and the cerebral machinations of highly placed politicians and bureaucrats acting on the world's stage. I have been struck by the extraordinary convergence that discourses about the environment displayed in
the two cases: positions on biodiversity in both instances were engendered by concepts of territoriality and sovereignty enshrined in the
nation-state.

It should be emphasized that I do not wish to exceptionalize Rio but
instead locate it as an instance of more profound changes occurring in
the world. The Earth Summit represented not a beginning but a focused
formalization of a series of piecemeal environmental treaties, of which
more than 170 had already been signed before the Earth Summit. A close
analysis of the different positions presented at Rio shows that taking the
high road in conceptualizing environmental problems in terms of "our
common future," in fact, universalized and naturalized existing global
hierarchies and inequalities. Critics from the South quite correctly saw
the environmentalism of the North as missing the point, insofar as it
failed to confront fully the fact that present consumption practices are
directly responsible for most of the world's environmental degradation
and therefore for the declining life chances of the world's poor. They
point out that the impersonality of markets and the invisibility of their
effects should not allow northern consumers to forget that we are wag-
ing a daily battle against those living on the margins of subsistence in
the far corners of the world. I argue that what makes this critique
powerful is, paradoxically, its commensurability with global environmentalism. In fact, "North versus South" views of environmental phenomena share common assumptions about territoriality and sovereignty encoded in the nation-state with "one world" views of those
questions.

As the participants in the debate themselves realized, these are the
very assumptions that environmental phenomena are making less ten-
able. I have suggested that the crisis of sovereignty be understood
in terms of an "unbundling" of the territorial basis of nation-states.
The hyphen between nation and state holds together a particular bundle
of phenomena that are increasingly in tension. It is this that makes
"the postcolonial condition" different from the order of nation-states
brought together by colonialism and nationalism. The new modes of
governmentality being instituted to regulate the relationship between
people and things on a global scale are operating across this "un-

bundled" space, creating novel sites and modes of resistance. Those who feel especially vulnerable to the disciplinary mechanisms instituted by this new mode of governance experience its impending arrival with a great deal of fear and uncertainty.[88] As manifest in farmers' protests against the regulation of biodiversity implicit in the Earth Summit and the GATT, they express these criticisms within contradictory logics. One strand of the critique draws on familiar analogies with nationalist struggles against colonial power. This represents a particular stock of knowledge, a familiar vocabulary, that can be marshaled to make sense of what is happening to them.

At the same time, the actions of various groups organizing against new modes of global regulation belie the conceptual and political frames of the nation-state (see in particular Wapner 1995). Even those organizations that have their origin in "local" movements have formed nongovernmental and postnational coalitions that are coming to grips with this new "unbundled" space in which they find themselves to be operating. This is clearly the case with the Karnataka Farmers Association, whose pronouncements and policies make some of these contradictory tendencies readily apparent. There are other organizations that have sprung up to launch and coordinate opposition. An international convention in Delhi in May 1993 drew two hundred representatives from trade unions, farmers groups, environmental organizations, academic institutions, and other popular movements from sixteen countries. The goal was to organize against what participants saw as a "massive power grab" by multinational corporations in the GATT negotiations. These corporations, they claimed, represented an enormous concentration of power that is neither accountable to popular democratic processes nor to the governments of the countries in which they operate.[89] Similar efforts to organize against "so-called free trade" and alternatives to destructive development include those citizens groups which issued the "Hamburg Declaration" in October 1992 and the Third World Network, which links peoples movements in Asia, Africa, and Latin America (Morehouse 1993).

In this final chapter, I have attempted to describe a process still in its incipient stages. This is a task fraught with many dangers, not the least of which is that of being proven wrong by subsequent events. Tilly argues that while the future path taken by European states is open, over the long run the power of the claim that every nation deserves a state is likely to diminish. The benign result of such a process, he says, "would take us back toward the world's diversity before the last two centuries of state consolidation and circumscription," but the most malign form that such a process could take would result in a "world of banditry, of hatred, of parochialism, and of gross inequality" (1992:717). In venturing to go into uncharted territory, I wish to pursue the implications of this new mode of governmentality for the types and forms of political organization that it enables. As long as peasants are viewed as being tied to the world economy primarily through the nation-state, the analytic importance of new modes of discipline that are not *singularly* mediated through the nation-state but have powerful impacts on peasant life will be missed. Both those who celebrate the new world "compact" and those who denounce it as imperialism on the part of the North fail to grasp adequately how these new modes of governmentality evade old geopolitical certainties. If the nation-state formed the basis for the projects of colonialism and nationalism, then the "unbundled" space that is being created by new forms of governmentality, embedded in global treaties such as the Earth Summit, characterizes "the postcolonial condition."

Epilogue

T he protests by farmers groups in India described in the last chapter, despite changing course, have continued unabated. The Kisan Union's rallies emphasized remunerative prices, equitable development of the countryside, and the end of corruption (described in Chapter 1); its joint agitations with the Karnataka Farmers Association were against the GATT, TRIP, and multinational seed companies (described in Chapter 5); and the latest series of agitations by the KRRS have been against restaurant chains owned by transnational corporations, the patenting of agricultural products, and neoliberal economic policies. Opening markets to international competition and dismantling the "permit-license raj" were high on the agenda of the Congress regime headed by Narasimha Rao (1991–96). Liberalization heralded a shift in the state's discourses of development, because the primary objective of "development" was no longer the attainment of national self-sufficiency and sovereignty. What effects did neoliberal policies have on rural areas? How were development policies changed by globalization? Why were policies opening up the food sector to multinationals resisted so vigorously by the Karnataka Farmers Association? In their opposition to the neoliberal paradigm, why did groups such as the KRRS draw on a discourse of nationalism to resist Cargill Seeds and Kentucky Fried Chicken restaurants? Finally, what relationship did resistance to changing modes of global governmentality, such as that offered by the Karnataka farmers, have to conditions of postcoloniality and to forms of identity?

I first describe a few incidents of peasant activism after the raid on Cargill detailed in the last chapter. Then I turn to the larger questions raised by the Karnataka farmers' opposition to changes in development strategies. I analyze why the KRRS has taken a nationalist position in attacking food-sector transnational corporations. Finally, I explore the implications of recent forms of peasant resistance for understandings of the condition of postcoloniality.

Since 1993, much of the attention given to peasant groups has turned on the farmers movement in the southern state of Karnataka. Professor Nanjundaswamy, leader of the KRRS, has spearheaded a series of attacks on the offices and restaurants owned by transnational corporations involved in the food sector. After June 1995, when Kentucky Fried Chicken (KFC), a subsidiary of Pepsico, opened a restaurant in Bangalore, the industrial center of Karnataka, Nanjundaswamy launched a campaign to discredit KFC so as to force it to shut down its operations. In late July, he gave KFC an ultimatum to leave the country within a week or face "direct action" for selling carcinogenic junk food. Nanjundaswamy's source of information was a U.S. Senate report identifying junk food as the cause of numerous cancers and other health problems such as obesity and high cholesterol. He also accused KFC of serving birds that suffered from leukosis, or chicken cancer. A controversy arose in the Indian Parliament when members of the opposition claimed that fast food caused health problems in eighty million Americans. A spokesperson for KFC denied that its food would lead to any health problems (*Agence France Presse,* July 31, 1995).

Nanjundaswamy maintained that fast-food chains such as KFC, Pizza Hut, and McDonald's would adversely affect the health of poor people. By increasing the demand for livestock, restaurant chains serving meat-based foods would divert grain from poor people to animal feed, which fetched higher profits. In their struggle against the multinational fast-food industry, farmers' leaders were joined by prominent environmentalists such as Maneka Gandhi, former minister for the environment. The KRRS then planned a massive rally to disrupt KFC's business on November 1, 1995. One of the activities leading up to the rally was to be the removal of Pepsi's billboards all over the state of Karnataka. Nanjundaswamy used the language of nonviolent protest [*satyagraha*] to describe his tactics for "disrupting" KFC's business (*Reuters Asia-Pacific Business Report,* October 15, 1995). Shortly after the antiglobalization rally, in which "speaker after speaker bludgeoned MNCs" (*PTI,* November 1, 1995), it was reported that the KRRS, quietly obtaining the support of labor unions and local organizations for an eventual raid on the restaurant, had prepared a strategic blueprint to attack multinational corporations (MNCs) so as to obtain the maximum mileage from the act. In response, police authorities stepped up the already tight, twenty-four-hour security around the restaurant, located in an upscale area of the city.

Despite delivering threats to take "direct action," the peasant group carefully bided its time. Several months later, on January 30, 1996, it struck. A group of 150 farmers burst into the restaurant at lunchtime and proceeded to break windows, smash furniture, burn ledgers, and throw utensils out from the two-storied restaurant onto the street (*Agence France Presse*, February 3, 1996). The restaurant was closed indefinitely.[1] Nanjundaswamy announced to reporters the following day: "This is our warning to McDonald's. There is no room for them in this country. Anyone setting up such a business will face the same kind of action" (*AFX News*, February 1, 1996). He promised to take similar measures against corporate poultry companies and industrial slaughterhouses (*Deutsche Presse-Agentur*, February 1, 1996). Two days later, Nanjundaswamy was arrested on charges of "instigating violence and rioting" (*Agence France Presse*, February 3, 1996). Because he was not physically involved in the raid, he was released in a few days after posting bail worth $1,070.[2] However, the court rejected the bail applications of the 101 KRRS supporters arrested during the incident (*Reuters*, February 9, 1996). In the aftermath of the raid, the police commissioner positioned five armed guards around the offices of all forty-seven transnational companies in Bangalore. The commissioner stated his resolve not to allow a repetition of the KFC incident anywhere else in the city (*Deutsche Presse-Agentur*, February 1, 1996).

The "success" of the KFC raid appeared to give Nanjundaswamy's campaign renewed vigor. When Pepsico announced that it would open a Pizza Hut restaurant in Bangalore in June, Nanjundaswamy defiantly stated: "Pizza Hut will have to pull down its shutters. We have attacked Cargill Seeds and Kentucky Fried Chicken because we wanted to initiate a debate on the role of multinationals" (*Agence France Presse*, June 25, 1996). However, he refused to reveal what form the protest against Pizza Hut would take (*Reuters*, June 8, 1996). Pepsico obtained a court order on June 15 preventing demonstrations from being held within the vicinity of the restaurant. Nanjundaswamy was quoted as saying that he would go ahead and make a speech at the street corner where the restaurant was located, because "freedom of expression cannot be restricted in a public place." The KRRS planned to petition the High Court to squash the order and, once again, threatened that it would resort to "direct action," as it had against Kentucky Fried Chicken (*Agence France Presse*, June 25, 1996).

Opposition to fast-food franchises was not limited to the farmers movement in Karnataka. During the preparations for Independence Day in 1995, the entire spectrum of opposition parties strongly criticized the ruling Congress Party's policies on this score. Consumer goods and fast-food transnationals became the focal point of dissatisfaction with "frivolous" foreign investment. "We want microchips, not potato chips," went the opposition's slogan. Digvijay Singh of the Samajwadi Party put the matter most succinctly: "In a country where ordinary people cannot get one square meal a day, we are inviting multinationals to prepare fast foods which only the affluent can afford" (*Deutsche Presse-Agentur*, August 13, 1995). Criticisms of the Congress Party's liberalization policies seem to have hit their mark. Although no party contesting the national elections (held in late April and early May 1996) seriously contemplated rolling back neoliberal reforms, the Congress Party was humiliated at the polls, finishing third behind the Bharatiya Janata Party (BJP) and the United Front. This followed serious losses in by-elections and state elections and appeared to indicate a disaffection with the direction, pace, and impact of neoliberal policies.

It was precisely this alienation that Nanjundaswamy's movement was seeking to tap. Well-to-do farmers had a direct interest in the rejection of neoliberal policies because cuts in government expenditure threatened to take away subsidies for agricultural inputs and support prices for farm output. Although farmers movements were active in various parts of the country, Nanjundaswamy had become the most visible symbol of rural dissatisfaction with the neoliberal agenda. Unlike Tikait, Nanjundaswamy moved easily in cosmopolitan circles within the country and abroad. A fifty-nine-year-old teacher of international law and a one-time member of the state legislature, he had quit his job in Germany in the 1980s to take up the cause of farmers in his native state of Karnataka (*Reuters Asia-Pacific Business Report*, October 15, 1995; *Agence France Presse*, February 3, 1996). It is important to note that the Karnataka farmers were not narrowly focused on neoliberal policies; instead, attacks on transnational corporations were a means to articulate a more far-reaching critique of development that went beyond the policies of the Indian state. Obviously, development agendas were implicit in neoliberal economic policies; however, there was no one-to-one correspondence between development programs and a market-oriented economic agenda. The Karnataka Farmers Association was, in some ways, very similar to the Kisan Union described in Chapter 1, and the two groups worked together quite closely to organize major rallies and protests.

The Karnataka farmers' criticism of neoliberal strategies of development had three aspects.[3] The first, closely connected to the attacks on fast-food outlets, had to do with the effects on the poor in India of a system oriented to the world market.[4] Unlike such peasant groups as the Shetkari Sangathana led by Sharad Joshi in Maharashtra, which welcomed open markets for the additional revenues that they expected access to world markets to generate, the Karnataka farmers expressed skepticism of the uneven effects of markets. The growth of meat consumption encouraged by fast-food chains among the upper classes in urban areas would increase the demand for livestock and its price. In turn, because the main source for high-quality feed for livestock is grain, this would exert an upward pressure on grain prices and set up a competition for the use of grain between feeding livestock and directly feeding humans. Given the ratios of conversion from grain to meat, far fewer people can be fed with a given quantity of grain if their diet is heavily meat-based than if their diet is largely cereal-based. However, rich consumers can afford to pay for the lost efficiencies of converting grain to meat, which translates into high prices for meat. In this manner, growing inequalities between small pockets of the urban economy hooked into global markets and the rest of the country have enabled a tiny number of affluent consumers to outbid the poor for grain. As Sen's (1981) analysis of the Bengal famine has revealed, unless mechanisms are in place to guarantee the poor a minimum level of entitlements, well-connected markets can remove food very effectively from their plates.

The second part of the Karnataka farmers' criticism of the neoliberal development agenda is that market-friendly policies have resulted in a greater concentration of wealth and have increased inequality in the country. Individuals with the capital to invest in agro-industries that catered to affluent consumers abroad or rich consumers in India's urban areas stood to benefit disproportionately from the "opening up" of markets.[5] The ability to sell goods and labor on the international market has clearly stratified the domestic economy, as those with educational and financial capital have captured the bulk of the benefits flowing from globalization. As new agro-industries have sprung up to produce food, flowers, fruit, and fish for the global market, this process has begun to affect rural areas. Karnataka, in particular, has been a leader in promoting horticultural exports, and so rural areas in that state have experienced the effects of liberalization earlier than those in other states. At a meeting of the Agrarian Way, an organization of one hundred producer and landless groups from forty-five countries in Mexico City, Nanjundaswamy railed against the concentration of wealth caused by neoliberal policies: "Putting land, wealth, and power in the hands of large landowners and transnational corporations unjustifiably, and injuriously, denies farmers the right to control their own destiny" (*InterPress Service*, April 26, 1996). In Nanjundaswamy's analysis, just as transnational corporations compromise the sovereignty of the nation, so do they undermine farmers' rights to self-determination.

The third and strongest aspect of farmers' criticism of neoliberal policies is aimed at its effects on human health and the environment. One of the main agendas of the Karnataka Farmers Association is to wean its members off their dependence on chemical farming. Such farming makes the soil infertile and reduces genetic diversity by making agriculture dependent on a small number of hybrid varieties. Similarly, the "broiler" chickens being raised for Kentucky Fried Chicken, "stuffed with hormones and chemicals" (*Washington Post*, October 1, 1995), are dangerous to the health of those who eat them. In its criticism of open market policies, the Karnataka Farmers Association brought together concerns about the health of consumers, threats to the economic viability of the peasantry, the loss of genetic diversity, and the degradation of the resource base, particularly land quality. These themes are closely connected to one another because biochemical farming is ecologically destructive and, through the transmission of its properties to the soil and the plant (as explained in Chapter 4), is detrimental to human health as well (see, in particular, Vasavi 1994).

It is significant that the critique of a neoliberal development strategy should focus so much on the role of transnational corporations. Why did the KRRS devote so much of its energy to physical attacks on multinational corporations? Why did it make such an explicit connection between actions aimed at protecting the rights of self-determination for farmers and safeguarding the sovereignty of the nation? As already indicated, the three major critiques of the model of development promoted during the tenure of the Congress government were that it was adversely affecting the poor, that it was increasing economic inequality, and that it was sacrificing the health of the environment and the population for the short-term profits of a few corporations. The KRRS's attack on foreign firms in the name of nationalism drew attention to the most important difference between earlier models of development and the current one. As a central justification for the postcolonial state, "development" was always envisioned as a process that would fortify and consolidate national sovereignty. Therefore, attacks on the strategy of development being pursued by the government, such as those described in Chapter 1, could be mounted in the name of the regime's accountability to the people. The legitimacy of the Kisan Union and other farmers groups lay precisely in their claim to speak for the rural areas, where the majority of people in India still live.[6]

We have to remember, however, that the Karnataka farmers' attack on neoliberal development in the name of the rural poor enacts its own sets of exclusions. Like the Kisan Union, the backbone of the KRRS was formed of relatively well-to-do agriculturists; it was thus unclear how much the populist gesture of attacking multinationals was a strategic weapon employed to legitimize its campaign and how inclusive the KRRS's own development agenda was intended to be. In challenging the neoliberal agenda for its effects on the poor, for increasing economic inequality, and for degrading the rural environment, did the KRRS intend to include all segments of the rural population in its alternative vision for development? What was the relationship between its base among the wealthier peasantry and its stated ideology? Opening markets to global trade has prompted varied responses even among the wealthier peasants. Crop regimes and regional variations may have important effects on peasant groups' support for such policies. For example, the Shetkari Sangathana in Maharashtra has supported neoliberal policies, whereas other groups of rich peasants in the same state have opposed such policies.

One of the main fears of the Karnataka farmers, as well as of other groups with whom they had formed a coalition on the issue of opposition to "frivolous" foreign investment, clearly lay in the loss of accountability that would accompany neoliberal policies (*Deutsche Presse-Agentur,* August 13, 1995). Policies of the national state could be opposed by democratic methods; however, no such avenues were available for opposing the policies of transnational corporations. By de-emphasizing the objective of national sovereignty, neoliberal models of development also made it more difficult for policies to be resisted and reformulated by democratic means at the national level (see also Sassen 1996).

Apart from employing a rhetoric of nationalism to attack neoliberal agendas, the KRRS pursued other avenues of resistance as well. Its call for reducing farmers' dependence on industrial inputs and the promotion of sustainable agriculture needs to be interpreted in this context. According to the KRRS, ecologically sustainable farming not only prevented the degradation of the soil, increased peasant profits, and preserved biodiversity but also reduced the farmer's dependence on transnational corporations for purchased inputs and for marketing output. Open market policies that encouraged transnational corporations to promote industrial agriculture and mass-produced processed food were bad for the health of the soil, environment, plants, the humans who consumed the food produced in this manner, and, by extension, the health of the nation itself. The call for a strategy for self-sufficient, ecologically sustainable farming has to be interpreted in this light. In addition to its efforts to promote healthy farming, the Karnataka Farmers Association attempted to forge transnational coalitions with other peasant groups, environmental organizations, and consumer associations around the world (a process documented in Chapter 5).

It is for this reason that it would be a mistake to see in the actions of the Karnataka farmers yet another example of "local" resistance to "global" processes of domination. All the chapters in this book, particularly Chapters 1 and 5, demonstrate that "global" discourses of development, markets, technology, and nationalism are part of "local" lives and "local" frames of meaning and are not, for example, externally imposed on the everyday lives of rural Indians.[7] In fact, I suggest that the dichotomy between the global and the local is largely predicated on the nation, for one pole of that dichotomy indicates that which is outside and the other that which is inside the nation.[8] A better way to understand the actions of farmers groups in India would be to see them as part of intermestic (international/domestic) coalitions that are attempting to resist forces of governmentality which are operating across and through the spaces of nation-states. To examine a particular site carefully, as I have done throughout the book, is not to do a "local" project. Persistent analytic confusion between place and space helps equate a "local" study with one that pays attention to place and a "global" study as one that lacks such a focus. It is for this reason that a fine-grained, historically nuanced, interpretive study can be praised or dismissed for being "particular." Issues of the scale of explanation, the location of the study, and the spatial frame of the analysis are thus collapsed into the confusing dichotomy of "particular" and "general."

Traversing different scales of explanation and different discursive spaces requires the kind of interdisciplinary approach that I have employed in this book. The benefit of pursuing such an interdisciplinary analysis is that it brings certain features of social life into view by opening up avenues to describe and interpret them. It is not my contention that *every* work on India ought to look at the kinds of features that I have identified in this book as being central to the condition of postcoloniality. But it is worthwhile to note that focusing on questions of hybridity, the role of the state (through discourses of development) in "village" India, and the presence of contradictory and incommensurable epistemologies reveals features of life that have largely escaped notice or comment in the scholarly literature. In this sense, interdisciplinarity has enabled us to ask a different set of questions and therefore to look for different kinds of empirical materials in the study of South Asian society. For example, seeing the relations between peasant movements and epistemologies of agriculture helps make connections between knowledge and power that traverse disciplines, scales of analysis, and spatial levels. Issues of mobilization and resistance run through the book, and it is to the relation between resistance and themes of postcoloniality that I now turn.

What are the implications of the shifts in peasant resistance documented in this epilogue for an understanding of postcoloniality? I have argued that any understanding of postcoloniality for rural people in India hinges on the articulation of discourses of development, global capitalism, and technologies of food production. I have endeavored to demonstrate that the green revolution and state development policies had a profound impact on the everyday lives of rural people. The effects of such phenomena could not possibly have been forecast or anticipated, given the manner in which they were transformed and reinterpreted by groups in rural society. More significant, developmentalism, agrarian capitalism, and technological change fundamentally transformed not merely the structural and material conditions of the lives of rural people but, very important, their epistemologies and identities as well. It is this mix of ingredients that I have indexed with the notion of the *condition* of postcoloniality.

Chapter 5 and the description of peasant activism in this epilogue document an important shift, whose implications for postcoloniality may be fundamental. At the very least, it would be fair to say that if there were forms of identity applicable to rural Indians that might have been termed "postcolonial," then those identities have now been thrown into some confusion. This is reflected in the divisions within the peasant movement itself, which had once achieved some coherence in fighting for preserving and extending subsidies and against an urban-centered model of national development but which has since dissolved into factions on opposite sides of the liberalization debate. Neoliberal development promises to reshape postcolonial identities in India, but from the perspective of the present (that is, from the end of the twentieth century) it is difficult to predict the form and shape that these identities will take in the future. In Chapter 5 I argued that new forms of global governmentality exhibited by treaties, accords, and institutions such as the Rio accords may indicate a deeper transformation in the order of nation-states that underlay colonialism. Such shifts do not necessarily augur an improvement in the life conditions for the rural poor in India; if anything, the reverse is more likely to occur. But changes in the order of nation-states do make the term "postcolonial" a more appropriate modifier to forms of identity, states of being, and modes of analysis than ever before.

Notes

All translations in this book are mine unless stated otherwise.

Introduction

1 Following usual anthropological practice, "Alipur" is a pseudonym.

2 Tube wells are so named because they consist of thin pipes of three inches or less in diameter that are sunk into the ground and then hooked to electric pumps to draw out groundwater.

3 In western Uttar Pradesh, most farms are irrigated by private tube wells, although lands adjacent to the Ganges, the Jamuna, or one of the many canals that flow from them use river water.

4 *Desi* (literally, "from the country") can mean a variety of things, depending on the context. In this case, it refers to farm-made or locally produced manure.

5 A *bigha* was the commonly used measure for land; 6.4 bighas equals one acre.

6 See Appadurai n.d. and Daniel 1993 for other examples of this kind of agronomical practice.

7 Among recent ethnographies that brilliantly tackle such redoublings as a central analytic task are Anna Tsing's *In the Realm of the Diamond Queen* (1993) and Marilyn Ivy's *Discourses of the Vanishing* (1995).

8 I am not arguing that hybridity is unique to postcoloniality but that it is a necessary feature of the postcolonial condition. See Bhabha 1994.

9 I do not mean to imply that overpopulation, rather than military force, is the chief explanation for colonialism. However, because "overpopulation" has become such an important explanation for "underdevelopment" and is now represented by First World "experts" as the chief threat to global environmental sustainability (see Chapter 5), it behooves us to keep in mind how Europe solved its "population problem."

10 Ahmad (1995:7) makes the opposite point, that the term "postcolonial" structures the history of the Third World around the axis of colonialism.

11 Shohat (1992:104) goes on to say, "The globalizing gesture of the 'postcolonial condition,' or 'post-coloniality,' downplays multiplicities of location and temporality, as well as the possible discursive and political linkages between 'post-colonial' theories

and contemporary anti-colonial theories and contemporary anti-colonial, or anti-neo-colonial struggles and discourses."

12 It should be clear that I do not think that poverty gives people an identity that necessarily or practically leads to cohesion and the formation of social movements.

13 Anthropologists and other social scientists have long observed this phenomenon but have struggled with the problem of accounting for it analytically. For example, to speak of "the modernity of tradition" is to remain caught within this dichotomy while attempting to break free of it (Rudolph and Rudolph 1967).

14 On governmentality, see Foucault 1991. On development institutions and discourses, see Ferguson 1990, Escobar 1995, and Cooper and Packard 1997.

15 The naturalization of the order of nation-states was symbolized most explicitly by the United Nations.

16 For example, the tropes of an "unchanging India" or of traditions that have existed for "centuries," of feeling that one is "back in the seventeenth century," and so forth are familiar enough in travel writing, but they recur with some regularity in development discourse and in professional (Western) social science. These tropes, stabilized during colonial rule, once again demonstrate the continuing salience of colonial discourse in the contemporary world. See Inden 1990 for a wonderful exposition.

17 Stuart Hall (1996:246) has put it aptly: "[Postcolonial] refers to a general process of decolonisation which, like colonisation itself, has marked the colonising societies as powerfully as it has the colonised (of course, in different ways). . . . Indeed, one of the principal values of the term 'post-colonial' has been to direct our attention to the many ways in which colonisation was never simply external to the societies of the imperial metropolis."

18 I use the term "modernity" rather than "postmodernity" because I believe that modernist narratives of progress are absolutely central to the experience of postcoloniality. In other words, the awareness of being behind, of being "underdeveloped," depends on modernist periodization. Similarly, hegemonic notions of space, public order, subjectivity, and so forth all depend on modernist, rather than postmodernist, sensibilities.

19 This question has been posed most acutely by Dirlik (1994) and Miyoshi (1993).

20 It may be helpful to emphasize that in referring to "narratives" of development and capital, I am not confronting "mere" discourse with "the real." Rather, I wish to draw attention to the ineluctable role played by narratives as symbolic technologies for the representation and understanding of social processes. For example, policies and plans of "development" rely on certain commonsensical stories that explain both why things are the way they are and how they can be changed. Explanations of development rely heavily on a stereotypical narrative of the individual nation, abstracted from a mythical history of "the West" and the statistical representation of sectors and of nations on the map of the world.

21 I am grateful to Jim Ferguson for pointing this out to me (telephone call, July 27, 1995).

22 It was only a *potentially* lucrative market because, in the mid-sixties, India did not have the foreign exchange reserves to pay for food imports in hard currency.

23 On the importance of a conjunctural understanding of postcoloniality, see Frankenberg and Mani 1993.

24 Some of these antimodern discourses are also antidevelopment. Thus, one finds the paradoxical situation that both supporters and critics of development make their arguments with the help of notions of "indigenousness."

25 Hall (1996:247) argues that the postcolonial obliges us "to re-read the very binary form in which the colonial encounter has for so long itself been represented. It obliges us to re-read the binaries as forms of transculturation, of cultural translation, destined to trouble the here/there cultural binaries for ever."

26 Hall brings out this aspect of theories of postcoloniality very well: "It follows that the term 'post-colonial' . . . re-reads 'colonisation' as part of an essentially transnational and transcultural 'global' process—and it produces a decentred, diasporic or 'global' rewriting of earlier, *nation-centred* imperial grand narratives" (1996:247; emphasis added).

27 I would not be mistaken to imply that the new global order is therefore kinder, gentler, or preferable to the previous one, merely that it is different and therefore will require different strategies of resistance and contestation. One example of contestation is presented in Chapter 5.

28 Such an account would have to take into consideration the fact that nationalism depends, as demonstrated in Chapter 1, on a revalorization of the binaries of colonialism. Therefore, one response to the historic failure of the nation (to bring about "development," for example) in the South Asian subcontinent is to throw into doubt the utility of colonial binaries.

29 The phrase is Hacking's (1982).

30 For a summary of the "mode of production" controversy, see Thorner 1982.

31 For Chiapas, see the excellent work by Collier (1994).

32 This is the central question that animates James C. Scott's magnificent work on rural Malaysia, *Weapons of the Weak* (1985).

33 The centrality accorded to participant-observation has a whole host of other implications that are more fully explored in Gupta and Ferguson 1997a.

34 It is not uncommon to find a text being praised for being "*seminal*," "displaying *mastery* over a wide range of material," "demonstrating *control* over many different fields of scholarship," being "the *authoritative* guide" to a subject, and so on. It is not incidental that metaphors of power and masculinity dominate evaluations of knowledge creation.

35 There are, of course, exceptions. A good example is provided by the work of Watts (1991, 1993a, 1993b, 1994).

36 Of course, this assumes that scholars with these different proclivities engage one another, which does not happen very frequently.

1 Agrarian Populism in the Development of a Modern Nation

1 Other examples are environmental treaties and global regulations of trade such as the General Agreement on Tariffs and Trade (GATT). The details of this argument are spelled out in Chapter 5.

2 "Structural adjustment" refers to a package of austerity programs intended to cut government expenditures; to remove subsidies, tariffs, and quotas; to promote ex-

ports; and to "get markets right." This package has been widely imposed by the International Monetary Fund (IMF) and the World Bank as a condition to receive multilateral "development" aid.

3   In this regard see Rich 1994. Criticisms of the damage done to the world's environment and its poor by the Bretton Woods institutions led to a nongovernmental organization–led movement, "Fifty Years Is Enough," to close them down.

4   As has already been argued, the Orientalism of development follows from its evolutionary assumptions, its essentialization of differences, and its ascription of homogeneity and in its use of totalizing narratives of progress.

5   A somewhat similar argument is made by Partha Chatterjee (1986) in his delineation of the difference between the *thematic* and *programmatic* of nationalism.

6   See, for example, Nandy 1980; Marglin and Marglin 1990; and Chatterjee 1986:97–101.

7   Readers will recognize that this point owes a great deal to the positions consistently articulated by Gayatri Chakravorty Spivak (1987, 1988a, 1990).

8   Stacy Leigh Pigg (1996) makes a fascinating argument using the case of Nepal, where development discourses seem to be employed in an even more aggressively self-reflexive manner.

9   See, for example, Johnston and Kilby 1975. The tremendous power of some narratives of "blueprint development" such as "the tragedy of the commons" is explored in Roe 1991.

10 It must be pointed out that "development" was added on, almost as an afterthought, in the title of what was going to be the Bank of Reconstruction. The primary purpose of the Bretton Woods institutions was to rebuild Europe, and "development" was added to its functions because the bank needed a more permanent function. Countries outside the North American/European axis were primarily interested in stabilizing prices in commodity markets, not in "development" or the eradication of poverty. It was not until the 1950s that attention began to be paid to poor countries. See Meier 1984 and Finnemore 1998 for a history of the World Bank's interest in poverty. Gunnar Myrdal (cited in Lumsdaine 1993:30) has pointed out that "the very idea that the developed countries, in all their dealings with underdeveloped countries, should show special consideration for their welfare and economic development, and should even be prepared to feel a collective responsibility for aiding them, is *an entirely new concept dating from after the Second World War*" (emphasis in original).

11 At the end of the Bretton Woods Conference, John Maynard Keynes, with his usual gift for prophecy, remarked: "There has never been such a far-reaching proposal [as that of the World Bank] on so great a scale. . . . I doubt if the world yet understands how big a thing we are bringing to birth" (quoted in Meier 1984:15). At the same time, however, he also realized that the institutions created in Bretton Woods needed to be "sold" to the rest of the world. In his speech moving the acceptance of the Final Act of the conference, he said: "Mr. President, we have reached this evening a decisive point. But it is only a beginning. We have to go from here as *missionaries,* inspired by zeal and faith. We have sold all this to ourselves. But the world at large still needs to be persuaded" (in Meier 1984:2; emphasis added). Perhaps for this reason, visits by World Bank teams to the Third World are still called "missions." The continuities with colonialism are not lost on those who have studied the role of missionaries in colonization (see Comaroff and Comaroff 1991).

12 Foreign aid in the form of concessional economic assistance to the Third World was little known before 1949 (Lumsdaine 1993:33).

13 See, however, Mason and Asher 1973 and Lumsdaine 1993. For critical studies of "development," see Apthorpe 1986; Corbridge 1991; Edwards 1989; Escobar 1984, 1991, 1992, 1995; Ferguson 1990; Mitchell 1991; Pieterse 1991; Roe 1991; Slater 1992; Watts 1993a, 1994; and Wood 1985.

14 Quoted in *Reassamblage,* a documentary film by Trinh T. Minh-ha (1982). The film does not attribute the quote to Illich: I am indebted to Arturo Escobar for this piece of information.

15 I am grateful to Sameer Pandya for this important insight.

16 A good example of this discourse was found in the crisis of the peso in early February 1995. The *San Jose Mercury News* (Zielenziger 1995:1A, 7A) explained the crisis in these terms: "In the past five years . . . savvy investors increasingly sought out young, growing markets to boost their returns. . . . Wall Street called these fledgling capitalists 'emerging markets.' Emerging because they resembled awkward teen-agers—growing in gigantic spurts, taking on new skills and responsibilities, but occasionally throwing tantrums or breaking windows."

17 Ludden points out that "imperial politicians project power from the heights of capitalist maturity and routinely speak as adults talking about children, in the rhetoric of national superiority, responsibility, philanthropy, and self-defense" (1992: 247–48).

18 It is in this sense that we can interpret Kothari's statement, "Where colonialism left off, development took over—in ways that proved even more pervasive and potent" (1990:143). See also Escobar 1995:156–59).

19 The heterogeneity of development discourse has been stressed by Sugata Bose, who argues that "these debates deserve a closer analysis, especially since the lines of division did not always reflect the dichotomies of modernity versus tradition, reason versus unreason, science versus superstition, or, most simplistically, Nehru versus Gandhi that many latter-day commentators have read into them" (1997:48–49).

20 The similarities between neoliberal strategies and colonial policies have also been noted by Peet and Watts (1993:236).

21 Chandra quotes Henry Sumner Maine on the progress of India between 1859 and 1887: "Taking the standards of advance which are employed to test the progress of Western countries, there is no country in Europe which, according to those criteria, and regard being had to the point of departure, has advanced during the same period more rapidly and farther than British India. . . . [There has occurred] a process of continuous moral and material improvement which in some particulars has attained a higher point than has yet been reached in England (1991:82–83)." A similar position has been espoused more recently by Morris et al. (1969). On the "deindustrialization debate," see also Bagchi 1982.

22 The justification for state involvement was provided by Lord Mayo in 1869: "The duties which in England are performed by a good landlord fall in India, in a great measure, upon the government. Speaking generally, the only Indian landlord who can command the requisite knowledge is the state" (cited in Ludden 1992:271).

23 Chandra (1991:134–60) has pointed to the essential similarity between nineteenth-century views of "progress" and those propagated in the 1930s and 1940s. Ludden (1992:268–76) makes a similar argument but extends his vision to the postcolonial state.

24 Thus, the renowned scientist Meghnad Saha asked the president of the Indian National Congress, Subhas Chandra Bose: "May I enquire whether the India of the future is going to revive the philosophy of village life, of the bullock-cart—thereby perpetuating servitude, or is she going to be a modern industrialised nation which, having developed all her natural resources, will solve the problems of poverty, ignorance and defence and will take an honoured place in the comity of nations and begin a new cycle of civilization?" (Bose 1962:51). Bose replied: "All Congressmen do not hold the same view on this question. Nevertheless, I may say without any exaggeration that the rising generation are [sic] in favour of industrialisation." (Bose 1962:55). In his Presidential Address to the Congress in 1938, Bose had argued that the economic problem could not be solved by agricultural improvement alone and that a program of industrialization coordinated by the state was necessary. "However much we may dislike modern industrialism and condemn the evils which follow in its train, we cannot go back to the pre-industrial era, even if we desire to do so" (1962:15). I am indebted to Sugata Bose's stimulating essay (1997) for these references to Subhas Chandra Bose.

25 Thus Gandhi wrote in *Hind Swaraj:* "India's salvation consists in unlearning what she has learnt during the past fifty years or so. The railways, telegraphs, hospitals, lawyers, doctors and such like have all to go, and the so-called upper class have to learn to live consciously and religiously and deliberately the simple life of a peasant" (cited in Bose 1997:50). Chandra, argues, however, that "in the 1930s, [Gandhi] repeatedly said that his position on modern industry had been grossly misinterpreted and that he was not opposed to modern large-scale industry so long as it augmented and lightened the burden of human labor and not displaced it [sic] and was owned by the state and not private capitalists" (1991:142).

26 These themes were also evident in the proceedings of the National Planning Committee, which was formed in 1938 with Nehru as its chair (Chandra 1991:144–60; Bose 1997:52–54).

27 See in particular Friedmann 1982:S256–60; 1990; and Friedmann and McMichael 1989:95–103. In her 1982 work, Friedmann periodizes the first international food order as lasting from 1870 to 1929. In the article coauthored with McMichael, however, she revises the periodization so that the first food regime stops before the First World War.

28 Friedmann suggests that U.S. support for policies that undermined its own markets could be understood with the strategic needs of the cold war. The importance of the livestock sector can be gauged by the figures for the United States. Beef consumption, which was steady for the first half of the twentieth century, increased by 50 percent after 1950, and the consumption of poultry, which had remained constant at sixteen pounds per person between 1910 and 1940, increased by 45 percent in the next decade and had reached seventy pounds per capita by 1985 (Friedmann and McMichael 1989:106).

29 By the early 1970s, imports contributed to more than a quarter of Third World wheat consumption, compared with less than 1 percent for other cereals (Friedmann 1990:21).

30 The importance of the Soviet model of planning is noted in Paul Brass 1994:275.

31 This statement was from one of Nehru's fortnightly letters to the chief ministers, May 10, 1956.

32 Varshney (1995:33) points out that Nehru sent a delegation to Israel to learn about cooperatives in the agricultural sector.

33 On this point, it might be useful to quote Nehru at greater length: "We can learn much from the industrially advanced nations of the West. But we have always to bear this fact in mind, that our country is differently situated. . . . We are not going to have 100 years in order to make good. Our problems, therefore, are essentially similar to those of other under-developed countries in Asia" (Letter to Chief Ministers, November 15, 1954, in Nehru 1988:72–73).

34 These quotes have been taken from two different letters to chief ministers: August 12, 1956, and November 15, 1954.

35 At the end of the First Plan, Nehru decided that his government needed to speed up the process of development and end unemployment in about ten years. In a letter to the chief ministers, he urged rapid action to implement his ideas regarding cooperative farming: "It has also to be remembered that, in the world of today, the pace is fast. Those who lag behind get left to fend for themselves in a world against them. Therefore, these changes to bring about cooperative farming cannot be slow" (August 12, 1956, in Nehru 1988:392). The Second Plan took the ten-year target to eliminate unemployment quite seriously. In retrospect, the naïveté of such ambitions is as astonishing as the hopes embodied in them are tragic.

36 Varshney (1995:47) points out that the Chinese model of productivity enhancement through intensifying labor inputs seemed to plateau in the 1960s.

37 I use the gendered category advisedly as they were overwhelmingly men.

38 I have been influenced by Pranab Bardhan (1984) for this theory of a dominant coalition fighting for and sharing the spoils of public policy. A similar argument is found in an embryonic form in Toye 1981:21–22. The small size of the dominant coalition at the center—and the importance of industrialists within it—was the reason why Mahalanobis acknowledged that it was easier for the central government to implement a heavy industrialization strategy than one that focused on agriculture and small-scale industry. The former "would involve only a small number of persons," whereas implementing policies in the rural sector "would depend on securing the willing cooperation or at least concurrence of millions of persons in the villages" (Mahalanobis 1961:70).

39 For the role of science and technology in development, see Escobar 1995:35–39.

40 The use of PL 480 wheat grew to 5 percent of Indian consumption by 1963, raising concerns in the United States Agency for International Development (USAID) that India was subsidizing its industrialization drive with foreign aid (Goldsmith 1988:182).

41 The debate has centered around the differences between those who emphasize the productivity gains that have flowed from the green revolution and those who point out its social costs, class implications, and so forth. See, for example, Sen 1975 and Frankel 1971. The green revolution provided the context for the famous "mode of production debate" about Indian agriculture (Thorner 1982).

42 It might be persuasively argued that it had equally "revolutionary" consequences for United States agriculture. In what is perhaps a similar case, the term "peasants" is almost never used to refer to family farmers or tenant farmers in the United States. Is it the fear that such a term injects the language of class into a society where the hegemonic ideology has decreed its absence?

43 Busch and Lacy point out that in 1920, the farm population in the United States stood at 32 million, about 30 percent of the total national population. By 1979, this figure had dropped to 6.2 million, or 3 percent of the total (1983:208–9).

44 Busch and Lacy (1983:209) put this point succinctly: "Farms today are fewer, larger, more specialized, and more capital intensive. They are more dependent on industrial inputs and many are even more highly in debt. . . . The number of farms fell to 2.37 million in 1979, down from nearly 7 million in the 1930s. . . . In 1978, just 7% of the farms generated 56% of the total value of all food and fiber production and controlled well over half of the farmland acreage in the country."

45 For example, in the introduction to his book, Kloppenburg (1988:xiv) has this to say: "The extensive social impacts—both positive and negative—stemming from the introduction of hybrid corn were clearly evident in the United States *before* the inauguration of the international Green Revolution of the 1960s. Had social scientists been attentive to those impacts, they would not have been so surprised by the appearance of certain negative consequences associated with the introduction of Green Revolution plant types." Although Kloppenburg is absolutely correct in pointing out this glaring contradiction, he does not attempt to explain its presence.

46 Not surprisingly, the commission's report to the Rockefeller Foundation emphasized work in exactly these areas: "The most acute and immediate problems, in approximate order of importance, seem to be the improvement of soil management and tillage practices; the introduction, selecting, or breeding of better-adapted, higher-yielding and higher-quality crop varieties; more rational and effective control of plant diseases and insect pests; and the introduction or development of better breeds of domestic animals and poultry, as well as better feeding methods and disease control" (Stakman, Bradfield, and Mangelsdorf 1967:32–33).

47 Busch and Lacy (1983:35) point out that a claim to scientific independence led to a preoccupation with increasing productivity, rather than to the questioning of the ends to be served by those increases. Negative consequences to "scientific advance" were dismissed as adjustment problems or the price to be paid for progress. These processes were abetted by commodity-specific organizations of client groups, whose interest was in obtaining seeds that would yield high outputs.

48 To appreciate the fact that this view has not been superannuated, see Mitchell 1991.

49 I will comment on the tendency to pose problems entirely in national terms later. Here, let me just point out that there is a difference between stating that "Mexico needed more food" and stating that "poor Mexicans needed more food." A country that is self-sufficient or even a surplus producer may still have people who are hungry. Poor people may not possess the purchasing power to feed themselves despite the existence of surpluses in the nation.

50 It is perhaps fitting that Norman Borlaug, one of the pioneers of the Mexico project, was awarded the Nobel Peace Prize. Giving Borlaug the prize for peace, rather than one for scientific achievement, testified to the enormous moral legitimacy enjoyed by purely technocratic solutions to the problem of poverty. See Mitchell 1991 for an example of how the same strategy continues to be used to deal with similar problems facing Egypt.

51 National food availability need not result only from greater production. It could, for example, be the result of higher imports.

52 I do not, by any means, intend to downplay the importance that these moral man-

dates had for the scientists who were doing this research. I have little doubt that they sincerely believed that their research would result in the eradication of hunger (Tolan 1994). The motivation that such a goal provided is not to be underestimated. Borlaug, for example, is described as working with an almost maniacal intensity, sometimes inspecting his experimental plots by the light of the moon (Stakman, Bradfield, and Mangelsdorf 1967:81). But it was to wheat, and not to the removal of hunger, that Borlaug was dedicated. He assumed that more of one would mean less of the other, therefore increasing wheat yields was *equivalent* to reducing hunger. From his very first job doing classified research in the fungicide testing laboratory of the multinational chemical giant DuPont, the resource-intensive and chemical-dependent *direction* of Borlaug's research effort was evident (41).

53 The notion of "comparative advantage" is itself dependent on the naturalization of the "national economy" and on the givenness of a world of nation-states that "freely" trade with one another. Mitchell (1994) has suggested that the idea of the "national economy" may have originated as recently as after the turn of this century. In other words, one has to accept the ideological premises of nationalism completely to accept the fiction of a "national economy." For dependent nation-states, this fiction has always appeared rather flimsy.

54 Mitchell provides good examples of the continued use of allochronistic discourses in discussing the development of Egypt (1991:24).

55 The same point is made with reference to environmental discourses in the 1990s in Chapter 5, thus heading off the temptation to adopt a teleological narrative of knowledge production ("that may have been true of the past but *no one* believes those things anymore").

56 In a section of the chapter on India entitled "Population Outstrips Food Production," Stakman, Bradfield, and Mangelsdorf (1967:238) state: "Clearly, India must either reduce the rate of human reproduction or increase her food production, or both, if she is to maintain even her present low level of subsistence. . . . India is in danger. Either she must produce more food or fewer people. But she already has too many people clamoring for the food that she now produces."

57 For a detailed scholarly demonstration of this point, see Sen 1981 and Greenough 1982. In Satyajit Ray's film of the Bengal famine, *Distant Thunder* Elite Video (New York: New York Film Annex [distributor]), the recurring motif is that of a pair of butterflies among green fields. Ray commented that the dancing butterflies were intended to communicate visually the fact that the famine occurred despite a good harvest. Nature's indifference to the suffering was conveyed to emphasize that the famine was entirely made by humans and was not the result of a bad harvest.

58 I should point out that Kloppenburg does not himself employ the term "imperialism" to refer to the process that he describes.

59 The debates surrounding "ecological imperialism" are dealt with at greater length in Chapter 5.

60 Subramaniam pointed out that no one argued for stopping industrial development on the grounds that it would lead to greater inequality and social tension (1979:27–28).

61 The output in 1964–65 stood at 89.0 million metric tons. It declined to 72.0 million tons in 1965–66 and increased slightly to 75.1 million in 1966–67 (Rudolph and Rudolph 1987:235).

62 U.S. exports of wheat accounted for approximately 50 percent of world wheat exports in 1961–65; 71 percent of these exports were in the form of aid (Friedmann 1982:S271).

63 An assessment of the green revolution is provided by Paul Brass (1994:309–20), who points out that cereal yields in India are still among the lowest in the world.

64 This short summary of an argument developed more fully in Chapter 2 is intended to give just enough of a background to make sense of the material that follows.

65 For an analysis of populism in Africa, see Low 1964.

66 Perhaps for this reason, some analysts have tended to regard these as essential ingredients of the populist recipe. Following Laclau 1977, however, I shall argue that there is no necessary correspondence between mass migration to urban areas, nationalism, and populism. That populism often took the form of *popular nationalism* in the Latin American context is very likely the result of a particular historical conjuncture and a specific geopolitical relationship to the United States.

67 Dornbusch and Edwards (1990) argue that populist economic policies followed in Allende's Chile and Peru under the Garcia administration led to both hyperinflation and the lowering of real living standards. They are careful, however, not to rule out the possibility that populist regimes could find some economic strategy that was sustainable. Tom Brass (1994b) sees populism as a particularistic response to the globalization of capital.

68 Peronism was seen as an eruption of barbarism when his supporters dropped their pants or made other obscene gestures in front of señoras in Buenos Aires and when they attacked cafés, university students, and newspapers that were hostile to him (Torre 1992:411–12). The Keynesian distributionist policies started by Perón included pension schemes, housing programs, and a system of collective bargaining and trade union rights for labor. Adelman (1994) suggests that the particular manner in which civil society was polarized and mobilized by Perón was not fiscally sustainable but, once achieved, effectively blocked the construction of an alternative dominant bloc in Argentina long after the Peronist coalition crumbled.

Torre (1992) suggests an important distinction between populist regimes and populist movements. Populist regimes may forge a ruling bloc by bringing together elements of a movement with other groups in a temporary coalition. Populist movements may outlive any particular populist regime, however, forming the basis for other ruling coalitions to be assembled in the future. Thus, Peronism continued to be a powerful force in Argentinian politics long after the demise of Perón (Adelman 1994). Regimes, in turn, may be distinguished from even shorter-lived populist electoral coalitions that do not translate electoral rhetoric into state action. Torre gives the examples of the coalitions that elected Alberto Fujimori and Fernando Collor de Mello to power in Peru and Brazil, respectively (1992:396).

69 Although "populism" is often used to describe Indira Gandhi's political strategy in the early elections of 1971, it is unclear which of the three forms mentioned above—regime, movement, or electoral coalition—is designated by the term. Sometimes the implication is that populism was a rhetorical position adopted by Indira Gandhi to forge a winning electoral coalition. Others point to the new set of redistributive policies put into place after the Congress swept into power to suggest that the populist agenda went beyond an electoral coalition and formed the basis of a *regime*. But no analyst has characterized Indira Gandhi's populism as the beginning of a new

movement, noting instead the almost complete absence of any organizing institutions, whether based in the party or among social groups affected by the government's policies. Even when populism is used in the manner described, there has been almost no analysis of what specifically makes a discourse or regime "populist" and how populism differs from other hegemonic blocs.

70 My account in this section relies heavily on Frankel 1978:388–549.

71 Only one out of four new voters at the national level in 1967 supported the party (Frankel 1978:353).

72 Indira Gandhi did manage to win the support of two thirds of the members of parliament (Rudolph and Rudolph 1987:134). It was with their help that she won the first major victory in her struggle with the old guard with the election of her candidate, V. V. Giri, to the presidency on August 20. The general election of 1972 loomed ahead, however, and it was there that the fate of the party would eventually be decided.

73 The entire slogan read "Kuch log kehten hai, Indira hatao; Main kehti hoon, garibi hatao" [Some people say, remove Indira; I say, remove poverty] (quoted in Frankel 1978:454–55).

74 Indira Gandhi too recognized the popular character of the victory which the Working Committee characterized as "the new consciousness of the people" (in Frankel 1978:460).

75 In the state elections that followed in early 1972, the Indira Congress made even more impressive gains, capturing 70 percent of the seats on 47 percent of the popular vote, both representing new highs in the history of the party (see Frankel 1978:477 and Rudolph and Rudolph 1987:130–31). Frankel points to the differences between the Congress and opposition strategies: " 'Theme' posters, films, records, cinema slides, tracts, leaflets, hoardings, and 'publicity materials of all kinds' were produced by the All India Congress Committee (AICC) in the various regional languages, and distributed among all sections of the electorate to establish the salience of broad national issues over local and state problems stressed by the opposition." She describes how Indira Gandhi, while warning about the need to be vigilant in the case of another war with Pakistan, nevertheless emphasized that she was focused on the bigger war against poverty: "Mrs. Gandhi elaborated the pledges of *Garibi Hatao* with promises to improve the income of the masses of the rural poor through new legislation to lower ceiling limits on landownership" to between ten and eighteen acres (Frankel 1978:476). Since agriculture is a state subject, Indira Gandhi, as a representative of the central government, was theoretically powerless to bring this about. If the state governments were also controlled by the Congress, however, the leader of the party could fulfill such a pledge.

76 The importance of party institutions in bringing about political reforms that help the poor has been emphasized by Kohli (1987).

77 The discussion in this paragraph borrows heavily from Frankel (1978:491–523), who characterizes the political effects of these welfare schemes this way: "Those who benefited or hoped to benefit from such new programs attributed their good fortune directly to 'Indraji,' whereas those who had not benefited blamed moneylenders, traders, or corrupt officials" (522).

78 The jatavs are one of the lowest-ranking castes whose occupational specialty was working with leather; however, in western Uttar Pradesh, their chief occupation did not derive from skinning and curing hide but from farming and agricultural labor.

79 See Wadley 1994:71, 163–64, 210–48 for similar reports of upper-caste resentment of their loss of privilege and lower-caste assertiveness in Karimpur, another village in western Uttar Pradesh.

80 There are "reservations" or quotas in government jobs for people belonging to the Scheduled Castes and Tribes.

81 The terms "Scheduled Caste" and "Backward Caste" are official categories employed by the Government of India. The former are untouchables who get the name from being on a "schedule" or list of untouchables made by the colonial government. "Backward Castes" are officially named as such to take account of those lower castes who are not untouchable but are "economically depressed" and who are thus under-represented in government institutions and offices.

82 The best guide to party politics in Uttar Pradesh is to be found in the work of Paul Brass (1965, 1984a, 1985). My own understanding of peasant mobilization has bene-fited tremendously from the work of Zoya Hasan (1989).

83 Although the party received a setback in the national elections of 1971, it rebounded and continued to receive approximately a fifth of the popular vote in the following decade.

84 Byres (1988) has called him an "organic" intellectual of the rich peasants.

85 This was when he had been elected (before independence) to the UP legislative assembly. He next targeted moneylenders, then called for a resolution to reserve 50 percent of the Congress Party posts "for the sons and dependents of the cultiva-tors . . . who formed the mass of our people" (Byres 1988:149).

86 This was followed by the land ceiling act of 1960, which attempted to reduce the size of the largest landholdings to 40 acres per individual. Since this still left very sub-stantial holdings in families, Indira Gandhi's government in 1971 established national guidelines that further reduced the ceiling to 27.5 acres per family. In 1973, the UP government modified the land ceiling act to conform to these guidelines (Brass 1980:396–97).

87 I use "him" for cultivator because the entire discourse of agricultural equity in zamindari abolition assumed a male cultivator. Legal changes thus normalized and justified male control over land (Bina Agarwal 1994).

88 One of the problems of implementing the law dispossessing large landowners was that the patwaris were under the authority of the zamindars. They could thus ma-nipulate the records to ensure that the former landlords managed to keep most of, if not all, their land by taking advantage of the loopholes in the law that allowed retention of self-cultivated lands. There were twenty-seven thousand patwaris in UP at that time (Byres 1988:151). They were replaced by others who would be less be-holden to the traditional landlords and, like the Congress itself, be more responsive to owner-cultivators.

89 Byres (1988:154) presents figures which suggest that the average number of fragments per acre varied from 0.70 for holdings over 25 acres to 2.2 for holdings below 2.5 acres. Thus, a household that owned 20–25 acres would find that land divided, on the average, into approximately 22 fragments! By the end of the Fourth Five-Year Plan in 1971, more than half the cultivable area in the state had been consolidated (Brass 1980:398).

90 Charan Singh also firmly opposed—and managed to scuttle—plans to increase the land tax on farmers. In fact, direct taxes on the agricultural sector are nonexistent

because agricultural income is exempt from taxation, and the land tax, nominally fixed, has declined in real terms to a token amount.

91 The information in this paragraph comes largely from Byres 1988.

92 Charan Singh maintained that the peasant proprietor was neither a capitalist nor a disguised proletarian: "Although he may occasionally employ others, he is both his own master and his own servant. . . . He does not exploit others, nor is he exploited by others; for he labours for himself and his children alone and he does not look for remuneration of his hard work at the farm in the way that a factory worker does" (given in Byres 1988:175).

93 As the "peasant movement" developed, some of these positions became less important. For example, as zamindari became a distant memory and the threat of collectivization receded, "peasant" leaders didn't feel the need to rail against these threats. Rather, they increasingly picked up on the theme of discrimination against rural areas by urban interests to create a powerful counterhegemonic project.

94 The difference between the BKD in 1969 and the Lok Dal in 1980 was that the former's strength was concentrated in the western part of UP, whereas the Lok Dal did equally well in the eastern half of the state (Brass 1985).

95 The output of all food grains increased to 108 million tons in 1970–71 and then to 121 million tons in 1975–76 from 72 million tons in 1965–66. Because most of this increase was due to wheat, the growth of wheat production was truly phenomenal, a 400 percent rise in the two decades since 1963–64 (Rudolph and Rudolph 1987: 235; Farmer 1986; Rudra 1982).

96 See Varshney 1995:88–89 for the changing composition of the lower house of Parliament.

97 Indira Gandhi's reaction is described in Byres (1982:59–60): "[The Planning Commission] had not bargained for the sharp rebuff that they received. . . . [T]he Prime Minister told the planners unequivocally that there was no question of taxing agriculture, adding that none of the experts in the Planning Commission and in the government or for that matter even outside the government seemed to her to have a realistic appreciation of the political factors and constraints applicable to these matters. Agriculture could not be taxed for *political* reasons" (emphasis added).

98 The information in this paragraph comes from Byres 1988.

99 Other demands included greater representation for farmers on government agencies dealing with their concerns, larger subsidies for inputs, greater support for exports, and equality between agricultural and industrial prices (see Varshney 1995:104–5).

100 The upper castes considered the jats to be a crude, rough, uneducated lot. The brahmin priest who was almost constantly employed by jats told me that "they don't possess any finesse. It is a thick-headed caste [*motee buddhi waali jati hai*]." Jats themselves, fully aware of these stereotypes, would employ them proudly. While describing how someone fought for his rights, a young jat told me: "Being a jat, he was not about to withdraw what he said. Once he said something, he stood by it," thereby implying something about the lack of trustworthiness of other castes.

101 Like Charan Singh, and unlike Tikait, these other "peasant" leaders have not always been farmers. Sharad Joshi was an Indian Administrative Service (IAS) officer, a member of the bureaucratic elite, who worked for the UN Postal Union in Berne,

Switzerland, in the 1970s before coming to peasant politics. Dr. Nanjundaswamy gave up a job in Germany teaching international law to serve as a member of the state legislature in Karnataka.

102 This bid at farmer unity, however, ended in failure over questions of leadership.

103 *India Today,* January 15, 1994, 19.

104 For example, the leader of the opposition in the UP assembly visited the town and declared that firing at the activists was "yet another example of police barbarism" because it was "totally unprovoked" (*Times of India,* June 21, 1989).

105 *Times of India,* June 21, 1989.

106 In this quote, the gender of the farmer is assumed to be male, except when complaining of ill treatment in a familiar metaphor, where it changes to "a stepdaughter." *Aaj,* July 19, 1989.

107 See R. S. Tiwari, "Farmers Unhappy—Whose Responsibility?" *Bijnor Times,* August 11, 1989, 3. The article is accompanied by a photograph of a large group of peasants armed with sticks [*lathis*]. The caption reads, "Oppressed peasants demonstrate their unhappiness by bringing sticks to face the guns and bullets of the police."

108 *Aaj,* July 19, 1989.

109 It must be remembered that the price of output was very high in 1967 because it was a year of shortfall of production.

110 *Bijnor Times,* August 11, 1989, 3.

111 Interestingly enough, the urban poor were completely erased in this discourse. Was it because it was difficult to fit them into the image of "India"? It was sometimes hinted that farmers and workers were in the same boat, that somehow they belonged together in "Bharat," but this suggestion was rarely explicated. For the most part, it remained a Manichaean discourse whose positive pole was agricultural and rural. Thus, sectoral concerns and constructions of place were fused together.

112 *Times of India,* July 31, 1989.

113 The effectiveness of Tikait's rhetoric lay in the fact that what he had to say also "made sense" to an urban reporter—that is, it appealed to the "common sense" of a middle-class urban dweller.

114 This point held for consumption more generally but was perhaps most severely marked by dress. Thus, acquiring items of household consumption such as TV sets, steel almirahs, beds, and so forth would perhaps evoke less envy, although acquiring something like a refrigerator, which was clearly "marked" as a luxury item of rich people in towns, very well might.

115 The implications of a singular "peasant" identity and its masculine form are further explored below.

116 *Times of India,* August 8, 1989.

117 It should also be pointed out that given the price of a tractor and the minimum amount of land necessary to justify purchasing it, only the biggest and most prosperous farmers could afford one.

118 *Times of India,* August 8, 1989.

119 The article goes on to contrast the evocation of peasant helplessness with the actions of Kisan Union activists: "On the ground, things are not quite as innocent

or fatalistic. Despite his innocuous exhortations, the Chaudary's [Tikait's] followers have repeatedly gone on the rampage; burnt down generators; refused to pay official levies and dues; and attacked the police, often hindering investigation into criminal offences. What matters, however, is the perceptions that all these actions are part of the kisan's 'helpless' resistance to the organized might of the state. That such a perception has existed from time immemorial is known; what is significant, even dangerous, is that Mr. Tikait has succeeded in channelising this perception into organized protest" (Chandan Mitra, "Tikait as Mini-Mahatma: Understanding the Rural Mind-Set," *Times of India,* August 9, 1989).

120 *Bijnor Times,* August 18, 1989.

121 Notions of pride, of course, were deeply gendered. If a man was caught stealing, the village council often prescribed what they considered the worst possible humiliation: being hit on the head with a slipper [*chappal*], in public and, on top of that, by a woman.

122 *Times of India,* August 9, 1989.

123 Ibid.

124 *Bijnor Times,* August 11, 1989, 3.

125 Rs 183 was approximately equal to ten dollars at prevailing exchange rates.

126 Most of the following information comes from the earlier period of the Kisan Union. The Kisan Union lost a great deal of its support among Muslims by indirectly supporting the Bharatiya Janata Party (BJP) in 1990; by 1992, it had virtually split because of factionalism (Banaji 1994:236). Lindberg (1994:114–15) provides a somewhat different picture.

127 "Maulana" is a form of address used in South Asia for one learned in Islamic holy texts.

128 The information in this paragraph comes from the *Times of India,* July 30 and August 8, 1989.

129 *Times of India,* August 9, 1989.

130 "Dalit" is the identity chosen by Scheduled Caste leaders to represent themselves.

131 For details, see Raman Nanda, "BKU Fosters 'Brotherhood,'" *Times of India,* July 30, 1989.

132 Quoted in Rashmee Z. Ahmed, "V.P. Singh Is Honest, but a Dabboo," *Times of India,* July 31, 1989.

133 Quoted in ibid.

134 Ranbir assumed that the landless laborer was male, thus ignoring women from lower-caste, landless households who worked primarily as wage laborers.

135 Village politics and social structure will be analyzed in greater detail in the next chapter.

136 Virendra was merely rearticulating a code of hospitality that largely continues to be upheld in the villages of western Uttar Pradesh.

137 Here Virendra was drawing on an upper-caste perception of the "crudeness" of jats.

138 Quoted in Ahmed, "V.P. Singh Is Honest."

139 Reported in the *Bijnor Times,* August 12, 1989. Robert Goldman has suggested to me (comments on oral presentation at South Asia Seminar, University of California, Berkeley) that Tikait might be implying that Rajiv Gandhi's father, an urban Parsi, belonged to that denationalized elite that constituted "India."

140 To speak of compulsory heterosexuality would be to understate the situation. Further, the pressure to produce a male heir, preferably within a year of marriage, weighs heavily on both bride and groom.

141 This discourse about "roots," which fuses patriarchy, genealogical descent, and location, is not peculiar to Chaudhary Tikait but is found, with various inflections, elsewhere. See, for example, Malkki 1992.

142 See *Bijnor Times,* August 18, 1989.

143 In fact, the story is headlined "BKU Supporters Will Be Happy When Farmer Unfurls Flag over Red Fort"; see *Aaj,* July 19, 1989.

144 The Hindi version is as follows: *Maa pay dhi / Pita pay chora / Bahut nahin / To thoda—thoda* (Ahmed, "V.P. Singh Is Honest"; my translation).

145 Quoted in Ahmed, "V.P. Singh Is Honest."

146 Peet and Watts note the *flexibility* of populist discourses, pointing out that they have been freely appropriated in neoliberal discourses against government intervention propagated by organizations such as the World Bank (1993:237–38).

147 My analysis in this section draws on Anderson 1992; Friedmann 1982, 1992; Lipietz 1989; McMichael 1993; McMichael and Buttel 1990; McMichael and Myhre 1991; Raynolds et al. 1993; Singh 1992; and Ufkes 1993a,b.

148 McMichael and Myhre, in fact, argue that "the current movement of liberalism substitutes global economism for national regulation" (1991:85). Goodman and Watts (1994), while sympathetic to the general argument about the role of multinational capital, caution against generalizations that fail to capture both the enormous variability of situations and the often contradictory outcomes that accompany changes in the organization of capital. They argue, for example, that GATT has provided the opportunity for national reregulation at the same time that it has brought down certain tariffs and subsidies and thereby created a more liberal trading environment.

149 The reactions of different farmers groups in India to GATT are explored in greater detail in Chapter 5. The struggle over biogenetic resources has become even more salient with the rise of plant genetic technology, which promises to become even more economically and politically important in the future.

2 Developmentalism, State Power, and Local Politics in Alipur

1 Apart from labor, control over the sexuality of women was extremely important. This took the form of controlling the circulation of thakur women, who were confined, as women of no other caste were, to the boundaries of their homes. It also meant the sexual availability of lower-caste women.

2 Sher Singh operated a slightly larger area, having confiscated some lands adjacent to his that were owned by harijans.

3 The UP Zamindari Abolition Act of 1952 forced landlords, who had been given the right to collect land revenue over a large area by ruling dynasties and later by the East India Company and the British colonial government, to get rid of land that exceeded a generous limit. See Chapter 1 for details.

4 The UP Zamindari Abolition Act was passed in 1952, so the Old Thakur's recollection of 1950 was a couple of years off.

5 At that time, there were no laws against bigamy.

6 Translating *naach-gaana* as "musical evenings" robs it of a connotation of licentiousness and masculine aesthetics, as it usually refers to male spectators enjoying female performances of music and dance.

7 Sharma (1978:142–43) also notes a similar process in a different village. The reason choosing sides took on additional significance was that a *public* declaration of one's sympathies could be traded for a share of benefits from government schemes if one's candidate won. I am grateful to James Brow for stressing the importance of this point to me.

8 Scott (1985:220–33) reports an identical series of events in the village of Sedaka in Malaysia. The supporters of the ruling party, who are for the most part relatively well-off, obtained almost all of the benefits of a Village Improvement Scheme despite the fact that a survey was conducted to determine need.

9 To give an idea of the concentration of land ownership, brahmins owned a quarter and thakurs nearly half the total land in the village (see Figure 1).

10 This perception of the police was widely shared in villages and small towns in western Uttar Pradesh. A landlord told me that he gladly rented his house to anyone except a policeman, because then he knew that he would never be able to collect rent.

11 The upper end of the cot is the more comfortable part, where higher-status people— that is, those who are upper-caste or older—sit.

12 See also Wadley 1994:52–55 for a discussion of veiling in western UP.

13 "Vote-bank" is the name given to the phenomenon of caste groups voting as a bloc. Politicians and journalists in India, as well as academics who study India, often assume bloc voting by caste groups in their calculations and analysis.

14 Drinking liquor, eating meat, and visiting prostitutes are seen as morally degenerate activities closely connected to one another.

15 For example, Rowe (1963:44) says: "The pressure upon the carpenter-blacksmith during plowing season is extreme. The individual farmer knows that regardless of the shortage of labor at peak seasons he has a firm claim."

16 In a survey of 334 villages in four states, Bardhan and Rudra (1980:299) found that production loans were given in almost half the cases. In Uttar Pradesh specifically, they found that production loans were given in 42 percent of cases, most of them with interest.

17 Michie (1981:31) reports a similar process taking place in the neighboring state of Rajasthan and argues that tenant rotation "protects the landlord but also breaks the diffuse patron-client tie." Miriam Sharma (1978:37) notes the same process in eastern Uttar Pradesh, in a village in Benaras District, at virtually the opposite end of the state from Alipur.

18 For further details, see Chapter 3. Michie (1981) and Bharadwaj (1985) corroborate these two features of tenancy for other areas. Byres (1982:41) supports tenant switching.

19 In this respect, the trends in Alipur go against those found in other green revolution areas (K. Bardhan 1977; Byres 1982).

20 An interesting example of the different implications of the same form of tenancy is given by Brow. He contrasts tenancy "in which a part of the product of subordinate tenants was recurrently appropriated by landlords of superior status" with tenancy

where there was to be found "a pattern or reciprocity and cyclical reproduction within the lower level community" (1980:64). This is the kind of contrast implied here.

21 There is some controversy over whether tenancy has been declining on a broader scale. Omvedt (1983:39) concludes, on the basis of nationwide National Sample Survey (NSS) data for the period 1950–72, that "the inescapable fact is that landlord-tenant relations are now a minor element in the relations of agricultural production, and tenanted land covers only a small proportion of the cultivated area."

22 In this light, it would not be inappropriate to speak of the "breakdown" of relations of patronage and dependence. Wadley (1994) has documented this process over sixty years for the village of Karimpur, which is, like Alipur, in the western part of Uttar Pradesh. Alavi too (1973:54) notes the phenomenon in a more general way. It goes without saying that the observed breakdown of patron/client ties is not peculiar to India. James Scott (1985) documents this process in great detail for Malaysia; Gilmore (1977) and Harding (1984) note the same phenomenon in different parts of Spain.

23 The remaining land was owned by institutions such as the UP state farm, was common land owned by the panchayat, or was owned by people who did not live in Alipur.

24 Brass (1984) provides evidence of lower-caste assertiveness from Deoria, another district of UP. Sharma (1978:172) also presents an interesting example of the same phenomenon from eastern UP.

25 For reports of very similar sentiments in another part of western Uttar Pradesh, see Wadley 1994:210–48.

26 See also Wadley 1994:101.

27 For another perspective on the decline of affection and its relation to ecology, see Gold forthcoming.

28 Scott, in his careful study of the ideology of patronage, points out (1985:138–83) that the higher classes emphasize features of the rapidly eroding system of patronage that are different from those emphasized by the lower classes. But because, in his opinion, it is those in the lower classes who have lost most in the transition to capitalist agriculture, they are more prone to employ the language of clientism than are rich farmers. "They have collectively created a *remembered village* and a *remembered economy* that serve as an effective ideological backdrop against which to deplore the present" (1985:178).

29 This conversation dates to late July 1992. Wage rates mentioned by Ranbir were those in effect at that time.

30 Brow reports a similar process for Sri Lanka, where "the spread of wage labor threatened to expose the hierarchical ideology that had masked traditional relations of production" (1981a:716). However, the increased insecurity accompanying the penetration of capitalism, he thinks, serves to inhibit the process of class formation.

31 Wadley reports almost identical reactions from lower-caste people in Karimpur (1994:151–53). Bardhan and Rudra (1986) point out that one of the ways in which rich peasants are combating the difficulty of controlling labor is by bringing in long-distance migrant labor during the peak harvesting season. Though their data are from Bengal, this has been happening in Punjab and Haryana too for several years now.

32 Although here I refer only to the green revolution areas of northwest India, the

growth of wage labor is a trend that holds broadly for the entire subcontinent. For India, see Bardhan 1970, 1980 and Omvedt 1983; for Bangladesh, Westergaard 1982; for Sri Lanka, Brow 1978, 1981b.

33 The fact that daughters do not inherit land keeps women from controlling the means of production. Bina Agarwal (1994) has argued that this is the chief cause of women's subordinate status in the subcontinent.

34 There were other causes of proletarianization as well—for example, confiscation of mortgaged land owing to inability to pay back loans, withdrawal from agriculture as a result of finding steady employment elsewhere, and so on. I am grateful to Miriam Sharma for pointing this out to me.

35 Appadurai has conceptualized the process of immiserization and marginalization in terms of the changing relationship between "entitlement" and "enfranchisement," "a change which gives poorer persons a wider voice in the conduct of public life, but fewer claims upon subsistence in local economic systems" (1989). For the record of increasing atrocities against the rural poor, see Joshi 1982; Frankel 1971:115; Byres 1982:56–57; Brass 1984b:93; and Michie 1981:36.

36 For the importance of seasonality in agriculture, see Appadurai n.d. and Chambers, Longhurst, and Pacey 1981.

37 See, for example, Hasan and Patnaik 1992, in which a similar argument is made.

38 For a review of the evidence, see Farmer 1986.

39 Land ceiling laws came much later than zamindari abolition and had as their explicit purpose not to give land to the tiller but to ensure more equitable distribution. Frankel (1971:4), listing the objectives of government planners, says, "The highest priority was assigned to rapid implementation of land reforms, including security of tenure, lower rents, transfer of ownership rights to tenants, and redistribution of land."

40 Prasad's younger brothers were either in high school or junior high at that time. A "joint family" is one in which the adult sons live together with their parents in one household.

41 Similar programs can be found in many developing countries where the agrarian sector is populous and electorally important. Scott notes, for instance: "If the conservative Malay elite is to continue benefiting from the privileges and opportunities the economy and the state provide, it must, as a basic precondition, maintain its political domination over the state. Given the semicompetitive election system that currently prevails, this objective requires the political support of the bulk of the Malay electorate. . . . It is in this context that one can understand the very considerable efforts in the field of development programs, grants, clinics, schools, loans, and infrastructure that the state has undertaken" (1985:314).

42 Government jobs are highly prized because employment is guaranteed for life, remuneration and benefits are generous, there are usually opportunities for making money "on the side," and the common perception is that one doesn't have to work very hard. When I asked one young man who came to me for help in finding employment if he would be interested in a private sector job, he said he would rather work for the government because then he would be paid without too much exertion on his part!

43 For example, Alipur's nongovernment primary and middle school was paid a certain sum to compensate for the tuition expenses of each Scheduled Caste student.

44 During my first extended stint of fieldwork in Alipur, I stayed in a room of the Manager's house. The reason why two of the state farm's fragments were situated near the thakurs' fields was that the land for the farm had been seized from them by the government because it exceeded the land ceiling, the maximum amount of land legally allowed to any one family.

45 Miriam Sharma (1978:58) gives many examples from the village in eastern UP where she did fieldwork. "The Seed Store Inspector, like the VLW [village-level worker], also regularly takes bribes. . . . Villagers who want an electrical connection . . . must bribe a multitude of officials. . . . In cases where money was received by the Pradhan for the village, such as loans and money for well and house construction, some amount was siphoned off." Other interesting examples follow later in the book (1978:113, 170). The VLW is a state official who is responsible for the implementation of development programs at the village level.

46 Opler, Rowe, and Stroop (1959:32) give an early example that demonstrates this process. Speaking of a local leader, they say: "His prestige and his political future depend upon gaining benefits and concessions for his village from government officials." As far as I know, the first person to have made the more general observation about the shift from patronage to brokerage is Mayer (1966, 1967)—in retrospect, an amazingly astute reading of the changing situation. Sharma (1978:109–14) sees this reflected in a change in the cultural category employed to refer to "big men"— from *rais* (a term emphasizing wealth) to *badaa aadmi* (a term emphasizing social capital). See also Sharma 1978:132, 157–58, 224. Scott (1985:311–13) documents an identical shift taking place in Malaysia: "What has occurred, however, is that the basis of their [larger farmers] domination has been transformed. Their control, which was once embedded in the primary dependencies of production relations, is now based far more on law, property, coercion, market forces, and political patronage. . . . Lacking the economic control that grew from earlier relations of production . . . *this elite will now sink or swim depending on the resources for patronage, profit, and control the state can put at its disposal*" (312–13; emphasis added).

47 None of these plots was distributed to landless women. In this way, state projects of land distribution completely reinforced gender hierarchies and exclusions in the village.

48 Six bighas would be a little less than one acre.

49 This is the official terminology used by the Government of India (GOI).

50 The "block" is an administrative unit consisting of approximately one hundred villages.

51 The political importance of marginal landholding in terms of the segmentation of small landholders from proletarians and the accompanying fracturing of class consciousness has been emphasized by Collier (1987).

52 The depth of this commitment varied. Some upper-caste men in Alipur firmly rejected a caste-based view of the world, whereas others just as strongly believed in it.

3 "Indigenous" Knowledges: Agronomy

1 On Ayurveda, see Bhagwan Dash 1989; Daniel 1984; Kakar 1982; Langford 1995; Leslie 1992; Obeyesekere 1992; and Trawick 1974, 1992.

2 In his careful study of "humoral" agronomy in Pakistan, Kurin states that the hu-

moral "system" he describes has its origins in "Greco-Arabic sources with Persian and Indian influences" (1983:285) and is "related" (but not identical) to Ayurvedic systems (293).

3 For an explanation of Ayurvedic terms, see Bhagwan Dash's *Fundamentals of Ayurvedic Medicine* (1989). Dash's text is a perfect example of what Obeyesekere has termed the "nineteenth-century synthesis," with a strong dose of nationalism and Hindu communalism thrown into its recounting of the "history" of Ayurveda.

4 I do not mean to imply that there was a period immediately before colonialism when a closed or static system of indigenous agronomy could be clearly observed.

5 My assessment of his reputation was, needless to say, based on what others told me about him. Knowing that I was Suresh's friend may have prevented people from speaking frankly about him in my presence. It was my experience, however, that the presence of a friend or a relative did not normally inhibit the full expression of free speech, especially if it was derogatory.

6 Suresh often related how economic necessity had forced brahmins, who were not supposed to touch the soil, into farming. Working with cow dung and the organisms of the soil, he maintained, was the work of *shudra* farming castes like the jats and chamaars. He also told me that women had "no caste" and were just like harijans for the same reason—because they regularly handled cow dung to make into cakes that are then used as cooking fuel. In this way, Suresh brought together the hierarchical ideology of caste with that of patriarchy. Other villagers, some of them brahmins, told me that Suresh was merely lazy and that he used his spiritual quest as an excuse for not working.

7 I was, after all, a representative of that most modern of nation-states, "America." I use "America" instead of the "United States," following common practice in Alipur.

8 Sompal was involved in a lawsuit filed by the brahmins after a fight in which the latter were beaten up. Sompal swore to me that he was not even at the scene of the incident and had been named in the lawsuit just because he was a thakur (it is not an uncommon procedure to name kin and friends who "deserve" to be punished along with the actual perpetrators). He was concerned that while his codefendants would get away with the alleged crime, he would be punished because he did not have the necessary "contacts" and resources to be acquitted.

9 The reasons for this unusual choice are described in some detail later in this chapter.

10 They did keep a number of goats that provided a small amount of milk and meat for domestic consumption. They also raised hens for eggs and meat.

11 All crop production figures were reported to me in mans/bigha. One man = 40 kg; 6.4 bighas = 1 acre. One man/bigha is approximately equal to 6.4 quintals/hectare. The average yield for maize in the village was 2.35 mans/bigha or 15 quintals/hectare (N = 108 households).

12 For this reason, there was much speculation as to why they had moved. Some were of the view that they had been kicked out of their home village; others surmised that they had moved because land was cheaper in Alipur.

13 His family proudly told me that this younger brother was a "bus conductor," but I later learned that he just hung out in the town and sometimes resorted to minor thievery on the bus route.

14 The rains were plentiful, so most farmers saw no need to supply irrigation water to the crops.

15 There was just one exception: a farmer who grew a little bit of traditional wheat for domestic consumption because the rotis made from it tasted better. Other people told me that at first they did not like rotis made from the new varieties because they looked less white than those made from traditional wheat. I was also informed that the new varieties were extremely heat producing, which, they claimed, was "to be expected" given the hot and dry fertilizers that had been applied to them.

16 On late capitalism, see Mandel's book (1975) with this title; the items listed to demonstrate "circulation" are taken from the influential essay by Appadurai (1990); and on time-space compression, see Harvey 1989.

17 The rise of "tropical rain forests" as a quite specific type of location, often detached from the messy geopolitical realities of nation-states, is worth independent investigation.

18 A historical narrative whose telos is independence makes it difficult to write a history of the postindependence period. In principle, of course, there is no reason why this *has* to be so: one could easily continue the narrative to demonstrate the full flowering of the nation, its gradual movement from incompleteness to perfection.

19 This section on representations of the Indian past leans heavily on the work of Chakravarti (1989) and Mani (1989). Both scholars make the point that these representations of the "glorious past," reconstructed through an examination of "ancient texts," positioned women in a very particular manner—that is, as bearers of an authentic culture and of "indigenous tradition" that had subsequently been corrupted. Chakravarti, Mani, and Chatterjee (1989) all stress another argument that is central to my brief summary—namely, that protonationalists, and later nationalists, largely took up this discourse about the fall from the glorious Vedic past and used it to narrate a different history, but one that shared some essential premises with Orientalist history.

20 For the larger context, see Cruikshank 1978:41–48.

21 Although the rediscovery in recent years of Gandhi as an astute critic of modernity sometimes implies that he stood on one side of this divide as against modernizing nationalists such as Nehru, I prefer to see Gandhi and Nehru as emphasizing different aspects of the split and embodying it in different ways.

22 Of course, the "savage" could also be a utopian figure, as in the "noble savage." Taussig has pointed out that the good savage/bad savage duality is absolutely central to "the West," for it allows "the whites of Europe and North America [to] purify themselves through using the good savage to purge the bad one" (1993:142).

23 A similar point is made in Mudimbe 1988:17. Although Trouillot brilliantly puts a set of structural oppositions at work to illuminate important tendencies in the construction of "the West," there is no hint in his work of how these categories were stabilized—that is, of the struggles that may have occurred to challenge, reform, or reformulate these structural positions. A different criticism of Trouillot's article is to be found in Marcus 1994:927–29.

24 One cannot push this analogy too far, however, because the relation of nationalism to colonial power is itself one of subalternity (see, for example, Luhrmann 1996). Aditya Behl has pointed out to me (conversation) that an additional complicating factor was that Hindu nationalists' version of the past included a dystopian position occupied by Muslim "invaders." Nationalism thus implies a much more complicated relationship to the triadic schema that Trouillot lays out for "the West."

25 By "natives," I mean the people who are positioned as such in the literature on indigenous knowledges, not the experts and government officials who form the national elite.

26 Brokensha and Riley do not explicitly consider the relationship between indigenous knowledge and folk beliefs—they make the substitution in commenting on the "accuracy" of Mbeere classifications.

27 Banuri and Marglin argue along similar lines: "Most descriptions of traditional knowledge systems emphasise the fact that they are embedded in the social, cultural and moral milieu of their particular community. In other words, actions or thoughts are perceived to have social, political, moral and cosmological implications, rather than possessing only, say, a purely technical dimension" (1993:11). I wish to thank Arun Agrawal for this reference.

28 See Brosius 1997 for a fascinating discussion of how environmentalists have employed representations of indigenous people in their campaigns to save the rain forests.

29 Posey (1983:227) uses almost identical language: "For many millennia Indians have *survived* in Amazonia. Their understanding of ecological zones, plant-human-animal relationships, and natural resource management has *evolved* through countless generations of trial and experimentation" (emphasis added).

30 It becomes difficult to understand how one can maintain both that indigenous knowledge systems are autonomous and form an alternative to science and that they have "irrational elements" or that they contain "dangerous practices along with beneficial ones" (Mathias-Mundy 1993b:8).

31 Arun Agrawal (1995:427–31) points out that a similar contradiction bedevils the enterprise of storing indigenous knowledge in databases that will serve as archives. He notes that such a project is built on notions of systematicness, reason, order, centralization, and bureaucratization, the very properties that indigenous knowledges supposedly lack.

32 Thus, Dirks (1990) argues that "tradition" is itself a modernist concept. Mani (1989) brilliantly demonstrates how women became the "ground" in struggles between "tradition" and "modernity," struggles that were possible because of the commensurability of the discourses of colonial officials and (male) nationalists.

33 This argument has to be understood in conjunction with Partha Chatterjee's (1993) demonstration that in the struggle between colonial and nationalist men, women were the safeguards of "tradition," and the household was the domain that was still "uncolonized."

34 Whereas traditionalists' attention to gender was a defensive move, Shiva (1988) takes the "ecofeminist" position that indigenous knowledge is "feminine" because women know how to nurture and care for the earth and because women suffer the most from environmental destruction. Shiva brings "the indigenous" and "the feminine" together in an essentialist manner, but her position flows from feminist critiques of Western science as patriarchal and dominating rather than from a defensive retreat into an uncolonized, hence authentic, domain. See also the critique by Bina Agarwal (1992).

35 I have already noted that this fact is recognized in at least some of the studies on "indigenous knowledge," for example, Brokensha and Riley 1980. The differences in knowledge between men and women flow from the fact that certain agricultural

operations such as plowing and seeding are done exclusively by men, postharvest operations like winnowing and processing are carried out exclusively by women, and operations such as weeding, harvesting, and threshing are done largely by women.

36 See Giddens's (1979:5) distinction between "discursive" and "practical" consciousness.

37 Kurin traces the origins of humoral agronomy to "Greco-Arabic sources with Persian and Indian influences. In this system, all material objects are composed of varying quantities of earth, air, fire, and water" (1983:285). For expositions of humoral understandings of the body, see Marriott 1989; Daniel 1984; and Trawick 1974.

38 A more recent addition to the literature, with a case study from Karnataka, is the excellent article by Vasavi (1994).

39 See also the classification in Crooke 1989 and Vasavi 1994. According to Crooke, "*rehar* or *usar* is land impregnated with *reh* or impure carbonate of soda" (1989:63).

40 Kurin explains: "Lighter soils are generally thought to be drier than heavier soils. They are also more seasonally variable, so that while the heaviest of soils might stay fairly close to moderate throughout the year, lighter soils will exhibit extreme variation—becoming cooler in the winter and hotter in the summer" (1983:287). See also Vasavi 1994.

41 For two of the most influential studies on farming practices in different parts of the world, see Conklin 1957 and Richards 1985.

42 See Agarwal 1994:311–15 for a discussion of the widespread taboo on women plowing. Agarwal reports that sowing is not exclusively a task done by males.

43 I have put "mistranslation" in quotation marks to emphasize that this is how the process appears from the vantage point of the analyst, not the farmers themselves.

44 For more details on the classification of soils, see Kurin 1983:287.

45 Because most farmers in Alipur purchased seed for their wheat harvest, I was unable to determine exactly why his family adopted this policy. Not borrowing or buying seed from someone else would be consistent with Delaney's (1991) analysis of Islamic cosmologies of seed and soil or lead one to psychoanalytic interpretations of "preserving the seed." I hesitate to make such inferences without more systematic data. Peasants in Alipur were even more reluctant to purchase fodder for their cattle than seed for their crops: clearly theories about "preserving the seed" would not explain the hesitation to purchase fodder. Yet the two attitudes are so similar that I would pause before explaining one by reference to cosmology and the other by drawing on theories of resource scarcity.

46 This point is elaborated in the next chapter on "indigenous" ecology.

47 Hoping to elicit a good myth or saying about the "prohibition" on women plowing, I asked both men and women in Alipur to explain this practice. No one could tell me anything else except that it was "customary" for women not to plow. One man did say that a widow he knew plowed her own fields and did not elicit any sanctions from the village council for her actions. It may have had to do with the association of patriarchy with control over "the seed," although this was never suggested to me by any of my respondents. Nonetheless, the absence of women from plowing and seeding operations was quite noticeable and systematic.

48 The flexibility of local moneylenders, often rich peasants in Alipur or neighboring villages, came at a price: interest rates were standardly 3 percent per *month*.

49 Theories of "satisficing" were introduced to explain why people stopped looking when they found strategies that were "good enough" rather than searching for those that were optimal (Elster 1983:74–75).

50 This is an unusual juxtaposition of terms, because *khayt* is typically masculine, and the term *sajaana* is almost always employed to refer to people or objects that are coded feminine or neutral.

51 It was a question that I never posed explicitly to anyone, and hence I can never be sure. I am grateful to Jim Scott for suggesting this point to me in a discussion (1993) of modernity and agriculture.

52 The implications of the extensive use of tube wells for water resources is explored in the next chapter.

53 There is a notion of the agency of the soil that is implicit in this statement that complements the agency of the crop mentioned earlier. In the next chapter I explore the agency of the land in greater detail.

54 One sack contains fifty kilograms.

55 The distinction that Suresh draws between the extension worker's measurements and his own approximation is very similar to Daniel's distinction between "agricultural approximations" and "agronomic precision" (1993:571–77). See also the insightful essay on measurement by Appadurai (n.d.).

56 The relationship between organic manure and chemical fertilizer is explored in greater depth in the next chapter.

57 The explosion took place in Pokhran, Rajasthan, on May 18, 1974.

58 Two hundred bighas equal approximately thirty acres.

59 Sharing water by the day of the week is more commonly found in cases in which several people jointly own the tube well. This form of allocation seems to be quite widespread. For an example from Maharashtra, see Appadurai 1984.

60 I later learned one possible reason for his parents' cool attitude toward him. As a teenager, Sompal had fallen passionately in love with his paternal cousin, the daughter of his father's elder brother, a relationship so taboo that it must have brought immense shame to his parents.

61 Sher Singh was the unsuccessful thakur candidate for headman mentioned in the previous chapter. By my second trip in 1989, he had eventually become the headman of Alipur.

62 This was in many ways an unusual practice because it combined two of the common forms of fixed-payment tenancy found in the village: peshagi, or cash rental, which is typically paid in its entirety up front; and jins, or a rental in kind, which is typically paid as a fixed amount of grain at the end of the rabi season.

63 The status of Dhani Singh's family as disempowered "nobodies" became evident when his younger brother was arrested for picking the pocket of an elderly villager. The constable offered to release the boy only on the guarantee that Sher Singh's uncle would bring him to the police station the next day. Sher Singh's uncle refused to do so despite profuse supplications by Dhani Singh's father. The boy was thus carted off to jail, the result of which, I was told, would be that he would be beaten badly and his family would have to pay a much larger bribe to the police to have him released. If he had been let off in the village, only the constable would have had to be paid off. But once he was taken to jail, the family would also have had to line the pockets of all the constable's superiors. This was an instance that most clearly

demonstrated, for all those who witnessed it, the relation of state power to local authority. Because Sher Singh and his uncle were appointed as "mediators" by the policeman, it reinforced their authority within the village.

64 Here is an interesting example of the cultural complexity of calculating Chayanovian dependency ratios. Neither the concept of "drudgery" nor that of "dependency" is available in culturally neutral terms. Interestingly enough, I did *not* find Jat women working in the fields in the absence of a man from their household.

65 For two studies that take a detailed and disaggregated look at the effects of mechanization on farming households, see Bina Agarwal 1983, 1985.

66 At the prevailing exchange rates in 1984–85, this amounted to eighty cents per day. In addition, a midday meal was normally provided. Translating wages in this manner understates their value, because ten rupees could, in terms of purchasing power, obtain a great deal more than eighty cents. For example, one day's wages could purchase a meager ration of food for an entire family of two adults and two or three children.

67 I am referring only to daily wages here. The actual wage per labor day might vary according to the prevalence of a different kind of labor contract. For instance, the form of sharecropping called *chauthaai* (or quarter share) is extremely common for the kharif maize crop. *Chauthaai* essentially involves the labor-intensive tasks of weeding and protection of the standing crop. The returns to labor implicit in this kind of "sharecropping" are extremely low, a fact that is masked by the formal difference in the type of labor contract. The lower "wage rate" can be explained by the paucity of alternative sources of employment at that time of the year and the low value of the output—that is, maize.

68 Suresh had a fourteen-year-old daughter who lived with the family for only half the time that I was in Alipur—her marriage was performed midway through my stay.

69 Suresh's justification for not working with the soil was drawn from the religious texts that he had read to prepare himself for his priestly role. Contact with the soil was polluting because the soil contained manure made from cow dung and other dirty substances that a brahmin priest must not touch. The books expressly prohibited brahmins from working with their own hands. Suresh once told me that it was a measure of the advance of *kalyuga* that brahmins had resorted to farming (kalyuga is the last, most degraded epoch in Hindu cosmology). As a priest, however, Suresh felt that he should keep himself as pure as possible.

70 Brahmin men were normally addressed as "panditji." Their wives were correspondingly called "panditaini."

71 A good reputation necessarily entailed not drinking or gambling, two of the quickest ways in which men lost money in the village. Several men in Alipur commented on Suresh's laziness, saying that he was irresponsible to his family by claiming to have given up working the soil. Suresh himself maintained that his sons were old enough to do all the work required and that he did supervise them to ensure that agricultural operations were being performed correctly.

72 Perhaps it should be stated the other way round. *Because* he did not have the support of fellow villagers, he could not effectively pin responsibility for the disaster on his uncles; hence, he could not make them pay their share.

73 Amit Rai (1993) has made an argument about theorizing "indigenous" discourses as possessing multivalent genealogies.

74 See especially the fine study of Gandhi by Richard Fox (1989:84–104).

75 For a fascinating discussion of the relation between technologies of cartography and representations of the "East" in the Renaissance construction of the "self," see Raman 1994.

76 Ivy makes a powerful argument *against* the claim that all traditions are invented (1995:21).

77 Although Bhabha is talking about colonial rule, the logic could easily be extended to colonization within the West.

4 "Indigenous" Knowledges: Ecology

1 In *Primitive Classification,* Durkheim and Mauss claim that this sort of connection is a feature of insufficiently developed faculties for classification: "It would be impossible to exaggerate, in fact, the state of indistinction from which the human mind developed. . . . Metamorphoses, the transmission of qualities, the substitution of persons, souls, and bodies, beliefs about the materialization of spirits and the spiritualization of material objects, are the elements of religious thought or of folklore. Now the very idea of such transmutations could not arise if things were represented by delimited and classified concepts" (1963:5). They seek to get rid of the confusion caused by religious thought or folklore by way of (ethnocentric) conceptual operation!

2 At first glance, a familiar gender bifurcation between masculine seed (*beej*) and feminine soil (*mitti*) appeared to be operative (Delaney 1991). Delaney uses seed and soil to analyze notions of creation and procreation in monogenetic religions such as Christianity and Islam. In Alipur, however, synonyms for the soil were both masculine and feminine. Thus, apart from mitti, there was the feminine term for land (zameen); farmers would interchange the terms for soil and land with the term for farm or plot (khayt), which is masculine.

3 Gudeman and Rivera (1989) report that Colombian peasants also use a notion of "force" or "strength" to talk about the land. The case they describe, however, differs quite significantly from that of Alipur in how the term is used and its relation to crops and humans.

4 The view of nature as raw material for culture has been well summarized by Haraway (1988:592): "Nature is only the raw material of culture, appropriated, preserved, enslaved, exalted, or otherwise made flexible for disposal by culture in the logic of capitalist colonialism."

5 At the same time, crops were deemed to act on the soil too; some crops weakened the soil more than others, some needed weak soil to grow well, whereas others could grow only on land that had a lot of strength, and so forth.

6 The relation between the crop cycle and sources of nutrition for different crops is analyzed in greater detail later in this chapter.

7 The extent of formal education of people in Alipur varied greatly but was especially stratified by class, age, and gender. In 1984–85, the generation over fifty included a few men who had more than a fifth grade education and no women who had more than a second grade education; as one went down the age grades, the levels of education increased for all classes and both genders. Even in 1984–85, however, very few men were educated beyond high school. There were only a handful of men with

college degrees, and of those, less than five lived in the village. Neither the high school nor the college curriculum included the study of agricultural subjects, following instead a standard set of subjects mandated by educational bureaucracies in Lucknow (the state capital) or Delhi (the national capital). Even as recently as 1991–92, very few girls were sent to school.

8   I have rendered Prasad's use of the English phrase "hand to hand," itself a transliteration of the Hindi phrase *haath-ki-haath,* as "immediately after." Haath-ki-haath is denotatively closest to "in its wake" or "at its heels."

9   The full quote has already been presented in Chapter 3.

10 On the uses of the past, see Bernard Cohn 1987b and Appadurai 1981.

11 Laahi, more popularly known as rāī, is a small mustard (*Brassica juncea*).

12 Gold (letter to author, 1996) reports that the term *saphed khaad* (white fertilizer) is also used in Rajasthan.

13 One man = 40 kg or 88 pounds. One hectare = 16 bighas. So the equivalent for 5 mans/bigha is 32 quintals/hectare.

14 DAP is usually applied at the time of sowing.

15 Weeding is usually done with family labor and generally involves all members of a household. Men, women, and children often go to the field to weed it together.

16 A view of culture as an integrated totality relies on its spatial encapsulation. For further development of this theme, see Gupta and Ferguson 1992, 1997a.

17 Compare this explanation to that presented in Gold forthcoming:12–13.

18 Similar data from Karnataka are reported in Rao 1993; Karnataka constitutes a very different agroclimatic zone.

19 As far as I could tell from listening to the taped conversation, the Subedar said "Assyria." At the time of the interview, however, I thought he had said "Australia."

20 I am not talking of inheritance laws here but of inheritance practices.

21 *Chars* refers to a skin bag used for drawing water out of a well.

22 Here, Ram Singh was probably referring to not having a regular surplus because the crop varied depending on whether the monsoons were plentiful. Even if one were to interpret Ram Singh's statement about a lack of surplus quite literally, this does not mean that farmers were not connected to markets earlier. Farmers were involved in purchasing inputs, obtaining credit, and buying household commodities through markets even when they were not selling their output.

23 The previous chapter, on indigenous theories of agronomy, spells out the properties of "hot" and "cold" in much greater detail.

24 Ann Gold (Gold and Gujar 1994 and Gold n.d., forthcoming) has recorded remarkably similar narratives and dispositions in a series of insightful papers.

25 For excellent explications of substantivism, see Daniel 1984; Kurin 1983; Marriott 1989; Obeyesekere 1992; and Trawick 1974.

26 Gold (forthcoming:18) reports a very similar statement about the declining strength of grain.

27 Some, but not all, of these cold-storage units had been set up by the government.

28 Gold (forthcoming:4) points out that the substantivist claim is not merely tied to physical health but has implications for moral decay as well.

29 This is parallel to the argument made by Heidegger in his discussion of "dwelling" in being-in-the-world—that is, Dasein and the World are not two separate things exterior to each other that then have to be reconciled.

30 The Gaia hypothesis similarly maintains a holistic vision of the earth as a globally integrated organism, in which human activity is balanced by the activity of other organisms in nature (Joseph 1990).

31 See Jacobs 1994 for a fascinating examination of a case in which the gender stratifications within aboriginal groups in Australia led to strategic alliances that simultaneously preserved a space for indigenous knowledges and forged a common ground with international feminism.

32 See Smitu Kothari 1985:387–89.

5 Peasants and Global Environmentalism: A New Form of Governmentality?

1 The lower estimate is from the *Times of India,* March 4, 1993. The *Indian Express* estimated the crowd to be 40,000 strong, and the highest estimate of 200,000 comes from Shiva and Holla-Bhar 1993.

2 The reason for this is that farmers' interests are much more strongly represented at the level of the regional state governments as compared with the federal or central government. The significance of this demand lies not only in that farmers groups would have greater say in state legislatures but also in that it would become more difficult for international agreements to be ratified.

3 This has been reported by Shiva and Holla-Bhar (1993). English can be read by only a small elite in the country. Apparently, the protesters suspected that the Indian government deliberately did not make drafts of the treaty available in the vernacular, as many more people would have read it and opposition to the treaty may have spread as a result. See also Tolan 1994.

4 Green shawls had been adopted as a symbol by the Karnataka farmers.

5 Sahai (1994:1573–74) argues that a strategic use be made of the concept of nations owning the biodiversity located on their territories, because this principle has been recognized in the Biodiversity Convention. See also Sahai 1996.

6 Shiva and Holla-Bhar (1993) point out that this is a form of "intellectual piracy," as in the case of the neem tree, whose medicinal and agricultural properties have been utilized by Indian villagers for millennia. Since 1985, over a dozen patents have been taken out by U.S. and Japanese firms on solutions and emulsions obtained from this tree so as to cater to the rapidly growing market for organic pesticides. Apart from the obvious question of whether the profits from widely held indigenous knowledge should be allowed to flow into private corporations, there is the problem of institutional inequities. An American patent would cost an individual or company in India Rs 20 lakhs (approximately $62,500), a sum that would allow one of the leading scientific institutions in the country to obtain a maximum of two patents a year (*Frontline,* January 14, 1994, 43).

7 To talk of a "series" of concepts is appropriate because they are linked to one another in such a way that reconsidering one has implications for thinking about the others.

8 Following conventional usage, I have labeled Third World countries as "the South" and the rich, industrialized nations as "the North." By doing this, I do not endorse this classification but treat it as a "material fact" that is an integral part of global environmental negotiations.

9   The United States refused to sign on the grounds that the treaty posed a threat to the U.S. biotechnology industry (Grubb et al. 1993:83).

10 In aligning the Biodiversity Convention with TRIPS, my intention is to follow the connections made by farmers groups in India and not to collapse the distinctions between the two accords. Similarly, in the rest of this chapter, I treat the three treaties signed at Rio as an example of global governmentality, because my goal is to problematize notions of sovereignty and territoriality. An investigation whose goal was to understand environmental treaties might pay greater attention to the fissures among the treaties as well as to their convergences.

11 In the case of the United States, only two multilateral environmental treaties were signed between 1940 and 1959; the number increased to ten between 1960 and 1979 and eleven in the 1980s (Cairncross 1992:6).

12 It was estimated that the thinning of the ozone layer over the United States would result in twelve million more cases of skin cancer over the next fifty years (ibid.:18).

13 The treaty also required that by 1992 emissions of halons, another ozone-depleting substance, be frozen in industrialized countries at 1986 levels.

14 The terms "fair" and "favorable" come from the protocol (Cairncross 1992:18).

15 For an explanation of why international and interstate treaties work—namely, why nation-states actually comply with environmental regimes—see Haas 1989.

16 Other examples of such North-South coalitions are provided by farmers groups described in the section "Peasant Protests," below, this chapter. I have not been able to deal with transnational coalitions of subaltern groups at any length in this book for reasons of space and time; however, I think such coalitions constitute some of the most important new global forces.

17 It is sometimes alleged that focusing on "just rhetoric" may miss the real point of international exchanges at world summits such as Rio. Such a position assumes that discourse is a smoke screen for "real interests," which can presumably be read off the structural positions occupied by nation-states and their leaders. I neither presume an identity between statements and interests nor do I assume that discourses are epiphenomenal to "real" interests. Both these positions are reductionist. It seems to be perfectly sensible that interested parties would employ discourses strategically so as to conceal, misstate, or otherwise modify the public "face" of their interests; at the same time, interests have to be articulated to be held, changed, and disputed or to persuade others to support them. Discourses, therefore, are the medium in which interests are articulated; representations of interests in discourses always have a strategic dimension. But that means that we have to pay attention to the manner in which discourses give shape and meaning to interests, rather than assume that they are the hollow form occupied by ontologically prior, well-shaped interests.

18 Most readers will recognize that I am referring to the title of the Brundtland Report (1987). See also the popular book by the International Institute for Environment and Development/Earthscan (1987).

19 Note the use of "historians" as an occupational category and the reference to Western epistemic breaks—this is a remarkably ethnocentric vision masquerading as a global statement. Who is the "we"? Which historians are being referred to here? Was the Copernician revolution such an extraordinary moment for "non-Western" peoples? Shiva (1992) argues that "the image of planet earth used as a visual in the

discourse on global ecology hides the fact that at the ethical level the global as construct does not symbolise planetary consciousness."

20 See Raman 1994 for a wonderful demonstration of the role that this new "vision" played as a technology that enabled and mediated colonial conquest.

21 I should explain that I am not, in principle, against attempts to define a "common good." The criticisms that I make here of the definition of "our common future" offered by First World leaders is that it barely conceals an ethnocentric, self-interested position that is being paraded as a "common good." I wish to thank Bob Baldwin for helping me clarify this point.

22 See Shiv Visvanathan's spirited critique (1991) of the Brundtland Commission report. I fully endorse Visvanathan's critique, from which I differ mainly in insisting on a more historically and critically informed understanding of "nature." Shiva (1992) argues that the notion of the global "does not represent the universal human interest, it represents a particular local and parochial interest which has been globalised through its reach and control."

23 It is striking how much the rhetoric of "sustainable development" parallels that of an earlier development paradigm, "growth with redistribution." Why is it significant that redistribution has dropped out of the picture in current models of development? Some analysts have suggested that the environmental movement itself needs to be held accountable for displacing ecological destruction to the Third World (Cockburn 1989:36; Baker 1984).

24 It is extraordinary that a "radical" First World environmental organization like Earth First! sold bumper stickers declaring "Malthus Was Right" (Tokar 1988:135). Stephens has pointed out the many ways in which images of children were racialized in the reporting of the Earth Summit. She notes, for instance, that the *Economist's* cover on the Rio conference featured a mass of black children who completely blotted out the environment (1992b:49–51).

25 The gender and racial qualities of each of these terms is intended. See also Stephens 1992b.

26 French, for example, says "international institutional development is not keeping pace with either the world's ever-growing interdependence or the rapidly deteriorating condition of the Earth" (1992:8).

27 Typical demands include strengthening the United Nations, more resources allocated to the United Nations Environment Programme (UNEP), and so on.

28 Interestingly enough, children played a very important symbolic role at Rio. The conference officially opened with the arrival of a ship full of children from different countries bearing messages and a United Nations International Children's Emergency Fund (UNICEF) banner, "Keep the Promise . . . For a Better World for All the Children" (for details, see Stephens 1992a, 1992b).

29 I am deeply indebted to Liisa Malkki's creative insights regarding "the family of nations" for this discussion: "The *Family* of Nations has senior and junior members, parents and children, just as it has masculine and feminine members" (1994:51). Cf. a Worldwatch paper *Planning the Global Family* (Jacobson 1987). An interesting twist to the metaphor of the family is provided by the repeated references to the birth of nuclear bombs as male offspring by scientists and defense intellectuals. Cohn remarks, "The nuclear scientists gave birth to male progeny with the ultimate power of violent domination over female Nature" (1987:701).

30 This is seen clearly in the remark made by a U.S. delegate in the face of Malaysia's refusal to bow to U.S. pressure on deforestation. He described Malaysia as "the bad boy" of the conference (*Far Eastern Economic Review*, June 25, 1992, 61). Carol Cohn makes a similar observation in her brilliant analysis of defense intellectuals: "The United States frequently appeared in discussions about international politics as 'father' . . . the metaphor used was that of parents needing to set limits for their children" (1987:697). Hilary French in a Worldwatch paper says "the deliberate setting of oil fires in Kuwait shows that the earth's environment is still highly vulnerable to *abuse* by *rogue* nations" (1992:30; emphasis added), thereby justifying the punishment meted out to the errant child (or perhaps Saddam Hussein was being compared to a rogue elephant, a wild beast that needed to be domesticated). If abuse of the environment is an index of immaturity or bestiality, one wonders where that would place the countries of the North, given that they are responsible for the overwhelming majority of environmental destruction to date.

31 See the insightful evaluation of Worldwatch by Wolfgang Sachs (1988). Agarwal (1992) has presented a careful, well-argued critique of essentializing arguments within ecofeminism. In a brilliant article, Nandy (1987b) has established the long-standing continuities between "development" and colonialism provided by familial humanism, with its ideology of "patriarchal suzerainty." See also Manzo 1991, whose work was cited in Chapter 1.

32 Sawyer is careful to note that the figure for the Amazonian rain forest is an approximation based on statistics that are, in the best case, extremely rough and uneven. Although much has been made of the effects of tropical deforestation on global warming, deforestation is many orders of magnitude more important for its implications for the loss of species diversity. If they have not done so already, we can expect large multinational drug companies to take up this worthy cause soon!

33 See Shiva's (1992) critique of Western versions of "globalism."

34 Speaking about the Rio declaration, *Newsweek* says "the declaration evolved into a lengthy charter spelling out the 'rights' of poor countries to develop in responsible ways. This, of course, is one of the things Darman warned Bush about: it's ecospeak for 'foreign aid'" (June 1, 1992, 22).

35 See especially Shiva 1992.

36 A World Health Organization (WHO) report on global environmental damage points out that safe drinking water and sanitation would have prevented a large proportion of the 3.2 million child deaths that occurred last year from diarrheal disease alone (*Newsweek*, June 1, 1992, 33).

37 Buttel (1992:20) goes on to say, "Some (e.g., Martinez-Alier), in fact, have devoted considerable attention to the fact that the 'North Atlantic ecological establishment' coexists so comfortably within the structural adjustment *Weltanschauung* of the official development community, which exists as much to ensure Third World debt repayment and to patch up the anarchic international monetary order as it does to achieve Third World development."

38 The relationship between particular strategies of development and the environment has been demonstrated in the case of the green revolution in Chapter 4.

39 It was precisely the overexploitation of land and water resources that worried farmers in Alipur.

40 It is not just sustainability that is being exported from the Third World. The *New*

York Times, in a report entitled "3d-World Funds: Wrong-Way Flow," says "the world's poorest and most indebted countries are beginning to get less in combined aid each year from the World Bank and the International Monetary Fund than they are paying in interest and principal . . . to the two organizations" (February 11, 1988).

41 See also Kothari and Kothari 1993.

42 "In 1985, the terms of trade of sub-Saharan countries (except oil-exporting countries) were 10 percent below 1970 levels" (Brundtland 1987:3–5). The same process was observed in Latin America: "In 1981, for instance, it took one Latin American country 9.8 times as much beef to buy a barrel of oil as it did in 1961" (A. Agarwal 1985:5). An estimate of the amount of money transferred from economies in the South to the North through debt payments and deteriorating raw materials prices (but not including the costs of consuming common environmental goods) is offered by Martin Khor of the Third World Network. He estimates the value of annual transfers from South to North to be in the range of $200 billion (Hertsgaard 1992:13).

43 In other words, more than 60 percent of the seed used by farmers is obtained from other farmers (Sahai 1993a).

44 The market for seeds in India has been estimated to be worth $235 million for 600,000 tons a year (*Times of India,* December 13, 1993).

45 See also Bandyopadhyay and Shiva 1988.

46 As the CSE statement puts it, "The billion dollar question is: are the rich prepared to pay the real costs of what they consume?" (CSE 1992:3).

47 The reason was the fear that reduction of carbon emissions would entail economic costs. As one U.S. negotiator at UNCED put it, "The United States' standard of living is not up for negotiation" (Hertsgaard 1992:13).

48 Tropical forests, which cover barely 7 percent of the world's land surface, harbor half the species of the world's flora and fauna. A fifteen-acre patch of rain forest in Brunei alone was found to have seven hundred species of trees, as many as in *all* North America (*India Today,* June 15, 1992, 82–84).

49 India's environment minister Kamal Nath argued: "How we deal with our forests is our business. This so-called globalising sinks idea stinks" (*India Today,* June 15, 1992, 87).

50 As Malaysian minister for primary industries Lim Keng Yaik put it: "The U.S. is saying: you lock up your carbon sink, and I am going to do nothing. [It] wants poor countries to sacrifice [revenues from selling wood] in order to maintain the consuming lifestyle of the rich" (*Far Eastern Economic Review,* June 25, 1992, 62). Representatives of the South point to the poor record of the North in conserving its forests: "Since Europeans first arrived in the New World, all but 5 percent of the virgin [sic] forests have been cut down" (*Newsweek,* June 1, 1992, 30).

51 D. S. Mahathir bin Mohamed made the point that "if we sincerely believe in equity and burden sharing, why not reforest the deserts of the world and the vast farms of Europe and America that are subsidized not to produce food? After all, all trees and not just tropical hardwoods provide oxygen" (1992:57). The other side of this picture is provided by José Lutzenberger, former Brazilian minister for environment, who says "the Malaysian minister of the environment is reputedly also one of the worst loggers in that country" (1992:56). In spite of the justifiable criticisms that the Malaysian prime minister makes here, I should not be taken to endorse his record of protecting Malaysia's rain forests, which is reportedly abysmal. However much Ma-

hathir's positions made sense as an advocate for the South, they were interpreted by the inhabitants of Malaysia's rain forests as yet another aggressive move by the national state against their existence.

52 In the section titled "Peasant Protests" below, this chapter, I consider the implications of changes in this modernist space for differentiation among peasant groups in the South, as well as for the formation of transnational coalitions between groups in the North and the South.

53 See, for example, Keck, who argues, "Such conflicts may raise issues that go well beyond a narrow vision of environmental problems, in questioning states' abilities to know and preside over the public good" (1994:91). Similarly, Walker and Mendlovitz (1990:1) contend that "in view of . . . a new awareness of the fragility of the planetary ecology, the organization of political life within a fragmented system of states appears to be increasingly inconsistent with emerging realities" (see also Agnew and Corbridge 1995:95). Contrarily, Krasner argues that the existing order was never a real condition for most Third World states. Despite this, he adds that the Westphalian state has become a reference point or convention that is "useful in some circumstances but not others" (1995:150). I think it is fair to say that the *premise* of national sovereignty has constituted a founding ideology for the global order of nation-states in which most Third World nation-states came into existence.

54 This led the *Economist* to complain, in an article entitled "Root of Evil at Rio": "After all the idealism, the Earth summit in Rio de Janeiro has turned out to be mainly about money and sovereignty" (June 13, 1992, 12).

55 The reporting in the South reflected this sense of defiance to northern domination. For example, an *India Today* report states, "The only time the South showed some grit and India leadership was when the North tried to push for a convention on saving forests. . . . [T]he South stood firm on the issue as they feared that such a convention would infringe on national sovereignty" (June 30, 1992, 31). Similarly, the *Far Eastern Economic Review* noted: "Malaysia's staunch refusal to bow to US pressure for a stronger statement on deforestation prompted one US delegate to describe the country as the 'bad boy' of the conference. 'So be it,' Razali [Malaysia's ambassador to the UN] says. 'Someone has to carry the can. We don't want to be *pushed aside and be bullied* like we have been for the past 45 years'" (June 25, 1992, 61; emphasis added).

56 French, for example, argues that "international laws and institutions have traditionally functioned as compacts between nations; but if they are to solve the problems of a rapidly deteriorating biosphere, they must also evolve into compacts *between people*" (1992:48; emphasis added).

57 The ideas in this paragraph owe a great deal to Ruggie 1993.

58 See Walker 1993:129 on the relationship between post-Renaissance ideas of state sovereignty and notions of sharply demarcated space.

59 Krasner (1995) identifies the distinctive features of the Westphalian state as being territoriality and autonomy.

60 Tilly traced the emergence of the familiar state system by contrasting it with possibilities that might have been: "In the thirteenth century, then, five outcomes may still have been open: (1) the form of national state which actually emerged; (2) a political federation or empire controlled, if only loosely, from a single center; (3) a theocratic federation—a commonwealth—held together by the structure of the

Catholic Church; (4) an intensive trading network without large-scale, central political organization; (5) the persistence of the 'feudal' structure which prevailed in the thirteenth century." He went on to argue: "The structure which became dominant in Europe after 1500, the national [sic] state, differed from these alternative possibilities in several significant ways: (1) it controlled a well-defined, continuous territory; (2) it was relatively centralized; (3) it was differentiated from other organizations; (4) it reinforced its claims through a tendency to acquire a monopoly over the concentrated means of physical coercion within its territory" (1975a:26–27). In a later work, Tilly admits that it was a mistake to characterize such states as "national" and that it might have been better to have called them "consolidated" states (1994:5).

61 Tilly's periodization was as follows: "The main rhythm, then, has three beats: (1) the formation and consolidation of the first great national states in commercial and military competition with each other, accompanied by their economic penetration of the remainder of Europe and of important parts of the world outside of Europe: roughly 1500 to 1700; (2) the regrouping of the remainder of Europe into a system of states, accompanied by the extension of European political control into most of the non-European world, save those portions already dominated by substantial political organizations (e.g., China and Japan): roughly 1650 to 1850; (3) the extension of the state system to the rest of the world, both through the acquisition of formal independence by colonies and clients, and through the incorporation of existing powers like China and Japan into the system: roughly 1800 to 1950. . . . Europeans played the major part in creating the contemporary international state-system, and presumably left the imprints of their peculiar political institutions on it" (1975b:637–38).

62 This shrinkage in the number of states was not restricted to Europe. When India became an independent nation-state in 1947, it was by the merger of more than four hundred independent princely states.

63 I am clearly referring here to what became the dominant conception of the order of nation-states.

64 The argument for the national/international connection has been developed at some length in Malkki 1994.

65 Of these twinned concepts, nationalism/internationalism and state/interstate, it is internationalism that has received the least attention. In fact, scholars of nationalism have so far paid more attention to ethnic or subnational identities than to transnational or international ones (Malkki 1994 is an exception; see also Gupta 1992). Given this fact, there is still a lot of ground to be covered before the emergence of studies that treat the interstate and international systems as being constitutive, rather than external, aspects of the nation-state (but see Wallerstein 1991a:139–57, 184–99).

66 Manzo points out that "reasoning man" has been the ultimate site of sovereignty in liberal thought, and the extension of sovereignty to other agencies like the state, the community, or the people has taken place either by extending the reach of "reasoning man" (for example, via the social contract to the state) or by drawing an analogy between the institution and the individual. It is for this reason that "a discussion of 'sovereign states' in anything other than individualist terms is so notoriously difficult" (1991:7).

67 The particular people who were representatives of that other sovereign republic (who enjoyed "diplomatic immunity") were also subject to the laws of their own

nation-states. The notion of "diplomatic immunity," with its medical metaphor of an infectable body, is itself worth closer analysis. I owe this example to Ruggie (1993).

68 See in particular Xenos 1996 for a discussion of refugees and the nation-state. Krasner (1995:117) goes further in suggesting that every major peace treaty has compromised the Westphalian model of territorial sovereignty.

69 The ethical questions raised in and by "the contemporary, unstable post-sovereign condition" are explored in Shapiro 1994.

70 I fully agree with Krasner (1995) that very few nation-states, particularly in the Third World, actually managed to accomplish all these tasks. I would argue, however, that these ideals are becoming problematic even for those powerful states which had come closest to the model of the Westphalian state.

71 Agnew and Corbridge state a very similar position when they write that "globalization and fragmentation do not signal their terminal decline; the Final Fall of the territorial state. But at the same time . . . the world that is in the process of emergence cannot be adequately understood in terms of the fixed territorial spaces of mainstream international relations theory (and international political economy)" (1995:99). In a similar vein, the argument about whether states will obstinately remain or become obsolete is criticized by Walker because these binary positions "share the same spatial imagery, an imagery rooted especially in seventeenth- and eighteenth-century ontological traditions" (1993:126). Walker and Mendlovitz (1990b:2) have put it very well: "State sovereignty offers only a misleading map of where we are and an even less useful guide to where we might be going."

72 If only for the purpose of scholarly persnicketiness, I note that the quote is from the drunken porter's speech in *Macbeth,* act 2, scene 3.

73 This last point would seem to indicate a situation that is "poststate" rather than "postnational."

74 Tilly argues that there are three possibilities for the future of European states: "(1) proliferation of states matching the more bellicose and/or diplomatically successful of those populations; (2) continuation of the long-term trend toward consolidation into a decreasing number of homogenizing states, the limit being a single homogenizing state; (3) detachment of the principle of cultural distinctness from that of statehood" (1992:705).

75 The same policies have been promoted in the rest of the world by North-controlled multilateral institutions through a neoliberal agenda.

76 Nandy says: "Some scattered non- or post-modern concepts of state have, however, begun to emerge in response to the crisis of the nation-state in our times. For while it is an open question what forms the post-modern state will take, there is little doubt that the dominant concept of the state will have to be drastically altered . . . in response to the larger processes of democratization going on all over the world" (1992:271). Walker (1993:154) makes much the same point, arguing that democracy cannot be rethought without fundamentally reconstituting ideas of state sovereignty.

77 Tilly contends that even in Europe, no large state "ever actually became a homogenous nation-state" (1992:710). See also the persuasive argument put forward by Krasner (1995) in this regard.

78 I do not think that Foucault naïvely believed that the economy was actually managed for the common welfare of all. However, it is significant that the rhetoric of

rule changed so that the ideal of government became one of management for the welfare of all.

79   Foucault (1991:100) says, "The population now represents more the end of government than the power of the sovereign; the population is the subject of needs, of aspirations, but it is also the object in the hands of the government, aware, *vis-à-vis* the government, of what it wants, but ignorant of what is being done to it."

80   The use of concepts such as "governmentality" and "discipline" to discuss global regulation is obviously similar, but not identical, to the concept of "international regimes" (Krasner 1978; Young 1989). For criticisms of the regimes literature, see Agnew and Corbridge 1995; Ruggie 1982; and Walker 1993. Keck and Sikkink (1993) propose the notion of an "issue network" to highlight the role of nonstate actors in global environmental and human rights issues.

81   I am referring to what Young (1989:13) has termed an international order rather than an international regime.

82   The description that follows of the setting up of the new institute is taken from Khor 1995.

83   The collaboration between the KRRS and the Third World Network is a good example of a process described by Keck: "The reconfiguration of social struggles as environmental issues opens up new political resources and new allies for their protagonists. Labeling struggles as 'environmental' can change the grid of political and social relations in which they are embedded" (1994:97).

84   I have borrowed the term "intermestic" from Sanjeev Khagram (dissertation proposal, 1993, Department of Political Science, Stanford). Coalitions of farmers, as well as the global activities of NGOs, indigenous groups, and others support Walker and Mendlovitz's (1990b:7–8) argument that political communities are being reshaped from their formalization in state sovereignty into a multiplicity of forms that are a response to "profound structural transformations on a global scale."

85   Because most of these protests have occurred after my last research trip to India, I am entirely dependent on reports in the press for the quotes that follow. These reports gave little indication of the structural positions of the "peasants" who participated in the rally, although the fact that they were followers of the BKU and the KRRS would tend to place them among the better-off, landowning segment of the rural population. As indicated in Chapter 1, many well-off farmers in Alipur, particularly jats, were enthusiastic supporters of the BKU.

86   Joshi's language befits a former UN official who returned to farming and took up the cause of agriculturists against urban and industrial interests.

87   Farmers in Karnataka (supporters of the KRRS) grow crops very different from those grown in western Uttar Pradesh, Punjab, or Haryana (supporters of the BKU). Sharad Joshi's followers are not the most powerful farmers in Maharashtra, the sugar barons who control rural politics and irrigation policies in the state, but from the stratum below them—that is, farmers who grow onions and other marketable food crops.

88   Tilly has framed the issue with particular cogency: "Anarchists who cheer the enfeeblement of their old enemy, the massive consolidated state, will have to think through what other changes in coercion, capital, states, and state systems are likely to accompany the huge mutations Europe and the world are now facing" (1992:716).

89 The fifteen largest transnational corporations have gross incomes greater than the gross domestic product of over 120 countries (Morehouse 1993:60).

Epilogue

1 Pepsico moved speedily to reopen the restaurant and thus established its determination not to be intimidated by such acts. The restaurant was back in business four days after it had been ransacked (*Reuters,* June 8, 1996).

2 The bail amount represents a substantial, but not outrageous, sum of money by Indian middle-class standards.

3 It should be clear that my explication of these criticisms is not intended to be an endorsement of the positions taken by the Karnataka Farmers Association.

4 Arun Kumar, an economist, has argued that production will shift to those commodities which can be sold in richer countries: "What the average Indian requires is unlikely to be produced. The Indian poor will suffer" (quoted in Tolan 1994).

5 In this light, attacking Kentucky Fried Chicken and Pizza Hut was also to target a particular type of conspicuous consumption practiced by newly affluent groups that had benefited from policies of economic liberalization.

6 Questions of their legitimacy are quite distinct from their success, or lack thereof, in achieving what they set out to do.

7 It may seem odd to have included nationalism among the list of "global" discourses; however, what I wish to emphasize is that, however different particular nationalisms are from one another, discourses of nationalism owe much to international and interstate relations—that is, to an order of nation-states.

8 Here I am drawing on R. B. J. Walker's *Inside/Outside.* Stuart Plattner (comment at American Ethnological Society Conference, Puerto Rico, April 19, 1996) suggested that the emphasis on the global/local dichotomy erases multiple levels of analysis between the local and the global, of which regional systems theory is a good example (Skinner 1964, 1965a, 1965b).

Works Cited

Abu-Lughod, Janet. 1989. *Before European Hegemony: The World System, A.D. 1250–1350*. New York: Oxford University Press.

Adelman, Jeremy. 1994. "Post-populist Argentina." *New Left Review*, no. 203:65–91.

Agarwal, Anil. 1985. *The Fifth World Conservation Lecture: Human-Nature Interactions in a Third World Country*. New Delhi: Centre for Science and Environment.

Agarwal, Anil, and Sunita Narain. 1992. "A Royalty for Every Potato." *Earth Island Journal* (Winter): 33.

Agarwal, Bina. 1983. *Mechanization in Indian Agriculture: An Analytical Study Based on the Punjab*. New Delhi: Allied.

———. 1985. "Women and Technological Change in Agriculture: Asian and African Experience." In *Technology and Rural Women: Conceptual and Empirical Issues*, ed. Ifthikar Ahmed, 67–114. London: George Allen and Unwin.

———. 1986. *Cold Hearths and Barren Slopes: The Woodfuel Crisis in the Third World*. New Delhi: Allied Publishers.

———. 1992. "The Gender and Environment Debate: Lessons from India." *Feminist Studies* 18, no. 1:119–58.

———. 1994. *A Field of One's Own: Gender and Land Rights in South Asia*. Cambridge: Cambridge University Press.

Aglietta, Michel. 1979. *A Theory of Capitalist Regulation: The US Experience*. Trans. David Fernbach. London: New Left Books.

Agnew, John, and Stuart Corbridge. 1995. *Mastering Space: Hegemony, Territory, and International Political Economy*. New York: Routledge.

Agrawal, Arun. 1995. "Dismantling the Divide between Indigenous and Scientific Knowledge." *Development and Change* 26:413–39.

Agrawal, Arun, and Suzana Sawyer. n.d. "Sexual Imagery and Racial Control: Disrobing the Gendered Discourse of Conservation and Overpopulation." Unpublished paper.

Ahmad, Aijaz. 1995. "The Politics of Literary Postcoloniality." *Race and Class* 36, no. 3:1–20.

Alavi, Hamza. 1973. "Peasant Classes and Primordial Loyalties." *Journal of Peasant Studies* 1, no. 1:23–62.

Alvares, Claude. 1992. *Science, Development, and Violence: The Revolt against Modernity*. Delhi: Oxford University Press.

Anderson, Benedict. 1992. "The New World Disorder." *New Left Review*, no. 193:3–13.

Anzaldúa, Gloria. 1987. *Borderlands/La Frontera: The New Mestiza.* San Francisco: Spinsters/Aunt Lute.

Appadurai, Arjun. 1981. "The Past as a Scarce Resource." *Man,* n.s., 16, no. 2:201–19.

———. 1984. "Wells in Western India: Irrigation and Cooperation in an Agricultural Society." *Expedition* 26, no. 3:3–14.

———. 1988. "Putting Hierarchy in Its Place." *Cultural Anthropology* 3, no. 1:36–49.

———. 1989. "Transformations in the Culture of Agriculture." In *Contemporary Indian Tradition,* ed. Carla M. Borden, 173–86. Washington, D.C.: Smithsonian Institution Press.

———. 1990. "Disjuncture and Difference in the Global Political Economy." *Public Culture* 2, no. 2:1–24.

———. 1991. "Global Ethnoscapes: Notes and Queries for a Transnational Anthropology." In *Recapturing Anthropology: Working in the Present,* ed. Richard G. Fox, 191–210.

———. 1993a. "The Heart of Whiteness." *Callaloo* 16, no. 4:796–807.

———. 1993b. "Number in the Colonial Imagination." In *Orientalism and the Postcolonial Predicament: Perspectives on South Asia,* ed. Carol A. Breckenridge and Peter van der Veer, 314–39. Philadelphia: University of Pennsylvania Press.

———. 1993c. "Patriotism and Its Futures." *Public Culture* 5, no. 3:411–29.

———. n.d. "The Terminology of Measurement in a Peasant Community in Maharashtra." Unpublished paper.

Appiah, Kwame Anthony. 1991. "Is the Post- in Postmodernism the Post- in Postcolonial?" *Critical Inquiry* 17 (Winter): 336–57.

Apthorpe, Raymond. 1986. "Development Policy Discourse." *Public Administration and Development* 6, no. 4:377–89.

Ashcroft, Bill, Gareth Griffiths, and Helen Tiffin, eds. 1995. *The Postcolonial Studies Reader.* New York: Routledge.

Babbitt, Bruce. 1992. "Free Trade and Environmental Isolationism." *New Perspectives Quarterly* 9, no. 3:35–37.

Bagchi, Amiya Kumar. 1982. *The Political Economy of Underdevelopment.* Cambridge: Cambridge University Press.

Baker, Randall. 1984. "Protecting the Environment against the Poor: The Historical Roots of the Soil Erosion Orthodoxy in the Third World." *Ecologist* 14, no. 2:53–60.

Balibar, Étienne. 1991. "*Es Gibt Keinen Staat in Europa:* Racism and Politics in Europe Today." *New Left Review,* no. 186:5–19.

Banaji, Jairus. 1994. "The Farmers' Movements: A Critique of Conservative Rural Coalitions." *Journal of Peasant Studies* 21, nos. 3–4:229–45.

Bandyopadhyay, Jayanta, and Vandana Shiva. 1988. "Political Economy of Ecology Movements." *Economic and Political Weekly* 23, no. 24:1223–32.

Banuri, Tariq, and Frédérique Apffel Marglin, eds. 1993. *Who Will Save the Forests? Knowledge, Power, and Environmental Destruction.* Atlantic Highlands, N.J.: Zed Books.

Bardhan, Kalpana. 1977. "Rural Employment, Wages, and Labour Markets in India: A Survey of Research." Parts 1–3. *Economic and Political Weekly* 12, no. 26:A34–A48; no. 27:1062–74; no. 28:1101–18.

Bardhan, Pranab K. 1980. "Interlocking Factor Markets and Agrarian Development: A Review of Issues." *Oxford Economic Papers* 32, no. 1:82–98.

———. 1984. *The Political Economy of Development in India.* Oxford: Basil Blackwell.

Bardhan, Pranab K., and Ashok Rudra. 1980. "Terms and Conditions of Sharecropping Contracts." *Journal of Development Studies* 16, no. 3:287.

——. 1986. "Labour Mobility and the Boundaries of the Village Moral Economy." *Journal of Peasant Studies* 13, no. 3:90–115.

Bate, Jonathan. 1991. *Romantic Ecology: Wordsworth and the Environmental Tradition.* New York: Routledge.

Baviskar, Amita. 1995. *In the Belly of the River: Tribal Conflicts over Development in the Narmada Valley.* Delhi: Oxford University Press.

Berreman, Gerald Duane. 1972. *Hindus of the Himalayas.* 2d ed., rev. and enl. Berkeley: University of California Press.

Bhabha, Homi K. 1984. "Of Mimicry and Man: The Ambivalence of Colonial Discourse." *October,* no. 28:125–33.

——. 1989. "Location, Intervention, Incommensurability: A Conversation with Homi Bhabha." *Emergences* 1, no. 1 (1989): 63–88.

——. 1993. "Interview: Homi Bhabha." *Stanford Humanities Review* 3, no. 1:1–6.

——. 1994. *The Location of Culture.* New York: Routledge.

Bharadwaj, Krishna. 1985. "A View on Commercialization in Indian Agriculture and the Development of Capitalism." *Journal of Peasant Studies* 12, no. 4:7–25.

Bidwai, Praful. 1992. "North vs. South on Pollution." *Nation,* June 22, 853–54.

Bijoy, C. R. 1993. "Emergence of the Submerged: Indigenous People at the U.N." *Economic and Political Weekly* 28, no. 26:1357–60.

Blyn, George. 1966. *Agricultural Trends in India, 1891–1947: Output, Availability, and Productivity.* Philadelphia: University of Pennsylvania Press.

Bose, Subhas Chandra. 1962. *Crossroads: The Works of Subhas Chandra Bose, 1938–1940.* Ed. Sisir K. Bose. New York: Asia Publishing House.

Bose, Sugata. 1997. "Instruments and Idioms of Colonial and National Development: India's Historical Experience in Comparative Perspective." In *Development Knowledge and the Social Sciences,* ed. Frederick Cooper and Randall Packard, 45–63. Berkeley: University of California Press.

Botkin, Daniel B. 1990. *Discordant Harmonies: A New Ecology for the Twenty-First Century.* New York: Oxford University Press.

Brass, Paul R. 1965. *Factional Politics in an Indian State: The Congress Party in Uttar Pradesh.* Berkeley: University of California Press.

——. 1980. "The Politicization of the Peasantry in a North Indian State: I." *Journal of Peasant Studies* 7 (July): 395–426.

——. 1984a. "Division in the Congress and the Rise of Agrarian Interests and Issues in Uttar Pradesh Politics, 1952 to 1977." In *State Politics in Contemporary India: Crisis or Continuity?* ed. John R. Wood, 21–51. Boulder, Colo.: Westview.

——. 1984b. "National Power and Local Politics in India: A Twenty-Year Perspective." *Modern Asian Studies* 18, no. 1:89–118.

——. 1985. *Caste, Faction, and Party in Indian Politics.* Vol. 2, *Election Studies.* Delhi: Chanakya Publications.

——. 1993. "Chaudhuri Charan Singh: An Indian Political Life." *Economic and Political Weekly* 28, no. 39:2087–90.

——. 1994. *The Politics of India since Independence.* 2d ed. New York: Cambridge University Press.

Brass, Tom. 1994a. "The Politics of Gender, Nature, and Nation in the Discourse of the New Farmers' Movements." *Journal of Peasant Studies* 21, nos. 3–4:27–71.

———. 1994b. "Post-Script: Populism, Peasants, and Intellectuals, or What's Left of the Future." *Journal of Peasant Studies* 21, nos. 3–4:246–86.

———, ed. 1994. "New Farmers' Movements in India." Special issue of *Journal of Peasant Studies* 21, nos. 3–4:1–286.

Brenner, Robert, and Mark Glick. 1991. "The Regulation Approach: Theory and History." *New Left Review,* no. 88:45–120.

Brokensha, David, and Bernard W. Riley. 1980. "Mbeere Knowledge of Their Vegetation and Its Relevance for Development: A Case-Study from Kenya." In *Indigenous Knowledge Systems and Development,* ed. David Brokensha, D. M. Warren, and Oswald Werner, 113–29. Lanham, Md.: University Press of America.

Brosius, J. Peter. 1997. "Endangered Forest, Endangered People: Environmentalist Representations of Indigenous Knowledge." *Human Ecology* 25, no. 1:47–69.

Brow, James. 1980. "The Ideology and Practice of Share-Cropping Tenancy in Kukulewa and Pul Eliya." *Ethnology* 19, no. 1:47–67.

———. 1981a. "Class Formation and Ideological Practice: A Case from Sri Lanka." *Journal of Asian Studies* 40, no. 4:703–18.

———. 1981b. "Some Problems in the Analysis of Agrarian Classes in South Asia." *Peasant Studies* 9, no. 1:26–39.

———. 1992. "The Education of Desire: Images of the Village Community in the Early Writings of Ananda Coomaraswamy." Paper presented at annual meeting of the Association for Asian Studies, Washington, D.C., April.

Brundtland, Gro Harlem, chair, United Nations World Commission on Environment and Development. 1987. *Our Common Future.* New York: United Nations.

Busch, Lawrence, and William B. Lacy. 1983. *Science, Agriculture, and the Politics of Research.* Boulder, Colo.: Westview.

Buttel, Frederick H. 1992. "Environmentalization: Origins, Processes, and Implications for Rural Social Change." *Rural Sociology* 57, no. 1:1–27.

———. 1993. "Twentieth Century Agricultural-Environmental Transitions: A Preliminary Analysis." Paper presented at Agrarian Studies Seminar, Yale University, August.

Byres, Terence J. 1982. "The Political Economy of Technological Innovation in Indian Agriculture." In *Science, Politics, and the Agricultural Revolution in Asia,* ed. Robert S. Anderson, Paul R. Brass, Edwin Levy, and Barrie M. Morrison, 19–75. AAAS Selected Symposium 70. Boulder, Colo.: Westview.

———. 1988. "Charan Singh, 1902–87: An Assessment." *Journal of Peasant Studies* 15, no. 2:139–89.

Cairncross, Frances. 1992. "The Environment: Whose World Is It, Anyway?" Special supplement, "Sharing a Survey of the Global Environment," *Economist,* May 30, 5–24.

Centre for Science and Environment (CSE). 1992. *The CSE Statement on Global Environmental Democracy.* New Delhi: CSE.

Chakrabarty, Dipesh. 1992. "Postcoloniality and the Artifice of History: Who Speaks for 'Indian' Pasts?" *Representations,* no. 37 (Winter): 1–26.

Chakravarti, Uma. 1989. "Whatever Happened to the Vedic *Dasi*? Orientalism, Nationalism, and a Script for the Past." In *Recasting Women: Essays in Colonial History,* ed. Kumkum Sangari and Sudesh Vaid, 27–87. New Delhi: Kali for Women.

Chambers, Robert, Richard Longhurst, and Arnold Pacey, eds. 1981. *Seasonal Dimensions to Rural Poverty.* London: Francis Pinter.

Chandra, Bipan. 1991. "Colonial India: British versus Indian Views of Development." *Review* 14, no. 1:81–167.

Chatterjee, Partha. 1986. *Nationalist Thought and the Colonial World: A Derivative Discourse?* London: Zed.

——. 1989. "The Nationalist Resolution of the Women's Question." In *Recasting Women: Essays in Colonial History,* ed. Kumkum Sangari and Sudesh Vaid, 233–53. New Delhi: Kali for Women.

——. 1993. *The Nation and Its Fragments: Colonial and Postcolonial Histories.* Princeton Studies in Culture/Power/History. Princeton, N.J.: Princeton University Press.

Chaudhury, Ranjit Roy, ed. 1991. "Holistic Health." Special issue of *India International Centre Quarterly* 18 (Summer–Monsoon).

Chengappa, Raj. 1992. "The Tower of Babble." Special Report. *India Today,* June 30, 30–32.

Clifford, James. 1988. *The Predicament of Culture: Twentieth-Century Ethnography, Literature, and Art.* Cambridge: Harvard University Press.

——. 1992. "Traveling Cultures." In *Cultural Studies,* ed. Lawrence Grossberg, Cary Nelson, and Paula A. Treichler. New York: Routledge.

Cockburn, Alexander. 1989. "Their Mullahs and Ours." *Zeta Magazine,* April, 33–40.

Cohn, Bernard S. 1987a. "The Census, Social Structure, and Objectification in South Asia." In *An Anthropologist among the Historians and Other Essays,* 224–54. Delhi: Oxford University Press.

——. 1987b. "The Pasts of an Indian Village" (1961). In *An Anthropologist among the Historians and Other Essays,* 88–99. Delhi: Oxford University Press.

Cohn, Carol. 1987. "Sex and Death in the Rational World of Defense Intellectuals." *Signs* 12, no. 4:687–718.

Collier, George A. 1987. "Peasant Politics and the Mexican State: Indigenous Compliance in Highland Chiapas." *Mexican Studies/Estudios Mexicanos* 3:71–98.

——. 1994. *Basta! Land and the Zapatista Rebellion in Chiapas.* With Elizabeth Lowery Quaratiello. Oakland, Calif.: Institute for Food and Development Policy.

Colwell, Robert K. 1985. "The Evolution of Ecology." *American Zoologist* 25:771–77.

Comaroff, Jean, and John L. Comaroff. 1991. *Of Revelation and Revolution: Christianity, Colonialism, and Consciousness in South Africa.* Chicago: University of Chicago Press.

Comaroff, John L. Forthcoming. "Ethnicity, Nationalism, and the Politics of Difference in an Age of Revolution." In *Ethnicity, Identity, and Nationalism in South Africa: Comparative Perspectives,* ed. Edward Wilmsen and P. McAllister.

Conklin, Harold C. 1957. *Hanunoo Agriculture: A Report on an Integral System of Shifting Cultivation in the Philippines.* Rome: Food and Agriculture Organization of the United Nations.

Cooper, Frederick, and Randall Packard, eds. 1997. *Development Knowledge and the Social Sciences.* Berkeley: University of California Press.

Corbridge, Stuart. 1991. "Third World Development." *Progress in Human Geography* 15, no. 3:311–21.

Crooke, William. 1989. *A Glossary of North Indian Peasant Life* (1879). Ed. Shahid Amin. Delhi: Oxford University Press.

Cruikshank, Margaret. 1978. "The Minute on Indian Education." In *Thomas Babington Macaulay*, 41–48. Boston: Twayne Publishers.

Dalby, Simon. 1992. "Security, Modernity, Ecology: The Dilemmas of Post–Cold War Security Discourse." *Alternatives* 17, no. 1:95–134.

Daniel, E. Valentine. 1984. *Fluid Signs: Being a Person the Tamil Way*. Berkeley: University of California Press.

——. 1993. "Tea Talk: Violent Measures in the Discursive Practices of Sri Lanka's Estate Tamils." *Comparative Studies in Society and History* 35, no. 3:568–600.

Das, Veena, ed. 1990. *Mirrors of Violence: Communities, Riots, and Survivors in South Asia*. Delhi: Oxford University Press.

Dash, Bhagwan. 1989. *Fundamentals of Ayurvedic Medicine*. 7th rev. ed. New Delhi: Konark Publishers.

Davis, Diane E. 1992. "Unlearning Languages of Development: From Rhetoric to Realism in Recent Studies of Latin America." *Latin American Research Review* 27, no. 1:151–68.

Davis, Mike. 1978. "'Fordism' in Crisis: A Review of Michel Aglietta's *Régulation et Crises: L'expérience des Etats-Unis*." *Review* 2, no. 2:207–69.

——. 1984. "The Political Economy of Late-Imperial America." *New Left Review*, no. 143:6–38.

Delaney, Carol. 1991. *The Seed and the Soil: Gender and Cosmology in Turkish Village Society*. Berkeley: University of California Press.

Dewey, Clive. 1972. "Images of the Village Community: A Study in Anglo-Indian Ideology." *Modern Asian Studies* 6, no. 3:291–328.

Dirks, Nicholas B. 1990. "History as a Sign of the Modern." *Public Culture* 2, no. 2 (1990):25–32.

Dirlik, Arif. 1994. "The Postcolonial Aura: Third World Criticism in the Age of Global Capitalism." *Critical Inquiry* 20, no. 2:328–56.

Di Tella, Torcuato. 1965. "Populism and Reform in Latin America." In *Obstacles to Change in Latin America*, ed. Claudio Véliz, 47–74. London: Oxford University Press.

Dornbusch, Rudiger, and Sebastian Edwards. 1990. "Macroeconomic Populism." *Journal of Development Economics* 32:247–77.

Duncan, Ian. 1988. "Party Politics and the North Indian Peasantry: The Rise of the Bharatiya Kranti Dal in Uttar Pradesh." *Journal of Peasant Studies* 16, no. 1:40–76.

Durkheim, Emile, and Marcel Mauss. 1963. *Primitive Classification*. Trans. Rodney Needham. Chicago: University of Chicago Press.

Edwards, Michael. 1989. "The Irrelevance of Development Studies." *Third World Quarterly*, no. 11:116–35.

Elster, Jon. 1983. *Explaining Technical Change: A Case Study in the Philosophy of Science*. Cambridge: Cambridge University Press.

Escobar, Arturo. 1984. "Discourse and Power in Development: Michel Foucault and the Relevance of His Work to the Third World." *Alternatives* 10:377–400.

——. 1991. "Anthropology and the Development Encounter: The Making and Marketing of Development Anthropology." *American Ethnologist* 18, no. 4:658–82.

——. 1992. "Reflections on 'Development': Grassroots Approaches and Alternative Politics in the Third World." *Futures*, June, 411–36.

——. 1995. *Encountering Development: The Making and Unmaking of the Third World*. Princeton, N.J.: Princeton University Press.

Esteva, Gustavo, and Madhu Suri Prakash. 1992. "Grassroots Resistance to Sustainable Development: Lessons from the Banks of the Narmada." *Ecologist* 22, no. 2:45–51.

Eyzaguirre, Pablo. 1992. "Farmer Knowledge, World Science, and the Organization of Agricultural Research Systems." In *Diversity, Farmer Knowledge, and Sustainability,* ed. Joyce Lewinger Moock and Robert E. Rhoades, 11–33. Ithaca, N.Y.: Cornell University Press.

Fabian, Johannes. 1983. *Time and the Other: How Anthropology Makes Its Object.* New York: Columbia University Press.

Farmer, B. H. 1986. "Perspectives on the 'Green Revolution' in South Asia." *Modern Asian Studies* 20, no. 1:175–99.

Ferguson, James. 1990. *The Anti-politics Machine: "Development," Depoliticization, and Bureaucratic Power in Lesotho.* Minneapolis: University of Minnesota Press.

Finnemore, Martha. 1997. "Redefining Development: The World Bank as an Arbiter of Development Norms." In *Development Knowledge and the Social Sciences,* ed. Frederick Cooper and Randall Packard, 203–27.

Fisher, William F., ed. 1995. *Toward Sustainable Development: Struggling over India's Narmada River.* Armonk, N.Y.: M. E. Sharpe.

Foucault, Michel. 1983. "The Subject and Power." Afterword to *Michel Foucault: Beyond Structuralism and Hermeneutics,* 2d ed., by Hubert L. Dreyfus and Paul Rabinow, 208–26. Chicago: University of Chicago Press.

——. 1991. "Governmentality." In *The Foucault Effect: Studies in Governmentality,* ed. Graham Burchell, Colin Gordon, and Peter Miller, 87–104. London: Harvester/Wheatsheaf.

Fox, Richard G. 1989. *Gandhian Utopia: Experiments with Culture.* Boston: Beacon.

Frank, Andre Gunder. 1993. "Bronze Age World System Cycles." *Current Anthropology* 34 (August–October): 383–429.

Frank, Andre Gunder, and Barry K. Gills, eds. 1993. *The World System: Five Hundred Years or Five Thousand?* New York: Routledge.

Frank, David John. 1994. "Global Environmentalism: International Treaties in World Society." Ph.D. diss., Stanford University.

Frankel, Francine R. 1971. *India's Green Revolution: Economic Gains and Political Costs.* Princeton, N.J.: Princeton University Press.

——. 1978. *India's Political Economy, 1947–1977: The Gradual Revolution.* Princeton, N.J.: Princeton University Press.

Frankenberg, Ruth, and Lata Mani. 1993. "Crosscurrents, Crosstalk: Race, 'Postcoloniality,' and the Politics of Location." *Cultural Studies* 7 (May): 292–310.

French, Hilary F. 1992. *After the Earth Summit: The Future of Environmental Governance.* Worldwatch Paper 107. New York: Worldwatch Institute.

Friedmann, Harriet. 1982. "The Political Economy of Food: The Rise and Fall of the Postwar International Food Order." *American Journal of Sociology* 88, supplement: S248–86.

——. 1990. "The Origins of Third World Food Dependence." In *The Food Question: Profits versus People?* ed. Henry Bernstein, Ben Crow, Maureen Mackintosh, and Charlotte Martin, 13–31.

——. 1992. "Distance and Durability: Shaky Foundations of the World Food Economy." *Third World Quarterly* 13, no. 2:371–83.

——. 1993. "The Political Economy of Food: A Global Crisis." *New Left Review*, no. 197:29–57.

Friedmann, Harriet, and Philip McMichael. 1989. "Agriculture and the State System: The Rise and Decline of National Agricultures, 1870 to the Present." *Sociologica Ruralis* 29, no. 2:93–117.

Garb, Yaakov Jerome. 1990. "Perspective or Escape? Ecofeminist Musings on Contemporary Earth Imagery." In *Reweaving the World: The Emergence of Ecofeminism*, ed. Irene Diamond and Gloria Feman Orenstein, 264–78. San Francisco: Sierra Club Books.

Geertz, Clifford. 1983. "Blurred Genres: The Reconfiguration of Social Thought." In *Local Knowledge: Further Essays in Interpretive Anthropology*, 19–35. New York: Basic.

Germani, Gino. 1978. *Authoritarianism, Fascism, and National Populism*. New Brunswick, N.J.: Transaction Books.

Ghosh, Amitav. 1989a. "The Diaspora in Indian Culture." *Public Culture* 2, no. 1:73–78.

——. 1989b. *The Shadow Lines*. New York: Viking.

——. 1993. *In an Antique Land*. New York: Knopf.

Giddens, Anthony. 1979. *Central Problems in Social Theory*. Berkeley: University of California Press.

Gill, Stephen. 1991. "Reflections on Global Order and Sociohistorical Time." *Alternatives* 16, no. 3:275–314.

Gilmore, David. 1977. "Patronage and Class Conflict in Southern Spain." *Man*, n.s., 13, nos. 3–4:446–58.

Gold, Ann Grodzins. n.d. "Foreign Trees: Lives and Landscapes in Rajasthan."

——. Forthcoming. "Sin and Rain: Moral Ecology in Rural North India." In *Ecological Concern in South Asian Religion*, ed. Lance Nelson, 1–36. Albany: State University of New York Press.

Gold, Ann Grodzins, and B. R. Gujar. 1994. "Drawing Pictures in the Dust: Rajasthani Children's Landscapes." *Childhood* 2:73–91.

Goldsmith, Arthur A. 1988. "Policy Dialogue, Conditionality, and Agricultural Development: Implications of India's Green Revolution." *Journal of Developing Areas* 22 (January): 179–98.

Goodman, David, and Michael J. Watts. 1994. "Reconfiguring the Rural or Fording the Divide? Capitalist Restructuring and the Global Agro-food System." *Journal of Peasant Studies* 22, no. 1:1–49.

Gordon, Colin. 1991. "Government Rationality: An Introduction." In *The Foucault Effect: Studies in Governmentality*, ed. Graham Burchell, Colin Gordon, and Peter Miller, 1–51. Chicago: University of Chicago Press.

Gough, Kathleen, and Hari P. Sharma, eds. 1973. *Imperialism and Revolution in South Asia*. New York: Monthly Review Press.

Greenough, Paul R. 1982. *Prosperity and Misery in Modern Bengal*. New York: Oxford University Press.

Grubb, Michael et al. 1993. *The "Earth Summit" Agreements*. London: Earthscan.

Gudeman, Stephen, and Alberto Rivera. 1989. "Colombian Conversations: The Strength of the Earth." *Current Anthropology* 30, no. 3:267–81.

Guha, Ramachandra. 1989. *The Unquiet Woods: Ecological Change and Peasant Resistance in the Himalaya*. Delhi: Oxford University Press.

Gupta, Akhil. 1988. "Technology, Power, and the State in a Complex Agricultural Society: The Green Revolution in a North Indian Village." Ph.D. diss., Stanford University.

——. 1992. "The Song of the Nonaligned World: Transnational Identities and the Reinscription of Space in Late Capitalism." *Cultural Anthropology* 7, no. 1:63–79.

Gupta, Akhil, and James Ferguson. 1992. "Beyond 'Culture': Space, Identity, and the Politics of Difference." *Cultural Anthropology* 7, no. 1:6–23.

——. 1997. "Culture, Power, Place: Ethnography at the End of an Era." In *Culture, Power, Place: Explorations in Critical Anthropology*, ed. Akhil Gupta and James Ferguson, 1–29. Durham, N.C.: Duke University Press.

——, eds. 1997a. *Anthropological Locations: Boundaries and Grounds of a Field Science.* Berkeley: University of California Press.

——. 1997b. *Culture, Power, Place: Explorations in Critical Anthropology.* Durham, N.C.: Duke University Press.

Haas, Peter M. 1989. "Do Regimes Matter? Epistemic Communities and Mediterranean Pollution Control." *International Organization* 43, no. 3:377–403.

Hacking, Ian. 1982. "Biopower and the Avalanche of Printed Numbers." *Humanities in Society* 5, no. 3:279–95.

Hall, Stuart. 1992. "The West and the Rest: Discourse and Power." In *Formations of Modernity*, ed. Stuart Hall and Bram Gieben, 275–320. Oxford: Polity.

——. 1996. "When Was the 'Post-Colonial'? Thinking at the Limit." In *The Post-Colonial Question: Common Skies, Divided Horizons*, ed. Iain Chambers and Lidia Curti, 242–60. New York: Routledge.

Haraway, Donna. 1988. "Situated Knowledges: The Science Question in Feminism and the Privilege of Partial Perspective." *Feminist Studies* 14, no. 3:575–99.

Harding, Susan Friend. 1984. *Remaking Ibieca: Rural Life in Aragon under Franco.* Chapel Hill: University of North Carolina Press.

Harold, Courtney, and C. Ford Runge. 1993. "GATT and the Environment: Policy Research Needs." Staff Paper P93-5. Department of Agriculture and Applied Economics, University of Minnesota, January.

Harvey, David. 1989. *The Condition of Postmodernity: An Enquiry into the Origins of Cultural Change.* New York: Blackwell.

Hasan, Zoya. 1989. *Dominance and Mobilization: Rural Politics in Western Uttar Pradesh, 1930–1980.* Newbury Park, Calif.: Sage Publications.

Hasan, Zoya, and Utsa Patnaik. 1992. "Aspects of the Farmers Movement in Uttar Pradesh in the Context of Uneven Growth of Capitalist Agriculture." Paper presented at School of Social Sciences (sss) seminar "Understanding Independent India," Jawaharlal Nehru University, New Delhi, March 6–8.

——. 1995. "Aspects of the Farmers Movement in Uttar Pradesh in the Context of Uneven Capitalist Development in Indian Agriculture." In *Industry and Agriculture in India since Independence*, ed. T. V. Sathyamurthy, 274–300. Delhi: Oxford University Press.

Hecht, Susanna, and Alexander Cockburn. 1992. "Rhetoric and Reality in Rio." *Nation*, June 22, 848–53.

Hertsgaard, Mark. 1992. "The View from 'El Centro del Mundo': Summing up the Summit." *Amicus Journal* 14, no. 3 (Fall): 12–14.

Hobsbawm, Eric. 1983. "Introduction: Inventing Traditions." In *The Invention of Tradition*, ed. Eric Hobsbawm and Terence Ranger, 1–14. New York: Cambridge University Press.

Inden, Ronald. 1990. *Imagining India.* Cambridge, Mass.: Blackwell.

International Institute for Environment and Development (IIED)/Earthscan. 1987. *Our Common Future: A Reader's Guide*. Washington, D.C.: IIED-Earthscan Publications.

Ivy, Marilyn. 1995. *Discourses of the Vanishing: Modernity, Phantasm, Japan*. Chicago: University of Chicago Press.

Jacobs, Jane M. 1994. "Earth Honoring: Western Desires and Indigenous Knowledges." In *Writing Women and Space: Colonial and Postcolonial Geographies*, ed. Alison Blunt and Gillian Rose, 169–96. New York: Guilford Press.

Jacobson, Jodi. 1987. *Planning the Global Family*. Worldwatch Paper no. 80. Washington, D.C.: Worldwatch Institute.

Johnson, Allen. 1980. "Ethnoecology and Planting Practices in a Swidden Agricultural System." In *Indigenous Knowledge Systems and Development*, ed. David W. Brokensha, D. M. Warren, and Oswald Werner, 49–66. Lanham, Md.: University Press of America.

Johnston, Bruce F., and Peter Kilby. 1975. *Agriculture and Structural Transformation*. New York: Oxford University Press.

Joseph, Lawrence E. 1990. *Gaia: The Growth of an Idea*. New York: St. Martin's.

Joshi, Barbara R. 1982. "Whose Law, Whose Order: 'Untouchables,' Social Violence, and the State in India." *Asian Survey* 22, no. 7:676–87.

Kakar, Sudhir. 1982. "Indian Medicine and Psychiatry: Cultural and Theoretical Perspectives on Ayurveda." In *Shamans, Mystics, and Doctors: A Psychological Inquiry into India and Its Healing Traditions*, 219–78. Chicago: University of Chicago Press.

Kalpavriksh. 1985. "The Narmada Valley Project—Development or Destruction?" *Ecologist* 15, nos. 5/6:269–85.

Kaviraj, Sudipta. 1994. "Crisis of the Nation-State in India." *Political Studies* 42:115–29.

Keck, Margaret E. 1994. "Sustainable Development and Environmental Politics in Latin America." In *Redefining the State in Latin America*, ed. Colin Bradford Jr., 91–110. Paris: Organization for Economic Cooperation and Development.

Keck, Margaret E., and Kathryn Sikkink. 1993. "International Issue Networks in the Environment and Human Rights," 1–38. Unpublished paper.

Keohane, Robert O., and Elinor Ostrom, eds. 1995. *Local Commons and Global Interdependence: Heterogeneity and Cooperation in Two Domains*. London: Sage Publications.

Khor, Martin. 1995. "India: From Green Revolution to Sustainable Agriculture." *Inter Press Service*, June 5.

Khoshoo, T. N. 1993. "Stopping the Great Gene Robbery." *Indian Express*, October 30.

Kloppenburg, Jack R., Jr. 1988. *First the Seed: The Political Economy of Plant Biotechnology, 1492–2000*. Cambridge: Cambridge University Press.

Kohli, Atul. 1987. *The State and Poverty in India: The Politics of Reform*. Cambridge: Cambridge University Press.

Kothari, Miloon, and Ashish Kothari. 1993. "Structural Adjustment vs Environment." *Economic and Political Weekly* 28, no. 11:473–77.

Kothari, Rajni. 1990. *Rethinking Development: In Search of Humane Alternatives*. Delhi: Aspect Publications.

Kothari, Smitu. 1985. "Ecology vs. Development: The Struggle for Survival." *Social Action* 35, no. 4:379–92.

Krasner, Stephen D. 1995. "Compromising Westphalia." *International Security* 20, no. 3:115–51.

——. 1978. *Defending the National Interest: Raw Materials Investments and U.S. Foreign Policy.* Princeton, N.J.: Princeton University Press.

Kurin, Richard. 1983. "Indigenous Agronomics and Agricultural Development in the Indus Basin." *Human Organization* 42 (Winter): 283–94.

Laclau, Ernesto. 1977. *Politics and Ideology in Marxist Theory.* London: Verso.

Lakshman, Nirmala. 1992. "Balance-sheet of Rio Conference." *Mainstream* 30, no. 36:5–6, 35.

Langford, Jean. 1995. "Ayurvedic Interiors: Person, Space, and Episteme in Three Medical Practices." *Cultural Anthropology* 10, no. 3:330–66.

Lenin, Vladimir Ilich. 1939. *Imperialism: The Highest Stage of Capitalism.* 1917. Reprint, New York: International Publishers.

Leslie, Charles. 1992. "Interpretations of Illness: Syncretism in Modern Ayurveda." In *Paths to Asian Medical Knowledge,* ed. Charles Leslie and Allan Young, 177–208. Berkeley: University of California Press.

Lindberg, Staffin. 1994. "New Farmers' Movements in India as Structural Response and Collective Identity Formation: The Cases of the Shetkari Sanghatana and the BKU." *Journal of Peasant Studies* 21, nos. 3–4:95–125.

Lipietz, Alain. 1985. *The Enchanted World: Inflation, Credit, and the World Crisis.* Trans. Ian Patterson. London: Verso.

——. 1986. "Behind the Crisis: The Exhaustion of a Regime of Accumulation. A 'Regulation School' Perspective on Some French Empirical Works." *Review of Radical Political Economics* 18, nos. 1–2:13–32.

——. 1989. "The Debt Problem, European Integration, and the New Phase of World Crisis." *New Left Review,* no. 178:37–50.

Lipschutz, Ronnie D., and Ken Conca. 1993. "The Implications of Global Ecological Interdependence." In *The State and Social Power in Global Environmental Politics,* ed. Ronnie D. Lipschutz and Ken Conca, 327–43. New York: Columbia University Press.

Loomba, Ania, and Suvir Kaul. 1994. "Introduction: Location, Culture, Post-coloniality." *Oxford Literary Review* 16:3–30.

Low, D. A. 1964. "The Advent of Populism in Buganda." *Comparative Studies in Society and History* 6, no. 4:425–44.

Ludden, David. 1992. "India's Development Regime." In *Colonialism and Culture,* ed. Nicholas B. Dirks, 247–87. Ann Arbor: University of Michigan Press.

Luhrmann, Tanya M. 1996. *The Good Parsi: The Postcolonial Anxieties of an Indian Colonial Elite.* Cambridge: Harvard University Press.

Lumsdaine, David Halloran. 1993. *Moral Vision in International Politics: The Foreign Aid Regime, 1949–1989.* Princeton, N.J.: Princeton University Press.

Lutzenberger, José. 1992. "Eco-imperialism and Bio-monopoly at the Earth Summit." *New Perspectives Quarterly* 9, no. 3:56–58.

Macaulay, Thomas Babington. 1952. "Indian Education: Minute of the 2nd of February, 1835." In *Macaulay: Prose and Poetry,* comp. G. M. Young, 719–30. Cambridge: Harvard University Press.

McClintock, Anne. 1992. "The Angel of Progress: Pitfalls in the Term 'Post-colonialism.'" *Social Text,* nos. 31–32:84–98.

——. 1994. "Closing Remarks." *Yale Journal of Criticism* 7, no. 1:239–43.

McMichael, Philip. 1993. "World Food System Restructuring under a GATT Regime." *Political Geography* 12, no. 3:198–214.

McMichael, Philip, and David Myhre. 1991. "Global Regulation vs. the Nation-State: Agro-food Systems and the New Politics of Capital." *Capital and Class*, no. 43:83–105.

McMichael, Philip, and Frederick H. Buttel. 1990. "New Directions in the Political Economy of Agriculture." *Sociological Perspectives* 33, no. 1:89–109.

Mahalanobis, P. C. 1961. *Talks on Planning*. Bombay: Asia Publishing House.

Malkki, Liisa. 1992. "National Geographic: The Rooting of Peoples and the Territorialization of National Identity among Scholars and Refugees." *Cultural Anthropology* 7, no. 1:24–44.

——. 1994. "Citizens of Humanity: Internationalism and the Imagined Community of Nations." *Diaspora* 3, no. 1:41–68.

Mandel, Ernest. 1975. *Late Capitalism*. Trans. Joris De Bres. New York: Verso.

Mani, Lata. 1989. "Contentious Traditions: The Debate on *Sati* in Colonial India." In *Recasting Women: Essays in Colonial History*, ed. Kumkum Sangari and Sudesh Vaid, 88–126. New Delhi: Kali for Women.

Manzo, Kate. 1991. "Modernist Discourse and the Crisis of Development Theory." *Studies in Comparative International Development* 26, no. 2:3–36.

Marcus, George E. 1994. "Review of *Recapturing Anthropology*." *American Ethnologist* 21, no. 4:927–29.

Marglin, Frédérique Apffel. 1990. "Smallpox in Two Systems of Knowledge." In *Dominating Knowledge: Development, Culture, and Resistance*, ed. Frédérique Apffel Marglin and Stephen A. Marglin, 102–44. Oxford: Clarendon.

Marglin, Frédérique Apffel, and Stephen A. Marglin, eds. 1990. *Dominating Knowledge: Development, Culture, and Resistance*. Oxford: Clarendon.

Marriott, McKim. 1989. "Constructing an Indian Ethnosociology." *Contributions to Indian Sociology* 23, no. 1:1–39.

Marx, Karl. 1976. *Capital: A Critique of Political Economy*. Vol. 1 (1883). Trans. Ben Fowkes. New York: Vintage.

Mason, Edward S., and Robert S. Asher. 1973. *The World Bank since Bretton Woods*. Washington, D.C.: Brookings Institution.

Mathias-Mundy, Evelyn. 1993a. "Background to the International Symposium on Indigenous Knowledge and Sustainable Development." With Gisèle Morin-Labatut and Shahid Akhtar. *Indigenous Knowledge and Development Monitor* 1, no. 2:2–5.

——. 1993b. "Aspects of Indigenous Knowledge." *Indigenous Knowledge and Development Monitor* 1, no. 2:6–10.

Mayer, Adrian C. 1966. "The Significance of Quasi-Groups in the Study of Complex Societies." In *The Social Anthropology of Complex Societies*, ed. Michael Banton, 97–122. London: Tavistock.

—— 1967. "Caste and Local Politics in India." In *India and Ceylon: Unity and Diversity*, ed. Philip Mason, 121–41. London: Oxford University Press.

Meier, Gerald M. 1984. *Emerging from Poverty: The Economics That Really Matters*. New York: Oxford University Press.

Merchant, Carolyn. 1980. *The Death of Nature: Women, Ecology, and the Scientific Revolution*. San Francisco: Harper and Row.

Metcalf, Thomas R. 1964. *The Aftermath of Revolt*. Princeton, N.J.: Princeton University Press.

Michie, Barry H. 1981. "The Transformation of Agrarian Patron-Client Relations: Illustrations from India." *American Ethnologist* 8, no. 1:21–40.

Mitchell, Tim. 1991. "America's Egypt: Discourse of the Development Industry." *Middle East Report* 29 (March/April): 18–36.

——. 1994. "At the Edge of the Economy." Paper presented at the "Languages of Development" workshop, University of California, Berkeley, October 28–30.

Miyoshi, Masao. 1993. "A Borderless World? From Colonialism to Transnationalism and the Decline of the Nation-State." *Critical Inquiry* 19, no. 4:726–51.

Morehouse, Ward. 1993. "For Trade Democracy: Growing Resistance to Dunkel's Design." *Frontline*, May 21, 60–61.

Morris, Morris D., Tapan Raychauduri, Bipan Chandra, and Toru Matsui. 1969. *Indian Economy in the Nineteenth Century: A Symposium*. Delhi: Indian Economic and Social History Association.

Morse, Bradford. 1992. *Sardar Sarovar: Report of the Independent Review*. Ottawa, Canada: Resource Futures International.

Mudimbe, V. Y. 1988. *The Invention of Africa: Gnosis, Philosophy, and the Order of Knowledge*. Bloomington: Indiana University Press.

Nandy, Ashis. 1980. *At the Edge of Psychology: Essays in Politics and Culture*. Delhi: Oxford University Press.

——. 1983. *The Intimate Enemy: Loss and Recovery of Self under Colonialism*. Delhi: Oxford University Press.

——. 1984. "Culture, State, and the Rediscovery of Indian Politics." *Economic and Political Weekly* 19, no. 49:2078–83.

——. 1987a. "Cultural Frames for Social Transformation: A Credo." *Alternatives* 12:113–23.

——. 1987b. "Reconstructing Childhood: A Critique of the Ideology of Adulthood." In *Traditions, Tyranny, and Utopias: Essays in the Politics of Awareness*, 56–76. Delhi: Oxford University Press.

——. 1992. "State." In *The Development Dictionary: A Guide to Knowledge as Power*, ed. Wolfgang Sachs, 264–74. London: Zed.

Nehru, Jawaharlal. 1988. *Letters to Chief Ministers, 1954–1957*. Vol. 4 of *Letters to Chief Minister, 1947–1964*, ed. G. Parthasarthi. New Delhi: Teen Murti House.

Obeyesekere, Gananath. 1991. "Hindu Medicine and the Aroma of Structuralism." *Journal of Religion* 71, no. 3:419–25.

——. 1992. "Science, Experimentation, and Clinical Practice in Ayurveda." In *Paths to Asian Medical Knowledge*, ed. Charles Leslie and Allan Young, 160–76. Berkeley: University of California Press.

O'Hanlon, Rosalind, and David Washbrook. 1992. "After Orientalism: Culture, Criticism, and Politics in the Third World." *Comparative Studies in Society and History* 34 (January): 141–67.

Omvedt, Gail. 1983. "Capitalist Agriculture and Rural Classes in India." *Bulletin of Concerned Asian Scholars* 15, no. 3:30–54.

Ong, Aihwa. 1987. *Spirits of Resistance and Capitalist Discipline: Factory Women in Malaysia*. Albany: State University of New York Press.

Onuf, Nicholas Greenwood. 1991. "Sovereignty: Outline of a Conceptual History." *Alternatives* 16, no. 4:425–46.

Opler, Morris E., William L. Rowe, and Mildred L. Stroop. 1959. "Indian National and State Elections in a Village Context." *Human Organization* 18, no. 1:30–34.

Peet, Richard, and Michael Watts. 1993. "Introduction: Development Theory and Environment in the Age of Market Triumphalism." *Economic Geography* 69, nos. 3–4:227–53.

Petulla, Joseph M. 1980. *American Environmentalism: Values, Tactics, Priorities.* College Station: Texas A&M University Press.

Pieterse, Jan Nederveen. 1991. "Dilemmas of Development Discourse: The Crisis of Developmentalism and the Comparative Method." *Development and Change* 22, no. 1:5–29.

Pigg, Stacy Leigh. 1996. "The Credible and the Credulous: The Question of 'Villagers' Beliefs' in Nepal." *Cultural Anthropology* 11, no. 2:160–201.

Pletsch, Carl E. 1981. "The Three Worlds, or the Division of Social Scientific Labor, circa 1950–1975." *Comparative Studies in Society and History* 23, no. 4:565–90.

Plucknett, Donald L., and Nigel J. H. Smith. 1982. "Agricultural Research and Third World Food Production." *Science* 217, no. 4556:215–20.

Posey, Darrell A. 1983. "Indigenous Ecological Knowledge and Development of the Amazon." In *The Dilemma of Amazonian Development,* ed. Emilio F. Moran, 225–57. Boulder, Colo.: Westview.

Posey, Darrell A., John Frechione, John Eddins, and Luiz Francelino Da Silva. 1984. "Ethnoecology as Applied Anthropology in Amazonian Development." With Debbie Myers, Diane Case, and Peter MacBeath. *Human Organization* 43 (Summer): 95–107.

Prakash, Gyan. 1992a. "Postcolonial Criticism and Indian Historiography." *Social Text,* nos. 31–32:8–19.

———. 1992b. "Writing Post-Orientalist Histories of the Third World: Indian Historiography Is Good to Think." In *Colonialism and Culture,* ed. Nicholas B. Dirks, 353–88. Ann Arbor: University of Michigan Press.

Prashad, Vijay. 1994. "Contract Labor: The Latest Stage of Illiberal Capitalism." *Monthly Review* 46, no. 5:19–26.

Rai, Amit S. 1993. "A Lying Virtue: Ruskin, Gandhi, and the Simplicity of Use Value." *South Asia Research* 13, no. 2:132–52.

Raman, Shankar. 1994. "Looking 'East': India and the Renaissance." Ph.D. diss., Stanford University.

Rao, D. S. K. 1993. "Ground Water Overexploitation through Borehole Technology." *Economic and Political Weekly* 28, no. 52:A129–34.

Raynolds, Laura T., David Myhre, Philip McMichael, Viviana Carro-Figueroa, and Frederick H. Buttel. 1993. "The 'New' Internationalization of Agriculture: A Reformulation." *World Development* 21, no. 7:1101–21.

Rich, Bruce. 1994. *Mortgaging the Earth: The World Bank, Environmental Impoverishment, and the Crisis of Development.* Boston: Beacon.

Richards, Paul. 1985. *Indigenous Agricultural Revolution: Ecology and Food Production in West Africa.* London: Hutchinson.

Roe, Emery M. 1991. "Development Narratives, or Making the Best of Blueprint Development." *World Development* 19, no. 4:287–300.

Rosaldo, Renato, Jr. 1988. "Ideology, Place, and People without Culture." *Cultural Anthropology* 3, no. 1:77–87.

———. 1989. "Imperialist Nostalgia." In *Culture and Truth: The Remaking of Social Analysis,* 68–87. Boston: Beacon.

Rowe, William L. 1963. "Changing Rural Class Structure and the Jajmani System." *Human Organization* 22, no. 1:41–44.

Rudolph, Lloyd I., and Susanne Hoeber Rudolph. 1967. *The Modernity of Tradition: Political Development in India*. Chicago: University of Chicago Press.

——. 1987. *In Pursuit of Lakshmi: The Political Economy of the Indian State*. Chicago: University of Chicago Press.

Rudra, Ashok. 1982. *Indian Agricultural Economics: Myths and Realities*. New Delhi: Allied Publishers.

Ruggie, John Gerard. 1982. "International Regimes, Transactions, and Change: Embedded Liberalism in the Postwar Economic Order." *International Organization* 36, no. 2:195–231.

——. 1993. "Territoriality and Beyond: Problematizing Modernity in International Relations." *International Organization* 47, no. 1:139–74.

Rushdie, Salman. 1980. *Midnight's Children*. New York: Knopf.

——. 1989. *The Satanic Verses*. New York: Viking.

Sachs, Wolfgang. 1988. "The Gospel of Global Efficiency: On Worldwatch and Other Reports on the State of the World." *IFDA Dossier*, no. 68 (November/December): 33–39.

Sahai, Suman. 1993a. "Dunkel Draft is Bad for Agriculture." *Economic and Political Weekly* 28, no. 25:1280–81.

——. 1993b. "Indian Patent Act and TRIPS." *Economic and Political Weekly*, 28, nos. 29–30:1495, 1497.

——. 1994. "Government Legislation on Plant Breeders' Rights." *Economic and Political Weekly* 29, no. 26:1573–74.

——. 1996. "How Do We Protect Our Genetic Resources?" *Economic and Political Weekly* 31, no. 27:1724–25.

Said, Edward W. 1979. "Zionism from the Standpoint of Its Victims." *Social Text*, no. 1:7–58.

——. 1983. *The World, the Text, and the Critic*. Cambridge: Harvard University Press.

Sassen, Saskia. 1996. *Losing Control? Sovereignty in an Age of Globalization*. New York: Columbia University Press.

Sawyer, Suzana. 1992. "Deforestation and Global Climate Change: How Do We Use What We Know and Don't Know?" Unpublished paper.

Schwarz, Adam. 1992. "Back Down to Earth: Global Summit Fails to Live Up to Expectations." *Far Eastern Economic Review*, June 25, 61–62.

Scott, David. 1995. "Colonial Governmentality." *Social Text*, no. 43:191–220.

Scott, James C. 1985. *Weapons of the Weak: Everyday Forms of Peasant Resistance*. New Haven: Yale University Press.

Sen, Amartya K. 1981. *Poverty and Famines: An Essay on Entitlement and Deprivation*. Oxford: Clarendon.

Sen, Geeti, ed. 1992. *Indigenous Vision: Peoples of India, Attitudes to the Environment*. New Delhi: India International Center.

Sen, Sudhir. 1975. *Reaping the Green Revolution: Food and Jobs for All*. Maryknoll, N.Y.: Orbis Books.

Shanmugaratnam, N. 1989. "Development and Environment: A View from the South." *Race and Class* 30, no. 3:13–30.

Shapiro, Michael J. 1991. "Sovereignty and Exchange in the Orders of Modernity." *Alternatives* 16, no. 4:447–77.

———. 1994. "Moral Geographies and the Ethics of Post-sovereignty." *Public Culture* 6, no. 3:479–502.

Sharma, Hari P. 1973. "The Green Revolution in India: Prelude to a Red One?" In *Imperialism and Revolution in South Asia*, ed. Kathleen Gough and Hari P. Sharma, 77–102. New York: Monthly Review Press.

Sharma, Miriam. 1978. *The Politics of Inequality: Competition and Control in an Indian Village*. Honolulu: University of Hawaii Press.

Shiva, Vandana. 1986. "Ecology Movements in India." *Alternatives* 11, no. 2:255–73.

———. 1988. *Staying Alive: Women, Ecology, and Survival in India*. New Delhi: Kali for Women.

———. 1991. *The Violence of the Green Revolution: Third World Agriculture, Ecology, and Politics*. Penang, Malaysia: Third World Network.

———. 1992. *The Greening of Global Reach*. Earth Summit Briefings, no. 12. Third World Network.

———. 1993a. "Farmers' Rights, Biodiversity, and International Treaties." *Economic and Political Weekly* 28, no. 14:555–60.

———. 1993b. *Monocultures of the Mind: Perspectives on Biodiversity and Biotechnology*. London: Zed.

Shiva, Vandana, and Radha Holla-Bhar. 1993. "Intellectual Piracy and the Neem Tree." *Ecologist* 23, no. 6:223–27.

Shohat, Ella. 1992. "Notes on the 'Post-colonial.'" *Social Text*, nos. 31–32:99–113.

Singh, Ajit. 1992. "The Lost Decade: The Economic Crisis of the Third World in the 1980s: How the North Caused the South's Crisis." *Contention* 1, no. 3:137–69.

Skinner, G. William. 1964. "Marketing and Social Structure in Rural China: Part I." *Journal of Asian Studies* 24, no. 1:3–43.

———. 1965a. "Marketing and Social Structure in Rural China: Part II." *Journal of Asian Studies* 24, no. 2:195–228.

———. 1965b. "Marketing and Social Structure in Rural China: Part III." *Journal of Asian Studies* 24, no. 3:363–99.

Slater, David. 1992. "Theories of Development and Politics of the Post-modern—Exploring a Border Zone." *Development and Change* 23, no. 3:283–319.

Sneddon, Chris. 1996. "Rethinking Sustainability: Toward an Integrative Conceptual Framework." Paper prepared for MacArthur Consortium Summer Institute, Stanford University, Palo Alto.

Sorsa, Piritta. 1992. "The Environment: A New Challenge to GATT?" Background paper for the *World Development Report 1992*, WPS 980. Washington, D.C.: World Bank.

Spivak, Gayatri Chakravorty. 1987. *In Other Worlds: Essays in Cultural Politics*. New York: Routledge.

———. 1988a. "Can the Subaltern Speak?" In *Marxism and the Interpretation of Culture*, ed. Cary Nelson and Lawrence Grossberg, 271–313. Urbana: University of Illinois Press.

———. 1988b. "Subaltern Studies: Deconstructing Historiography." In *Selected Subaltern Studies*, ed. Ranajit Guha and Gayatri Chakravorty Spivak, 3–32. New York: Oxford University Press.

———. 1990. *The Post-colonial Critic: Interviews, Strategies, Dialogues*. Ed. Sarah Harasym. New York: Routledge.

Srivastava, Ravi. 1989a. "Interlinked Modes of Exploitation in Indian Agriculture during Transition: A Case Study." *Journal of Peasant Studies* 16, no. 4:493–522.

——. 1989b. "Tenancy Contracts during Transition: A Study Based on Fieldwork in Uttar Pradesh (India)." *Journal of Peasant Studies* 16, no. 3:339–95.

Stakman, Elvin C., Richard Bradfield, and Paul C. Mangelsdorf. 1967. *Campaigns against Hunger.* Cambridge: Belknap Press.

Stephens, Sharon. 1992a. "'And a Little Child Shall Lead Them': Children and Images of Children at the UN Conference on Environment and Development." Dragvoll, Norway: Norwegian Centre for Child Research.

——. 1992b. "Children at the UN Conference on Environment and Development: Participants and Media Symbols." *Barn,* nos. 2–3:44–51.

Subramaniam, C. 1979. *The New Strategy in Agriculture.* New Delhi: Vikas.

Taussig, Michael. 1987. *Shamanism, Colonialism, and the Wild Man: A Study in Terror and Healing.* Chicago: University of Chicago Press.

——. 1993. *Mimesis and Alterity: A Particular History of the Senses.* New York: Routledge.

Thomas, Keith. 1983. *Man and the Natural World: A History of the Modern Sensibility.* New York: Pantheon.

Thorner, Alice. 1982. "Semi-Feudalism or Capitalism? Contemporary Debate on Classes and Modes of Production in India." Parts 1–3. *Economic and Political Weekly* 17, no. 49:1961–68; no. 50:1993–99; no. 51:2061–66.

Tilly, Charles. 1992. "Futures of European States." *Social Research* 59, no. 4:705–17.

——. 1975a. "Reflections on the History of European State-Making." In *The Formation of National States in Western Europe,* 3–83. Princeton, N.J.: Princeton University Press.

——. 1975b. "Western State-Making and Theories of Political Transformation." In *The Formation of National States in Western Europe,* 601–38. Princeton, N.J.: Princeton University Press.

——. 1994. *Cities and the Rise of States in Europe, A.D. 1000 to 1800.* Boulder, Colo.: Westview.

Tokar, Brian. 1988. "Social Ecology, Deep Ecology, and the Future of Green Political Thought." *Ecologist* 18, nos. 4–5:132–41.

——. 1989. "Politics under the Greenhouse." *Zeta Magazine,* March, 90–96.

Tolan, Sandy. 1994. "Against the Grain: Multinational Corporations Peddling Patented Seeds and Chemical Pesticides Are Poised to Revolutionize India's Ancient Agricultural System, but at What Cost?" *Los Angeles Times,* July 10, 18.

Torre, Carlos de la. 1992. "The Ambiguous Meanings of Latin American Populisms." *Social Research* 59 (Summer): 385–414.

Toye, John. 1981. *Public Expenditure and Indian Development Policy, 1960–1970.* Cambridge: Cambridge University Press.

Trawick, Margaret. 1974. "Principles of Continuity in Three Indian Sciences: Psychology of Samkhya and Yoga, Biology of Ayurveda, Sociology of Dharma-Sastra, and Their Concentric Domains." Master's thesis, University of Chicago.

——. 1992. "Death and Nurturance in Indian Systems of Healing." In *Paths to Asian Medical Knowledge,* ed. Charles Leslie and Allan Young, 129–59. Berkeley: University of California Press.

Trinh, T. Minh-ha. 1982. *Reassemblage: From the Firelight to the Screen.* Berkeley.

Trouillot, Michel-Rolph. 1991. "Anthropology and the Savage Slot: The Poetics and Politics of Otherness." In *Recapturing Anthropology: Working in the Present,* ed. Richard G. Fox, 17–44. Santa Fe: School of American Research Press.

Tsing, Anna Lowenhaupt. 1993. *In the Realm of the Diamond Queen: Marginality in an Out-of-the-Way Place.* Princeton, N.J.: Princeton University Press.

Udall, Lori. 1995. "The International Narmada Campaign: A Case of Sustained Advocacy." In *Toward Sustainable Development: Struggling over India's Narmada River,* ed. William F. Fisher, 201–27. Armonk, N.Y.: M. E. Sharpe.

Ufkes, Frances M. 1993a. "The Globalization of Agriculture." *Political Geography* 12, no. 3:194–97.

———. 1993b. "Trade Liberalization, Agro-food Politics, and the Globalization of Agriculture." *Political Geography* 12, no. 3:215–31.

Van Beek, Walter E. A., and Pieteke M. Banga. 1992. "The Dogon and Their Trees." In *Bush Base, Forest Farm: Culture, Environment, and Development,* ed. Elisabeth Croll and David Parkin, 57–75. New York: Routledge.

Varshney, Ashutosh. 1989. "Ideas, Interest, and Institutions in Policy Change: Transformation of India's Agricultural Strategy in the Mid-1960s." *Policy Sciences* 22, nos. 3–4:289–323.

———. 1995. *Democracy, Development, and the Countryside: Urban-Rural Struggles in India.* New York: Cambridge University Press.

Vasavi, A. R. 1994. " 'Hybrid Times, Hybrid People': Culture and Agriculture in South India." *Man* 29, no. 2:283–300.

Visvanathan, Shiv. 1988. "On the Annals of the Laboratory State." In *Science, Hegemony, and Violence,* ed. Ashis Nandy, 257–88. Delhi: Oxford University Press.

———. 1991. "Mrs. Brundtland's Disenchanted Cosmos." *Alternatives* 16, no. 3:377–84.

Vyasulu, Vinod. 1993. "New Economic Policy and Technological Change: Towards New Initiatives." *Economic and Political Weekly* 28, nos. 29–30:1515–20.

Wadley, Susan S. 1994. *Struggling with Destiny in Karimpur, 1925–1984.* Berkeley: University of California Press.

Walker, R. B. J. 1993. *Inside/Outside: International Relations as Political Theory.* Cambridge: Cambridge University Press.

Walker, R. B. J., and Saul H. Mendlovitz. 1990. "Interrogating State Sovereignty." In *Contending Sovereignties: Redefining Political Community,* ed. R. B. J. Walker and Saul H. Mendlovitz, 1–12. Boulder, Colo.: Lynne Rienner.

———, eds. 1990. *Contending Sovereignties: Redefining Political Community.* Boulder, Colo.: Lynne Rienner.

Wallerstein, Immanuel. 1974. *The Modern World-System I: Capitalist Agriculture and the Origins of the European World-Economy in the Sixteenth Century.* New York: Academic Press.

———. 1991a. *Geopolitics and Geoculture: Essays on the Changing World-System.* New York: Cambridge University Press.

———. 1991b. "National and World Identities and the Interstate System." With Peter D. Phillips. In *Geopolitics and Geoculture: Essays on the Changing World-System,* 139–57. New York: Cambridge University Press.

Wapner, Paul. 1995. "Politics beyond the State: Environmental Activism and World Civic Politics." *World Politics* 47:311–40.

Watts, Michael. 1991. "Visions of Excess: African Development in an Age of Market Idolatry." *Transition,* no. 51:124–41.

———. 1993a. "Development I: Power, Knowledge, Discursive Practice." *Progress in Human Geography* 17, no. 2:257–72.

———. 1993b. "The Geography of Post-colonial Africa: Space, Place, and Development in Sub-Saharan Africa (1960–93)." *Singapore Journal of Tropical Geography* 14, no. 2: 173–90.

———. 1994. "Development II: The Privatization of Everything?" *Progress in Human Geography* 18, no. 3:371–84.

Westergaard, Kirsten. 1982. *State and Rural Society in Bangladesh: A Study in Relationship.* London: Curzon.

Williams, Patrick, and Laura Chrisman, eds. 1993. *Colonial Discourse and Postcolonial Theory: A Reader.* New York: Harvester/Wheatsheaf.

Wolf, Diane L. 1992. *Factory Daughters: Gender, Household Dynamics, and Rural Industrialization in Java.* Berkeley: University of California Press.

Wood, Geof. 1985. "The Politics of Development Policy Labelling." *Development and Change* 16, no. 3:347–73.

Xenos, Nicholas. 1996. "Refugees: The Modern Political Condition." In *Challenging Boundaries: Global Flows, Territorial Identities,* ed. Michael J. Shapiro and Hayward R. Alker. Minneapolis: University of Minnesota Press.

Young, Crawford. 1988. "The African Colonial State and Its Political Legacy." In *The Precarious Balance: State and Society in Africa,* ed. Donald Rothchild and Naomi Chazan, 25–66. Boulder, Colo.: Westview.

Young, Ovan R. 1982. *Resource Regimes: Natural Resources and Social Institutions.* Berkeley: University of California Press.

———. 1989. *International Cooperation: Building Regimes for Natural Resources and the Environment.* Ithaca, N.Y.: Cornell University Press.

Young, Robert. 1990. *White Mythologies: Writing History and the West* London: Routledge.

Zielenziger, Michael. 1995. "How Mexico's Ills Grew into Global Problem." *San Jose Mercury News,* February 5, 1A, 7A.

Zimmerer, Karl S. 1994. "Human Geography and the 'New Ecology': The Prospect and Promise of Integration." *Annals of the Association of American Geographers* 84, no. 1:108–25.

Zimmermann, Francis. 1987. *The Jungle and the Aroma of Meats: An Ecological Theme in Hindu Medicine.* Berkeley: University of California Press.

Index

China. *See* India: development in other countries and, 49–50

Chrisman, Laura, 8

Class: agricultural technology and, 14–15, 27, 285; crops grown and, 243–44; divisions among peasants by, 94–96, 137–40, 150, 360 n.51; green revolution, 26–27, 61; village politics and, 107–8, 150. *See also* Caste; Green revolution; Wage labor

Clifford, James, 229–31

Cockburn, Alexander, 297, 371 n.23

Cohn, Bernard S., 26, 368 n.10

Cohn, Carol, 371 n.29

Collier, George, 63, 360 n.51

Colonialism: administrative and economic control during, 10; decay of Indian civilization by, 170; reconstituted features of, 22, 43, 57, 342 n.16, 345 n.18. *See also* Development discourse, colonial genealogy of; Postcolonial condition

Colwell, Robert K., 235

Comaroff, John, 318

Community. *See* Indigenousness: definition of community and

Conca, Ken, 304

Congress Party, 78, 144; development and, 44, 335; divisions within, 63, 66–68, 76; neoliberalism and, 330, 333; populism and, 63, 65, 73, 91, 351 n.75

Consumerism, 354 n.114; dowry and, 96; indigenousness and, 167–68; Western, 310, 373 n.50

Cooper, Frederick, 342 n.14

Coparcenary inheritance, 274

Corbridge, Stuart, 316–18, 376 n.71

Corn, 154–55; hybrid varieties of, 52–53. *See also* Crops; High yielding varieties

Corruption: bureaucratic, 73–74, 88–89, 98, 351 n.77, 360 n.45; lower castes and, 73–74, 108; village politics and, 125, 145–49, 365–66 n.63

Crops: choice of, 186–91, 240–41, 243, 275–79; fertilizers and, 210–13; land quality and, 236–46; monsoons and, 205–6; preparation of field for, 191–94; rotation of, 246–60; sowing, 198–201; weeding, 201–4; wind and, 213–16. *See also* Agricultural practices; Agriculture; Agronomy, humoral; Corn; Green revolution; Wheat

Cropping, multiple. *See* Agricultural practices: multiple cropping

Dalby, Simon, 318

Daniel, E. Valentine, 235, 341 n.6, 364 n.37, 365 n.55, 368 n.25

Das, Veena, 23

Davis, Diane E., 63

Davis, Mike, 302, 319

Decolonization, 23–24, 45, 57, 152. *See also* Neocolonialism; Postcolonial condition

Delaney, Carol, 364 n.45, 367 n.2

Desai, Morarji, 67

Development: assistance, 344 n.10, 345 n.12, 347 n.40, 350 n.62; failure of, 88–91, 286, 347 n.35; industrialization and agriculture in, 13, 35, 44, 47–50, 52, 61, 324, 346 n.24, 347 n.38, 349 n.60; nationalism and, 152–53; regime of, 39, 290, 304; rural, 143, 148–49; social justice and, 73, 144, 353 n.93; stages of, 40; sustainable, 173, 235, 292, 304, 306, 341 n.9, 371 n.23. *See also* India: development programs in

Development discourse, 6, 342 n.20, 344 n.4; agricultural research and, 54–56; colonial genealogy of, 9–11, 42–43, 345 nn.21, 22, 23; colonization of nature in, 265, 371 n.29; constitution of subjects through, 39–40; critique of, 5, 286, 345 n.13; definition of, 36–37; essential difference and, 33; globalizing power of, 16; lifecycle in, 41, 57, 345 nn.16, 17, 371 n.29, 372 nn.30, 31; populism and, 34, 63, 70, 74, 91; representations of past in, 40–42; shifts in, 12–13, 345 n.19; world food economy and, 15, 34

Dewey, Clive, 171

and, 120; village politics and, 121–24
General Agreement on Tariffs and Trade
(GATT), 36, 103, 291–92, 299, 308–9,
321, 324, 330, 356 nn.148, 149. *See
also* Capitalism, global; Environmen-
talism, global
Germani, Gino, 64
Ghaznavi, Dawood, 307–8
Ghosh, Amitav, 178–79, 230
Giddens, Anthony, 364 n.36
Gill, Stephen, 304, 321
Gills, Barry K., 178–79
Glick, Mark, 302, 319
Globalization: environmentalism and,
293–95, 371 n.26; global/local
dichotomy and, 24–25, 337, 378 n.8;
governmentality and, 25, 320–21, 328–
29. *See also* Capitalism, global;
Environmentalism, global
Gobar gas plants, 255–56
Gold, Ann, 358 n.27, 368 n.17, 24, 26,
28
Goodman, David, 103
Gorbachev, Mikhail, 302
Gordon, Colin, 320
Gough, Kathleen, 27
Governmentality, 320–21; development
and, 33; new global forms of, 25, 293,
298–99, 315–17, 321, 328–29, 337;
resistance to, 301
Gramsci, Antonio, 91
Great Depression, 45
Green revolution, 2, 14–15, 101, 347
n.41; class formation and, 26–27, 61,
354 n.117; consumerism and, 136,
139; continuity with past, 45;
fertilizers and, 2–4, 20; narratives of,
53; national development and, 16, 52;
population and, 75; populism and,
142; precursor of, 48, 77; rural health
and, 285; success of, 60, 353 n.95;
support for, 5, 61; in U.S., 53, 348
n.45; water resources and land quality
issues in, 20
Griffiths, Gareth, 8
Grubb, Michael, 296

Gupta, Akhil, 28, 183, 230

Haeckel, Ernst, 287
Hall, Stuart, 8, 36, 342 n.17, 343 nn.25,
26
Haraway, Donna, 367 n.4
Harijans, 72–74, 133, 356 n.2, 361 n.6
Harold, Courtney, 309
Harvey, David, 101, 321, 362 n.16
Haryana, 75
Hasan, Zoya, 96, 352 n.82
Health: indigenous theories of 158–59,
227–28; of poor, 334–35; relationship
of human to plant, 234–35, 279–85,
335, 337
Hecht, Susanna, 297
Herbicides, 260–64; governmental
promotion of, 260, 264
Hertsgaard, Mark, 302
High-yielding varieties (HYVS): of corn,
52–53; health and, 282, 285; of wheat,
58, 77, 106, 155, 194–96, 262, 276,
285, 362 n.15
History: of agricultural practices, 236;
colonial versus nationalist, 169–72,
362 n.19; of village politics, 108–25
Hybridity, 5–6; of agricultural discourse,
157, 159–60, 176, 186; colonialism
and, 230; postcolonial condition and,
18, 20, 157

Identity: clothing and, 85; indigenous,
323; postcoloniality and, 158, 170,
319; underdevelopment and, 11, 40–
41; Western, 229–231, 362 n.22, 367
n.75. See also Hybridity; Postcolonial
condition
Illich, Ivan, 39
Inden, Ronald, 342 n.16
India: Bangalore, 323, 332; consumption
rates in, 310–11; contrast between
Bharat and, 75, 80, 81–88, 100–1, 275,
354 n.111, 355 n.139; development
programs in, 69–70, 98, 142, 148;
development in other countries and,
49–51, 346 n.30, 347 n.33; develop-

ment strategies in (*see* Development: industrialization and agriculture in); food crisis of 1966–67, 66, 77; Karnataka, 334–35, 364 n.38, 368 n.18, 369 n.4, 377 n.87; Uttar Pradesh, 75–80, 106, 126, 353 n.94, 354 n.104, 357 nn.16, 17, 358 nn.22, 23, 24, 377 n.87

Indian National Congress. *See* Congress Party

Indigenous knowledge, 17, 158–60, 172–79, 181, 288–89, 363 nn.25, 26, 27, 30, 31; hybridity of, 19–20, 213. *See also* Agronomy, humoral; Scientific knowledge; Substantivist theories

Indigenousness, 18, 165–83, 363 n.28; Amazon and, 175, 363 n.29; authenticity and, 19, 178–79, 229; in colonial and nationalist discourse, 168–72; definition of community and, 174; global capitalism and, 166–68; polysemic quality of, 166, 172, 343 n.24; as residual category, 180

Intellectual property rights, 291–92. *See also* Sovereignty: genetic resources

International Maize and Wheat Improvement Center (CIM-MYT), 58

Internationl Monetary Fund (IMF), 39, 102, 233, 299, 343–44 n.2

International Symposium on Indigenous Knowledge and Sustainable Development, 173

Irrigation, 204–10, 265–79; demise of fallowing and, 248; soil quality and, 278–79; sowing seed and, 199–200; weeds and, 263–64. *See also* Agricultural practices; Crops; Green revolution; Tube wells

Ivy, Marilyn, 341 n.7, 367 n.76

Jain, A. P., 52

Jins. *See* Sharecropping

Johnson, Allen, 177

Johnson, Lyndon B., 60–61

Joseph, Lawrence E., 235

Joshi, Sharad, 80, 83, 325, 334, 353–54

n.101, 377 nn.86, 87

Kalpavriksh, 301

Karnataka Rajya Ryota Sangha (KRRS; Karnataka Farmers Association), 80, 291, 310, 313, 322, 324, 328–37, 377 nn.83, 87, 378 n.2

Kaul, Suvir, 8

Kaviraj, Sudipta, 317

Keck, Margaret, 374, n.53, 377 nn. 80, 83

Kennedy, John F., 39

Kentucky Fried Chicken (KFC), 330–35, 378 n.5. *See also* Capitalism, global; Multinational corporations

Keynes, John Maynard, 344 n.11

Keohane, Robert O., 315

Khagram, Sanjeev, 377 n.84

Khor, Martin, 324, 373 n.42, 377 n.82

Khoshoo, T. N., 310

Kisan Union. See Bharatiya Kisan Union (BKU)

Kloppenburg, Jack R. Jr., 53–54, 59, 348 n.45, 349 n.58

Knowledge. *See* Agronomy, humoral; Indigenous knowledge; Scientific knowledge

Kohli, Atul, 68, 351 n.76

Kothari, Rajni, 23

Krasner, Stephen, 374 nn.53, 59, 376 nn.68, 70, 77, 377 n.80

Kurin, Richard, 182, 235, 360–61 n.2, 364 nn.37, 40, 44, 368 n.25

Laborers, landless, 93–95, 126, 139–41

Laclau, Ernesto, 63–65, 350 n.66

Lacy, William B., 54, 348 nn.43, 44, 47

Land quality. *See* Soil

Land reform, 48–49, 51, 55, 77, 142, 146, 351 n.75, 352 nn.86, 88, 359 n.39, 360 n.44; gender hierarchies and, 359 n.33, 360 n.47

Land tenancy. *See* Sharecropping

Lawsuit, 361 n.8

Legitimacy: of caste and class privilege, 150, 352 n.79; lineage and, 98–100; of patronage, 358 n.28, of peasant parties,

378 n.7; noble savage and, 171; peasant challenges to, 17; population and, 56; postcolonial critiques of, 179

Nations, family of, 57, 371 n.29

Nation-state: comparative advantage and, 349 n.53; decline of, 21–23, 320; formation of, 316–17, 320, 375 n.65; populism and, 63; telos of, 23, 362 n.18; unbundling of, 314, 318–19, 326, 327, 329, 376 nn.71, 76. *See also* Sovereignty

Nehru, Jawaharlal, 49–51, 60–61, 345 n.19, 346 nn.26, 31, 347 nn.32, 33, 35, 362 n.21

Neocolonialism, 13, 293; theories of, 22. *See also* Colonialism; Decolonization; Postcolonial condition

Neoliberalism, 36, 292–93, 323, 330, 333–36, 356 nn.146, 148, 376 n.75, 378 n.5. See also Capitalism, global; Globalization

New Deal, 45

Nostalgia: imperialist, 18, 168; for origins, 249; for village harmony, 132, 136. *See also* Indigenousness; Nationalism; Village politics

Obeyeskere, Gananath, 158–59, 212, 361 n.3, 368 n.25

O'Hanlon, Rosalind, 8

Omvesh, Swami, 92

Ong, Aihwa, 230

Onuf, Nicholas Greenwood, 317

Orientalism, 169–71, 344 n.4

Ostrom, Elinor, 315

Packard, Randall, 342 n.14

Panchayat system. *See* Village politics

Patnaik, Utsa, 96

Patriarchy. *See* Caste; Gender

Patronage, 126–41, 358 n.28; bureaucratic, 145; change to brokerage from, 146, 149–50, 360 n.46, 358 nn.22, 28; development programs and, 126

Peasants: divisions among, 91–97, 354 n.102; political mobilization of, 75–76,

79–80, 86–87, 354 n.107, 354–55 n.119, 369 n.1; transnational alliances and, 301, 328, 337, 370 n.16, 377 nn. 83, 84

Pepsico, 331–32. *See also* Capitalism, global; Multinational corporations

Peronism, 63, 66, 350 n.68. *See also* Populism

Peshagi. *See* Sharecropping

Petulla, Joseph M., 235

Pigg, Stacy Leigh, 344 n.8

Pizza Hut, 331–32, 378 n.5. *See also* Capitalism, global; Multinational corporations

Planning. *See* India; Development

Pletsch, Carl E., 39

Plucknett, Donald L., 58–59, 60

Population: displacement of U.S. farm, 53, 348 nn.43, 44; as governable object, 320, 377 n.79; threat of increasing, 43, 54–58, 283, 297, 304, 308, 341 n.9, 349 n.56. *See also* Environmentalism

Populism: caste and, 69–74; definition of, 350 nn.66, 68, 69; development discourse and, 34, 63, 70, 74–75; division of society by, 66, 69, 71; flexibility of, 350 n.67, 356 n.146; mass media and, 73; opposition groups and, 34–35, 75–79, 80, 97, 260; underdevelopment and, 35, 63–66; welfare programs and, 69–70; world food economy and, 35. *See also* Green revolution; Village politics

Posey, Darrell A., 170, 175

Postcolonial condition, 6–12, 15, 104, 299, 338, 341–42 n.11; changing social relations and, 107; colonialism and, 7, 10, 342 n.17; controversy surrounding, 6–8; global capitalism and, 11, 15; hybridity and, 6, 12; indigenous knowledge and, 264–65; modernity and, 342 n.18, nation-state and, 293, 319, 320, 327; versus postmodern condition, 10; space and, 326

Postcolonial theory, 7–11, 20–24;

indigenousness and, 167, 227–33
Poverty: food and, 284–85; health, 334–35; political rhetoric of, 67–69, 84–85, 87, 351 n.75; state programs to fight, 17, 126. *See also* Populism
Prakash, Gyan, 8, 169
Prakash, Madhu Suri, 301
Prashad, Vijay, 230
Progress, ideas of. *See* Development Discourse
Punjab, 75
Punjab Agricultural University, 61

Rai, Amit, 366 n.73
Raman, Shankar, 303, 367 n.75, 371 n.20
Rao, Narasimha, 325, 330
Ray, Satyajit (filmmaker), 349 n.57
Resistance: indigenousness and, 19, 168, 229; intellectuals and, 31; peasant, 13, 15, 27, 61, 74, 79, 89, 237, 331, 336–38, 353 n.99, 354–55 n.119; new transnational modes of, 301, 326, 328, 335, 337, 377 nn.83, 84. *See also* Governmentality; Peasants
Riley, Bernard W., 174, 177–78
Rio Accords. *See* Earth Summit
Rockefeller Foundation, 52–53, 56–61, 299
Rosaldo, Renato, Jr., 168, 170
Rudolph, Lloyd I., 63, 66–68, 342 n.13, 351 n.72
Rudolph, Susanne Hoeber, 63, 66–68, 342 n.13, 351 n.72
Rudra, Ashok, 357 n.16, 358 n.31
Ruggie, John Gerard, 303, 316–18, 374 n.57, 375–76 n.67
Runge, C. Ford, 309
Rushdie, Salman, 23, 230

Sachs, Wolfgang, 372 n.31
Sahai, Suman, 310, 369 n.5
Said, Edward W., 230
Samajwadi Party, 333
Savage slot, 171, 228. *See also* Indigenousness
Sawyer, Suzana, 304-6

Scheduled Caste (sc). *See* Harijans
Scientific knowledge: 175, 303–4, 348 n.47, 363 n.30; ecology as, 235–36; patriarchy and, 180, 343 n.34. *See also* Agricultural research; Indigenous knowledge
Scott, James C., 34, 357 n.8, 358 nn.22, 28, 359 n.41, 360 n.46
Seed selection. *See* Agricultural practices: seed selection in
Sen, Amartya K., 55, 172, 334, 349 n.57
Shanmugaratnam, N., 308
Shapiro, Michael J., 317–18, 376 n.69
Sharecropping, 127–30, 221–22, 358 n.21, 365 n.62, 366 n.67
Sharma, Hari P., 27
Sharma, Miriam, 357 nn.7, 17, 358 n.24, 360 nn.45, 46
Shastri, Lal Bahadur, 60
Shetkari Sangathana, 80, 325–26, 334, 336. *See also* Peasants: political mobilization of; Resistance: peasant
Shiva, Vandana, 23, 293, 310, 363 n.34, 369 nn.1, 3, 6, 370–71 n.19, 371 n.22, 373 n.44
Shohat, Ella, 8, 341–42 n.11
Singh, Ajit, 100
Singh, Chaudhary Charan, 75–80, 100, 352 n.85, 90, 353 nn.92, 101
Singh, Digvijay, 333
Singh, V. P., 355 nn.132, 138
Smith, Nigel J. H., 58–60
Sneddon, Chris, 235
Soil, 236–46; classification of, 182, 185, 364 n.40; irrigation and, 278–79; strength of, 241–42, 246, 250, 367 nn.3, 5
Sorsa, Pivitta, 308
Sovereignty, 324, 375 n.66, 376 n.69; development and, 51, 61, 336; environmental issues and, 21, 313, 374 nn.53, 54, 56; genetic resources and, 291–92, 295–97, 304, 310, 313; of nation-state, 59–60, 293, 314, 316; territoriality and, 21, 294, 316, 376 nn.68, 71

Akhil Gupta is Associate Professor of Anthropology at
Stanford University. He is coeditor, with James Ferguson,
of *Culture, Power, Place: Explorations in Critical Anthropology* (Duke, 1997) and *Anthropological Locations: Boundaries and Grounds of a Field Science.*

Library of Congress Cataloging-in-Publication Data
Gupta, Akhil
Postcolonial developments: agriculture in the making of
modern India / Akhil Gupta.
Includes bibliographical references and index.
ISBN 0-8223-2183-1 (cloth: alk. paper).
ISBN 0-8223-2213-7 (paper: alk. paper)
1. Agriculture—India.   2. Agriculture and state—India.
3. Rural development—India.   4. Ethnoscience—India.
5. Environmental policy—India.   I. Title.
S279.G86   1998   307.1'412'09542—dc21   97-43036 CIP